THE MINOR PLEASURES
OF LIFE

THE

MINOR

PLEASURES

OF LIFE

Selected and Arranged
by
ROSE MACAULAY

LONDON
VICTOR GOLLANCZ LTD
Covent Garden

First published 1934
Second impression December 1934
First Cheap Edition Autumn 1936
Reprinted September 1936

'Tis most undoubtedly true, that all men are equally given to their pleasure, only thus, one mans pleasure lyes one way, and anothers another. Pleasures are all alike, simply considered in themselves, he that hunts, or he that governs the Commonwealth, they both please themselves alike, he that takes pleasure to hear Sermons, enjoys himself as much as he that hears Plays.

Whilst you are upon Earth, enjoy the good things that are here (to that end were they given) and be not melancholly, and wish yourself in Heaven.

JOHN SELDEN

There should be a joyous set of elegant extracts—a *Literatura Hilaris* or *Gaudens*.

LEIGH HUNT

PREFACE

I feel that a few apologies to readers should precede this book, which has been so laboriously charming to compile, and which seems to me, now I look through it, slimmed though it is of much that I hoped it would contain, to be so full of agreeable reading. First, then, there may be those who will seek in it in vain their own favourite pleasures, and will perhaps find some things that are not to them pleasures at all, such as gossip, football, chess, sprunking, catching animals, taking umbrage, or what not. I must refer them to my motto from Selden—one man's pleasure lies one way, another's another. There is here no pleasure which I have not either observed, or read, to be such to some of mankind, though not all are so to me. Secondly, there may be those who will complain that this book wears an air disproportionately 17th century ; and, now I look at it, I see they will have grounds. But, apart from this being the literary period most familiar to me, and therefore coming most readily to my mind, its literature, from the rich and sonorous prose and lovely verse of its earlier years, through the graceful Latinized elegance of its middle period, to the lounging, easy urbanity of its close, is so entrancing that it lures one, like a siren, to dwell with it. I have even tagged the Roman dignity of Cicero's *De Senectute* with the lively man-about-town idiom of Mr. Samuel Parker, who makes Socrates exclaim briskly " Bless me, what do you mean, Sir ? " like a coffee-house wit. And this brings me to my next apology—for translations. When I could, I have used the great translators—Chapman, Florio, Holland, North, Golding, Greneway, Dryden, Pope, and the rest, who have created in their renderings living English prose or verse. To those who may think that apart from these, I should have left such familiar languages as Latin and French untranslated, I can but say that I think them very likely right, and apologise for offering them English versions of my own where they could have made as good, or better, themselves.

As to the spelling of authors writing before the last quarter of the 18th century, my aim has been to follow the text of some edition published in the author's lifetime, or immediately after ; or, if none was published, to follow the manuscript where it is accessible. I did not succeed in seeing the Pepys MS., so have followed the inconsistent orthography of those who have up till now edited him. When I have taken my text from an edition considerably later than the first, I have given the edition's date.

I wish I could be sure that no inaccuracies have crept into my transcriptions, made in the British Museum from texts often dim, in a handwriting always bad, and typed afterwards. If any have, I apologise ; also (to any reader who dislikes it), for the contemporary spelling. This seems to be a matter of taste ; if more editors of our older literature had shared mine, they would have spared me much trouble. Even Arber modernised ; even Mr. Norman Ault, whose scholarly *Seventeenth Century Lyrics* so bristles with invaluable and generous sign-posts to good collections of verse. I dare say they are right; it is obviously an arguable point, and each anthologist must do as he prefers. The only unpardonable method is, as it seems to me, compromise.

There is here one little 17th century poem (on p. 22) which has not, I believe, been printed before; if any one knows of it, I should be glad to hear. Several poems and prose extracts have not, so far as I know, been published since the century of their first appearance, so may be unfamiliar to many readers; among these are what seem to me the two delightful ballads of young women bathing, not the whole of which proved, however, discreet enough for a modern anthology.

Finally, I should like to thank several friends who have made intelligent and happy suggestions, and some who have supplied material, (to Miss Antonia White, for instance, I owe a sentence from an unpublished letter of Jane Welsh's), and to acknowledge the unfailing and kindly help of the superintendents of the British Museum Reading Room, and the staff of the London library. I should also like to express gratitude for the work of all the scholarly editors who so greatly lighten the task of anthologists, such, for instance, as Miss Marjorie Hope Nicholson, whose patient skill in deciphering several miles of the abominable handwriting of Henry More for her *Conway Letters* filled me with admiration when I wrestled with it myself.

CONTENTS

CONTENTS

CONTENTS

13

CONTENTS

THE MINOR PLEASURES
OF LIFE

AGREEABLE ENCOUNTERS

Elephants

If Elephants see a man comming against them that is
out of the way in wildernes, for they would not afray
him, they will draw themselves somewhat out of the way,
and then they stint, and pass little and little before him,
and teach him the way, and if a dragon come against
him, they fight with the dragon and defend the man, and
put them forth to defend the man strongly and mightily.

BARTHOLOMEW ANGLICUS
De Proprietatibus Rerum (c. 1240)
Trans. John Trevisa (1398, modernised 1582)

Burgundian Jews

I was brought acquainted with a Burgundian Jew,
who had married an apostate Kentish woman. I asked

15

him divers questions : he told me, amongst other things, that the World should never end ; that our soules transmigrated, and that even those of the most holy persons did pennance in the bodyes of bruits after death, and so he interpreted the banishment and salvage life of Nebuchadnezzar ; that all the Jews should rise againe and be led to Jerusalem ; that the Romans only were the occasion of our Saviour's death ; . . . that when the Messias came, all the ships, barkes, and vessells of Holland should, by the powere of certain strange whirle winds, be loos'd from their ankers and transported in a moment to all the desolat ports and havens throughout the world, wherever the dispersion was, to convey their breathren and tribes to the Holy Citty ; with other such like stuff. He was a merry drunken fellow, but would by no means handle any money (for something I purchas'd of him) it being Saturday ; but desired me to leave it in the window, meaning to receive it on Sunday morning.

JOHN EVELYN
Diary (Leyden, Aug. 28, 1641)

COLONELS

I remember in those Times, an admired Original of that Vocation, sitting in a Coffee-house near two Gentlemen, whereof one was of the Clergy, who were engag'd in some Discourse that savoured of Learning ; this Officer thought fit to interpose, and professing to deliver the Sentiments of his Fraternity, as well as his own . . . turning to the Clergy-Man, spoke in the following Manner, " D—n me, Doctor, say what you will, the Army

is the only School for Gentlemen. Do you think my lord
Marlborough beat the French with Greek and Latin ?
D—n me, a Scholar when he comes into good Company,
what is he but an Ass ? D—n me, I would be glad, by
G—d, to see any of your Scholars with his Nouns, and his
Verbs, and his Philosophy, and Trigonometry, what a
Figure he would make at a Siege or Blockade, or ren-
countring, d—n me," etc. After which he proceeded with
a Volley of Military Terms . . . harder to be understood
than any that were coined by the Commentators upon
Aristotle.

JONATHAN SWIFT
Essay on Modern Education (c. 1723)

POETS

Some days after this conversation I walked to Lausanne,
to breakfast at the hotel with an old friend. . . . He presently came in, accompanied by two English ladies. . . .
The husband of one of them soon followed. I saw by
their utilitarian garb, as well as by the blisters and blotches
on their cheeks, lips and noses, that they were pedestrian
tourists, fresh from the snow-covered mountains. . . .
The man was evidently a denizen of the north, his accent
harsh, skin white, of an angular and bony build, and self-
confident and dogmatic in his opinions. The precision and
quaintness of his language, as well as his eccentric remarks
on common things, stimulated my mind. Our icy islanders
thaw rapidly when they have drifted into warmer lati-
tudes : broken loose from its anti-social system, mystic
casts, côteries, sets and sects, they lay aside their

17

purse-proud, tuft-hunting, and toadying ways, and are very apt to run riot in the enjoyment of all their senses....

We talked as loud and as fast as if under the exhilarating influence of champagne, instead of such a sedative compound as *café au lait*.... The stranger expressed his disgust at the introduction of carriages into the mountain districts of Switzerland, and at the old fogies who used them.

" As to the arbitrary, pitiless, Godless wretches," he exclaimed, " who have removed nature's landmarks by cutting roads through Alps and Apennines, until all things are reduced to the same dead level, they will be arraigned hereafter with the unjust ; they have robbed the best specimens of what men should be, of their freeholds in the mountains ; the eagle, the black cock, and the red deer they have tamed or exterminated. The lover of nature can nowhere find a solitary nook to contemplate her beauties. Yesterday," he continued, " at the break of day, I scaled the most rugged height within my reach ; it looked inaccessible ; this pleasant delusion was quickly dispelled ; I was rudely startled out of a deep reverie by the accursed jarring, jingling, and rumbling of a calèche, and harsh voices that drowned the torrent's fall."

The stranger, now hearing a commotion in the street, looked out of the window, and rang the bell violently.

" Waiter," he said, " is that our carriage ? Why did you not tell us ? Come, lasses, be stirring, the freshness of the day is gone. You may rejoice in not having to walk ; there is a chance of saving the remnants of skin the sun has left on our chins and noses." ...

On their leaving the room to get ready for their journey, my friend told me the strangers were the poet Wordsworth, his wife and sister. Who could have divined this ? I could see no trace, in the hard features and weather-stained

18

brow of the outer man, of the divinity within him. In a few minutes the travellers re-appeared. . . . Now that I knew that I was talking to one of the gentle craft, as there was no time to waste, I asked him abruptly what he thought of Shelley as a poet ?

" Nothing," he replied, as abruptly.

Seeing my surprise, he added, " A man who has not produced a good poem before he is twenty-five, we may conclude cannot and never will do so."

" The Cenci ! " I said eagerly.

" Won't do," he replied, shaking his head, as he got into the carriage : a rough-coated Scotch terrier followed him.

" This hairy fellow is our flea-trap," he shouted out, as they started off.

When I recovered from the shock of having heard the harsh sentence passed by an elder bard on a younger brother of the Muses, I exclaimed, After all, poets are but earth.

E. J. TRELAWNY

Recollections of the Last Days of Shelley and Byron (1858)

I drove to Pisa . . . and . . . hastened to the Tre Palazzi . . . where the Shelleys and Williamses lived on different flats under the same roof, as is the custom on the Continent. The Williamses received me in their earnest cordial manner . . . we were in loud and animated conversation, when I was rather put out by observing in the passage near the open door, opposite to where I sat, a pair of glittering eyes steadily fixed on mine ; . . . Mrs. Williams's eyes followed the direction of mine, and going to the doorway, she laughingly said,

"Come in, Shelley, it's only our friend Tre just arrived."

Swiftly gliding in, blushing like a girl, a tall thin stripling held out both his hands ; and although I could hardly believe, as I looked at his flushed, feminine and artless face, that it could be the Poet, I returned his warm pressure. . . . I was silent from astonishment : was it possible this mild-looking, beardless boy could be the veritable monster at war with all the world ?—excommunicated by the Fathers of the Church, deprived of his civil rights by the fiat of a grim Lord Chancellor, discarded by every member of his family, and denounced by the rival sages of our literature as the founder of a Satanic school ? I could not believe it : it must be a hoax. He was habited like a boy, in a black jacket and trowsers, which he seemed to have outgrown, or his tailor, as is the custom, had most shamefully stinted him in his "sizings." Mrs. Williams saw my embarrassment, and to relieve me asked Shelley what book he had in his hand ? His face brightened, and he answered briskly.

"Calderon's Magico Prodigioso, I am translating some passages in it."

"Oh, read it to us ! "

Shoved off from the shore of common-place incidents that could not interest him, and fairly launched on a theme that did, he instantly became oblivious of everything but the book in his hand. The masterly manner in which he analysed the genius of the author, his lucid interpretation of the story, and the ease with which he translated into our language the most subtle and imaginative passages of the Spanish poet, were marvellous, as was his command of the two languages. After this touch of his quality, I no longer doubted his identity; a dead silence ensued; looking up, I asked,

" Where is he ? "

Mrs. Williams said, " Who ? Shelley ? Oh, he comes and goes like a spirit, no one knows when or where."

Presently he re-appeared with Mrs. Shelley. She . . . welcomed me to Italy, and asked me the news of London and Paris, the new books, operas, and bonnets, marriages, murders, and other marvels. The Poet vanished, and tea appeared.

Ibid.

VISITORS FROM THE MOON

We find our Air consists of thicker and grosser Vapours than the Air of the Moon. So that one of her Inhabitants arriving at the Confines of our World, as soon as he enters our Air will inevitably drown himself, and we shall see him fall dead on the Earth.

I should rejoyce at a Wreck, *said the Countess*, as much as my Neighbours on the Coast of *Sussex* ; how pleasant would it be to see 'em lie scatter'd on the ground, where we might consider at our ease their extraordinary Figures ! But what, *said I*, if they could swim on the outward surface of our Air, and be as curious to see us, as you are to see them ; should they Angle or cast a Net for us, as for so many Fish, would that please you ? Why not ? *said the Countess ;* For my part I would go into their Nets of mine own accord, were it but for the pleasure to see such strange Fishermen.

BERNARD DE FONTENELLE
A Plurality of Worlds. Trans. John Glanvill (1688)

Anno 1670, not far from *Cyrencester*, was an Apparition
Being demanded, whether a good Spirit or a bad? returned no answer, but disappeared with a curious Perfume
and a most melodious Twang. Mr. *W. Lilly* believes it
was a Farie. So *Propertius*.

JOHN AUBREY
Miscellanies (1696)

A COUNTRY LASS

I saw a Countrey lasse
did lye upon the grass,
her hatt of Strawe was made,
To keepe her in the Shade,
Her Band of plated haire
Scorning what els to ware, . . .

Her purfled Sleeves were white
lik Sunn dazling my Sight
her mayden Ribbon ty'de
to shew a Virgin Bride
her Petticoate the die
just like an Azure skye
Sheapheards to shew thiere Loves
offer'd Kidds Leather Gloves.

Skynn white as Mornings milke
softer then downe, or Silke

Brest Rocks of Curds all Seas
not prest yet for a Cheese.
haire brown as is the Berry,
her lookes modistly merry
her face still did renew
washt in each Mornings dew

Some Rurall folke did say
Her breath tasted like whay
When lipps with mine did meete,
Butter milke sugar'd sweete
Her dewy lipps Loves Streame
Fresh Strawberryes and Creame. . .

Her Waterpoole the Glasse,
bracelets redd berries was
flowers for Jewells wore
All Arts her Love for bore . . .
her Bedd the fresher grasse
her Pillowe Rushes bough'd
Trees, Curtaines for her Shroud. . . .

for Hoboyes shee did keepe
a Quire of Birds did sing
thinking she was the Spring
the murmurring Rivolettes playd,
Loves Spiritts then Obey'd,
The Brookes did dropping Weepe
while shee did gently sleepe.

? JOHN GAMBLE
I saw a Country Lasse (a. 1687)

As I left that place, and enterd into the next field, a second pleasure entertained me, 'twas a handsom milk-maid, that had cast away all care, and sung like a *Nightinghale*, her voice was good, and the Ditty fitted for it, 'twas that smooth song which was made by *Kit Marlowe* now at least fifty yeers ago : and the Milk-Maids mother sung an answer to it, which was made by *Sir Walter Raleigh* in his younger daies. They were old-fashioned Poetrie, but choicely good, I think much better then that now in fashion in this critical age. Look yonder, on my word, yonder they be both a milking againe ; I will give her the *chub*, and perswade them to sing these two songs to us.

PISCATOR : God speed, good woman, I have been a fishing, and am going to *Bleak Hall* to my bed, and having caught more fish then will sup my self and friend, will bestow this upon you and your daughter. . . .

MILKWOMAN : Marrie God requite you Sir, and we'l eat it cheerfully : and if you come this way a fishing two months hence, a grace of God Ile give you a Sillibub of new Verjuice, in a new-made Hay-Cock, and my *Maudlin* shall sing you one of her best *Ballads*, for she and I both love all *Anglers*, they be such honest, civil, quiet men : in the mean-time, will you drink a draught of *Red Cowes milk*, you shall have it freely.

PISC : No, I thank you, but I pray you do us a Courtesie that shall stand you and your daughter in nothing, and we wil think our selves stil something in your debt ; it is but to sing us a song, that was sung by you and your daughter when I last past over this meadowe about eight or nine daies since.

IZAAK WALTON
The Compleat Angler (1653)

24

Sir G. Carteret, Sir W. Pen and I walked forth, and I spied Mrs Pierce and another lady passing by. So I left them and went to the ladies, and walked with them up and down, and took them to Mrs Stephens, and there gave them wine and sweetmeats, and were very merry; and then comes the Doctor, and we carried them by coach to their lodging, which was very poor, but the best they could get, and such as made much mirth among us. So I appointed one to watch when the gates of the town were ready to be shut, and to give us notice; and so the Doctor and I staid with them playing and laughing, and at last were forced to bid good night for fear of being locked into the town all night. So we walked to the yard, designing how to prevent our going to London to-morrow, that we might be merry with these ladies, which I did.

SAMUEL PEPYS
Diary (April 29, 1662)

AUTHORSHIP

ENJOYING ONE'S BOOK

'Twill be a pretty thing, and I am glad you putt me on it. I doe it playingly. This morning being up by 10, I writt two lives: one was Sir John Suckling, of whom I wrote a leafe and a ½ in folio. . . .

My memoires of lives is now a booke of 2 quires, close
written : and after I had begun it, I had such an impulse
on my spirit that I could not be at quiet till I had done
it. . . .

My booke of lives . . . they will be in all about six
score, and I beleeve never any in England were delivered
so faithfully and with so good authority.

JOHN AUBREY
Letter to Anthony Wood (1680)

REVENGE

I am writing a comedy for Thomas Shadwell. . . . And I
shall fit him with another, *The Countrey Revell*, . . . but
of this, mum ! for 'tis very satyricall against some of my
mischievous enemies which I in my tumbling up and
downe have collected.

Ibid.

THE BLISS OF EXCESSIVE FONDNESS

He [Richardson] was delighted by his own works. No
author enjoyed so much the bliss of excessive fondness.
. . . The extreme delight which he felt on a review of his
own works, the works themselves witness. Each is an
evidence of what some will deem a violent literary vanity.
To *Pamela* is prefixed a letter from the editor (whom we
know to be the *author*) consisting of one of the most
minutely laboured panegyrics of the work itself, that ever

the blindest idolater of some ancient classic paid to the object of his frenetic imagination. . . . To the author's own edition of his *Clarissa* is appended an alphabetical arrangement of the sentiments dispersed throughout the work ; and such was the fondness that dictated this voluminous arrangement, that such trivial aphorisms as, "habits are not easily changed," "men are known by their companions," etc. seem alike to be the object of their author's admiration. And in *Sir Charles Grandison*, is not only prefixed a complete *index*, with as much exactness as if it were a History of England, but there is also appended a list of the similes and allusions in the volume. . . . Literary history does not record a more singular example of that self-delight which an author has felt on a revision of his works. It was this intense pleasure which produced his voluminous labours.

ISAAC DISRAELI
Curiosities of Literature (1792–1823)

AN AGREEABLE DELIRIUM

The mere act and habit of writing, without probably even a remote view of publication, has produced an agreeable delirium. . . . Petrarch exhibits no solitary instance of this passion of the pen. "I read and I write night and day it is my only consolation. . . . On the table where I dine, and by the side of my bed, I have all the materials for writing; and when I awake in the dark, I write, although I am unable to read the next morning what I have written." Petrarch was not always in his perfect senses.

The copiousness and the multiplicity of the writings of

many authors have shown that too many find a pleasure in the act of composition which they do not communicate to others. . . . At the early period of printing, two of the most eminent printers were ruined by the volumes of one author ; we have their petition to the pope to be saved from bankruptcy. . . . We are astonished at the fertility and the size of our own writers of the seventeenth century, when the theological war of words raged, spoiling so many pages and brains. . . . They went on with their work, sharply or bluntly, like witless mowers, without stopping to whet their scythes. They were inspired by the scribbling demon of that rabbin, who, in his oriental style and mania of volume, exclaimed that were " the heavens formed of paper, and were the trees of the earth pens, and if the entire sea run ink, these only could suffice " for the monstrous genius he was about to discharge on the world. . . .

The pleasure which authors of this stamp experience is of a nature which, whenever certain unlucky circumstances combine, positively debarring them from publication, will not abate their ardour one jot ; and their pen will still luxuriate in the forbidden page which even booksellers refuse to publish.

Ibid.

VOLUMINOUS PRYNNE

He may be well intituled *Voluminous Prynne*, as Tostatus Abulensis was 200 years before his time called *Voluminous Tostatus* ; for I verily believe, that if it be rightly computed, he wrot a sheet for every day of his life, reckoning from the time when he came to the use of reason and the

28

state of Man. His custom when he studied was to put on
a long quilted cap which came an inch over his eyes,
serving as an *Umbrella* to defend them from too much
light, and seldom eating a dinner, would every 3 hours or
so be maunching a roll of bread.

ANTHONY WOOD
Athenae Oxoniensis (1692)

WAITING FOR REVIEWS

Next Thursday I shall be delivered to the World, for
whose inconstant and malicious levity I am coolly but
firmly prepared.

EDWARD GIBBON
Letter to his Stepmother, before publication of vols 2 and 3
of the Decline and Fall (1781)

PATRONS

Let there be Patrons ; patrons like to thee,
Brave *Porter* ! Poets ne'r will wanting be ;
Fabius, and *Cotta, Lentulus,* all live
In thee, thou Man of Men ! who here do'st give
Not onely subject-matter for our wit,
But likewise Oyle of Maintenance to it :
For which, before thy Threshold, we'll lay downe
Our Thyrse, for Scepter ; and our Baies for Crown.
For, to say truth, all Garlands are thy due ;
The *Laurell, Mirtle, Oke,* and *Ivie* too.

ROBERT HERRICK
To the Patron of Poets, Mr. Endymion Porter
Hesperides (1648)

Vapid. Now do take my advice and write a play—if any accident happens, remember, it is better to have written a damn'd play than no play at all—it snatches a man from obscurity.

FREDERICK REYNOLDS
The Dramatist (1793)

•

ROYAL APPRECIATION

The Duke of Gloucester, brother of King George III, permitted Mr Gibbon to present to him the first volume of the History of the Decline and Fall of the Roman Empire. When the second volume of that work appeared, it was quite in order that it should be presented to His Royal Highness in like manner. The Prince received the author with much good nature and affability, saying to him, as he laid the quarto on the table, "Another d-mned thick square book! Always scribble, scribble! Eh! Mr Gibbon?"

Does not every reader of this anecdote judge it to be a most ingenious example of *persiflage*? How admirably does the prince *quiz* the vo-luminous Historian! . . . We must suppose Mr Gibbon to be a very silly man, if he could be flattered by the leave given to lay his works before so incompetent a personage.

H. D. BEST
Personal and Literary Memorials (1829)

He walked much and contemplated, and he had in the head of his staffe a pen and inke-horne, carried alwayes a note-booke in his pocket, and as soon as a thought darted, he presently entered it into his booke, or otherwise he might perhaps have lost it.

JOHN AUBREY
Brief Lives. Thomas Hobbes (c. 1680)

THE ARDOR SCRIBENDI

He has the ardor scribendi upon him so strong, that he would rather you'd ask him to write an epilogue to a new play, than offer him your whole estate—the theatre is his world, in which are included all his hopes and wishes.—In short—he is a dramatic maniac.

FREDERICK REYNOLDS
The Dramatist (1793)

NOURISHMENT OF AUTHORS

Every animal has an aliment peculiarly suited to its constitution. The heavy ox seeks nourishment from earth ; the light cameleon has been supposed to exist on air ; a sparer diet than even this will satisfy the man of true genius, for he makes a luxurious banquet on empty applause. It is this alone which has inspired all that was ever truly great and noble among us. It is, as Cicero finely calls it, the echo of virtue. Avarice is the passion of inferior natures ; money the pay of the common herd. The author who draws his quill merely to take a purse, no more deserves success than he who presents a pistol.

OLIVER GOLDSMITH
Inquiry into the present state of polite learning (1759)

BEING TRANSLATED INTO RUSSIAN

He called to us with a sudden air of exultation, as the thought darted into his mind, " O ! Gentlemen, I must tell you a very great thing. The Empress of Russia has ordered the *Rambler* to be translated into the Russian language : so I shall be read on the banks of the Wolga. Horace boasts that his fame would extend as far as the banks of the Rhone ; now the Wolga is farther from me than the Rhone was from Horace." BOSWELL. " You must be pleased with this, Sir." JOHNSON. " I am pleased, Sir, to be sure." I have since heard that the report was not well founded ; but the elation discovered by Johnson in the belief that it was true, shewed a noble ardour for literary fame.

JAMES BOSWELL
Life of Johnson (1791)

JOHNSON : But wilt thou do me a favour, now ?

BAYES : Ay, Sir : What is't ?

JOHNS. : Why, to tell him the meaning of thy last Play.

BAYES : How, Sir, the meaning ? do you mean the Plot.

JOHNS. : Ay, ay ; any thing.

BAYES : Faith, Sir, the Intrigo's now quite out of my head ;
but I have a new one, in my pocket, that I may say is a
Virgin ; 't has never yet been blown upon. I must tell you
one thing. 'Tis all new Wit ; and, though I say it, a better
than my last : and you know well enough how that took.
In fine, it shall read, and write, and act, and plot, and
shew, ay, and pit, box and gallery, I gad, with any play
in *Europe*. . . .

BAYES : My next Rule is the Rule of Record, and by way
of Table-Book. Pray observe.

JOHNS. : Well, we hear you : go on.

BAYES : As thus. I come into a Coffee-House, or some
other place where wittie men resort, I make as if I minded
nothing ; (do you mark ?) but as soon as any one speaks,
pop I flap it down, and make that, too my own.

JOHNS. : But, Mr *Bayes*, are not you sometimes in danger
of their making you restore, by force, what you have
gotten thus by Art ?

BAYES : No, Sir ; the world's unmindful : they never take
notice of these things. . . .

BAYES : Whereupon they all clapping—

SMITH : But, suppose they do not.

BAYES : Suppose ! Sir, you may suppose what you please,

I have nothing to do with your suppose, Sir, nor am not at all mortifi'd at it; not at all, Sir; I gad, not one jot. Suppose, quoth a !—(*Walks away.*)

JOHNS. : Phoo! pr'ythee, *Bayes*, don't mind what he says : he's a fellow newly come out of the Country, he knows nothing of what's the relish, here, of the Town.

BAYES : If I writ, Sir, to please the Country, I should have follow'd the old plain way; but I write for some persons of Quality, and peculiar friends of mine, that understand what Flame and power in writing is; and they do me the right, Sir, to approve of what I do.

JOHNS. : Ay, ay, they will clap, I warrant you; never fear it.

BAYES : I'm sure the design's good; that cannot be deny'd. And then, for language, I gad, I defie 'em all, in nature, to mend it. Besides, Sir, I have printed above a hundred sheets of papyr, to insinuate the Plot into the Boxes : and withal, have appointed two or three dozen of my friends, to be readie in the Pit, who, I'm sure, will clap, and so the rest, you know, must follow; and then, pray, Sir, what becomes of your suppose ? Ha, ha, ha.

JOHNS. : Nay, if the business be so well laid, it cannot miss.

BAYES : I think so, Sir. . . . If I could engage 'em to clap, before they see the Play, you know 'twould be so much the better; because then they were engaged : for, let a man write never so well, there are, now-a-days, a sort of persons, they call Critiques, that, I gad, have no more wit in 'em than so many Hobby-horses; but they'l laugh you, Sir, and find fault, and censure things that, A gad, I'm sure they are not able to do themselves. A sort of envious persons, that emulate the glories of persons of parts, and think to build their fame, by calumniating of persons that,

I gad, to my knowledge, of all persons in the world are, in nature, the persons that do as much despise all that, as—a—in fine, I'l say no more of 'em.

JOHNS. : Ay, ay, you have said enough of 'em in conscience : I'm sure more than they'l ever be able to answer.

BAYES : Why, I'l tell you, Sir, sincerely and *bona fide* ; were it not for the sake of some ingenious persons, and choice female spirits, that have a value for me, I would see 'em all hang'd before I would e'er more set pen to paper ; but let 'em live in ignorance like ingrates.

JOHNS. : Ay marry ! that were a way to be reveng'd on 'em indeed : and, if I were in your place, now, I would do it.

BAYES : No, Sir ; there are certain tyes upon me, that I cannot be disengag'd from ; otherwise, I would. . . .

BAYES : That's very good, i'faith : ha, ha, ha. . . . How, do you not like it now, Gentlemen ? Is not this pure Wit ?

SMITH : 'Tis snip snap, Sir, as you say ; but, methinks, not pleasant, not to the purpose, for the Play does not go on.

BAYES : Play does not go on ? I don't know what you mean : why, is not this part of the Play ?

SMITH : Yes, but the Plot stands still.

BAYES : Plot stand still ! why, what a Devil is the Plot good for, but to bring in fine things ?

SMITH : O, I did not know that before.

BAYES : No, I think you did not : nor many things more, that I am Master of. Now, Sir, I gad, this is the bane of all us writers : let us soar never so little above the common pitch, I gad, all's spoil'd ; for the vulgar never understand us, they can never conceive you, Sir, the excellencie of these things.

JOHNS : 'Tis a sad fate, I must confess : but you write on still ?

BAYES : Write on ? I gad, I warrant you. 'Tis not their talk shall stop me : if they catch me at that lock, I give 'em leave to hang me. As long as I know my things to be good, what care I what they say ?

GEORGE VILLIERS, DUKE OF BUCKINGHAM
The Rehearsal (1672)

SUCCESS

The volume of my history . . . was now ready for the press. . . . During this awful interval, I was neither elated by the ambition of fame, nor depressed by the apprehension of contempt. My diligence and accuracy were attested by my own conscience. . . .

I am at a loss how to describe the success of the work without betraying the vanity of the writer. The first impression was exhausted in a few days ; a second and third edition were scarcely adequate to the demand, and the bookseller's property was twice invaded by the pyrates of Dublin. My book was on every table, and almost on every toilette ; the historian was crowned by the taste of fashion of the day ; nor was the general voice disturbed by the barking of any profane critic. . . .

. . . Twenty happy years have been animated by the labour of my history; and its success has given me a name, a rank, a character, in the World, to which I should not otherwise have been entitled. The freedom of my writings has, indeed, provoked an implacable tribe ; but as I was safe from the stings, I was soon accustomed to the buzzing of the hornets ; my nerves are not tremblingly alive ; and my literary temper is so happily framed, that I am more sensible of pleasure than pain. The rational pride of an author may be offended rather than flattered by vague indiscriminate praise ; but he cannot, he should not, be indifferent to the fair testimonies of private and public esteem. . . .

EDWARD GIBBON
Autobiography (1789)

EASY MONEY

All on a sudden he changed his mode of life, shut himself up in his rooms, and rarely associated with any one. In the course of a few weeks, " A Ramble through Italy, by the Rev. William Moore, Fellow of King's College," was announced for publication. As he was a well-known character, many persons were very desirous to see the book. The adventures related (which were all imaginary, as he had never been out of England) were amusing enough, although some of them were highly improbable. . . . Moore netted three hundred guineas by his Travels, and as he spent nothing during his tour, he became comparatively a rich man, and was enabled to compound with some of the most urgent of his creditors. He was subsequently appointed to a living, by which he was enabled to launch again into the gay world ; but his conduct was so notorious that his companions were of a less respectable class than formerly. (1796)

HENRY GUNNING
Reminiscences of Cambridge (1852)

BOSWELL : " But I wonder, Sir, you have not more pleasure in writing than in not writing."
JOHNSON : " Sir, you *may* wonder."

JAMES BOSWELL
Life of Johnson (1791)

POSTHUMOUS GLORY

O, if my lot should give me such a friend, who knows so well how to honour the men of Phoebus ! . . . When at last, having traversed the years of a life not silent, and being full of years, I yield to my ashes their rights, this friend would stand, with wet eyes, beside my bier, and it will be enough if I say to him, standing there, " Let me be thy care." He would carefully and gently dispose in a little urn my limbs, loosened by livid death. And perhaps he would carve my face in marble, binding my locks with a wreath of Paphian myrtle or laurel of Parnassus, and I should rest in secure peace. Then, so far as there is any faith, any certain reward for the good, I myself, removed to the heaven of the sky-dwelling gods, to wherever toil and a pure heart and flaming excellence are borne, shall watch in some degree, (so far as the fates permit) from that retired world this world here, and, with my mind calmly smiling, shall have my face suffused with glorious light, and at the same time shall joyfully applaud myself in heavenly Olympus.

JOHN MILTON
Mansus (1639) (Trans. from Latin)

I have completed all things so exquisitely to my minde that I would not for all the world but that I had had this opportunity of revising them, so fond am I of the frutes of my own minde, which yet I think I should not be, did I not hope that they will be very serviceable to the World in their chiefest concernes.

HENRY MORE
Letter to Lady Conway (1662)

BATHING

PLEASURES OF SWIMMING

From the twentieth day of *May* unto the twentieth of *August*, we may commodiously adventure our Bodies in the water. . . .

If you can swim, leap into the water ; but if not, then walk gently in, till you have waded so deep that the water covers your belly, and is up to your middle : then spread your body flat upon the waters, and endeavour to swim with a good courage. . . .

He that does them [swimming exercises] with dexterity, and can exercise them all as easily as he can see the Sun, all persons will call him *Neptunes Nephew*, The Captain of the Sea ; and will never cease filling their minds with his praise. . . .

Besides the delight of the mind that the party swimming hath, there is much profit or use ; for he may swim to any shoar, and view it all the time he is Swimming. . . .

Touch your Toes [while swimming] and handle them as you please, and pare them at pleasure, for you may safely do it, and without danger.

WILLIAM PERCY
The Compleat Swimmer, or the Art of Swimming (1658)
Adapted from Everard Digby's *De Arte Natandi*
(1587)

NIGHT BATHE

It was in *June*, and 'twas on *Barnaby* Bright too,
A time when the days are long, and nights are short,
A crew of merry Girles, and that in the night too,
Resolv'd to wash in a river, and there to sport ;
And there (poore things) they then resolv'd to be merry
    too,
And with them did bring good store of junketting stuffe,
As Bisket, and Cakes, and Sugar, and Syder, and Perry
    too,
Of each such a quantity, that was more than enough.

But mark what chanct unto this innocent crew then,
Who thought themselves secure from any eare ;
They knew twas dark, that none coud take a view then,
And all did seem to be voyd of any feare ;

Then every one uncas'd themselves, both smock and all
And each expected first who should begin ;
And that they might stay but an houre, they told the
    Clock and all ;
Then all in a Te-he-ing vaine did enter in.

But now comes out the Tale I meant to tell ye,
For a Crew of Jovial Lads were there before,
And finding there some viands for their belly,
They eas'd em then poor hearts of all their store ;
Then every Lad sate down upon the Grasse there,
And whisper'd thanks to th' Girls for all their good
    Cheare.
In which they drank a health to every Lass there,
That then were washing and rinsing without any fear.

And when they had pleas'd (and fill'd) their bellies and
    pallats too,
They back did come unto the foresaid place,
And took away their Smocks, and both their Wallets
    too,
We brought their good Bubb, and left them in pittifull
    case,
For presently they all came out to th' larder there,
That it put 'em unto their shifts their Smocks to find ;
I think, says one, my shift is a little farder there,
I, I, sayes another, for yours did lye by mine.

At last, says one, the Divel a smock is here at all,
The Devil, a bit of bread, or drop of drink,
They've took every morsel of our good cheare and all,
And nothing but Gowns and Petticoats left, as I think,

At last, says one, if they'd give us our Smocks agen,
And likewise part of what we hither brought,
We shall be much obliegd, and think 'em Gentlemen,
And by this foolish example be better taught.

Although in the River they were as merry as crickets
    there,
Twixt laughing and fretting their state they did con-
    dole ;
And then came one of the Lads from out of the thickets
    there,
And told 'em hee'd bring 'em their smocks, and what
    was stole ;
They only with Petticoats on, like Jipsies were clad in
    then,
He brought 'em their Smocks, and what he had
    promis'd before ;
They fell to eat, and drink as if they'd been mad there,
And glad they were all, they'd got so much of their
    store.

And when they all had made a good repast there,
They put on their cloths, and all resolv'd to be gone ;
Then out comes all the ladds in very great hast there,
And every one to the other then was known ;
The girles did then conjure the ladds that were there,
To what had past their lipps should still be seald,
Nay more than that they made 'em all to swear there,
To which they did, that nothing should be reveald.

Then each at other did make a pass at kissing then,
And round it went to every one level coile,
But thinking that at home they might be missing then,
And fear'd that they had stay'd too great a while,

Then hand in hand they alltogether marcht away,
And every lad convey'd his Mistris home,
Agen they kist, then every Lass her man did pray,
That what had past, no more of that but *Mum.*

ANON

The Bathing of the Girles (Westminster Drollery, II,
1672)

USES OF SWIMMING

The skill and art of swimming is also very requisite in
every Noble and Gentleman, especially if he looketh for
employment in the warres, for hereby (besides the pre-
serving of his owne life upon infinite occasions), he may
many wayes annoy his enemy. *Horatius Cocles* onely by
the benefit of swimming saved his country, for when
himselfe alone had long defended and made good the
Bridge over *Tyber* against the *Hetruscans,* the *Romanes*
brake it downe behind him, wherewith, in his Armour
he cast himselfe into the River and . . . swam with safetie
into the Citie, which rewarded him with a Statue erected
in the Market place. . . .

And as resolute was that attempt . . . of *Gerrard* and
Harvey, two Gentlemen of our own Nation, who in
eightie eight in the fight at Sea, swam in the night time,
and pierced with Awgers, or such like instruments, the
sides of the Spanish Galleons, and returned back safe to
the Fleete.

HENRY PEACHAM
The Compleat Gentleman (1622)

A FEAT

Julius Caesar being hard put to it neere Alexandria leaped into the sea and laying some bookes on his head made shift to swimme a good way with one hand.

SIR THOMAS BROWNE
Notes from Commonplace Books (undated)

THE PRIVATE BATHE

The four and twentieth Day of May,
    of all times in the Year,
A Virgin Lady bright and gay,
    did privately appear
Close by the River side, which she
    did single out the rather,
Cause she was sure, it was secure,
    and had intent to Bathe her.

With glittering Glance, her jealous Eyes,
    did slyly look about,
To see if any lurking Spies,
    were hid to find her out :
And being well resolv'd that none
    could view her Nakedness ;
She puts her Robes off, one by one,
    and doth her self undress. . . .

Into a fluent stream she leapt,
    which look'd like Liquid Glass ;
The Fishes from all quarters crept,
    to see what Angel 'twas ;

44

She did so like a Vision look,
   or Fancy in a Dream,
'Twas thought the Sun the Sky forsook;
   and dropt into the stream. . . .

Thus was the Rivers Diamond head,
   with Pearls and Saphir crown'd:
Her Legs did shove, her Arms did move,
   her Body did rebound:
She then did quaff the Juice of Joy,
   fair Venus Queen of Love
With Mars did never in more ways,
   of melting motion move! . . .

ANON

The Swimming Lady : . . . Being a true Relation of a
Coy Lady . . . Swimming in a River near Oxford
(late 17th c.)

IN THE HELLESPONT

When I who was *Amans,* which we translate
A Lover, stole out of my Fathers Gate,
And having put off all my cloathes strait way,
My armes through the moyst sea did cut their way,
The Moone did yeeld a glimmering light to me,
Which all the way did beare me company.
I looking on her said, Some favour have
Towards me, and thinke upon the *Latmain* Cave.
O favour me! for thy *Endymions* sake,
Prosper this stollen journey which I take. . . .

   When I these words, or else the like had said,
My passage through the sea by night I made.

45

The Moones bright beames were in the water seene,
And 'twas as light as if it day had beene,
No noise or voyce unto my eares did come.
But the murmure of the water when I swum.
Only the *Alcyons* soe lov'd *Coeyds* sake
Seemed by night a sweet complaint to make.
But when my armes to grow tir'd did begin,
Unto the top of the waves I did spring
But when I saw thy torch, O then quoth I,
Where that fire blazeth, my faire love doth lye.
For that same shore, said I, doth her containe
Who is my goddesse, my fire, and my flame.
These words to my armes did such strength restore,
Me thought the Sea grew calmer than before.
The coldnesse of the waves I seem'd to scorne,
For love did keepe my amorous heart still warme.
The neerer I came to the shoare, I find
The greater courage and more strength of mind.
But when I could by thee discerned be
Thou gav'st me courage by looking on me.
Then to please thee, my Mistresse, I begin
To spread my armes abroad, and strongly swim.
Thy Nurse from leaping downe could scarce stay
        thee ;
This without flattery I did also see,
And though she did restraine thee, thou didst come
Downe to the shoare, and to the waves didst run,
And to imbrace and kiss me didst begin:
The gods to get such kisses sure would swim.

OVID

Heroides XVIII (C. 15 B.C.)
Trans. Wye Saltonstall (1639)

I shall never forget my surprise and delight on first behold-
ing the bottom of the sea. The water within the reef was
as calm as a pond ; and as there was no wind, it was quite
clear, from the surface to the bottom, so that we could see
down easily even at a depth of twenty or thirty yards.
When Jack and I dived in shallower water, we expected to
have found sand and stones, instead of which we found
ourselves in what appeared really to be an enchanted
garden. The whole of the bottom of the lagoon, as we
called the calm water within the reef, was covered with
coral of every shape, size and hue. Some portions were
formed like large mushrooms ; others appeared like the
brain of a man, having stalks or necks attached to them ;
but the most common kind was a species of branching
coral, and some portions were of a lovely pale pink colour,
others pure white. Among this there grew large quantities
of sea-weed of the richest hues imaginable, and of the most
graceful forms ; while innumerable fishes—blue, red,
yellow, green and striped—sported in and out among the
flower-beds of this submarine garden, and did not appear to
be at all afraid of our approaching them. . . . When Jack
reached the bottom, he grasped the coral stems, and crept
along on his hands and knees, peeping under the sea-weed
and among the rocks. I observed him pick up one or two
oysters . . . so I also gathered a few.

R. M. BALLANTYNE
The Coral Island (1860)

Diana and her Darlings dear,
   went walking on a day,
Throughout the Woods and Waters clear,
   for their disports and play
The leaves aloft were very green
   and pleasant to be hold ;
These Nymps then walkt the trees between
   under the shadows cold,
So long, at last they found a place
   of Springs and Waters clear,
A fairer Bath there never was
   found out this thousand year :
Wherein *Diana*, daintily,
   herself began to bathe,
And all her Virgins fair and pure,
   themselves do wash and lave :
And as the Nymps in water stood,
   Acteon passed by,
As he came running thro the Wood,
   on them he cast his Eye, . . .
You hunters all, that range the Woods,
   although you rise up rath,
Beware you come not nigh the Flood,
   were Virgins use to bathe :
For if *Diana* you espy,
   among her Darlings dear,
Your former Shape she will disguise
   and make you horns to wear.

And so do I conclude my Song,
    having nothing to alledge :
If *Acteon* had Right or Wrong,
    let all true Virgins judge.

ANON
*An excellent New Sonnet, Shewing how the Goddess
Diana Transform'd Acteon into the Shape of a Hart*
(late 17th c.)

AT SCARBOROUGH

Betwixt the well and the harbour, the bathing machines
are ranged along the beach, with all their proper utensils
and attendants—you have never seen one of these
machines. Imagine to yourself a small, snug, wooden
chamber, fixed upon a wheel-carriage, having a door at
each end, and on each side a little window above, a bench
below,—the bather, ascending into this apartment by
wooden steps, shuts himself in, and begins to undress,
while the attendant yokes a horse to the end next the sea,
and draws the carriage forwards, till the surface of the
water is on a level with the floor of the dressing-room. . . .
The person within being stripped, opens the door to the
seaward, where he finds the guide ready, and plunges headlong in the water—After having bathed, he re-ascends into
the apartment . . . and puts on his clothes at his leisure,
while the carriage is drawn back again upon the dry land ;
. . . The guides who attend to the ladies in the water, are
of their own sex, and they and the female bathers have
a dress of flannel for the sea ; nay, they are provided with
other conveniences for the support of decorum. A certain

number of the machines are fitted with tilts, that project from the seaward end of them, so as to screen the bathers from the view of all persons whatsoever—. . . For my part, I love swimming as an exercise, and can enjoy it at all times of the tide, without the formality of an apparatus —You and I have often plunged together into the Isis ; but the sea is a much more noble bath, for health as well as pleasure. You cannot conceive what a flow of spirits it gives, and how it braces every sinew of the human frame. Were I to enumerate half the diseases which are every day cured by sea-bathing, you might justly say you had received a treatise, instead of a letter.

TOBIAS SMOLLETT
Humphrey Clinker (1771)

HOLY WATER

As I was troubled with fits, she advised me to bathe in the loff, which was holy water ; and so I went in the morning to a private place along with the housemaid, and we bathed in our birth-day soot, after the fashion of the country ; and behold, whilst we daddled in the loff, Sir George Coon started up with a gun ; but we clapt our hands to our faces, and passed by him to the place where we had left our smocks—A civil gentleman would have turned his head another way.—My comfit is, he new not which was which, and, as the saying is, *All cats in the dark are grey*.

Ibid.

The King bathes, and with great success; a machine
follows the Royal one into the sea, filled with fiddlers,
who play " God Save the King," as His Majesty takes
his plunge !

FANNY BURNEY
Diary (July 8, 1879)

A TUSCAN FOREST POOL

In the middle of the day, I bathe in a pool or fountain
formed in the middle of the forests by a torrent. It is surrounded on all sides by precipitous rocks, and the waterfall
of the stream which forms it falls into it on one side with
perpetual dashing. Close to it, on the top of the rocks, are
alders, and above, the great chestnut trees, whose long and
pointed leaves pierce the deep blue sky in strong relief.
The water of this pool . . . is as transparent as the air, so
that the stones and sand at the bottom seem, as it were,
trembling in the light of noonday. It is exceedingly cold
also. My custom is to undress and sit on the rocks, reading Herodotus, until the perspiration has subsided, and
then to leap from the edge of the rock into this fountain
—a practice in the hot weather exceedingly refreshing.
This torrent is composed, as it were, of a succession of
pools and waterfalls, up which I sometimes amuse myself
by climbing when I bathe, and receiving the spray all over
my body, whilst I clamber up the moist crags with
difficulty.

P. B. SHELLEY
Letter to T. L. Peacock (1818)

51

BEING FLATTERED

BY POLYPHEMUS

I heard the Ruffian-Shepherd rudely blow,
Where, in a hollow cave, I sate below ;
On *Acis*' bosom I my Head reclin'd :
And still preserve the Poem in my Mind.
    Oh, lovely *Galatea*, whiter far
Than falling Snows, and rising Lilies are ;
More flowery than the Meads, as Crystal bright :
Erect as Alders, and of equal Height :
More wanton than a Kid, more sleek thy Skin,
Than Orient Shells, that on the Shore are seen.
Than Apples fairer, when the Boughs they lade ;
Pleasing, as Winter Suns, or Summer Shade :
More grateful to the Sight, than goodly Plains ;
And softer to the Touch, than Down of Swans ;
Or Curds new-turn'd ; and sweeter to the Taste
Than swelling Grapes, that to the Vintage haste :
More clear than Ice, or running Streams, that stray
Through Garden Plots, but ah ! more swift than they.
    Yet, *Galatea*, harder to be broke
Than Bullocks, unreclaim'd, to bear the Yoke,
And far more stubborn, than the knotted Oak :

Like sliding Streams, impossible to hold ;
Like them, fallacious, like their Fountains, cold,
More warping, than the Willow, to decline
My warm Embrace, more brittle than the Vine ;
Immoveable, and fixt in thy Disdain :
Rough as these Rocks, and of a harder Grain.
More violent than is the rising Flood :
And the prais'd Peacock is not half so proud.
Fierce as the Fire, and sharp, as Thistles are,
And more outragious than a Mother-bear :
Deaf as the Billows, to the Vows I make ;
And more revengeful than a trodden Snake.
In Swiftness than the flying Hind,
Or driven Tempests, or the driving Wind.
All other Faults with Patience I can bear ;
But swiftness is the Vice I only fear.

JOHN DRYDEN
Acis, Polyphemus and Galatea (1700)
From Ovid, *Metamorphoses* (c. 5 B.C.)

BY ENGLISH LADIES

Byron says that the number of anonymous amatory
letters and portraits he has received, and all from English
ladies, would fill a large volume. He says he has never
noticed any of them ; but it is evident he recurs to them
with complacency.

LADY BLESSINGTON
Journal of Conversations with Lord Byron
(1834)

Mr. John Herne of Exeter, the senior proctor for the last year, made a speech for his farewell, wherein he flattered the undergraduates, stiling them " florentissimi juvenes," men that are examples rather than to be made examples. Soe Shepen also flattered them which made them the ruder and debaucht. So impudent they were at this time that they kicked a barrell or a kidderkin that lay in the street up Kat Street and to Wadham College gate even with the proctors.

ANTHONY WOOD
Life and Times (1665)

By Foreign Visitors

He was mightily importuned to goe into France and Italie. Foraigners came much to see him, and much admired him, and offered him great preferments, to come over to them, and the only inducement of severall foreigners that came over into England, was chiefly to see O. Protector and Mr. J. Milton, and would see the house and chamber where he was borne : he was much more admired abrode then at home.

JOHN AUBREY
Brief Lives : John Milton (c. 1680)

March 5, 1668. I began our defence most acceptably and smoothly, and continued at it without any hesitation or loss, but with full scope, and all my reason free about me, as if it had been at my own table . . . till past three in the afternoon ; and so ended, without any interruption from the Speaker. . . . And all the world that was within hearing did congratulate me, and cry up my speech as the best thing they ever heard ; and my Fellow Officers overjoyed in it . . . and everybody says I have got the most honour that any could have had the opportunity of getting.

March 6. Up betimes, and . . . to Sir W. Coventry's chamber ; where the first word he said to me was, " Good-morrow, Mr. Pepys, that must be Speaker of the Parliament-house : " and did protest I had got honour for ever in Parliament. He said that his brother, that sat by him, admires me ; and another gentleman said that I could not get less than £1,000 a year if I would put on a gown and plead at the Chancery-bar ; but, what pleased me most, he tells me that the Sollicitor-Generall did protest that he thought I spoke the best of any man in England. . . . I to the Duke of York's lodgings . . . and, as soon as he saw me, he told me with great satisfaction that I had converted a great many yesterday, and did, with great praise of me, go on the discourse with me. And, by and by, over-taking the King, the King and Duke of York come to me both and he said, " Mr. Pepys, I am very glad of your success yesterday ; " and fell to talk of my well speaking, and many of the Lords there. My Lord Barkeley did cry me up for what they had heard of it ; and others, Parliament-men there, about the King, did say that they never heard such a speech in their lives delivered in that manner. Progers, of the Bedchamber, swore to me . . . that he did tell the King that he thought I might teach the Solicitor-General. Everybody that saw me almost come to me, as Joseph Williamson and others, with such eulogy as cannot be expressed. From thence I went to Westminster Hall, where I met Mr G. Montagu, who come to me and kissed me, and told me that he had often heretofore kissed my hands, but now he would kiss my lips : protesting that I was another Cicero, and said all the world said the same of me. . . . Every creature I met there of the Parliament, or that knew anything of the Parliament's actings, did salute me with this honour : . . . Mr Sands, who swore he would go twenty mile, at any time, to hear the like again, and that he never saw so many sit four hours together to hear any man in his life. . . . Mr Chichly,—Sir John Duncomb, —and everybody do say that the kingdom will ring of my abilities, and that I have done myself right for my whole life : and so Captain Cooke, and others of my friends, say that no man had ever such an opportunity of making his abilities known ; . . . Mr Lieutenant of the Tower did tell me that Mr Vaughan did protest to him . . . that he had sat twenty-six years in Parliament and never heard such a speech there before : for which the Lord God make me thankful ! and that I may make use of it not to pride and vain-glory, but that, now I have this esteem, I may do nothing that may lessen it ! I spent the morning thus walking in the Hall, being complimented by everybody with admiration : . . . and after dinner with Sir W. Pen, who come to my house to call me, to White Hall, to wait on the Duke of York, where he again and all the company magnified me, and several in the Gallery : among others my Lord Gerard, who never knew me before or

spoke to me, desires his being better acquainted with me ;
and that, at table where he was, he never heard so much
said of any man as of me, in his whole life.

March 8. (Lord's Day). Sir J. Robinson, Lieutenant of
the Tower, did call me with his coach, and carried me to
White Hall, where met with very many people still that
did congratulate my speech the other day in the House
of Commons, and I find the world almost rings of it.

SAMUEL PEPYS
Diary (March, 1668)

BY A WOODEN FIGURE

Who would believe the proud Person I am going to speak
of, is a Cobler upon *Ludgate-Hill* ? This Artist being
naturally a Lover of Respect, and considering that no Man
living will give it him, has contrived the Figure of a Beau
in Wood, who stands before him in a bending Posture,
with his Hat under his Left Arm, and his Right Hand
extended in such a Manner as to hold a Thread, a Piece
of Wax, or an Awl, according to the particular Service in
which his Master thinks fit to employ him. When I saw
him, he held a Candle in this obsequious Posture. I was
very well pleased with the Cobler's Invention, that had
so ingeniously contrived an Inferior, and stood a little
while contemplating this inverted Idolatry, wherein the
Image did Homage to the Man.

RICHARD STEELE
Lucubrations of Isaac Bickerstaff
Tatler, No. 127 (1709)

If there was an Occasion for the Experiment, I would not
question to make a proud Man a Lunatick in three Weeks
Time, provided I had it in my Power to ripen his Phrensy
with proper Applications. . . . When I was in France (the
Region of Complaisance and Vanity) I have often observed
That a great Man who has entered a Levy of Flatterers
humble and temperate, has grown so insensibly heated by
the Court which was paid him on all sides, that he has
been quite distracted before he could get into his Coach.

Ibid.

BY FOREIGN AMBASSADORS

A foreign minister of no very high talents, who had been
in his company for a considerable time quite overlooked,
happened luckily to mention that he had read some of his
Rambler in Italian, and admired it much. This pleased him
greatly ; . . . and finding that this minister gave such a
proof of his taste, he was all attention to him, and on the
first remark which he made, however simple, exclaimed,
" The Ambassador says well ;—his Excellency observes—"
And then he expanded and enriched the little that had
been said in so strong a manner that it appeared something
of consequence. This was exceedingly entertaining to the
company who were present. . . . " *The Ambassador says
well* " became a laughable term of applause, when no
mighty matter had been expressed.

JAMES BOSWELL
Life of Johnson (1791)

BOSWELL : " No quality will get a man more friends than a disposition to admire the qualities of others. I do not mean flattery, but a sincere admiration." JOHNSON : " Nay, Sir, flattery pleases very generally. In the first place, the flatterer may think what he says to be true : but in the second place, whether he thinks so or not, he certainly thinks those whom he flatters of consequence enough to be flattered."

Ibid.

BEING SENT DOWN

AGREEABLE EXILE

I am in that city which the Thames washes with its flowing waters ; I am detained, and not unwillingly, in my delightful home. I have now no anxiety to revisit the reedy Cam, nor does desire for my rooms there, which have been for some time denied me, trouble me. Bare fields, that refuse pleasant shade, don't please me ; how ill that place suits the disciples of Phoebus ! I don't care to put up continually with the threats of a harsh master, and the other things that my nature won't endure. If it be exile to be in one's father's home, and, free from worries, to pursue the pleasures of leisure, then I don't refuse the name, nor yet the state, of exile ; I enjoy its conditions cheerfully. Would that the lamenting poet who was exiled in Tomi had never endured anything worse. . . . For here I can give free time to the gentle Muses, and books, which are my very life, seize me wholly. From these, when I am tired, the spectacle of the rounded theatre summons me, and the garrulous stage calls me to applause, whether it be the sagacious old man who is on the boards, or the prodigal heir, or the suitor, or the soldier with his helmet laid aside, or whether the advocate, enriched by a ten-years' law-suit, thunders out his barbarous words to an ignorant court, or (as often) the cunning servant is aiding the lover son, and tricking the nose of the hard father. . . . Or furious Tragedy shakes her bloody sceptre, and rolls her eyes, with wild locks, and it is painful to look, yet I look, and in looking find pleasure while it pains me, for sometimes there is sweet bitterness in tears. . . .

But I do not always hide indoors, nor in the city, nor does the spring pass by me unused. I go also to a grove near by, planted with elms, and to the noble shade of a suburb. Here very often you may see troops of virgins go by, stars breathing forth enticing flames. Ah, how often have I been astounded by some marvellous figure, which might even rejuvenate the old age of Jupiter ! Ah, how often have I seen eyes that surpassed jewels and whatever stars revolve about either pole; and necks more ivory than the arms of twice-living Pelops, or than the way which flows with pure nectar ; and extraordinary beauty of forehead, and shaking locks, the golden nets which treacherous Love spreads. And seductive cheeks, compared with which the hyacinth's purple and the blush of your own flower, Adonis, seem contemptible. Yield, you often praised heroines of old, and whatever mistress ever captured wandering Jove ! Yield, you Persian girls with turbaned brows, and you who dwell in Susa and Memnonian Nineveh ! And you too, nymphs of Greece, lower your *fasces*, and you, young matrons of Troy and of Rome. . . . The first glory is due to British maidens ; enough for you, foreign women, to follow them. You, London, the city built by Trojan colonists, seen far and wide by your towered head, you enclose (too happy !) within your walls whatever beauty the pendulous earth holds. The stars that sparkle over you in the clear sky, the ministering host of Endymion's goddess, are not so many as the girls who, conspicuous in person and gold, shine in a troop through your streets. . . .

But I, while the indulgence of the blind boy yet allows it, am preparing to leave these happy walls as soon as possible, and, using the help of the divine moly, to flee far from the ignominy of the treacherous Circe. Besides, it is fixed that I go back to the reedy marshes of the Cam, and to the noise of the raucous school again.

JOHN MILTON
Elegia Prima ad Carolum Diodatum (1626)
(Trans. from Latin Elegiacs)

BELLS

On The Road to Oxford

Famous rings of bells in Oxfordshire called the Crosse-ring

He travelleth to *Tames* ; where passing by those Townes
Of that rich Country neere, whereas the mirthful clownes
With Taber and the pipe, on holydayes doe use,
Upon the May-pole Greene, to trample out their shooes :
And having in his eares the deepe and solemne rings
Which sound him all the way, unto the learned Springs.

MICHAEL DRAYTON
Poly-Olbion. Song XV (1613)

Great Tom

Bee dum ye infant chimes, thump not the mettle
That nere outrung a tinker and his kettle.
Cease all your petty larums, for to day
Is yonge Tom's resurrection from the clay.
And know when Tom shal ring his loudest knells
The big'st of you'll be thought but Dinner Bells. . . .

Rejoyce with Christ Church—look higher Oseney,
Of Gyante Bells the famous treasury ;
The base vast thunderinge Clocke of Westminster,
Grave Tom of Linconne—Hugh Excester—
Are but Tom's eldest Brothers, and perchance
Hee may cal cozen with the bell of Ffrance.

RICHARD CORBET

Oxford Great Tom (1612)

Oh the bonny *Christchurch* Bells,
  1, 2, 3, 4, 5, 6 ;
They sound so wond'rous great
  So woundy sweet,
And they trowl so merrily, merrily,
Oh ! the first and second Bell,
That every day at Four and Ten,
Cry, Come, come, come, come, come to Pray'rs ;
And the Virger troops before the Dean.
Tinkle, tinkle, ting, goes the small Bell at Nine,
To call the Beerers home ;
But the Dev'l a man ;
Will leave his Can,
'Till he hears the mighty *Tom*.

HENRY ALDRICH

Christchurch Bells (1673)

ENCHANTING MELODY

What Musick is there that compar'd may be
To well-tun'd Bells enchanting melody !

FABIAN STEDMAN

Tintinnalogia (Edition 1671)

CATCHING ANIMALS

TIGER CUBS

They diligently seek out the caves and dens of the Tigers where their young ones are lodged, and then upon some swift horses they take and carry them away : when the female Tiger returneth and findeth her den empty, in rage she followeth after them by the foot, whom she quickly overtaketh, by reason of her celerity. . . . For this occasion, the Hunters do devise certain round spheres of glass, wherein they picture the young ones very apparent to be seen by the dam ; one of these they cast down before her at her approach ; she looking upon it is deluded, and thinketh that her young ones are enclosed therein, and the rather, because through the roundness thereof it is apt to rowl and stir at every touch, this she driveth along backwards to her den, and there breaketh it with her feet and nails, and so, seeing she that she is deceived, returneth back again after the Hunters for her true Whelps ; whilest they in the mean season are safely harbored in some house, or else gone on some shipboard.

EDWARD TOPSELL
History of Four-Footed Beasts and Serpents (1607)

It is said that Unicorns above all other creatures do reverence Virgins and young Maids, and that many times at the sight of them they grow tame, and come and sleep beside them, for there is in their nature a certain savour, wherewithal the Unicorns are allured and delighted : for which occasion the *Indian* and *Ethiopian* hunters use this stratagem to take the beast. They take a goodly strong and beautiful young man, whom they dress in the apparel of a woman, besetting him with divers odoriferous flowers and spices.

The man so adorned, they set in the Mountains or Woods where the Unicorn hunteth, so as the winde may carry the savour to the beast, and in the mean season the other Hunters hide themselves : the Unicorn deceived with the outward shape of a woman and sweet smells, cometh unto the young man without fear, and so suffereth his head to be covered and wrapped within his large sleeves, never stirring but lying still and asleep, as in his most acceptable repose. Then when the Hunters by the sign of the young man perceive him fast and secure, they come upon him, and by force cut off his horn, and send him away alive : but concerning this opinion we have no elder authority than *Tzetzes*,* who did not live above five hundred years ago, and therefore I leave the Reader to the freedom of his own judgment, to believe or refuse this relation ; neither was it fit that I should omit it, seeing that all Writers since the time of *Tzetzes* do most constantly believe it.

Ibid.

* Topsell was, of course, wrong here ; unicorns had been snared by virgins at least since the 2nd century A.D.

Ofte Bees gather honie in hollowe trees, and the Beare
findeth honie by smell, and goeth up to the place that the
honie is in, and maketh a waye into the Tree with his
clawes, and draweth out the honie and eateth it, and
commeth ofte by custome unto such a place, when he is
an hungred : And the Hunter taketh heed thereof . . . and
hangeth craftely a right heavie hammer or wedge before
the open way to the honie, then the Bear commeth and is
an hungred, and the logge that hangeth ther on high
letteth him : and he putteth awaye the wedge with violence, but after the removing, the wedge falleth againe and
hitteth him on the eare, and he hath indignation thereof,
and putteth away the wedge fiercely, and then the wedge
falleth and smiteth him harder than it did before ; and he
striveth so long with the wedge, untill his feeble head
doth fayl by oft smiting of the wedge, and then he falleth
downe . . . and slayeth himselfe in that wise. Theophrastus
telleth this manner Hunting of Beares, and learned it of
the Hunters in the country of Germanie.

BARTHOLOMEW ANGLICUS
De Proprietatibus Rerum (c. 1240)
Trans. John Trevisa (1398, modernised 1582)

DRAGONS

Now the manner how the *Indians* kill the Mountain Dragons is thus : they take a garment of Scarlet, and picture
upon it a charm in golden letters, this they lay upon the

mouth of the Dragon's den, for with the red colour and the gold, the eyes of the Dragon are overcome, and he falleth asleep, the *Indians* in the mean season watching, and muttering secretly words of Incantation ; when they perceive he is fast asleep, suddenly they strike off his neck with an Ax, and so take out the balls of his eyes, wherein are lodged those rare and precious stones which contain in them vertues unutterable, as hath been evidently proved by one of them, that was included in the Ring of Gyges. . . . As for the flesh, it is of a vitrial or glassie colour, and the *Ethiopians* do eat it very greedily, for they say it hath in it a refrigerative power. And there be some which by certain inchanting verses do tame Dragons, and rideth upon their necks, as a man would ride upon a Horse, guiding and governing them with a bridle.

EDWARD TOPSELL
History of Four-Footed Beasts and Serpents (1607)

ELEPHANTS

When they be taken, they are made tame and mild with Barley : and a cave or ditche is made under the earth, as it were a pitfall in the elephaunt's waye, and unawares he falleth therein. And then one of the hunters commeth to him and beateth and smiteth him, and pricketh him full sore. And then another hunter cometh and smiteth the first hunter and doth him away, and defendeth the elephaunt, and giveth him Barley to eate, and when he hath eaten thrice or foure times, then he loveth him that defendeth him, and is afterward milde and obedient to him. . . . Elephants lie never downe in sleeping; but when they be wearye they leane to a tree and so rest somewhat. And men lye in a waite to aspy their resting places prively, for to cut the tree in the other side : and the Elephaunt commeth and is not ware of the fraud, and leaneth to the tree and breaketh it with the weight of his body, and falleth downe with the breaking, and lieth there.

BARTHOLOMEW ANGLICUS
De Proprietatibus Rerum (c. 1240)
Trans. John Trevisa (1398, modernised 1582)

Apes

All the kinde of these Apes approch neerest of all beasts to the resemblance of a mans shape, but they differ one from another in the taile. Marvellous crafty and subtill they be to beguile themselves : for by report, as they see hunters doe before them, they will imitate them in every point, even to besmear themselves with glew and birdlime, and shoo their feet between gins and snares, and by that means are caught.

PLINY THE ELDER
Natural History (c. 77)
Trans. Philemon Holland (1601)

Crocodiles

It hath been seldom seen that Crocodiles were taken, yet it is said that men hunt them in the waters, for *Pliny* saith, that there is an assured perswasion, that with the gal and fat of a Water-adder, men are wonderfully holpen, and as it were armed against Crocodiles, and by it enabled to take and destroy them, especially when they carry also about them the herb *Potamegeton*. There is also a kinde of thorny wilde Bean growing in Egypt, which hath many sharp prickles upon the stalks, this is a great terrour to the Crocodile, for he is in great dread of his eyes, which are very tender and easie to be wounded. Therefore he avoideth their sight, being more unwilling to adventure upon a man that beareth them, or one of them, than he is to adventure upon a man in compleat Armour, and therefore all the people plant great store of these, and also bear them in their hands when they travail. . . .

Peter Martyr hath also other means of taking Crocodiles. Their nature is, that when they goe to the land to forrage and seek after a prey, they cannot return back again but by the same footsteps of their own which they left imprinted in the sand : wherefrom, when the Countrey people perceive their footsteps, instantly with all the hast they can make, they come with spades and mattocks and make a great ditch, and with boughs cover the same, so as the Serpent may not espy it, and upon the boughs they also again lay sand to avoid all occasion of deceit and suspicion of fraud at his return : then when all things are thus prepared, they hunt the Crocodile by the foot untill they finde him, then with noises of bells, pans, kettels, and such like things, they terrifie and make him return as fast as fear can make him run towards the waters again, and they follow him as near as they can, until he falleth into the ditch, where they all come about him and kill him . . . and so being slain, they carry him to the great City *Cair*, where for their reward they receive ten pieces of gold. . . .

We do read that Crocodiles have been taken and brought alive to *Rome*. The first that ever brought them thither was *Marcus Scaurus*, who in the games of his aedility, brought five forth and shewed them to the people in a great pond of water (which he had provided only for that time) and afterward *Heliogabalus* and *Antoninus Pius*.

EDWARD TOPSELL
History of Four-footed Beasts and Serpents (1607)

TURTLES

There be found Tortoises in the Indian sea so great, that one only shel of them is sufficient for the roofe of a dwelling house. And among the Islands, principally in the red sea, they use Tortoise shells ordinarily for boats and wherries upon the water.

Many waies the fisher-men have to catch them ; but especially in this manner : They use in the mornings, when the weather is calm and still, to flote aloft upon the water, with their backs to be seen all over : and then they take such pleasure in breathing freely and at libertie, that they forget themselves altogether : insomuch as their shell in this time is so hardened and baked with the sun, that when they would they cannot dive and sinke under the water againe, but are forced against their wills to flote above, and by that meanes are exposed as a prey unto the fishermen. Some say that they go forth in the night to land for to feed, where, with eating greedily, they be wearie ; so that in the morning, when they are returned again, they fall soon asleep above the water, and keepe such a snorting and routing in their sleepe, that they bewray where they be, and so are easily taken : and yet there must be three men about every one of them : and when they have swom unto the Tortoise, two of them turne him upon his backe, the

third casts a cord or halter about him, as hee lyeth with
his belly upward and then is he haled by many more
together, to the land.

PLINY THE ELDER
Natural History (c. 77)
Trans. Philemon Holland (1601)

COCKATRICES

It is a question whether the Cockatrice dye by the sight of
himself : some have affirmed so much, but I dare not
subscribe thereunto, because in reason it is unpossible
that any thing should hurt it self, that hurteth not another
of his own kinde ; yet if in the secret of nature GOD have
ordained such a thing, I will not strive against them that
can shew it.

. . . I cannot without laughing remember the old Wives
tales of the Vulgar Cockatrices that have been in *England*,
for I have oftentimes heard it related confidently, that
once our Nation was full of Cockatrices, and that a certain
man did destroy them by going up and down in Glasse,
whereby their own shapes were reflected upon their own
faces, and so they dyed.

EDWARD TOPSELL
History of Four-footed Beasts and Serpents (1607)

SATYRS

Yet said *Apollonius*, there is a remedy to quail these
wanton leaping beasts, which men say *Midas* used (for
Midas was of kindred to Satyres, as appeared by his ears).

71

This *Midas* heard his mother say that Satyres loved to be drunk with wine and then sleep soundly, and after that be so moderate, mild and gentle, that a man would think they had lost their first nature.

Whereupon he put wine into a fountain neer the highway, whereof when the Satyre had tasted he waxed meek suddenly, and was overcome.

PLINY THE ELDER
Natural History (c. 77)
Trans. Philemon Holland (1601)

MULLETS

In Languedoc within the province of Narbon . . . there is a standing poole or dead water called Laterra, wherein men and Dolphins together, use to fish : for at one certain time of the yeare, an infinite number of fishes called Mullets, taking the vantage of the tide when the water doth ebbe at certain narrow weares and passages, with great force break forth of the said poole into the sea : and by reason of that violence no nets can be set and pitched against them strong enough to abide and beare their huge weight and the streame of the water together, if so be men were not cunning and craftie to wait and espie their time to lay for them and to entrap them. . . . The fisher men being ware thereof, and all the people besides (for the multitude knowing when fishing-time is come, run thither, and the rather for to see the pleasant sport) crie as lowd as ever they can to the Dolphins for aid, and call *Simo, Simo*, to help to make an end of this their game and pastime of fishing. The Dolphins soon get the eare of their crie, and know what they would have, and the better if the North-winds blow and carrie the sound unto them. . . . The Dolphins resort thither flock-meale, sooner than a man would thinke, for to assist them in their fishing. And a wondrous pleasant sight it is to behold the squadrons as it were of those Dolphins, how quickly they take their places and be arranged in battell array even against the very mouth of the said poole, where the Mullets use to shoote into the sea : to see (I say) how from the sea they oppose themselves and fight against them, and drive the Mullets (once affrighted and skared) upon the shelves. Then come the fishers and beset them with net and toile . . . howbeit for all that the Mullets are so quick and nimble, that a number of them whip over, get away, and escape the nets. But the Dolphins then are readie to receive them. . . . And so the conflict being ended, and all the fishing sport done . . . the Dolphins retire not presently into the deepe againe, but stay until the morrow, as if they knew very well that they had so carried themselves, as that they deserved a better reward than one daies refection and victuals : and therefore contented they are not and satisfied, unlesse to their fish they have some sops and crums of bread given them soaked in wine, and that their bellies full. *Mutianus* makes mention of the semblable manner of fishing in the gulfe of Iassos ; but herein is the difference, for that the Dolphins come of their own accord without calling, take their part of the bootie at the fishers' hands ; and every boat hath a Dolphin attending upon it as a companion, although it be in the night season and at torch light.

PLINY THE ELDER
Natural History (c. 77)
Trans. Philemon Holland (1601)

The Mullets have a naturall ridiculous qualitie by themselves, to be laughed at : for when they be afraid to be caught, they wil hide their head, and then they think they be sure enough, weening that all their body is likewise hidden. These Mullets neverthelesse are so lecherous, that in the season when they use to ingender, in the coasts of Phoenice and Languedock, if they take a milter out of their stews or pooles where they use to keep them, and draw a long string or line through the mouth and gils, and so tie it fast, and then put him into the sea, holding the other end of the line still in their hands, if they pull him again unto them, they shal have a number of spawners or femals follow him hard at taile to the bank side. Semblably, if a man do the same with a female in spawning time, hee shall have as many milters follow after her. And in this manner they take an infinite number of Mullets.

Ibid.

HARES

The man whose vacant mind prepares him for the sport,

The Hare-Finder The Finder sendeth out, to seeke out nimble *Wat*,

Which crosseth in the field, each furlong, every Flat,

Till he this pretty Beast upon the Forme hath found,

A description of a Course at the Hare Then viewing for the Course, which is the fairest ground,

The Greyhounds foorth are brought, for coursing then in case,

And choycely in the Slip, one leading forth a brace :

The Finder puts her up, and gives her Coursers law.

And whilst the eager dogs upon the Start doe draw,

Shee riseth from her seat, as though on earth she flew,
Forc'd by some yelping Cute to give the Greyhounds view, A Curre
Which are at length let slip, when gunning out they goe,
As in respect of them the swiftest wind were slow.
When each man runnes his Horse, with fixed eyes, and notes
Which Dog first turnes the Hare, which first the other When one
    coats . . . Greyhound
    outstrips
And turne for turne againe with equall speed they ply, the other in
Bestirring their swift feet with strange agilitie : the Course

MICHAEL DRAYTON
Poly-Olbion. Song XXIII (1622)

HARES

Starrs Enamour'd with Pastimes Olympicall,
Starrs and Planets that beautifull shone ;
Would no longer that earthly men only shall
Swim in pleasure, and they but look on.

Round about horned *Lucina* they stormed,
And her informed how minded they were ;
Each God and Goddesse, to take humane bodyes,
As Lords and Ladies, to follow the Hare.

Chast *Diana* applauded the Motion,
And pale *Proserpina*, set in her place,
Lights the Welkin, and governs the Ocean,
While she conducted her Nephewes in chace,

75

And by her Example, her Father to trample
The old and ample earth, leave the aire,
Neptune the Water, the Wine *Liber Pater*,
And *Mars* the slaughter, to follow the Hare.

Light god *Cupid* was hors'd upon *Pegasus*,
Borrow'd of *Muses* with kisses and prayers,
Strong *Alcides* upon cloudy *Caucasus*,
Mounts a Centaure that proudly him beares.

Postillian of the skye, light heel'd *Mercury*,
Makes his Courser fly fleet as the aire,
Yellow *Apollo*, the Kennel doth follow,
With whoop and hollow after the hare.

Hymen ushers the ladies ; *Astraea*
The Just, took hands with *Minerva* the bold ;
Ceres the brown, with bright *Cytherea*,
With *Thetis* the wanton, *Bellona* the old ;

Shamefac't *Aurora*, with subtil *Pandora* ;
And *May* with *Flora*, did company beare ;
Juno was stated, too high to be mated,
But yet she hated not hunting the hare.

Drown'd *Narcissus*, from his *Metamorphosis*,
Rais'd by *Eccho*, new manhood did take ;
Snoring *Somnis* upstarted *Cineris*,
That this thousand year was not awake.

To see club-footed old *Mulciber* booted,
And *Pan* promoted on *Chirons* Mare ;
Proud *Faunus* pouted, and *Aeolus* shouted,
And *Momus* flouted, but follow'd the Hare.

Deep *Melompus* and cunning *Ichnobates*,
Nape and *Tigre*, and *Harpyre*, the Skyes
Rend wit roaring, whilst huntsman-like *Hercules*
Winds the plentifull horne to their cryes,

Till with varieties, to solace their Pieties,
The weary Deities repos'd them where
We shepheards were seated, and there we repeated,
What we conceited of their hunting the Hare.

Young *Amintas* suppos'd the Gods came to breath
(After some battels) themselves on the ground,
Thirsis thought the starrs came to dwell here beneath,
And that hereafter the earth would go round,

Coridon aged, with *Phillis* ingaged,
Was much inraged with jealous despaire;
But fury vaded, and he was perswaded,
When I thus applauded the hunting the Hare.

Starr's but Shadows were, State were but sorrow,
Had they no Motion, nor that no delight;
Joyes are Jovial, delight is the marrow
Of life, and Action the Axle of might.

Pleasure depends upon no other friends,
And yet freely lends to each vertue a share;
Only as measures, the jewell of pleasures,
Of pleasure the treasures of hunting the Hare.

Three broad Bowles to the Olympical Rector,
His *Troy* borne Eagle he brings on his knee,
Jove to *Phoebus* carowses in *Nector*,
And he to Hermes, and Hermes to me;

Wherewith infused, I pip'd and I mused,
In songs unused this sport to declare ;
And that the Rouse of *Jove*, round as his Sphere may
move,
Health to all that love hunting the hare.

ANON
The hunting of the Gods
(*Westminster Drollery*, 1672)

FOXES

I could have set them right on several subjects, Sir ; for
instance, the gentleman who said he could not imagine
how any pleasure could be derived from hunting,—the
reason is, because man feels his own vacuity less in action
than when at rest.

JAMES BOSWELL
Life of Johnson (Croker's ed. 1831)

He certainly rode on Mr Thrale's old hunter with a
good firmness, and though he would follow the hounds
fifty miles on end sometimes, would never own himself
either tired or amused. " I have now learned," (said he)
" by hunting, to perceive, that it is no diversion at all, nor
ever takes a man out of himself for a moment ; the dogs
have less sagacity than I could have prevailed on myself
to suppose ; and the gentlemen often call to me not to ride
over them. It is very strange, and very melancholy that
the paucity of human pleasures should persuade us ever
to call hunting one of them."

HESTHER LYNCH PIOZZI
Anecdotes of Dr. Johnson (1786)

I know not love (quoth he) nor will not know it,
Unless it be a boare, and then I chase it. . . .

Thou hadst been gone (quoth she) sweet boy ere this,
But that thou toldest me thou wouldst hunt the boare.
O be advis'd, thou knowest not what it is
With Javelines poynt a churlish swine to goare,
Whose tushes never sheath'd he whetteth still,
Like to a mortall butcher, bent to kill. . . .

But if thou needs will hunt, be rul'd by mee,
Uncouple at the timorous flying Hare,
Or at the fox, which lives by subtilty,
Or at the Roe, which no encounter dare :
Pursue these fearefull creatures o're the downs,
And on they well-breath'd horse keepe with thy
  hounds.

W. SHAKESPEARE

Venus and Adonis (1593. Edition 1607)

D U C K S

To take such wilde duckes as are about your pondes to
make them tame, you must cast the lees of wine or red
wine in that verie place of the pond side, where you have
accustomed to cast them meat of wine and corne, with
leaven and flower tempered together, and you shall take

them when you see them drunke. Or else to take of the roote and seed of Henbane a good quantitie, and lay it to steepe in a basen full of water a whole day and a night ; afterward put thereinto wheat, and boile all together untill the said corne be well steept and swelled, . . . the wilde duckes will runne unto it, and as soone as they shall have eaten it they will fall downe all astonished and giddie.

CHARLES ESTIENNE
La Maison Rustique (1572)
Trans. Richard Surflet (1600)

BIRDS

The *Greeke* Emperours began it, and now nothing so frequent : he is no body, that in the season hath not a Hawke on his fist. A great Art, and many bookes written of it.

ROBERT BURTON
The Anatomy of Melancholy
(1621. Edition 1632)

BUTTERFLIES

The *Persian* Kings hawke after Butterflies with sparrowes.

Ibid.

MOLES

Take a live one in March, and put the same into a verie deepe and hollow bason at night after sunne set. Burie the said bason in the earth up to the brims, that so the moules may easily tumble into it, when they heare the captive crie in the night time. For all such as shall heare her (and this kind of cattell is of a verie light hearing) comming neer to their food, they will into the bason one after another; and by how many moe go in, by so much will they make the greater noise (not one being able to get out againe) because the bason within is smooth, slike, and slipperie.

CHARLES ESTIENNE
La Maison Rustique (1572)
Trans. Richard Surflet (1600)

JACKDAWS

At Oxford Mr T. H. used, in the summer time especially, to rise very early in the morning, and would tye the leaden-counters (which they used in those dayes at Christmas, at post and payre) with pacthreds, which he did besmere with birdlime, and bayte them with parings of cheese, and the jack-dawes would spye them a vast distance up in the aire, and as far as Osney-abbey, and strike at the bayte, and so be harled in the string, which the wayte of the counter would make cling about ther wings.

JOHN AUBREY
Brief Lives. Thomas Hobbes (c. 1680)

Many Gentlemen . . . will wade up to the Arme-holes
upon such occasions, and voluntarily undertake that, to
satisfie their pleasure, which a poor man for a good stipend
would scarce be hired to undergoe. . . . Hawking and hunting are very laborious, much riding and many dangers accompany them ; but this is still and quiet : and if so be the
angler catch no Fish, yet he hath a wholesome walk to the
Brooke side, pleasant shade by the sweet silver streames ;
he hath good Aire, and the melodious harmony of Birds ;
hee sees the swannes, herons, ducks, water-hens, cootes,
&c. and many other fowle with their brood, which he
thinketh better than the noise of Hounds, or blast of
Hornes, and all the sport that they can make.

ROBERT BURTON
The Anatomy of Melancholy (1621. Edition 1632)

Fisherman's Art

O Sir, doubt not but that *Angling* is an Art, and an Art
worth your learning : The question is rather whether you
be capable of learning it; for *Angling* is something like
Poetry, men are to be born so ; I mean with inclinations
to it, though both may be heightened by practice and experiment, but he that hopes to be a good *Angler* must not
onely bring an inquiring, searching, observing wit, but
he must bring a large measure of hope and patience, and a
love and propensity to the Art it self; but having once got
and practis'd it, then doubt not but Angling will prove to

be so pleasant, that it will prove like Vertue, a reward to it selfe. . . .

He that views the ancient Ecclesiastical Canons, shall find *Hunting* to be forbidden to Church-men, as being a toilsom, perplexing Recreation, and shall find *angling* allowed to *Clergy-men*, as being a harmlesse Recreation, that invites them to *contemplation* and *quietness*. . . .

IZAAK WALTON
The Compleat Angler (1653)

Fisherwoman's Luck

The Fishes in the Flood,
    when she doth Angle,
For the Hooke strive a good
    them to entangle,
And leaping on the Land
    from the cleare water
Their scales upon the sand
    lavishly scatter.

MICHAEL DRAYTON
The Shepheards Sirena (1627)

Chubs

Have with you (Sir !) on my word I have him. Oh it is a great logger-headed *Chub*. Come, hang him upon that willow twig, and lets be going. But turn out of the way a

little, good Scholer, towards yonder high hedg ; we'll sit
whilst the shower falls upon the teeming earth, and gives
a sweeter smell to the lovely flowers that adorn the verdant
medowes.

IZAAK WALTON
The Compleat Angler (1653)

OTTERS

VENATOR : Now, now *Ringwood* has him. Come bring him
to me. Look, 'tis a Bitch *Otter*, and she has lately whelp'd,
let's go to the place where she was *put down*, and not far
from it you will find all her young ones, I dare warrant
you, and kil them all too.

HUNTSMAN : Come gentlemen, come all, lets go to the
place where we *put down* the *Otter*. Look you, hereabout
it was she kenell'd, look you, here it was indeed, for her's
her young ones, no less then five ; come lets kill them all.

PISCATOR : No, I pray Sir, save me one, and I'le try if I
can make her tame, as I know an ingenious Gentleman
in *Leicester-shire* (Mr *Nich. Seagrave*) has done; who hath
not onely made her tame, but to catch fish, and do many
things of much pleasure.

HUNTSMAN : Take one with all my heart ; but let us kill
the rest. And now lets go to an honest Alehouse, where
we may have a cup of good barley wine and sing *Old Rose*,
and all of us rejoyce together.

Ibid.

FLEAS

Vex'd with a Thousand *Pigmy* friends, and such
As dare not stand the onset of a touch.
Strange kind of Combatants, whose Conquest lies
In nimbly skipping from their Enemies,
While these, with eager fiercenesse, lay about
To catch the thing they faine would be without.
These sable furies bravely venture on,
But when I 'gin t'oppose them, whip, th'are gone.
Doubtlesse I think each is a *Magick Dauncer*,
Bred up by some infernall *Necromauncer*,
But that I doe believe none e'er scarce knew
(Mongst all their spirits) such a damned crew.

SIR JOHN MENNIS (?)
Musarum Deliciae (1655)

FLIES

Domitian the Emperour was much delighted with catching
flies.

ROBERT BURTON
The Anatomy of Melancholy (1621. Edition 1632)

PRACTICALLY ANYTHING

What pleasure doth man take in hunting the stately *Stag*,
the generous *Buck*, the *Wild Boar*, the cunning *Otter*, the
crafty *Fox*, and the fearful *Hare*. And if I may descend to
a lower Game, what pleasure is it sometimes with gins to
betray the very Vermin of the earth, as namely the *Fichet*,

the *Fulimart*, the *Feret*, the *Pole-cat*, the *Mould-warp*, and the like creatures that live upon the face and within the bowels of the Earth. . . .

Hunting is a Game for Princes and noble persons; it hath been highly prized in all ages. Hunting trains up the younger Nobility to the use of manly exercises.

IZAAK WALTON
The Compleat Angler (1653)

Eusebius is of opinion, that wilde beasts were of purpose created by God, that men by chasing and encountring them, might be fitted and enabled for warlike exercises.

HENRY PEACHAM
The Compleat Gentleman (1622)

CELESTIAL

A Rash Attempt

Who would ever have believed that man could voyage the paths of the air? He arranges in a row feathers, the oars of birds, and binds together the light structure with flax cords; the lower part is bound together with wax melted by fire, and now the labour of this remarkable piece of work was finished. The boy, laughing, handled the feathers and wax, ignorant that the implements were prepared for his own shoulders. To whom said his father,

" It is with these ships that we must go to our own country ; with this contraption we must flee from Minos. . . . But do not gaze up at the Bear, or at sworded Orion, the comrade of Boötes ; follow me, with the wings you will be given ; I will go in front, you take care to follow ; you will be safe with me as guide. For if we go through the higher air near the sun, the wax will be unable to bear the heat ; or if we beat low wings nearer the sea, the moving feathers will be wet with sea water. Fly between the two ; mind the winds too, my son, and where the breezes carry you, spread sail to them." While he admonishes, he fits his work on to the boy, and shows him how to move, as their mother instructs the weak birds. Then he fits to his own shoulders the wings he has made, and nervously launches his body on its new journey. And now, about to fly, he gave his little son a kiss. . . . There was a hill less than a mountain, higher than the level fields ; from this the two take off for their ill-starred flight. Daedalus moves his own wings, and at the same time looks back at his son's, and keeps ever on his course. And now the novel journey delights them, and Icarus, having put aside fear, flies more boldly, with audacious skill. A man catching fish on a quivering rod saw them, and his hand dropped from the task he had begun. Now Samos lay on their left (Naxos and Paros had been left behind, and Delos, beloved of Apollo) ; on their right was Lebynthos, and wood-shaded Calymne, and Astypalea encircled by fishy seas ; when the boy, too rash in his incautious years, made his way higher, and left his father. . . .
[*Here this flight loses its status as a Pleasure, and must end.*]

OVID
Ars Amatoria. Bk. II (c. 2 B.C.)

So from the turf outsprang two steeds jet-black,
Each with large dark blue wings upon his back.
The youth of Caria placed the lovely dame
On one, and felt himself in spleen to tame
The other's fierceness. Through the air they flew,
High as the eagles. Like two drops of dew
Exhaled to Phoebus' lips, away they are gone,
Far from the earth away, unseen, alone,
Among cool clouds and winds. . . .

JOHN KEATS
Endymion (1818)

WITCH TRANSPORT FOR HIRE

There are foure severall ways wherby this flying in the
aire, hath beene or may be attempted. . . . 1. By spirits
or Angels. 2. By the help of Fowls. 3. By wings fastened
immediately to the body. 4. By a flying chariot. . . . We
read of divers that have passed swiftly in the air, by the
help of spirits and Angels. . . . Thus witches are commonly
related to passe unto their usuall meetings . . . and as they
doe sell windes unto Mariners, so likewise are they sometimes hired to carry men speedily through the open air.
Acosta affirms that such kind of passage are usuall among
divers sorcerers with the Indians at this day.

JOHN WILKINS
Mathematicall Magick (1648)

The day being arrived on which Mr Lunardi had informed the public . . . that he would ascend with the Air Balloon . . . at a very early hour of the day, about a hundred and fifty thousand spectators . . . assembled together at the Artillery Ground, Moorfields, where the machine was to be launched . . . forming together of themselves, perhaps, one of the grandest spectacles ever seen, there being . . . the Prince of Wales, Mr Fox, Colonel Fitzpatrick, Lord North, Lord Robert Spenser, Colonel North, Mr Burke, Lord Surry, Mr Sheridan, and many other persons of distinction, and as great a display of female beauties as ever, at any one time, feasted the eye of admiration.

The novelty of a man ascending to the clouds by the assistance of a quantity of inflammable air, contained in a balloon of thirty three feet diameter, was a curiosity which this country had never beheld, and of course both the credulous and the infidel attended. . . .

About one o'clock, Mr Lunardi and a Mr Biggins, who intended to ascend with Mr Lunardi in the balloon, came upon the spot. . . . It was found, to the regret of all, that the enterprising spirit of Mr Biggins must remain, for a time at least, ungratified. The globe had not capacity and strength enough to elevate them both. . . .

The machine mounted with slow and gradual majesty into the air. When it had risen about the height of an hundred feet, it descended again very low . . . but Mr Lunardi, with great presence of mind, threw out with his feet a large quantity of ballast from his sand bags, when the immense machine overcame the pressure of the atmosphere, disappointed the gloomy wisdom of the splenetic, and rose with the most beautiful and even progress to the skies. The clearness of the day, and the grandeur of the machine, added to the novelty, made it a luxury to the most untutored mind; but to the philosopher and the man of letters it was an occasion of the most rational delight—thus to see a new element subdued by the talents of man.

Mr Lunardi was accompanied in his aerial passage by a couple of pigeons, a cat, and a favourite lap-dog. . . . When the grand machine appeared superbly floating in the newly subdued element, and the cradle containing the bold Aerial Navigator was seen depending from it, astonishment filled the multitude, and *awful silence filled the air*, which the next instant was in tremulation with the most impassioned bursts of applause. . . . Mr Lunardi appeared perfectly composed, and as the balloon went up, bowed most gracefully, and calmly waved his flag to the admiring and wonder-struck spectators. . . . Being evidently too much encumbered, he threw it out. Soon after one of his oars broke from the pivot, and he threw that down also ; but . . . made use of the other occasionally to direct his course. . . .

In about a quarter of an hour, sailing over Pall Mall at an immense height, he met with a counter current of air, which carried him rapidly a north easterly course, over Highgate. . . . The globe was visible from various parts of the town till near five o'clock, appearing then not larger than a tennis ball, soon after which it became invisible. . . .

When Mr Lunardi had gained the utmost altitude of his ascension, he felt so strong a propensity for sleeping, that it was with the utmost difficulty he could keep himself awake ; the cold at this time became so intensely piercing, as to render Mr Lunardi's situation in it almost insupportable. . . . The cat was . . . benumbed . . . and had not Mr Lunardi's regard for his dog led him to afford him the warmth of his bosom, the animal would inevitably have perished.

The prospects were grand and awful beyond the power of imagination. . . .

The oar which dropped was dexterously caught by Mr Season, master of the Magpye alehouse, the corner of Mutton Lane ; one of the wings or sails . . . was taken up by . . . a servant at the Baptist's Head, St. John's Lane : but it was seized and torn to pieces and divided among the populace. The poor woman, with streaming eyes and wringing hands, declared that the loss of her husband or one of her children would scarcely have given her more affliction than she felt at being so cruelly despoiled. . . .

After Mr Lunardi had been up . . . about an hour and a half, the thermometer stood at 35 degrees, when the atmosphere was so cold, that icicles were upon his clothes, and he was fearful his balloon would burst ; at this time he drank several glasses of wine . . . on throwing out some air the thermometer rose to 50, when the atmosphere was delightful. . . . At Northaw . . . he threw out his cat . . . which was taken up alive. . . .

He descended a little past five o'clock, at a place called Colliers-end. . . . It is computed that his course was at the rate of twenty miles an hour, and that at times he was . . . full three miles from the earth. . . .

The evening previous to his ascending in the balloon, Mr Lunardi impelled by that common prudence every man ought to be actuated by, and not through the impulse of fear . . . signed his will, with a degree of composure that strongly marked the philosopher and the Christian.

Without attempting to enquire, whether aerostatic

experiments have a further tendency than to amuse the mind and gratify curiosity, the occurrence here related may probably have an effect highly salutary both to religion and morality. It had an extraordinary influence on the vulgar uninformed, who had been almost unanimous in declaring the project impracticable. Demonstration having convinced them of their error, they will in future be careful not obstinately to persevere in opinions hastily and inconsiderately adopted. Having beheld the ingenuity of man accomplish an exploit which they had not conceived to be within the scope of possibility, by a natural transition, the *firmament fretted with golden fires* will become an object of their enquiry, and as often as Mr Lunardi's achievement recurs to their recollection, ideas connected with the Heavenly system will arise in their minds ; and . . . it may be presumed, will be a powerful means of leading the mind of man to contemplate the stupendous works of the creation, and consequently to revere and venerate the great and omnipotent Author of our being.

ANON

Lunardi's Grand Aerostatic Voyage through the Air,
containing a complete and circumstantial Account of the
Grand Aerial Flight made by that enterprising Foreigner,
in his Air Balloon, on Sept. 15, 1784.

SUBLIME PLEASURE

The whole scene before me filled the mind with a sublime pleasure. . . . I uncorked my bottle, eat, drank, and wrote, just as in my study. . . . The broom-sticks of the witches, Ariostos flying-horse, even Milton's sunbeam conveying the angel to the earth, have all an idea of effort . . . which do not affect a voyage in the Balloon. Thus tranquil, and thus situated, how shall I describe to you a view, such as the antients supposed Jupiter to have of the earth ? . . .

At half after three o'clock, I descended in a cornfield, on the common of South Mimms, where I landed the cat. . . . At twenty minutes past four, I descended in a meadow. . . . Some labourers were at work in it. I requested their assistance ; they exclaimed, they would have nothing to do with one who came on the Devil's horse . . . I at last owed my deliverance to the spirit and generosity of a female. A young woman . . . took hold of a cord which I had thrown out, and calling to the men, they yielded their assistance. . . .

The interest which the spectators took in my voyage was so great, that the things I threw down were divided and preserved, as our people would relicks of the most celebrated saints. And a gentlewoman, mistaking the oar for my person, was so affected with my supposed destruction, that she died in a few days. This circumstance being mentioned . . . when I had the honour of dining with the Judges . . . I was very politely requested . . . not to be concerned at the involuntary loss I had occasioned ; that I had certainly saved the life of a young man who might possibly be reformed and be to the public a compensation for the loss of the lady. For the jury was deliberating on the fate of a criminal whom . . . they must have condemned, when the Balloon appeared, and a general inattention and confusion ensued. The jury . . . acquitted the criminal immediately, on which the court adjourned to indulge itself in observing so novel a spectacle.

V. LUNARDI

Letter to Gherardo Compagni, in Naples (Sept. 24, 1784)

I went, with a light heart, to the Parliament House [Edinburgh] where my Balloon is exhibited, being in a happy frame of mind for enjoying the conversation of the ladies, no less than 200 of whom have honoured me with their company this morning. Happy mortal ! you exclaim : —and well you might, could you form any adequate idea of the Scottish Beauties ! . . . Ah ! what glory to ascend my AERIAL CHARIOT in their view ! to be the object of their admiration ! to have all their eyes turned to me ! all their prayers and wishes breathed forth for my safety ! and to hear their united acclamations ! Oh Heaven ! my very brain turns giddy with the thought, and my whole soul anticipates the happy moment !

I have just received letters from *three* ladies, expressing their wishes to accompany me on my voyage. . . . How unfortunate that the Balloon should be too small to ascend with more than one person ! And I have not time to enlarge it, or else—

Ibid.
(Oct. 4, 1785)

M. BLANCHARD AND M. BOBY

I took my departure from Rouen with M. Boby, at a quarter past five. . . . While we were ascending vertically in a majestic manner, we continually saluted the Spectators with our flags. . . .

We found ourselves becalmed. . . . Having attentively

surveyed the vast expanse and contemplated the beauty of the clouds, which rolled over each other like a tempestuous sea, we congratulated ourselves on the occasion. . . . The rarefied air gave M. Boby an appetite. He ate, and I followed his example . . . we drank to the health of the city of Rouen and the Earth in general. . . .

It was now, for the first time, that we opened the Valve, in order to descend ; it produced the desired effect. . . . What was the astonishment of my Companion when he perceived himself resting lightly on the tops of the leaves ! . . . Looking at me, he exclaimed with rapture, *Ah, what a majestic descent !* Observing a great number of peasants running towards us, he expressed a desire to reascend, as it was impossible to know their intentions. . . . The outcries of the peasants invited our return . . . and we accosted them about the height of one hundred feet. . . . The most courageous contemplated us and exclaimed, " Are you Men, or Gods ? What are you ? Make yourselves known ! " We replied. We are men like you, and here is a proof of it. We took off our coats, and threw them down ; they seized on them eagerly, and began to divide them in pieces. . . . We came lightly down on a piece of corn, the ears of which supported us ; we floated for some time in that situation, and nothing surely, could be more majestic than to see us glide along the surface of it. At last we rested upon the Earth.

JEAN PIERRE BLANCHARD
An exact Narrative of his
3rd Aerial Voyage, accompanied by M.
Boby (July 18, 1784)

1

Tho' Miracles cease yet Wonders increase,
Imposition plays up her old tune,
Our old gallic Neighbours' scientifical labours
Have invented the Air Balloon.

2

This puff'd up Machine, most Frenchmen have seen,
And perhaps as a very great boon
Our wide gaping Isle Sir, may expect in short while
  Sir,
The wonderful Air Balloon.

3

It will mount up on high, almost to the Sky,
You may peep if you please in the Moon :
All Mathematicians, and deep Politicians,
Admire the Air Balloon.

6

Should war 'gain break out, as it is not a doubt
With Some that it may happen soon,
The French will invade us, their Troops all parade
  us,
Brought o'er in an Air Balloon.

7

Then Ships will appear, not in Water but Air,
And come in a twinkling down :
From Calais to Dover, how quick they'll be over,
Blown up with the Air Balloon.

8

Blood and Oons then, says Pat, but I can't believe that,
'Tis the tale of some hum-bugging loon :
So I say Botheration to the Frog-eating Nation,
Likewise to the Air Balloon.

MR. OAKMAN
(1784)

An Airgonaut

Yesterday sevennight, as I was coming down stairs at
Strawberry, to my chaise, my housekeeper told me, that
if I would go into the garden, I might see a balloon ; so I
did, and so high, that though the sun shone, I could scarce
distinguish it, and not bigger than my snuff box. It had
set out privately from Moulsey, in my neighbourhood, and
went higher than any airgonaut had yet reached. But Mr.
Windham, and Sadler his pilot, were near meeting the fate
of Icarus ; and though they did land safely, their bladder-
vessel flew away again, and may be drowned in the moon
for what we know ! Three more balloons sail to-day ; in
short, we shall have a prodigious navy in the air, and then
what signifies having lost the empire of the ocean ?

HORACE WALPOLE
Letter to Sir Horace Mann (1785)

Before me I could see the pearl-grey water netted with tiny ripples, the yellow sands, and ahead of me the sunshine falling dimly through the mussel-shell slate mother-of-pearl mist, thickened here and there in curdled spots of white cloud. The mouth of the Ouse ran like a bar of silver through the wriggling mud-flats to King's Lynn. As I passed over the town, flying almost directly into the sun, the distant cuts, drains, dykes, waterways and rivers gleamed high up, suddenly startling me with the dazzle of ghostly silver Zeppelins on my own level in the air. I was flying just below the clouds, and when I reached the Bedford River I pressed back the stick to go up through them. Clouds cloaked me in shapelessness, the machine bumped gently, I opened the throttle a trifle as the r.p.m. fell off a little, shreds of vapour passed by me and the sun shone more radiant and more golden. At 3,000 I was above the plain of vapour. The sun shone brilliantly, black shadows of struts and wires striped my wings. On my left a vast area of milk was ruffled here and there with white-cap breakers. A wall of skimmed milk stretched facing me across the sky. But on my right the milky sea was calm : no cloud clotted, with curdled white, the almost transparent whey. Yet even that sea was not absolutely uniform, but watered and laced with long, low, gentle waves that divided the pacific calm. I was alone, and a happy forgetfulness came over me as I gazed at this mood of Nature's.

Plane, engine, oil and air-speed were forgotten, as a car is forgotten, and at 5,000 feet I floated in a soundless disembodied dream, waking occasionally, it is true, to put my head into the cockpit and peer blindly until my sun-dazzled eyes could make the compass out. I was on my course—and there on my left was Ely and before me—rising up as high as my own level—the sunlit loops of the Cam, somewhere near Cambridge, seen sparkling through the bank of pearl-grey mist. . . . I shut the throttle and glided down. . . . The machine bumped as I passed through cloud. The air-speed fell to 60 as I glided slowly down. . . . I did a big side-slip, but even so I overshot and went round again. This time my approach was perfect, and my landing curiously soft and dreamlike. I was on the earth, but the earth was unreal : a limbo of haze and softened sunlight. Reality was far above me. There were no shadows here on earth and scarcely any sounds except that my ear squeaked suddenly as the air rushed into the eustachian tube.

DAVID GARNETT
A Rabbit in the Air (1932)

Among the Stars

He climbed and it grew easier to correct the plunges for the stars gave him his bearings. Their pale magnet drew him up ; after that long and bitter quest for light, for nothing in the world would he forgo the frailest gleam. If the glimmer of a little inn were all his riches, he would turn around this token of his heart's desire until his death ! So now he soared towards the fields of light. . . .

In a flash, the very instant he had risen clear, the pilot found a peace that passed his understanding. Not a ripple tilted the plane but, like a ship that has crossed the bar, it moved within a tranquil anchorage. In an unknown and secret corner of the sky it floated, as in a harbour of the Happy Isles. Below him still the storm was fashioning another world, thridded with squall and cloudbursts and lightnings, but turning to the stars a face of crystal snow.

Now all grew luminous, his hands, his clothes, the wings, and Fabien thought that he was in a limbo of strange magic ; for the light did not come down from the stars but welled up from below, from all that snowy whiteness.

The clouds beneath threw up the flakes the moon was pouring on them ; on every hand they loomed like towers of snow. A milky stream of light flowed everywhere, laving the plane and crew. When Fabien turned he saw the wireless operator smile.

" That's better ! " he cried.

But his words were drowned by the rumour of the flight ; they conversed in smiles. I'm daft, thought Fabien, to be smiling ; we're lost.

And yet—at last a myriad dark arms had let him go ; those bonds of his were loosed, as of a prisoner whom they let walk a while in liberty amongst the flowers.

" Too beautiful," he thought. Amid the far-flung treasure of the stars he roved, in a world where no life was, no faintest breath of life, save his and his companion's. Like plunderers of fabled cities they seemed, immured in treasure-vaults whence there is no escape. Amongst these frozen jewels they were wandering, rich beyond all dreams, but doomed.

ANTOINE DE SAINT-EXUPÉRY
Vol de Nuit
Trans. by Stuart Gilbert (1932)

Nakar and Damilcar descend in Clouds, and sing

NAKAR :

Merry, merry, merry, we sail from the East
Half tippled at a Rain-bow Feast.

DAM :

In the bright Moon-shine while winds whistle loud,
Tivy, tivy, tivy, we mount and we fly,
All racking along in a downy white Cloud :
And lest our leap from the Skie should prove too far,
We slide on the back of a new-falling Star.

NAKAR :

And drop from above
In a Gelly of Love !

DAM :

But now the Sun's down, and the Element's red,
The Spirits of Fire against us make head !

NAKAR :

They muster, they muster, like Gnats in the Air,
Alas ! I must leave thee, my Fair ;
And to my light Horse-men repair.

DAM :

O stay, for you need not to fear 'em to-night ;
The wind is for us, and blows full in their fight :
And o're the wide Ocean we fight !
Like leaves in the Autumn our foes will fall down,
And hiss in the water—

NAKAR :

But their men lye securely intrench'd in a Cloud :
And a Trumpeter-Hornet to battel sound loud.

JOHN DRYDEN
Tyrannick Love (1670)

What you say is true, *said she*, I love the Stars, there is somewhat charming in them, and I could almost be angry with the Sun for effacing 'em. I can never pardon him, *I cry'd*, for keeping all those Worlds from my sight : What Worlds, *said she*, looking earnestly upon me, what Worlds do you mean ? . . . Alas, *said I*, I am asham'd, I must own it, I have had a strong Fancy every Star is a World. I will not swear it is true, but must think so, because it is so pleasant to believe it : 'Tis a fancy come into my head, and is very diverting. If your folly be so diverting, *said the Countess*, Pray make me sensible of it ; provided the Pleasure be so great, I will believe of the Stars all you would have me. It is, *said I*, a diversion, Madam, I fear you will not relish, 'tis not like one of *Molière's* Plays, 'tis a Pleasure rather of the fancy than of the Judgment. . . .

> BERNARD DE FONTENELLE
> *A Plurality of Worlds*
> Trans. John Glanvill (1688)

I am glad, *said the Lady*, I have learnt the Genealogie of the Sciences, and am convinc'd I must stick to Astronomy, my Soul is not mercenary enough for Geometry, nor is it tender enough for Poetry ; but I have as much time to spare as Astronomy requires, beside, we are now in the Countrey, and lead a kind of Pastoral life, all which suits best with Astronomy. . . . Give me as little trouble as you can to comprehend you. Fear it not, Madam, *said I*. . . . Imagine then a *German* call'd *Copernicus* confounding every thing, tearing in pieces the beloved Circles of Antiquity, and shattering their Crystal Heavens like so many Glass Windows: seiz'd with the noble Rage of Astronomy, he snatcheth up the Earth from the Centre of the Universe, sends her packing, and placeth the Sun in the Centre. . . . All now turns round the Sun, the Earth herself goes round the Sun, and *Copernicus* to punish the Earth for her former lazyness makes her contribute all he can to the Motion of the Planets and Heavens, and now stripp'd of all the heavenly Equipage with which she was so gloriously attended, she hath nothing left her but the Moon, which still turns round her . . . and doth not leave her, but as the Earth advanceth in the Circle which she describeth about the Sun, and if the Moon turns round the Sun, it is because she will not quit the Earth. I understand you, *said she*, and I love the Moon for staying with us when all the other Planets do abandon us ; nay, I fear your German would have willingly taken her away too if he could, for in all his proceedings, I find he had a great spight to the Earth. 'Twas well done of him, *said I*, to abate the Vanity of Mankind, who had taken up the best place in the Universe, and it pleaseth me to see the Earth in the croud of the Planets. Sure, *said she*, you do not think their Vanity extends it self as far as Astronomy ! Do you believe you have humbled me, in telling me the Earth goes round the Sun ? For my part, I do not think my self at all the worse for't. . . .

I told her of a third Systeme, invented by *Ticho Brahe*, who had fix'd the Earth in the Centre of the World, turn'd the Sun round the Earth, and the rest of the Planets round the Sun. . . . But the Countess, who had a quick apprehension, said, she thought it was too affected, among so many great Bodies, to exempt the Earth only from turning round the Sun . . . and that tho' this Systeme was to prove the immobility of the Earth, yet she thought it very improbable. So we resolv'd to stick to *Copernicus*, whose opinion we thought most Uniform, Probable, and Diverting.

Ibid.

Let us leave *Mars*, he is not worth our stay : But what a pretty thing is *Jupiter*, with his four Moons, or Yeomen of the Guard ; they are four little Planets that turn round him, as our Moon turns round us.

Ibid.

STAR-GAZING

Look at the stars ! look, look up at the skies !
  O look at all the fire-folk sitting in the air !
The bright boroughs, the circle-citadels there !
Down in dim woods the diamond delves ! the elves' eyes !
The grey lawns cold where gold, where quickgold lies !
  Wind-beat whitebeam ! airy abeles set on a flare !
  Flake-doves sent floating forth at a farmyard scare !—
Ah well ! it is all a purchase, all is a prize.
Buy then ! bid then !—What ?—Prayer, patience, alms, vows.
Look, look ; a May-mess, like on orchard boughs !
  Look ! March-bloom, like on mealed-with-yellow sallows !
These are indeed the barn ; withindoors house
The shocks. This piece-bright paling shuts the spouse
  Christ home, Christ and his mother and all his hallows.

GERARD MANLEY HOPKINS
The Starlight Night (1877)

But the *Nightinghale* (another of my airy creatures) breathes such sweet loud musick out of her little instrumental throat, that it might make mankind to think miracles are not ceased. He that at midnight (when the very laborer sleeps securely) should hear (as I have very often) the clear aires, the sweet descant, the natural rising and falling, the doubling and redoubling of her voice, might well be lifted above earth, and say, Lord, what musick hast thou provided for the Saints in Heaven, when thou affordest men such musick on earth !

And this makes me the lesse to wonder at the many *Aviaries* in Italy, or at the great charge of *Varro* his Aviarie, the remaines of which are yet to be seen in *Rome*. . . .

This for the birds of pleasure, of which very much more might be said.

IZAAK WALTON
The Compleat Angler (1653)

RAPHAEL DESCENDS

> Nor delaid the winged saint
After his charge receivd ; but from among
Thousand Celestial Ardors, where he stood
Vaild with his gorgeous wings, up springing light
Flew through the midst of Heav'n ; th' angelic Quires
On each hand parting, to his speed gave way
Through all th' Empyreal road ; . . . .
>   . . . . Down thither prone in flight,

He speeds, and through the vast Ethereal Skie
Sailes between the worlds and worlds, with steddie wing
Now on the polar windes, then with quick Fann
Winnows the buxom Air ; till within soare
Of Towring Eagles, to all the Fowles he seems
A *Phoenix*, gaz'd by all, as that sole Bird
When to enshrine his reliques in the Sun's
Bright Temple, to *Ægyptian Theb's* he flies.
At once on th' Eastern cliff of Paradise
He lights, and to his proper shape returns
A Seraph winged ; six wings he wore, to shade
His lineaments Divine ; the pair that clad
Each shoulder broad, came mantling o're his brest
With regal Ornament ; the middle pair
Girt like a Starrie Zone his waste, and round
Skirted his loines and thighes with downie Gold
And colours dipt in Heav'n ; the third his feet
Shaddowd from either heele with featherd maile
Skie-tinctur'd grain. Like *Maia's* son he stood,
And shook his Plumes, that Heav'nly fragrance filld
The circuit wide. Strait knew all the Bands
Of Angels under watch ; and to his state,
And to his message high in honour rise ;
For on som message high they guessed him bound.
Thir glittering Tents he passd, and now is come
Into the blissful field, through Groves of Myrrhe,
And flouring Odours, Cassia, Nard, and Balme ;
A Wilderness of sweets ; for Nature here
Wantond as in her prime, and plaid at will
Her Virgin Fancies, pouring forth more sweet,
Wilde above rule or Art ; enormous bliss.

JOHN MILTON
Paradise Lost. Book V (1667)

CHRISTMAS

Dancing in Church

Captain Potter (born in the north of Yorkshire) sayes
that in the country churches, at Christmas, in the Holy-
daies after Prayers, they will dance in the Church, and
as they doe dance they cry (or sing)

"Yole, Yole, Yole, etc."

JOHN AUBREY
Remains of Gentilism and Judaism (1687)

The Yule Log

In the west riding of Yorkshire on Xmass Eve, at night,
they bring in a large Yule-log, or Xmass block, and set it
on fire, and lap their Christmas ale, and sing,
"Yule, Yule,
A pack of new cards and Xmass stool."

Ibid.

On Christmas eve I went not to bed, being desirous of seeing the many extraordinary ceremonies performed then in their churches, as midnight masses and sermons. I walked from church to church the whole night in admiration at the multitude of sceanes and pageantry which the friars had with much industry set out, to catch the devout women and superstitious sort of people, who never parted without dropping some money into a vessell set on purpose ; but especially observable was the pupetry in the Church of the Minerva, representing the Nativity. I thence went and heard a sermon at the Apollinare ; by which time it was morning.

JOHN EVELYN
Diary (Rome 1644)

THE MYRTH OF THE HONEST

It is now Christmas, and not a Cup of drinke must passe without a Caroll, the Beasts, Fowle and Fish, come to a generall execution, and the Corne is ground to dust for the Bakehouse, and the Pastry : Cards and Dice purge many a purse, . . . now good cheere and welcome, and God be with you, and I thanke you : and against the new yeere, provide for the presents : the Lord of Mis-rule is no meane man for his time, and the ghests of the high Table must lacke no Wine : the lusty bloods must looke about them like men, and piping the dauncing puts away much melancholy : stolne Venison is sweet, and a fat Coney is worth money : . . . a good fire heats all the house, and a full Almes-basket makes the Beggers Prayers : the Maskers and Mummers make the merry sport : . . . Swearers and Swaggerers are sent away to the Ale-house, and unruly Wenches goe in danger of Judgement : Musicians now make their Instruments speake out, and a good song is worth the hearing. In summe, it is holy time, a duty in Christians, for the remembrance of Christ, and custome among friends, for the maintenance of good fellowship : in briefe, I thus conclude of it : I hold it a memory of the Heavens Love, and the worlds peace, the myrth of the honest, and the meeting of the friendly.

NICHOLAS BRETON
Fantasticks (1626)

CLOTHES

A WELL-DRESSED MAN

LADY TOWNLEY : He's very fine.

EMILIA : Extream proper.

SIR FOPLING : A slight suit I made to appear in at my first arrival, not worthy your consideration, Ladies.

DORRIMANT : The Pantaloon is very well mounted.

SIR FOP. : The Tassels are new and pretty.

MEDLEY : I never saw a Coat better cut.

SIR FOP. : It makes me show long-wasted, and I think slender.

DOR. : That's the shape our Ladies doat on.

MED. : Your breech, though, is a handfull too high, in my eye, Sir *Fopling*.

SIR FOP. : Peace, *Medley*, I have wish'd it lower a thousand times, but a Pox on't, 'twill not be.

LADY TOWN. : His Gloves are well fring'd, large and graceful.

SIR FOP. : I was always eminent for being bien ganté.

EMILIA : He wears nothing but what are Originals of the most famous hands in *Paris*.

SIR FOP. : You are in the right, Madam.

LADY TOWN. : The Suit ?

SIR FOP. : Barroy.

EMILIA : The Garniture ?

SIR FOP. : Le Gras.

MED. : The Shooes ?

SIR FOP. : Piccar.

DOR. : The Perriwig ?

SIR FOP. : Chedreux.

LADY TOWN. and EMILIA : The Gloves ?

SIR FOP. : Orangerie ! You know the smell, Ladies !

SIR GEORGE ETHEREGE
The Man of Mode (1676)

In the second yeere of Queen Elizabeth, 1560, her *silke woman*, Mistris Montague, presented her majestie for a new yeere's gift, a *paire of black knit silk stockings*, the which, after a few dayes wearing, pleased her highness so well, that she sent for Mistris Montague, and asked her where she had them, and if she could help her to any more; who answered, saying, " I made them very carefully of purpose onely for your majestie, and seeing these please you so well, I will presently set more in hand." "Do soe (quoth the queene) for *indeed I like silke stockings so well, because they are pleasant, fine, and delicate, that henceforth I will wear no more* CLOTH STOCKINGS "—and from that time unto her death the queene never wore any more *cloth hose*, but onely silke stockings.

JOHN STOW
Annals (1580–1605)

YOUNG GENTLEMEN'S CLOTHES

LADY (to her sons) : Come hether both of you, doe you weare your cloathes Gentle-men like ? Where is your hat-band ? . . . Have you taken cleane shirts this morning ? Your bands be not cleane. Why have you taken your wast-coates ? Is it so colde ? Button your Dublet, are you not ashamed to be so untrussed ? Where is your Jerkin ? for this morning is somewhat colde : And you also, take your coate, are you ungirt ? Boy Neuf-a-Bien, heere you ?

You do nothing but play trickes there, Goe fetch your Masters silver hatched Daggers, you have not brushed their breeches, Bring the brushes and brush them before me, Lord God how dustie they are ! They are full of dust, what stockins have you ? Your silke stockins or your wosted hose ? Put on your garters embroidered with silver, for it may be that yee shall goe foorth with me, where are your Cuffes and your falles ? Have you cleane handkerchers ? Take your perfumed gloves that are lyned, Put on your gownes untill we goe, and then you shall take your cloakes lyned with Taffate, and your Rapiers with silver hiltes. Tye your shooe-stringes. Well, take your bootes, your boot-hosen, and your gilt spurres. Ri(chard) Neuf-a-Bien, have you made cleane their shooes to-day ?

RICHARD NEUF-A-BIEN : Yea, Madame.

LADY : Truely so it seemes, come hether you brasen-facte lyer, art thou not ashamed to affirme so apparent a lye before me ? The myre and durt sticke on them yet. Seest thou not that they are all durtie ?

PIERRE ERONDELL
The French Garden (1605)

FEMALE CONVERSATION

In a Room where both Sexes meet, if the Men are discoursing upon any general Subject, the Ladies never think it their business to partake in what passes, but in a separate Club entertain each other, with the price and choice of Lace and Silk, and what Dresses they liked or disapproved at the Church or the Play-House. And when you

are among yourselves, how naturally, after the first Com-
plements, do you apply your hands to each other's Lap-
pets and Ruffles and Mantuas, as if the whole business of
your Lives, and the publick concern of the World, depended
upon the Cut and colour of your Dresses. As Divines say,
that some People take more pains to be damned, than it
would cost them to be Saved ; so your Sex employs more
thought, memory, and application to be Fools, than would
serve to make them wise and useful. When I reflect on this,
I cannot conceive you to be Human Creatures, but a sort
of Species hardly a degree above a Monkey ; who has more
diverting Tricks than any of you ; is an Animal less mischievous and expensive, might in time be a tolerable
Critick in Velvet and Brocade, and for ought I know
wou'd equally become them.

I would have you look upon Finery as a necessary Folly,
as all great Ladies did whom I have ever known : I do
not desire you to be out of the fashion, but to be the last
and least in it : . . . and in your own heart I would wish you
to be an utter Contemner of all Distinctions which a finer
Petticoat can give you ; because it will neither make you
richer, handsomer, younger, better natur'd, more vertuous, or wise, than if it hung upon a Peg.

JONATHAN SWIFT
Letter to a Young Lady (1727)

FRUIT ON THE HEAD

Again I am annoyed by the foolish absurdity of the present
mode of dress. Some ladies carry on their heads a large
quantity of fruit, and yet they would despise a poor useful

member of society, who carried it there for the purpose of selling it for bread. Some, at the back of their perpendicular caps, hang four or five ostrich feathers, of different colours, etc. Spirit of Addison! thou pure and gentle shade, arise! thou, who with such fine humour, and such polished sarcasm, didst lash the cherry-coloured hood, and the party patches, and cut down, with a trenchant sickle, a whole harvest of follies and absurdities awake! for the follies thou didst lash were but the beginning of follies; and the absurdities thou didst censure, were but the seeds of absurdities! Oh, that thy master-spirit, speaking and chiding in thy graceful page, could recall the blushes, and collect the scattered and mutilated remnants of female modesty!

HANNAH MORE
Letter to her sister (1776)

FEW BUT FIT

The women here . . . when they go abroad, though they be naked, yet they are laden with gold and precious stones hanging at their Ears, Necks, Legs, Armes, and upon their Breasts.

JOHN BULWER
Anthropometamorphosis : or, The Artificial Changeling
(1650)

COLLECTING

SERPENTS' EGGS

In Summer time yerely, you shall see an infinit number of
snakes, gather round together into an hoape, entangled
and enwrapped one within another so artificially, as I am
not able to expresse the manner thereof; by the means
therfore of the froth or salivation which they yeeld from
their mouths . . . there is engendred the egg aforesaid.
The priests of France called Druidae, are of opinion, and
so they deliver it, that these serpents when they have
thus engendred this egg, do cast it up on high into the
aire, by the force of their hissing, which being observed,
there must be one ready to catch and receive it in the fall
again (before it touch the ground) within the lappet of a
coat of arms or soldiers cassocks. They affirme also that
the party who carrieth this egg away had need to be wel
mounted upon a good horse and to ride away upon the
spur, for that the foresaid serpents will pursue him still,
and never give over until they meet with some great river
between him and them. . . . They ad moreover and say,
that the onely marke to know the egg whether it be right
or no, is this, That it will swim aloft above the water
even against the stream, yea though it were bound and

enchased in a plate of gold. Over and besides, these
Druidae ... do affirme, That there must be a certaine
speciall time of the Moones age espied, when this business
is to be gone about.

PLINY
Natural History (c. 77)
Trans. Philemon Holland (1601)

BIRDS' EGGS

Next morning I went to see Sir Thomas Browne. . . .
His whole house and garden being a paradise and cabinet of
rarities, and that of the best collection, especially medails,
books, plants, and natural things. Amongst other curiosities, Sir Thomas had a collection of the eggs of all the
foule and birds he could procure, that country (especialy
the promontory of Norfolck) being frequented, as he said,
by severall kinds which seldome or never go farther into
the land, as cranes, storkes, eagles, and variety of water-
foule.

JOHN EVELYN
Diary (Oct. 17, 1671)

BOOKS

The Bishop [More, of Ely] collected his library by
plundering those of the clergy in his diocese ; some he
paid with sermons or more modern books ; others, less
civilly, only with a quid illiterati cum libris ?

RICHARD GOUGH
Anecdotes of British Topography (1768)

116

A gentleman calling on a friend who had a very choice library, found him unusually busy in putting his best books out of sight : upon asking his view in this, he was answered, Don't you know the Bishop of Ely dines with me to-day ?

Ibid.

For this is my mynde this one pleasoure have I
Of bokes to have grete plenty and aparayle. . . .

Still am I besy bokes assemblynge
For to have plenty it is a pleasaunt thynge
In my conceyt and to have them ay in honde
But what they mene do I nat understonde.

But yet I have them in great reverence
And honoure savynge them from fylth and ordure
By often brusshynge and moche dylygence
Full goodly bounde in pleasaunt coverture
Of damas satyn or else of velvet pure.
I kepe them sure ferynge lyst they sholde be lost
For in them is the connynge wherin I me bost.

ALEXANDER BARCLAY
The Shyp of Folys (1509)
(Trans. from Brandt)

The personal dislike which Pope Innocent X bore to the French had originated in his youth, when a cardinal, from having been detected in the library of an eminent French collector of having purloined a most rare volume.

The delirium of a collector's rage overcame even French politesse ; the Frenchman not only openly accused his illustrious culprit, but was resolved that he should not quit the library without replacing the precious volume— from accusation and denial both resolved to try their strength : but in this literary wrestling-match the book dropped out of the cardinal's robes—and from that day he hated the French.

ISAAC DISRAELI
Curiosities of Literature (1791–1823)

I have made Mr Bodley acquainted with your kinde and friendly offer, who accepteth of it in most thankful manner : and if it pleaseth you to appoint to-morrow . . . wee will not fayle to bee with you at your house for that purpose. And remember I give you fayre warning that if you hold any booke so deare as that you wold be loth to have him out of your sight, gett him aside beforehande ; for myne owne part, I will not doe wronge to my judgement as to chuse of the worst, if bettere bee in place. And beside you wold account mee a simple man. . . .

True it is that I have raysed some expectations of the quality of your gift in Mr Bodley, whom you shall find a gentle man, in all respects very worthy of your acquayntance.

SIR HENRY SAVILE
Letter to Sir Robert Cotton (c. 1600)

NOTE. As an example of the garbling methods of literary anecdotists, it is instructive to compare this letter with the account of it given by Isaac Disraeli in *Curiosities of Literature*, which runs, " Sir Robert Saville writing to Sir Robert Cotton, appointing an interview with the founder of the Bodleian Library, cautions Sir Robert, that ' If he held any book so dear as he would be loath to lose it, he should *not let Sir Thomas out of his sight*, but set " the boke " aside beforehand.' "

MANUSCRIPTS

One of the Ptolemies refused supplying the famished
Athenians with wheat, until they presented him with
the original manuscripts of Æscylus, Sophocles, and
Euripides.

ISAAC DISRAELI
Curiosities of Literature (1792–1823)

CONVERSATION

CHAT

In various talk th'instructive hours they past,
Who gave the ball, or paid the visit last.
One speaks the glory of the British Queen,
And one describes a charming Indian screen ;
A third interprets motions, looks, and eyes ;
At ev'ry word a reputation dies.
Snuff, or the fan, supply each pause of chat,
With singing, laughing, ogling, *and all that.*

ALEXANDER POPE
The Rape of the Lock (1712)

At table I had very good discourse with Mr Ashmole, wherin he did assure me that frogs and many insects do often fall from the sky, ready formed.

SAMUEL PEPYS
Diary (May 23, 1661)

Tossing and Goring

When I called upon Dr Johnson next morning, I found him highly satisfied with his colloquial prowess the preceding evening. " Well (said he) we had good talk." Boswell : " Yes, Sir ; you tossed and gored several persons."

JAMES BOSWELL
Life of Johnson (1791)

About Cowley

Belinda : Come, Mr. *Sharper*, you and I will take a Turn, and laugh at the Vulgar—Both the great Vulgar and the small—Oh Gad ! I have a great passion for *Cowley*— Don't you admire him ?

Sharper : Oh Madam ! He was our *English Horace*.

Belinda : Ah so fine ! So extreamly fine ! So every thing in the World that I like—Oh Lord, walk this Way—I see a Couple, I'll give you their History.

WILLIAM CONGREVE
The Old Batchelor (1693)

CARELESS : Where are the Women ? I'm weary of guzz-
ling, and begin to think them the better Company ?

MELLEFONT : Then thy Reason staggers, and thou'rt
almost Drunk.

CARELESS : No Faith, but your Fools grow noisie—and
if a Man must endure the Noise of Words without Sense,
I think the Women have more Musical Voices, and
become Nonsense better.

MELLEFONT : Why, they are at the end of the Gallery ;
retir'd to their Tea and Scandal ; acording to their
Ancient Custom after Dinner.

WILLIAM CONGREVE
The Double-Dealer (1693)

IMPROVING THE MIND

If you are in company with Men of learning, though they
happen to discourse of Arts and Sciences out of your compass, yet you will gather more advantage by list'ning to
them than from all the nonsense and frippery of your own
Sex ; but, if they be Men of Breeding as well as Learning,
they will seldom engage in any Conversation where you
ought not to be a hearer, and in time have your part. If they
talk of the Manners and Customs of the several Kingdoms
of Europe, of Travels into remoter Nations, of the state of
their own Country, or of the great Men and Actions of
Greece and Rome ; if they give their judgment upon English
and French Writers, either in Verse or Prose, or of the

nature and limits of Virtue and Vice, it is a shame for an English Lady not to relish such Discourses, not to improve by them, and endeavour by Reading and Information, to have her share in those Entertainments ; rather than turn aside, as it is the usual custom, and consult with the Woman who sits next her, about a new Cargo of Fans.

JONATHAN SWIFT
Letter to a Young Lady (1727)

EDUCATED TALK

One of the greatest pleasures of life is conversation ;— and the pleasures of conversation are of course enhanced by every increase of knowledge : not that we should meet together to talk of alkalis and angles, or to add to our stock of history and philology,—though a little of these things is no bad thing in conversation ; but let the subject be what it may, there is always a prodigious difference between the conversation of those who have been well educated and of those who have not enjoyed this advantage. Education gives fecundity of thought, copiousness of illustration, quickness, vigour, fancy, words, images and illustrations ;— it decorates every common thing, and gives the power of trifling without being undignified and absurd. . . . Now, really, nothing can be further from our intention than to say anything rude and unpleasant ; but we must be excused from observing, that it is not now a very common thing to be interested by the variety and extent of female knowledge.

SYDNEY SMITH
Female Education (1809)

If they have a story to relate, they must needs make its beginning rise with the Beginning of the World, and they dwell so long upon frivolous circumstances that they are insensibly drawne to other matters, into which they hop like birds from branch to branch, and sometimes in the very middle of their relation they wander so far from the Subject they had in Hand, that they are forc'd to seek about for it againe, as the young lad did for his Fathers Asses.

J. B.
Heroick Education (1657)

HOW TO CONVERSE

I have passed, perhaps, more time than any other man of my age and country in visits and assemblies, where the polite persons of both sexes distinguish themselves ; and could not without much grief observe how frequently both gentlemen and ladies are at a loss for questions, answers replies and rejoinders. . . . How often do we see at Court, at publick visiting-days, at great men's levées, and other places of general meeting that the conversation falls and drops to nothing, like a fire without supply of fuel. This is what we all ought to lament; and against this dangerous evil I take upon me to affirm, that I have, in the following papers, provided an infallible remedy. . . .

The curious reader will observe, that, when conversation appears in danger to flag . . . I took care to invent some sudden question, or turn of wit to revive it ; such as

these that follow : " What ? I think here's a silent meeting !
Come, Madam, a penny for your thought " ; with several
others of the like sort. . . .

When this happy art of polite conversing shall be
thoroughly improved, good company will be no longer
pestered with dull, dry, tedious story-tellers, nor brangling
disputers ; for a right scholar of either sex in our science
will perpetually interrupt them with some sudden sur-
prising piece of wit, that shall engage all the company in a
loud laugh ; and if, after a pause, the grave companion
resumes his thread in the following manner, " Well, but
to go on with my story," new interruptions come from the
left and right, till he is forced to give over.

JONATHAN SWIFT

*Introduction to A Compleat Collection of Genteel and
Ingenious Conversation* (1738)

AT THE TEA-TABLE

Lady Smart's antichamber. Miss Notable comes in.

MR. NEVEROUT : Miss, your slave : I hope your early
rising will do you no harm. I find you are but just come
out of the cloth market.

MISS : I always rise at eleven, whether it be day or no.

COL. ATWITT : Miss, I hope you are up for all day.

MISS : Yes, if I don't get a fall before night.

COL. : Miss, I heard you were out of order ; pray, how
are you now ?

MISS : Pretty well, Colonel, I thank you.

COL. : Pretty and well, miss ! that's two very good things . . .

MISS (*to* LADY SMART) : Pray, Madam, give me some more sugar to my tea.

COL. : Oh ! Miss, you must needs be very good-humour'd, you love sweet things so well.

NEVEROUT : Stir it up with the spoon, miss ; for the deeper the sweeter.

LADY SMART : I assure you, Miss, the Colonel has made you a great compliment.

MISS : I am sorry for it ; for I have heard say, complimenting is lying. . . .

LADY SMART : Lord, miss, how can you drink your tea so hot ? sure your mouth's paved. How do you like this tea, colonel ?

COL. : Well enough, madam ; but methinks it is a little more-ish.

LADY SMART : Oh colonel ! I understand you. Betty, bring the canister ; I have very little of this tea left ; but I don't love to make two wants of one ; want when I have it, and want when I have it not. He, he, he, he.

LADY ANSWERALL (*to the* MAID) : Why, sure, Betty, you are bewitched, the cream is burnt too.

BETTY : Why, madam, the bishop has set his foot in it.

LADY SMART : Go, run, girl, and warm fresh cream.

BETTY : Indeed, madam, there's none left ; for the cat has eaten it all.

LADY SMART : I doubt it was a cat with two legs. . . .

COL. : Miss, when will you be married ?

MISS : One of these odd-come-shortly's, colonel.

NEVEROUT : Yes ; they say the match is half made, the spark is willing, but miss is not.

MISS : I suppose the gentleman has got his own consent for it.

LADY A. : Pray, my Lord, did you walk through the Park in the rain ?

LORD SPARKISH : Yes, madam, we were neither sugar nor salt, we were not afraid the rain would melt us. He, he, he

COL. : It rain'd, and the sun shone at the same time. . . .

LADY S. : Miss, dear girl, fill me out a dish of tea, for I'm very lazy.

MISS *fills a dish of tea, sweetens it, and tastes it.*

LADY S. : What, miss, will you be my taster ?

MISS : No, madam ; but they say it's an ill cook that can't lick her own fingers.

NEV. : Pray, miss, fill me another.

MISS : Will you have it now, or stay till you get it ?

LADY A. : But, colonel, they say you went to court last night very drunk : nay, I'm told for certain, you had been among the Philistines : no wonder the cat winked when both her eyes were out.

COL. : Indeed, madam, that's a lye.

LADY A. : 'Tis better I should lye than you should lose your good manners besides, I don't lie, I sit. . . .

LADY S. : Well, I fear Lady Answerall can't live long, she has so much wit. . . .

MISS : But pray, Mr Neverout, what lady was that you were talking with in the side-box last Tuesday ?

NEV. : Miss, can you keep a secret ?

MISS : Yes, I can.

NEV. : Well, miss, and so can I.

JONATHAN SWIFT
A Compleat Collection of Genteel and Ingenious Conversation (1738)

CONVERSION

To the Church of England

It is honorable, both for that by this meanes infinite nombers of soules may be brought from theyr idolatry, bloody sacrifices, ignoraunce and incivility, to the worshipping of the true God aright to civill conversation, and also theyr bodyes freed from the intollerable tirrany of the Spaniards whereunto they are already or likely in shorte space to be subjected, unlesse her excellent Majestie or some other christian prince doe speedily assiste, and afterward protect them in their just defensive wars against the violence of usurpers. . . .

Likewise it is profitable, for heereby the Queens dominions may bee exceedingly enlarged, and this Realme inestimably enriched, with pretious stones, gold, silver, pearle, and other commodityes which those countryes yeald, and (God giving good successe to the voiage) an entrance made thereby to many other Empyres (which happily may prove as rich as this) and it may bee to Peru its selfe and other Kingdomes of which the Spaniards bee now possessed. . . .

To be shorte, all sound Christians . . . do repute the Kings of Castile and Portugall meere usurpers in Africke and America. . . . Christians may not warrantably conquer Infidells upon pretence only of their infidelity. But I hould it very reasonable and charitable to send preachers safely guarded if need bee, to offer Infidells the gladd tidings of the Gospell. . . .

The condicions to be required of them are these. First to renounce their Idolatry, and to worship the only true God. . . .

2. That the Inga of Manoa . . . surrender the ensignes of his Empire to her Majestie. . . . Also her Majesties Lieuetenantes to direct the Guianians in their conclusions both of warr and peace : Rendring yearly to Her Majestie and her successors a great tribute allotting to her use some rich mines and rivers of gold, pearle, silver, rocks of pretious stone, etc. with some large fruitfull countryes for the planting of her Colonyes. . . .

Wee may make choise to arme and instructe such of them as we find most trusty and most prone to Christianity, reserving the powder and shott in our own custody. . . .

Besids this easy and compendious way of possessing Guiana by arming the inhabitants, there is speciall choise to be had in sending preachers of good discrecion and behavior for their conversion.

SIR WALTER RALEIGH
Of the Voyage for Guiana (c. 1598)

He the Duke of Norfolk renounced " the errors of Popery " . . . he said, " I cannot be a good Catholic ; I cannot go to Heaven; and if a man is to go to the devil, he may as well go thither from the House of Lords as from any other place on earth."

When he qualified for some office, perhaps that of Lord Lieutenant of the county—of Gloucester, I think—which qualification consists in receiving the Lord's Supper according to the rite of the Church of England, he returned the cup out of which he drank the sacramental wine, saying in hardly an under voice, "Port, by G——!" What does the Church of England gain by conversions such as these ?

H. D. BEST
Personal and Literary Memorials (1829)

TO PRESBYTERIANISM

> Yesterday I went
> To see a lady that has a parrott ; my woman
> While I was in discourse, converted the fowle,
> And now it can speak naught but Knox's words ;
> So there's a parrot lost.

JASPER MAYNE
The City Match (1639)

TO ROMAN CATHOLICISM

In the river of *Pato* otherwise called *Orinoque*, in the principall part thereof called *Warismero*, the 23 of Aprill 1593, *Domingo de Vera* Master of the Campe and . . . Captaine generall for our Lorde the King . . . commanded all the soldiers to be drawne together and put in order of battaile, the Captaines and soldiers and master of the campe standing in the middest of them, said unto them : Sirs, Soldiers and Captaines, you understand long since that our Generall *Anth. de Berreo*, with the travell of 11 yeares,

EP   129

and expence of more than 100000 pesoes of Gold, discovered the noble provinces of *Guiana* and *Dorado* : On the which he tooke possession to governe the same. . . . Now they had sente me to learne out and discover the ways most easily to enter and to people the saide provinces, and where the Campes and Armies may best enter the same. By reason whereof I entend to do so in the name of his Majesty, and the said governour *Antho. de Berreo*, and in token thereof I require you, *Fran. Carillo*, that you aide me to advance this crosse that lieth here on the ground, which they set on end towardes the east, and the said Master of the Campe, the Captains and soldiers kneeled down and did due reverence unto the said crosse, and thereupon the Master of the Campe . . . drew out his sworde and cut the grasse of the ground, and the boughs of the trees, saying, I take this possession in the name of *Don Philip* our master, and of his governour *Antho : de Berreo* . . . And the said Master of the Campe kneeled downe . . . and all the Captaines and soldiers saide that the possession was wel taken, and that they would defend it with their lives, upon whosoever would say the contrary. . . . And in prosecution of the said possession . . . the Master of the Camp entered by little and little, with all the Campe and men of warre, more then two leagues into the Inland, and came to a towne of a Principall, and conferring with him did let him understand . . . that his Majesty . . . had sent him to take the said possession. And the said fryer *Francis Carillo* by the Interpretor delivered him certain thinges of our holy Catholique faith, to al which he answered, that they understood him well and would becom Christians, and that with a very good wil they should advance the crosse, in what part or place of the towne it pleased them, for he was for the governour *Anth : de Berreo*, who was his Master. Thereupon the said master of the Campe tooke a great crosse, and set it on ende toward the east, and requested the whole Campe to witnesse it.

RODRIGO DE CARANCA, Register of the Army
Report to King of Spain of the discovery of Nuevo Dorado. Taken at sea by Captain Popham and trans. by Sir Walter Raleigh (1594)

TO CHRISTIANITY

For when the *Saxons* first receaved the Christian Faith,
Paulinus of old *Yorke*, the zealous Bishop then,
In *Swales* abundant streame Christned ten thousand men,
With women and their babes, a number more beside,
Upon one happy day, whereof shee boasts with pride.

MICHAEL DRAYTON
Poly-Olbion. Song XXVIII

TO AND FRO

Upon the dissolution of the abbeys, he [Henry VIII] gave him the abbey of Wilton, and a country of lands and mannours therabout belonging to it. . . .

In queen Mary's time, upon the returne of the Catholique religion, the nunnes came again to Wilton abbey, and this William, earl of Pembroke came to the gate . . . with his cappe in his hand, and fell upon his knee to the lady abbesse and the nunnes, crying peccavi. Upon queen

Mary's death the earle came to Wilton (like a tygre) and
turned them out, crying, " Out, ye whores, to worke, to
worke, ye whores, goe spinne."

JOHN AUBREY
Brief Lives : William Herbert, 1st earle of Pembroke
(c. 1680)

To Royalism

The day of restoration of K.Ch.2 observed. . . . They
were freed from the chaines of darkness and confusion
which the presbyterians and phanaticks had brought upon
them . . . some of them seeing what mischiefe they had
done, tack'd about to participate of the universal joy, and
at length clos'd with the royal partie.

ANTHONY WOOD
Life and Times (1660)

To Orangery

O falsnes ! He that ran with the humour of King James II
now forsakes him, to cring to prince of Orange in hopes
to keep his bishoprick.

Ibid.
(1689)

To Holy Orders

Such strifes as these S. *Augustine* had, when S. *Ambrose*
indeavoured his conversion to Christianity, . . . Our learned
Author . . . did the like. And declaring his intention to

132

his deare friend D. *King*, the then worthy *Bishop of London* . . . That Reverend Bishop most gladly received the news ; and, with all convenient speed ordained him Deacon and Priest.

Now the English Church had gained a second S. *Augustine*, for I think none was so like him before his conversion : none so like S. *Ambrose* after it. And if his youth had the infirmities of the one Father, his age had the excellencies of the other, the learning and holiness of both.

Now all his studies (which were occasionally diffused) were concentred in Divinity. Now he had a new calling, new thoughts, and a new employment for his wit and eloquence. Now all his earthly affections were changed into divine love, and all the faculties of his soule were ingaged in the conversion of others. . . .

Presently after he enterd into his holy Profession, the King made him his Chaplaine in ordinary, and gave him other incouragements, promising to take a particular care of him.

IZAAK WALTON
Life of Dr. John Donne (1640)

TO SCORN OF MONEY

Who could imagine that Diogenes in his yonger dayes should bee a falsifier of mony who in the after-course of his life was so great a contemner of metall, as to laugh at all that loved it. Butt men are not the same in all divisions of their ages.

SIR THOMAS BROWNE
Notes from Commonplace Books (Undated)

Dr —— *Twiss*, . . . told me, that his father (Dr *Twiss*, polocutor of the Assembly of Divines, and Author of *Vindiciae*) when he was a school-boy at *Winchester*, saw the phantome of a Scool-fellow of his, deceased, (a rake-hell) who said to him, " *I am damned*." This was the occasion of Dr *Twiss's* (the father's) Conversion, who had been before that time, as he told his Son, a very wicked Boy, he was hypochondriacal. There is a Story like this, of the Conversion of St *Bruno*, by an Apparition : upon which he became mighty devout, and founded the Order of the *Carthusians*.

JOHN AUBREY
Miscellanies (1696)

To a State of Grace

But about the 14th Year of his Age, being under some more than usual Convictions of Sin, after his having robb'd a Neighbour's Orchard, it pleas'd God he met with *Parsons Of Resolution*, (as Corrected by *Bunny*) in the reading of which such Impressions were made upon his Spirit, as never wore off to the Day of his Death. . . . He had often formerly had tho'ts of this kind Stirring in his Mind, but now they came in another manner, with Sense and Power and Seriousness to his Heart. This cast him into Fears about his Condition, and they drove him to Cordial Contrition, Confession, and Prayer ; and issu'd in a serious Resolution of altering his Course. Meeting afterwards with Dr. Sibb's *Bruised Reed*, . . . by the reading also of Mr. Perkins *of Repentance*, . . . and some other of his Treatises, he was further inform'd and confirm'd. . . . The reading of Mr. Ezek. Culverwel *Of Faith* at this time gave him much Relief. . . .

Upon further search, he found that the first Degree of Special Grace was usually very small, and therefore not easily distinguishable in the season of its first Prevalence from Preparatory Grace : . . . But that which most perplex'd him, and which created him the Greatest Difficulty, was the finding himself Guilty of known and deliberate Sin, after that he had tho't himself Converted : This he for a long time could not tell how to Reconcile with true Grace. Every known Sin he committed, in this respect, renew'd his Doubt. . . .

It much encreas'd his Peace to find others in the like Condition : He found his Case had nothing Singular.

EDMUND CALAMY
Life of Richard Baxter (1702)

TO QUAKERISM

Mrs Knowles mentioned, as a proselyte to Quakerism, a young lady well known to Dr Johnson . . . JOHNSON (frowning very angrily) : " Madam, she is an odious wench. She could not have any proper conviction that it was her duty to change her religion. . . . She knew no more of the Church which she left, and that which she embraced, than she did of the difference between the Copernican and Ptolemaic systems." MRS KNOWLES: " She had the New Testament before her." JOHNSON : " Madam, she could not understand the New Testament."

JAMES BOSWELL
Life of Johnson (1791)

CORRESPONDENCE

A Use for Letters

MRS FAINALL : You were dress'd before I came abroad.

MILLAMANT : Ay, that's true—— O but then I had— *Mincing*, what had I ? Why was I so long ?

MINCING : O Mem, your Laship staid to peruse a Pacquet of Letters.

MILL. : O ay, Letters—I had Letters—I am persecuted with Letters—I hate Letters—— No Body knows how to write Letters ; and yet one has 'em, one does not know why—— They serve one to pin up one's Hair.

WITWOUD : Is that the way ? Pray, Madam, do you pin up your Hair with all your Letters ? I find I must keep Copies.

MILL. : Only with those in Verse, Mr *Witwoud*. I never pin up my Hair with Prose. I think I try'd once, *Mincing*.

MINCING : O Mem, I shall never forget it.

MILL. : Ay, poor *Mincing* tift and tift all the Morning.

MINCING : Till I had the Cramp in my Fingers, I'll vow, Mem. And all to no purpose. But when your Laship pins

it up with Poetry, it sits so pleasant the next Day as any
Thing, and is so pure and so crips.

WITWOUD : Indeed, so crips ?

MINCING : You're such a Critick, Mr *Witwoud*.

WILLIAM CONGREVE
The Way of the World (1700)

ANOTHER USE

The manuscripts of Pope's version of the Iliad and
Odyssey . . . are written chiefly on the backs of letters.

ISAAC DISRAELI
Curiosities of Literature (1792–1823)

TO AN EXACTING CORRESPONDENT

Well, my dear, what's the matter with you, that you cry
out like an eagle ? Pray wait to judge me until you are
here. What is there so dreadful in the words, " my days
are full " ? When I have been gadding abroad and get
home, I find there M. de la Rochefoucauld, whom I
haven't seen all day : can I write ? M. de la Rochfoucauld
and M. Gonville are here : can I write ? But when they
have gone ? Ah, when they have gone, it's eleven o'clock,
and I go out myself ; I am sleeping at my neighbour because building is going on in front of my windows. But
the afternoon ? I have a headache then. The morning ?
A headache again, and I take a herb broth which makes me

drunk. You are in Provence, my dear : your time is clear, and your head still more so ; the lust to write to everyone presses on you ; from me it's gone ; and if I had a lover who wanted letters from me every morning, I should break with him. Don't, then, measure our friendship by letters ; I should love you as much, only writing you a page in a month, as you love me writing ten a week. When I am at Saint-Maur, I can write, because I have more head and more leisure, but . . . Paris kills me.

MADAME DE LA FAYETTE
Letter to Madame de Sevigné (1673) (Trans.)

More Welcome than a Diamond

I have expected your letter all this day with the greatest impatience that was possible, and at last resolved to goe out and meet the fellow, and when I came downe to the Stables, I found him come, had sett up his horse, and was sweeping the Stable in great Order. I could not imagin him so very a beast as to think his horses were to bee served before mee, and therfor was presently struck with an apprehension hee had no letter for mee, it went Colde to my heart as Ice, and hardly left mee courage enough to aske him the question, but when hee had drawled it out that hee thought there was a letter for mee in his bag I quickly made him leave his broome. Twas well tis a dull fellow, hee could not but have discern'd else that I was strangely overjoyed with it, and Earnest to have it, for though the poor fellow made what hast hee coulde to unty his bag, I did nothing but chide him for being soe slow. At Last

I had it, and in Earnest I know not whither an intire diamond of the bignesse on't would have pleased mee half
soe well.

DOROTHY OSBORNE
Letter to Sir William Temple (1653)

CARRIED BY BIRDS

I think 'tis not to be doubted that Swallowes have been
taught to carry Letters betwixt two Armies. But 'tis certain that when the Turks besieged *Malta* or *Rodes* (I now
remember not which 'twas) *Pigeons* are then related to
carry and recarry Letters. And Mr *G. Sander* in his
Travels (*fol.* 269) relates it to bee done betwist *Aleppo* and
Babylon.

IZAAK WALTON
The Compleat Angler (1653)

TOO ARDENT

I have moreover read your letter. For *it* I do *not* thank
you. It afforded me neither pleasure nor amusement. Indeed, my Friend, this Letter of yours has, to my mind,
more than one fault. I do not allude to its being egotistical.
To speak of onself is, they say, a privilege of Friendship.
. . . There is about your Letter a *mystery* which I detest.
It is so full of *meaning* words underlined, *meaning* sentences half finished ; *meaning* blanks with notes of admiration; and *meaning* quotations from foreign languages, that

really in this abundance of meaning . . . I am somewhat
at a loss to discover what you would be at. I know how
you will excuse yourself on this score : you will say that
you knew my Mother would see your Letter ; and that, of
course, you cared not what difficulties I as Interpreter
might be subjected, so that you got your feelings towards
me expressed. Now, Sir, once for all, I beg you to understand that I dislike as much as my Mother disapproves
your somewhat too ardent expressions of friendship towards me ; and that if you cannot write to me as to a man
who feels a deep interest in your welfare, who admires
your talents, respects your virtues, and for the sake of these
has often—perhaps too often—overlooked your faults ;—
if you cannot write to me as if—as if you were married,
you need never waste ink or paper on me more.

JANE WELSH
Letter to Thomas Carlyle (1822)

COURTESY

THE MASTER

I wish further that he carie himselfe pleasant and courteous unto his folke, not commanding them any thing in his
choler. Boisterous and rough handling will prevaile as
little with men, as with stiffenecked jades. Let him speake

familiarly unto them, let him laugh and jest with them sometimes, and also either give them occasion, or else suffer them to laugh and be merrie. For their uncessant paines are somewhat mitigated, when they are vouchsafed some gentle and courteous intreatance of their maister towards them.

Notwithstanding I wish him not to be too familiar with them for the avoiding of contempt. Neither would I have him to acquainte them with his purposes, except it be sometimes to aske their counsell in a matter, and let him not spare sometimes to seeme to doe after their advise, though he had determined the same course before : for they will worke with more cheerfulness, when they thinke that the matter is caried according to their invention. . . .

Let him patiently and quietly beare their tedious and troublesome natures, whom he knoweth to envie and repine at him, never falling out with them, or giving them any just occasion of displeasure : but winking at that ever which he knoweth of their nature and naturall inclination, let him pleasure them to the utmost that he can, and seeme to be at one with them. . . . And thus he may purchase rest and peace.

CHARLES ESTIENNE
La Maison Rustique (1572)
Trans. Richard Surflet (1600)

THANKS FOR A BOOK

Worthy Sir,

I have receaved . . . the booke of Sir George Ent of the Use of Respiration. It is a very learned and ingeniose booke full of true and deepe philosophy. I pray you to present unto him my most humble service. Though I recieved it but three dayes since, yet, drawen-on by the easinesse of the style and elegancy of the language, I have read it all over, and I give you most humble thankes for sending it me. I pray you present my service to Mr Hooke.

I am, Sir, your most obliged and humble servant,

Tho: Hobbes.

THOMAS HOBBES
Letter to John Aubrey (1679)

DIFFERING POLITELY

It is as uncharitable a point in us to fall upon those popular scurrilities and opprobrious scoffs of the Bishop of Rome, to whom, as a temporal Prince, we owe the duty of good language. I confess there is cause of passion between us : by his sentence I stand excommunicated ; Heretick is the best language he affords me ; yet can no ear witness I ever returned him the name of Antichrist, Man of Sin, or Whore of Babylon. It is the method of Charity to suffer without reaction ; those usual Satyrs and invectives of the Pulpit may perchance produce a good effect on the vulgar, whose ears are opener to Rhetorick than Logick ; yet do they in no wise confirm the faith of wiser Believers, who know that a good cause needs not to be patron'd by passion, but can sustain it self upon a temperate dispute.

SIR THOMAS BROWNE
Religio Medici (1642)

CREDULITY

To Cure the Gout

Madame de Bouxols, Marshal Berwick's daughter, assured me that there was nothing so good for the gout, as to preserve the parings of my nails in a bottle close-stopped.

HORACE WALPOLE
Letter to Thomas Gray (1765)

A Peculiar People

There are two rivers *Atoica* and *Caora*, and on that braunch which is called *Caora* are a nation of people whose heades appeare not above their shoulders, which though it may be thought a meere fable, yet for mine owne parte I am resolves it is true, because every child in the provinces of *Arromaia* and *Canuri* affirme the same : they are called *Ewaipanoma :* they are reported to have their eyes in their shoulders, and their mouths in the middle of their breasts, and that a long train of haire groweth backward betwen their shoulders. . . . For mine owne part I saw them not, but I am resolved that so many people did not all combine, or forethinke to make the report.

SIR WALTER RALEIGH
The Discoverie of Guiana (1596)

SPIRITS ON THE STAIRS LIKE BEES

In those darke [Elizabethan] times astrologer, mathematician, and conjurer, were accounted the same things ; and the vulgar did verily beleeve him to be a conjurer. He had a great many mathematicall instruments and glasses in his chamber, which did also confirme the ignorant in their opinion, and his servitor (to impose on freshmen and simple people) would tell them that sometimes he should meet the spirits comeing up his staires like bees. . . . Now there is to some men a great lechery in lying, and imposing on the understandings of simple people, and he thought it for his credit to serve such a master. . . . One time . . . he happened to leave his watch in the chamber windowe— (watches were then rarities). The maydes came in to make the bed, and hearing a thing in a case cry *Tick, Tick, Tick,* presently concluded that that was his Devill, and tooke it by the string with the tongues, and threw it out of the windowe into the mote (to drowne the Devill). It so happened that the string hung upon a sprig of an elder that grew out of the mote, and this confirm'd them that 'twas the Devill. So the good old gentleman gott his watch again.

JOHN AUBREY
Brief Lives : Thomas Allen (c. 1680)

For my part, I have ever believed, and do now know, that there are Witches : they that doubt of these, do not onely deny them, but Spirits, and are obliquely and upon consequence a sort not of Infidels, but Atheists.

SIR THOMAS BROWNE
Religio Medici (1642)

A Monster

By and by we are called to Sir W. Batten's to see the strange creature that Captain Holmes hath brought with him from Guiny ; it is a great baboon, but so much like a man in many things that though they say there is a species of them, yet I cannot believe but that it is a monster got out of a man and a she-baboon. I do believe that it already undestands much English, and I am of the mind it might be taught to speak or make signs.

SAMUEL PEPYS
Diary (Aug. 24, 1661)

Very Strange

At noon to my Lord Crew's, where one Mr. Templer (an ingenious man and a person of honour he seems to be) dined ; and, discoursing of the nature of serpents, he told us some that in the waste places of Lancashire do grow to a great bigness, and that do feed upon larks, which they take thus :—They observe when the lark is soared to the highest, and so crawl till they come to be just underneath them ; and there they place themselves with their mouths uppermost, and there, as it is conceived, they do eject poyson up to the bird ; for the bird do suddenly come down again in its course of a circle, and falls directly into the mouth so of the serpent ; which is very strange.

Ibid. (Feb. 4, 1662)

DELIGHTING TO TERATOLOGIZE

I think (if you can give me leave to be free with you), that you are a little inclineable to credit strange relations. I have found men that are not skilfull in the history of Nature very credulous and apt to impose upon themselves and others, . . . or delight to teratologize (pardon the word) and to make shew of knowing strange things.

JOHN RAY
Letter to John Aubrey (1691)

CURING THE AGUE

I took, early in the morning, a good dose of Elixir, and hung three spiders about my neck, and they drove my ague away—*Deo gratias.*

ELIAS ASHMOLE
Life (April 11, 1681)

Mr. Noel has the Letter of Resolution concerning Origen to convey to your Ladiship. I am persuaded it will please you better than any Romance.

HENRY MORE
Letter to Lady Conway (1661)

CURIOUS SIGHTS

REMARKABLE RIVERS

And one of no lesse credit than *Aristotle* tells us of a merry River, the River *Elusina*, that dances at the noise of Musick, for with Musick it bubbles, dances, and growes sandy, and so continues til the musick ceases, but then it presently returnes to its wonted calmnesse and clearnesse. . . . And . . . one of no lesse authority than *Josephus* that learned Jew, tells us of a River in *Judea*, that runs swiftly all the six dayes of the week, and stands still and rests all their *Sabbath*.

IZAAK WALTON
The Compleat Angler (1653)

147

In another chamber are divers sorts of instruments of musiq : amongst other toys that of a satyre, which so artificially expressed a human voice, with the motion of eyes and head, that it might easily affright one who was not prepared for that most extravagant sight. They shewed us also a chayre that catches fast any who sitts downe in it, so as not to be able to stirr, but, by certaine springs concealed in the arms and back thereoff, which at sitting downe surprizes a man on the suddaine, locking him in by the armes and thighs, after a true trecherous Italian guise. . . . Here stands a rare clock of German worke ; in a word, nothing but what is magnificent is to be seene in this paradise.

JOHN EVELYN
Diary (Villa Borghese, Nov. 17, 1644)

CORPSE OF A YOUNG LADY

In one of these monuments Pancirollus tells us that, in the time of Paul III, there was found the body of a young lady, swimming in a kind of bath of precious oyle or liquor, fresh and entire as if she had been living, neither her face discolour'd, nor her hair disorder'd ; at her feet burnt a lamp, which suddenly expir'd at the opening of the vault ; having flam'd, as was computed, now 1500 years, by the conjecture that she was Tulliola, the daughter of Cicero, whose body was thus found, as the inscription testified.

Ibid.
(Fossa Nuova, Jan. 28, 1645)

DANCING

1

Where lives the man that never yet did heare
Of chaste *Penelope*, *Ulisses'* Queene ? . . .

3.

Homer doth tell in his aboundant verse,
The long laborious travailes of the *Man* ;
And of his lady too he doth reherse
How shee illudes with all the art she can,
Th' ungratefull love which other lords began ; . . . .

4.

All this he tells, but one thing he forgot,
One thing most worthy his eternall song ;
But he was old, and blind, and saw it not,
Or else he thought he should *Ulisses* wrong,
To mingle it his tragike acts among ;
 Yet was there not in all the world of things
 A sweeter burden for his Muse's wings.

5.

The courtly love *Antinous* did make :
Antinous that fresh and jolly knight,
Which of the gallants that did undertake

149

To win the widdow, had most wealth and might,
Wit to perswade, and beautie to delight :
  The courtly love he made unto the Queene,
  Homer forgot, as if it had not beene.

7.

One onely night's discourse I can report,
When the great Torch-bearer of Heaven was gone
Downe in a maske unto the Ocean's Court,
To revell it with Thetis all alone ;
Antinous disguisèd and unknowne,
  Like to the Spring in gaudie ornament,
  Unto the Castle of the Princesse went.

11.

Only *Antinous* when at first he view'd
Her starbright eyes, that with new honour shind ;
Was not dismayd, but there-with-all renew'd
The noblesse and the splendour of his mind ;
And as he did fit circumstances find,
  Unto the throne he boldly gan advance,
  And with faire maners wooed the Queene to dance.

12.

" Goddesse of women, sith your heav'nlinesse
Hath now vouchsaft it selfe to represent
To our dim eyes, which though they see the lesse
Yet are they blest in their astonishment ;
Imitate heav'n, whose beauties excellent
  Are in continuall motion day and night,
  And move thereby more wonder and delight.

13.

Let me the moover be, to turne about
Those glorious ornaments, that Youth and Love

Have fixed in you, every part throughout;
Which if you will in timely measure move,
Not all those precious jemms in heav'n above,
  Shall yeeld a sight more pleasing to behold,
  With all their turnes and tracings manifold."

14.

With this the modest Princesse blusht and smil'd,
Like to a cleare and rosie eventide,
And softly did returne this answer mild :
" Faire Sir, you needs must fairely be denide
Where your demaunde cannot be satisfide :
My feet, which onely Nature taught to goe,
  Did never yet the art of footing know.

15.

But why perswade you me to this new rage ?
(For all disorder and misrule is new)
For such misgovernment in former age
Our old divine Forefathers never knew ; . . ."

16.

" Sole heire of Vertue and of Beautie both,
Whence cometh it " (*Antinous* replies)
" That your imperious vertue is so loth
To grant your beauty her chiefe excercise ?
Or from what spring doth your opinion rise
  That da700uncing is a frenzy and a rage,
  First known and us'd in this new-fangled age ?

17.

Da   uncing (bright Lady) then began to bee,
When the first seeds whereof the World did spring
The fire, ayre, earth, and water—did agree,
By Love's perswasion,—Nature's mighty King—

The
antiquitie
of Dancing.

151

To leave their first disordred combating ;
   And in a daunce each measure to observe,
   As all the world their motion should preserve.

19.

Like this, he fram'd the gods' eternall Bower,
And of a shapelesse and confused masse,
By his through-piercing and digesting power,
The turning vault of heaven formèd was ;
Whose starry wheeles he hath so made to passe,
   As that their moovings do a musicke frame,
   And they themselves still daunce unto the same.

22.

How justly then is Dauncing tearmèd new,
Which with the World in point of time begun ?
Yea Time it selfe (whose birth *Jove* never knew,
And which indeed is older then the sun)
Had not one moment of his age outrunne,
   When out leapt Dauncing from the heap of things,
   And lightly rode upon his nimble wings." . . .

28.

The
original of
Dancing.

When Love had shapt this World,—*this great faire Wight*,
That all wights else in this wide womb containes ;
And had instructed it to daunce aright,
A thousand measures with a thousand straines,
Which it should practise with delightfull paines,
   Untill that fatall instant should revolve,
   When all to nothing should againe resolve :

29.

The comely order and proportion faire
On every side, did please his wandring eye :
Till glauncing through the thin transparent ayre,
A rude disordered rout he did espie

152

Of men and women, that most spightfully
  Did one another throng, and crowd so sore,
  That his kind eye in pitty wept therefore.

30.

And swifter then the lightning downe he came,
Another shapelesse Chaos to digest ;
He will begin another world to frame,
(For Love till all be well will never rest)
Then with such words as cannot be exprest,
  He cutts the troups, that all asunder fling,
  And ere they wist, he casts them in a ring.

33.

" If Sence hath not yet taught you, learne of me
A comely moderation and discreet ;
That your assemblies may well ordered bee
When my uniting power shall make you meet,
With heav'nly tunes it shall be tempered sweet :
  And be the modell of the World's great frame,
  And you, Earth's children, *Dauncing* shall it name.

The speech
of Love,
perswading
men to learn
Dancing.

34.

Behold the *World*, how it is *whirled round*,
And for it is so *whirl'd*, is named so ;
In whose large volume many rules are found
Of this new Art, which it doth fairely show ;
For your quicke eyes, in wandring too and fro
  From East to West, on no one thing can glaunce,
  But if you marke it well, it seemes to daunce.

35.

First you see fixt in this huge mirrour blew
Of trembling lights, a number numberlesse :
Fixt they are nam'd, but with a name untrue,
For they all moove, and in a Daunce expresse

By the
orderly
motion of
the fixed
stars.

That *great long yeare*, that doth containe no lesse
   Then threescore hundreds of those yeares in all,
   Which the sunne makes with his course naturall.

37.

Under that spangled skye, five wandring flames
Besides the King of Day, and Queene of Night,
Are wheel'd around, all in their sundry frames,
And all in sundry measure doe delight,
Yet altogether keepe no measure right;
   For by it selfe each doth it selfe advance,
   And by it selfe each doth a galliard daunce.

39.

For that brave Sunne the Father of the Day,
Doth love this Earth, the Mother of the Night;
And like a revellour in rich aray,
Doth daunce his galliard in his lemman's sight,
Both back, and forth, and sidewaies, passing light;
   His princely grace doth so the gods amaze,
   That all stand still and at his beauty gaze.

40.

But see the Earth, when he approcheth neere,
How she for joy doth spring and sweetly smile;
But see againe her sad and heavy cheere
When changing places he retires a while;
But those blake cloudes he shortly will exile,
   And make them all before his presence flye.
   As mists consum'd before his cheereful eye.

41.

Who doth not see the measures of the Moone,
Which thirteene times she daunceth every yeare?
And ends her pavine thirteene times as soone
As doth her brother, of whose golden haire

154

She borroweth part and proudly doth it weare ;
  Then doth she coyly turne her face aside,
  Then half her cheeke is scarse sometimes discride.

43.

And now behold your tender nurse the *Ayre*   Of the Ayre.
And common neighbour that ay runs around ;
How many pictures and impressions faire
Within her empty regions are there found ;
Which to your sences Dauncing doe propound.
  For what are *Breath, Speech, Ecchos, Musicke, Winds,*
  But Dauncings of the Ayre in sundry kinds ?

46.

And thou sweet *Musicke,* Dauncing's onely life,
The eare's sole happinesse, the ayre's best speach ;
Loadstone of fellowship, charming-rod of strife,
The soft mind's Paradice, the sicke mind's leach ;
With thine own tong, thou trees and stons canst teach,
  That when the Aire doth dance her finest measure,
  Then art thou borne, the gods and mens sweet pleasure.

47.

Lastly, where keepe the *Winds* their revelry,
Their violent turnings, and wild whirling hayes,
But in the Ayre's tralucent gallery ?
Where shee herselfe is turnd a hundreth wayes,
While with those Maskers wantonly she playes ;
  Yet in this misrule, they such rule embrace,
  As two at once encomber not the place.

49.

For loe the *Sea* that fleets about the Land,   Of the sea.
And like a girdle clips her solid waist,
Musicke and measure both doth understand ;
For his great chrystall eye is alwayes cast

Up to the Moone, and on her fixèd fast;
   And as she daunceth in her pallid spheere,
   So daunceth he about his Centre heere.

50.

Sometimes his proud greene waves in order set,
One after other flow into the shore;
Which, when they have with many kisses wet,
They ebbe away in order as before;
And to make knowne his courtly love the more,
   He oft doth lay aside his three-forkt mace,
   And with his armes the timorous Earth embrace.

51.

Onely the Earth doth stand for ever still:
Her rocks remove not, nor her mountaines meet:
(Although some wits enricht with Learning's skill
Say heav'n stands firme, and that the Earth doth fleet,
And swiftly turneth underneath their feet)
   Yet though the Earth is ever stedfast seene,
   On her broad breast hath Dauncing ever beene.

52.

Of the rivers.

For those blew vaines that through her body spred,
Those saphire streames which from great hils do spring,
(The Earth's great duggs, for every wight is fed
With sweet fresh moisture from them issuing):
Observe a daunce in their wilde wandering;
   And still their daunce begets a murmur sweet,
   And still the murmur with the daunce doth meet.

53.

Of all their wayes I love *Meander's* path,
Which to the tunes of dying swans doth daunce;
Such winding sleights, such turns and tricks he hath,
Such creeks, such wrenches, and such daliaunce;

That whether it be hap or heedlesse chaunce,
   In this indented course and wriggling play
   He seemes to daunce a perfect cunning *hay*.

55.

See how those flowres that have sweet beauty too,

Of other
things upon
the earth.

(The onely jewels that the Earth doth weare,
When the young Sunne in bravery her doth woo) :
As oft as they the whistling wind doe heare,
Doe wave their tender bodies here and there ;
   And though their daunce no perfect measure is,
   Yet oftentimes their musicke makes them kis.

59.

But why relate I every singular ?
Since all the World's great fortunes and affaires
Forward and backward rapt and whirled are,
According to the musicke of the spheares :
And Chaunge herself her nimble feete upbeares :
   On a round slippery wheele that rowleth aye,
   And turnes all States with her imperious sway.

60.

Learne then to daunce, you that are Princes borne,
And lawfull lords of earthly creatures all ;
Imitate them, and therof take no scorne,
For this new art to them is naturall—
And imitate the starres celestiall :
   For when pale Death your vital twist shall sever,
   Your better parts must daunce with them for ever."

61.

Thus Love perswades, and all the crowde of men
That stands around, doth make a murmuring ;
As when the wind loosed from his hollow den
Among the trees a gentle base doth sing,

157

Or as a brooke through pebbles wandering ;
　　But in their looks they uttered this plain speach,
　　That they would learn to daunce, if Love would teach

64.

Rounds or Country Dances.

Thus when at first Love had them marshalled,
As earst he did the shapelesse masse of things,
He taught them *rounds* and winding *heyes* to tread,
And about trees to cast themselves in rings :
As the two Beares, whom the First Mover flings
　　With a short turn about heaven's axeltree,
　　In a round daunce for ever wheeling be.

70.

Lavoltaes.

Yet is there one, the most delightfull kind,
A loftie jumping, or a leaping round ;
Where arme in arme two dauncers are entwind
And whirle themselves with strict embracements bound,
And still their feet an *anapest* do sound ;
　　An *anapest* is all their musick's song,
　　Whose first two feet are short, and third is long.

71.

As the victorious *twinnes* of *Loeda* and *Jove*
That taught the Spartans dauncing on the sands
Of swift *Eurotas*, daunce in heavn above,
Knit and united with eternall hands ;
Among the starres their double image stands,
　　Where both are carried with an equall pace,
　　Together jumping in their turning race.

76.

Thus Love taught men, and men thus learn'd of Love
Sweet Musick's sound with feet to counterfaite ; . . .

77.

Since when all ceremonious misteries,
All sacred orgies and religious rights,

All pomps, and triumphs, and solemnities,
All funerals, nuptials, and like publike sights,
All Parliaments of peace, and warlike fights,
    All learned arts, and every great affaire
    A lively shape of dauncing seems to beare.

The use and
formes of
dauncing in
sundry
affaires of
man's life.

87.

For after townes and kingdomes founded were,
Betweene greate States arose well-ordered War ;
Wherein most perfect measure doth appeare,
Whether their well-set ranks respected are
In quadrant forme or semicircular :
    Or else the march, when all the troups advance,
    And to the drum, in gallant order daunce.

88.

And after Warrs, when white-wing'd Victory
Is with a glorious tryumph beautified,
And every one doth *Io Io* cry,
Whiles all in gold the conquerour doth ride ;
The solemne pompe that fils the Citty wide
    Observes such ranke and measure everywhere,
    As if they altogether dauncing were.

97.

The Queene, whose dainty eares had borne too long
The tedious praise of that she did despise ;
Adding once more the musicke of the tongue
To the sweet speech of her alluring eyes,
Began to answer in such winning wise,
    As that forthwith *Antinous'* tongue was tyde,
    His eyes fast fixt, his eares were open wide.

98.

" Forsooth " (quoth she), " great glory you have won
To your trim minion, Dauncing, all this while,
By blazing him Love's first begotten sonne ; . . .

What meane the mermayds when they daunce and sing
But certaine death unto the marriner?
What tydings doe the dauncing dilphins bring,
But that some dangerous storme approcheth nere?
Then sith both Love and Dauncing lyveries beare
  Of such ill hap, unhappy may I prove,
  If sitting free, I either daunce or love."

102.

Yet once again *Antinous* did reply ; . . .

106.

" Love in the twinckling of your eylids daunceth,
Love daunceth in your pulses and your vaines,
Love when you sow, your needle's point advanceth
And makes it daunce a thousand curious straines
Of winding rounds, whereof the forme remaines ;
  To shew, that your faire hands can daunce the hey,
  Which your fine feet would learne as well as they.

III.

If they whom sacred Love hath link't in one,
Doe as they daunce, in all their course of life,
Never shall burning griefe nor bitter mone,
Nor factious difference, nor unkind strife,
Arise between the husband and the wife ;
  For whether forth or bake or round he goe,
  As the man doth, so must the woman doe.

116.

Who sees an Armie all in ranke advance,
But seemes a wise Commaunder is in place,
Which leadeth on that brave victorious daunce?
Much more in Dauncing's Art, in Dauncing's grace,

Blindness it selfe may Reason's footstep trace ;
  For of Love's maze it is the curious plot,
  And of Man's fellowship the true-love knot.

117.

But if these eyes of yours, (load-starrs of Love,
Shewing the World's great daunce to your mind's eye !)
Cannot with all their demonstrations move
Kinde apprehension in your fantasie,
Of Dauncing's vertue and nobilitie ;
  How can my barbarous tongue win you there to,
  Which Heav'n and Earth's faire speech could never do ?

118.

O Love my king : if all my wit and power
Have done you all the service that they can,
O be you present in this present hower,
And help your servant and your true Leige-man
End that perswasion which I earst began ;
  For who in praise of Dauncing can perswade
  With such sweet force as Love, which Dancing made ? "

SIR JOHN DAVIES, *Orchestra* (1594)

WICKED DANCING

COMUS *enters with a Charming Rod in one hand, his
Glass in the other, with him a rout of Monsters, headed
like sundry sorts of wilde Beasts, but otherwise like Men
and Women, their Apparel glistering, they come in making
a riotous and unruly noise, with Torches in their hands.*

COMUS :

  The Star that bids the Shepherd fold,
  Now the top of Heav'n doth hold,

FP   161

And the gilded Car of Day,
His glowing Axle doth allay
In the steep *Atlantick* stream,
And the slope Sun his upward beam
Shoots against the dusky Pole,
Pacing toward the other gole
Of his Chamber in the East.
Mean while welcom Joy, and Feast,
Midnight shout, and revelry,
Tipsie dance, and Jollity.
Braid your Locks with rosie Twine
Dropping odours, dropping Wine.
Rigor now is gon to bed,
And Advice with scrupulous head,
Strict Age, and sowre Severity,
With their grave Saws in slumber lie.
We that are of purer fire
Imitate the Starry Quire,
Who in their nightly watchfull Sphears,
Lead in swift round the Months and Years.
The Sounds, and Seas with all their finny drove
Now to the Moon in wavering Morrice move,
And on the Tawny Sands and Shelves,
Trip the pert Fairies and the dapper Elves ;
By dimpled Brook, and Fountain brim,
The Wood-Nymphs deckt with Daisies trim,
Their merry wakes and pastimes keep :
What hath night to do with sleep ? . . .
Com, knit hands, and beat the ground,
In a light fantastick round. . . .
   The LADY *enters.*
LADY :
   This way the noise was, if mine ear be true,

My best guide now, me thought it was the sound
Of Riot, and ill-manag'd Merriment,
Such as the jocund Flute, or gamesom Pipe
Stirs up among the loosse unletter'd Hinds,
When for their teeming Flocks, and granges full
In wanton dance they praise the bounteous *Pan*,
And thank the gods amiss. I should be loath
To meet the rudeness, and swill'd insolence
Of such late Wassailers.

JOHN MILTON
Comus (1634)

IMMODERATION

Now it chanced that those of the wooers pleased him most
who had come from Athens, and of these Hippocleides
the son of Tisander was rather preferred, both by reason
of manly virtues and also because he was connected by
descent with the family of Kypselos at Corinth. Then
when the appointed day came for the marriage banquet
and for Cleisthenes himself to declare whom he selected
from the whole number, Cleisthenes sacrificed a hundred
oxen and feasted both the wooers themselves and all the
people of Sikyon ; and when the dinner was over, the
wooers began to vie with one another both in music and
in speeches for the entertainment of the company ; and
as the drinking went forward and Hippocleides was very
much holding the attention of the others, he bade the
flute-player play for him a dance-measure ; and when the
flute-player did so, he danced : and it so befell that he
pleased himself in his dancing, but Cleisthenes looked on
at the whole matter with suspicion. Then Hippocleides

after a certain time bade one bring in a table ; and when
the table came in, first he danced upon it Laconian figures,
and then also Attic, and thirdly he planted his head upon
the table and gesticulated with his legs. Cleisthenes mean-
while, when he was dancing the first and second time,
though he abhorred the thought that Hippocleides should
now become his son-in-law, because of his dancing and
his shamelessness, yet restrained himself, not desiring to
break out in anger against him ; but when he saw that he
thus gesticulated with his legs, he was no longer able to
restrain himself, but said : " Thou hast danced away thy
marriage, nevertheless, son of Tisander ! " and Hippocleides answered and said " Hippocleides cares not ! "
and hence comes this saying.

HERODOTUS
History (5th cent. B.C.)
Trans. G. C. Macaulay

ELVES

> Or Faerie Elves,
> Whose midnight Revels, by a Forrest side
> Or Fountain some belated Peasant sees,
> Or dreams he sees, while over head the Moon
> Sits Arbitress, and neerer to the Earth
> Wheels her pale course, they on thir worth and dance
> Intent, with jocond Music charm his ear ;
> At once with joy and fear his heart rebounds.

JOHN MILTON
Paradise Lost, Book I (1667)

The first mundaye in Lent . . . my selfe, thats I, otherwise called Cavaliero Kemp, head-master of Morrice-dancers . . . began frolickly to foote it from the right honourable the Lord Mayors of London towards the right worshipfull (and truely bountifull) Master Mayors of Norwich. My setting forward was somewhat before seaven in the morning ; my Taberer stroke up merrily ; and as fast as kinde people thronging together would give me leave, thorow London I leapt.

[And so to Norwich in nine days.]

WILLIAM KEMP
Nine Daies Wonder (1600)

Hey ! who comes heere all-along,
With bag-piping and drumming ?
'Tis the Morris daunce a-comming.
Come, come, ladies, come ladies out ;
O ! come, come quickly,
And see how trim they daunce, how trim and trickly.

Hey ! there againe, there again ; hey ho there agayne
Hey ! there againe, how the bells they shake it,
Now for our town once, and take it.
Soft awhile, not so fast ; they melt them :
What ho Piper ! Piper be hang'd awhile :
Knave, seest not the dauncers how they swelt them?
Out there awhile you come : I say you are too farr in;
There, give the hobby horse more room to play in.

THOMAS MORLEY
Madrigalls to foure Voyces (1594)

When thou dos't dance the Spheares doe play,
By Night Starrs torches, Sunn by day
Each stepp soe loath to wrong thy Birth,
Affraide to hurt thy Mother Earth,
  The tender blades of Grass when thou
  dos't dance upon them doe not bowe.

The falling dew to doth thee Wooe
When tripps't on it scarse wetts thy shoe,
Then Lady like doth Change thy minde
and Dances on the Wavering wind
  The thynner Ayre strives thine to meete
  to Tread it with thy Gentle feete.

JOHN GAMBLE (?)
When thou dost dance (before 1687)

DANCING TREES

NIGHT:
  Tis now a time when (*Zephyrus*) all with dancing
  Honor me, above day my state advancing.
  Ile now be frolicke, all is full of hart,
  And ev'n these trees for joy shall beare a part:
  Zephyrus they shall dance.
ZEPHYRUS:
  Daunce, Goddesse? how?
NIGHT:
  Seemes that so full of strangenes to you now?
  Did not the Thracian harpe long since the same?
  And (if we ripp the ould records of fame)

166

Did not *Amphions* lyre the deafe stones call,
When they came dancing to the Theban wall ? . . .
Dauncing, and musicke must prepare the way,
Ther's little tedious time in such delay.

    This spoken, the foure SILVANS *played on their instruments the first straine of this song following : . . . the trees of gould . . . began to move, and dance according to the measure of the time which the musitians kept in singing . . .*

        Move now with measured sound
        You charmed grove of gould,
        Trace forth the sacred ground
        That shall your formes unfold.

Diana, and the starry night for your Apollos sake
Endue your Silvan shapes with powre this strange
    delight to make
Much joy must needs the place betide where trees for
    gladnes move,
A fairer sight was nere beheld, or more expressing love,

        Yet neerer *Phoebus* throne
        Mete on your winding waies,
        Your Brydall mirth make knowne
        In your high-graced Hayes.

Let Hymen lead your sliding rounds, and guide them
    with his light,
While we do Io Hymen sing in honour of this night
Joyne three by three, for so the night by triple spel
    decrees
Now to release *Apollos* knights from these enchanted
    trees.

*This dancing-song being ended, the goulden trees stood in
rankes three by three. . . . . . .*

Tell me, gentle howre of night
Wherein dost thou most delight ?
Not in sleepe . . . wherein then ?
In the frolicke vew of men ?
Lovest thou musicke ? *Howre.* O, tis sweet.
Whats dauncing ? *Howre.* Ev'n the mirth of feete.
Joy you in Fayries and in elves ?
We are of that sort our selves.

THOMAS CAMPION

Maske . . . in honour of the Lord Hayes, and his Bride
(1607)

CUMBERLAND DANCING

After Skiddaw we walked to Ireby, the oldest market town
in Cumberland, where we were greatly amused by a country dancing-school holden at the Tun ; it was indeed no
new cotillon fresh from France ; No, they kickit and jumpit
with mettle extraordinary, and whiskit and friskit, and
toed it and go'd it, and twirl'd it and whirl'd it, and
stamped it and sweated it, tatooing the floor like mad. The
difference between our country dances and these Scottish
figures is about the same as leisurely stirring a cup o' tea
and beating up a batter pudding. I was extremely gratified
to think that, if I had pleasures they knew nothing of,
they had also some into which I could not possibly
enter.

JOHN KEATS

Letter to Thomas Keats (1818)

DAY-DREAMS

GOING TO MARYLAND

Now if I would be rich, I could be a prince. I could goe into Maryland, which is one of the finest countrys of the world ; same climate with France ; between Virginia and New England. I can have all the favour of my lord Baltemore I could wish. His brother is his lieutenant there, and a very good natured gentleman. Plenty of all things : ground there is 2000 miles westwards.

I could be able I believe to carry a colony of rogues ; another of ingeniose artificers ; and I doubt not one might make a shift to have 5 or 6 ingeniose companions, which is enough.

JOHN AUBREY
Brief Lives : William Butler (c. 1680)

A MELODRAMATIC LIFE

I sometimes feel a little uneasy about that imagined self of mine—the Me of my daydreams—who leads a melodramatic life of his own, quite unrelated to my real existence. So one day I shadowed him down the street. He

169

loitered along for a while, and then stood at a shop-window and dressed himself out in a gaudy tie and yellow waistcoat. Then he bought a great sponge and two stuffed birds and took them to lodgings, where he led for a while a shady existence. Next he moved to a big house in Mayfair, and gave grand dinner-parties, with splendid service and costly wines. His amorous adventures in this region I pass over. He soon sold his house and horses, dismissed his retinue of servants, and went—saving two young ladies from being run over on the way—to live a life of heroic self-sacrifice among the poor.

I was beginning to feel encouraged about him, when in passing a fishmongers, he pointed with his stick at a great salmon and said, " I caught that fish."

LOGAN PEARSALL SMITH
Trivia (1918)

DECANAL

A Good Dish

The King appointed Doctor *Donne* to waite on him at dinner the next day ; and his Majesty (being set down) before he eat any meat, said (after his pleasant manner) *Doctor Donne, I have invited you to dinner, and though you sit not downe with me, yet I will carve to you of a dish*

that I know you love ; you love London well, I doe there-
fore make you Deane of Pauls, and, when I have dined, take
your meate home to your study, say grace, and much good
may it doe you.

IZAAK WALTON
The Life and Death of Dr. Donne (1640)

DEPLORING THE
DECADENCE OF THE AGE

WORSE AND WORSE

Damnosa quid non imminuit dies ?
Aetas parentum, peior avis, tulit
Nos nequiores, mox daturos
Progeniem vitiosiorem.

HORACE
In Romanos moribus corruptos. Carmina, Bk III
(c. 20 B.C.)

THE HUMOUR OF MANY HEADS

Which very absurdity is daily committed amonst us, even
in the esteem and censure of our own times. And to speak
impartially, old Men, from whom we should expect the

greatest example of Wisdom, do most exceed in this point of folly ; commending the days of their youth, which they scarce remember, at least well understood not ; extolling those times their younger ears have heard their Fathers condemn, and condemning those times the gray heads of their posterity shall commend. And thus is it the humour of many heads, to extol the days of their Fore-fathers, and declaim against the wickedness of times present. Which notwithstanding they cannot handsomly do, without the borrowed help and Satyrs of times past ; condemning the vices of their own times, by the expressions of vices in times which they commend ; which cannot but argue the community of vice in both.

SIR THOMAS BROWNE
Pseudodoxia Epidemica (1646)

What We Were Before, and What We Are Now

Consider with thy selfe (gentle Reader) the olde discipline of Englande, mark what we were before, and what we are now : . . . cast thine eye backe to thy Predecessors, and tell mee howe wonderfully wee have beene chaunged, since wee were schooled with these abuses. *Dion* sayth, that english men could suffer watching and labor, hunger and thirst, and beare of al stormes with hed and shoulders, they used slender weapons, went naked, and were good soldiours, they fed uppon rootes and barkes of trees, they would stand up to the chin many dayes in marishes without victualles : and they had a kind of sustenaunce in time of neede, of which if they had taken but the quantitie of a

172

beane, or the weight of a pease, they did neyther gape after meate, nor long for the cuppe, a great while after. The men in valure not yeelding to *Scithia*, the women in courage passing the *Amazons*. The exercise of both was shootyng and dancing, running and wrestling, and trying such maisteries, as eyther consisted in swiftnesse of feete, agilitie of body, strength of armes, or Martiall discipline. But the exercise that is nowe among us, is banqueting, playing, pipyng, and dauncing, and all suche delightes as may win us to pleasure, or rocke us a sleepe.

Oh what a woonderfull chaunge is this ? Our wreastling at armes is turned to wallowyng in Ladies laps, our courage, to cowardice, our running to ryot, our Bowes into Bolles, and our Dartes to Dishes. We have robbed *Greece* of Gluttonie, *Italy* of wantonnesse, *Spaine* of pride, *Fraunce* of deceite, and *Dutchland* of quaffing. Compare *London* to *Rome*, and *England* to *Italy*, you shall finde the Theaters of the one, the abuses of the other, to be rife among us. *Experto crede*, I have seene somewhat, and therefore I thinke may say the more. STEPHEN GOSSON

The Schoole of Abuse (1579)

OUR SPARKFULL YOUTH

Hitherto will our sparkefull Youth laugh at their great grandfathers *English*, who had more care to do wel than to speake minion-like, and left more glorie to us by their exploiting of great actes, than we shall doe by our forging anew words and uncouth phrases. WILLIAM CAMDEN

Remains concerning Britain (1605)

... We flourisht long,
E're idle Gentry up in such aboundance sprong,
Now pestring all this Ile : whose disproportion drawes
The publique wealth so drie, and only is the cause
Our gold goes out so faste, for foolish foraine things
Which upstart Gentry still into our Country brings ;
Who their insatiate pride seek chiefly to maintaine
By that, which only serves to uses vile and vaine :
Which our plaine Fathers earst would have accounted
    sinne,
Before the costly Coach, and silken stock came in ;
Before that *Indian* weed so strongly was imbrac't ;
Wherein such mighty summes we prodigally waste ;
That Merchants long train'd up in gayn's deceitfull
    schoole,
And subtly having learn'd to soothe the humorous
    foole,
Present their painted toyes unto this frantique gull,
Disparaging our Tinne, our Leather, Corne, and Wooll;
When Forrainers, with ours them cloath and feed,
Transporting trash to us, of which we nere had need.
    But whilst the angry Muse thus on the Time
    exclames,
Sith every thing therin consisteth in extreames,
Lest she inforc't with wrongs her limits should trans-
    cend,
Here of this present Song she briefly makes an end.

MICHAEL DRAYTON
Poly-Olbion. Song XVI
(1613)

'Tis strange to see the folly that possesses the young People of this Age, and the libertys they take to themselv's; I have the Charrity to beleeve they appear very much worse than they are, and that the want of a Court to govern themselv's by is in great part the cause of theire Ruine; Though that was noe perfect scoole of Vertue, yet Vice there wore her maske, and apeard soe unlike herselfe that she gave noe scandall. Such as were realy as discreet as they seem'd to bee, gave good Example, and the Eminency of theire condition made others strive to imitate them, or at least they durst not owne a contrareary course. All who had good principles and inclinations were incouraged in them, and such as had neither were forced to put on a handsome disguise that they might not bee out of countenance at themselves.

DOROTHY OSBORNE
Letter to Sir William Temple (1654)

FRIVOLOUS LITERARY TASTE OF THE COMMONWEALTH

Plain poetry is now disesteem'd, it must be Drollery, or it will not please.

HENRY HERRINGMAN, bookseller
Preface to Musarum Deliciae (1655)

CONTEMPLATING OUR FOREFATHERS

'Tis opportune to look back upon old times, and contemplate our Forefathers. Great examples grow thin, and to be fetched from the passed world. Simplicity flies away, and iniquity comes at long strides upon us.

SIR THOMAS BROWNE
Epistle Dedicatory to Hydrotaphia (1658)

Decay of Learning, Preaching, Conversation, and Manners

A reason why learning hath decayed in these later times and now, is the nation of England her too much admiring the manners and fashions of the French nation, when as there is not a gentleman of a considerable estate in England but must have a French man or woman to breed up their children after their way. . . .

A neglect now of the Fathers and none but foolish vaine and florid preaching. One that discourseth in company scolar-like (viz. by quoting the Fathers, producing an antient verse from the poets suitable to his discours) is accounted pedanticall and pedagogicall. Nothing but news and the affaires of Christendom is discoursed off, and that also generally at coffee-houses. And clubbs at alehouses and coffee houses have not bin up above 14 years before this time. . . .

Decay of learning. Before the warr wee had scholars that made a thorough search in scholasticall and polemicall divinity, in humane authors, and naturall philosophy. But now scholars studie these things not more than what is just necessary to carry them throug the exercises their respective colleges and the Universitie. Their aime is not to live as students ought to do, viz. temperat, abstemious, and plaine and grave in apparell ; but to live like gents, to keep dogs and horses, to turne their studies and coleholes into places to receive bottles, to swash it in apparell, to weare long periwigs, etc., and the theologists to ride abroad in grey coats with swords by their sides.

The masters have lost their respect by being themselves scandalous and keeping company with undergraduates.

Fresh nights, caroling in public halls, Christmas sports, vanished, 1661.

ANTHONY WOOD
Life and Times (Dec. 1661)

This Folly of Laughing At

An age wherein a zealous concernment in studies is laught at and many wonder at the folly of those before the warr time that spent so much time and broke their braines in schol. divinity and metaphis. This folly of laughing at continued wors and worse till 1679. . . . An age given to brutish pleasure and atheisme. . . . This year [1662] such a saying come up in London, " The Bishops get all, the Courtiers spend all, the Citizens pay for all, the King neglects all, and the Divells take all."

Ibid.

Meaner Travelling

When I was a youth many great persons travelled with 3 horses, butt now there is a new face of things.

SIR THOMAS BROWNE
Letter to his son Edward (1680)

177

In those days (Elizabetha regina) . . . when a senator went
to the Parliament-house a-foote, or a horse-back with his
foot-cloath, he had at his heeles ½ a dozen or 10 tall
fellowes with blew coates and badges and long basket-hilt
swords. Now forsooth only a laquey and a little spitt-pig.

The advantage that king Charles I had: gentlemen then
kept good horses, and many horses for a man-at-armes,
and men that could ride them; hunting-horses. Now we
are come all to our coaches forsooth ! . . . Now young men
are so farre from managing good horses, they know not
how to ride a hunting nag nor handle their weapons. . . .

In Sir Philip Sidney's time 'twas as much disgrace for a
cavalier to be seen in London rideing in a coach in the
street as now 'twould be to be seen in a petticoate and
wastcoate. They rode in the streets then with their rich
foot-cloathes, and servants wayting on them with blewe
coates and badge. . . .

T.T., an old gentleman that remembers Queen Elizabeth's raigne and court. . . . He hath seen much in his time
both at home and abroade; and with much choler in-
veighes against things now :—" Alas ! o' God's will !
Now-a-dayes every one, forsooth ! must have coaches,
forsooth ! In those dayes gentlemen kept horses for a
man-at-armes, besides their hackney and hunting-horses.
This made the gentry robust and hardy and fitt for service ; were able to be their owne guides in case of a rout
or so, when occasion should so require.

Our gentry forsooth in these dayes are so effeminated
that they know not how to ride on horseback. Then when
the gentry mett, it was not at a poor blind sordid ale-house,

to drinke up a barrell of drinke and lie drunke there two
or three dayes together; fall together by the eares.
They mett then in the fields, well-appointed, with their
hounds or their hawkes; kept up good hospitality; and
kept a good retinue, that would venture that bloud and
spirit that filled their vaines which their masters' tables
nourisht; kept their tenants in due respect of them. We
had no depopulacion in those dayes.

You see in me the ruines of time. The day is almost at
end with me, and truly I am glad of it : I desire not to live
in this corrupt age. I foresawe and fortold the late changes,
and now easily foresee what will follow after. Alas ! o'
God's will ! It was not so in Queen Elizabeth's time : then
youth had respect to old age.

Revels—then the elders and better sort of the parish
sate and beheld the pastimes of the young men, as wrast-
ling, shooting at butts, bowling, and dancing. All this is
now lost; and pride, whoring, wantonnesses, and drunken-
nesses. Then the charity of the feast, St Peter's box,
mantayned the old impotent poore."

JOHN AUBREY
Brief Lives : Thomas Tyndale (c. 1680)

LUXURY IN COLLEGE

About 1638 or 1640, when he was at Trinity College,
Dr Kettle, preaching as he was wont to do on Trinity Sunday, told 'em that they should keepe their bodies chast
and holy: "but," said he, "you fellows of the College here
eate good commons and drinke good double-beer. . . ."

How would the good old Dr. have raunted and beat-up his kettle-drum, if he should have seen such luxury in the college as there is now! Tempora mutantur!

Ibid.
Ralph Kettell

DECLINE OF CHEMISTS

Meredith Lloyd tells me that, three or 400 yeares ago, chymistry was in a greater perfection, much, than now; their process was then more seraphique and universall: now they looke only after medicines.

Ibid.
Brief Lives : Saint Dunstan (c. 1680)

WHAT A WRETCHED PASS

What a wretched Pass is this wicked Age come to, when *Ben. Johnson* and *Shakespear* won't go down with 'em, without these Baubles to recommend 'em, and nothing but *Farce* and *Grimaces* will go down. . . . In short, Mr *Collier* may save himself the trouble of writing against the Theatres, for, if these lewd Practices are not laid aside, and Sence and Wit come in play again, a Man may easily foretell, without pretending to the Gift of Prophesie, that the Stage will be short-liv'd.

TOM BROWN
Letter to Mr Moult (1699)

An Undoubted Truth

I know it is reckoned but a form of speech, when Divines complain of the Wickedness of the Age. However, I believe, upon a fair Comparison with other Times and countries, it would be found an undoubted Truth.

JONATHAN SWIFT
*Project for the Advancement of Religion
and Reformation of Manners* (1709)

No Pancakes

It hath been an old custom in Oxford for the scholars of all houses, on Shrove Tuesday, to go to dinner at ten clock, (at which time the little bell, called *pan-cake bell*, rings, or at least should ring, at St Maries), . . . and it was always followed in Edmund hall, as long as I have been in Oxford, till yesterday, when they went to dinner at twelve, and to supper at six, nor were there any fritters at dinner, as there used always to be. When laudable old customs alter, 'tis a sign learning dwindles.

THOMAS HEARNE
Diary (Feb. 27, 1723)

Everything that's Old

HARDCASTLE : In my time, the follies of the town crept slowly among us, but now they travel faster than a stage-coach. . . .

MRS HARDCASTLE : Ay, your times were fine times indeed ; you have been telling us of them for many a long year.

Here we live in an old rambling mansion, that looks for all the world like an inn, but that we never see company . . . and all our entertainment your old stories of Prince Eugene and the Duke of Marlborough. I hate such old-fashioned trumpery !

HARD : And I love it. I love every thing that's old : old friends, old times, old manners, old books, old wines ; and, I believe, Dorothy you'll own I have been pretty fond of an old wife.   OLIVER GOLDSMITH
She Stoops to Conquer (1772)

TASTE OVER

English living poets I have avoided mentioning ; we have none who will not survive their productions. Taste is over with us ; and another century will sweep our Empire, our literature, and our name, from all but a place in the annals of mankind.   LORD BYRON
Memorandum (1807)

MODERN SQUEAMISHNESS

I am delighted with your approbation of my " Cenci." . . . I confess I cannot approve of the squeamishness which excludes the exhibition of such subjects from the scene, a squeamishness the produce, as I firmly believe, of a lower tone of the public mind, and foreign to the majestic and confident wisdom of the golden age of our country.   P. B. SHELLEY
Letter to Thomas Medwin (1819)

No-one can describe the splendour and excitement of the early days of Crockford's. A supper of the most exquisite kind . . . was provided gratis. The members of the Club included all the celebrities of England . . . and at the gay and festive board . . . the most brilliant sallies of wit, the most agreeable conversation, the most interesting anecdotes, interspersed with grave political discussions and acute logical reasoning on every conceivable subject, proceeded from the soldiers, scholars, statesmen, poets, and men of pleasure. . . . The tone of the Club was excellent. A most gentlemanlike feeling prevailed, and none of the rudeness, familarity, and ill-breeding, which disgrace some of the minor clubs of the present day, would have been tolerated for a moment.

CAPTAIN R. H. GRONOW
Reminiscences, 1810–60 (1861)

THE SHAMELESS 1860's

How astonished and horror-struck would be the great ladies of the Restoration [of the Bourbons] if they could rise from their graves and behold their granddaughters emulating the *demi-monde* in their dress, language and manners ; *affichant* their *liaisons* in the sight of the sun ; walking into their lovers' houses unveiled, undisguised, or riding with them publicly, and having their carriages called under their own names at the restaurants or small theatres where they have been tête-à-tête !

The dignified, artful, proud, but perhaps not more virtuous grandmother would have been unutterably disgusted, not so much at the immorality as at the bad taste displayed in such arrangements, which then existed just as much as now, but were supposed to be unknown.

Ibid.

A Copious and Pleasant Conversation

The last time I saw Southey was on an evening at Taylor's [1839]. . . . We sat on the sofa together; our talk was long and earnest; topic ultimately the usual one, steady approach of democracy, with revolution (probably *explosive*) and a *finis* incomputable to man—steady decay of all morality, political, social, individual, this once noble England getting more and more ignoble and untrue in every fibre of it, till the *gold* . . . would *all* be eaten out, and noble England would have to collapse in shapeless ruin, whether *for ever* or not none of us could know. Our perfect consent on these matters gave an animation to the Dialogue, which I remember as copious and pleasant. Southey's last word was in answer to some tirade of mine about universal Mammon-worship, gradual accelerating decay of mutual humanity, of piety and fidelity to God or man, in all our relations, performances—the whole illustrated by examples, I suppose—to which he answered, not with levity, yet with a cheerful tone in his seriousness, " It will not, and it cannot, come to good " !

THOMAS CARLYLE
Reminiscences (1867)

Again, as the train drew out of the station, the old gentleman pulled out of his pocket his great shining watch ; and for the fifth, or as it seemed to me, the five hundredth, time, he said . . . " To the minute, to the very minute ! It's a marvellous thing, the railway ; a wonderful age ! "

Now I had long been annoyed by the old gentleman's smiling face, platitudes, and piles of newspapers ; I had no love for the Age ; and an impulse came on me to denounce it.

" Allow me to tell you," I said, " that I consider it a wretched, an ignoble age. Where's the greatness of Life, where's dignity, leisure, stateliness ; where's Art and Eloquence ? Where are your great scholars, statesmen ? Let me ask you, Sir," I cried, glaring at him, " where's your Gibbon, your Burke or Chatham ? "

LOGAN PEARSALL SMITH
Trivia (1918)

MOTOR-BICYCLES AND PROHIBITIONS

" England," said my friend, " in spite of everything, is probably a happier country to-day than it has ever been in history." The sun was shining at the moment, a lark was singing above a buttercup meadow with a stream winding through it, and an invisible cuckoo was shouting over a distant wood ; but even so I wondered if he could be serious. I do not object to a man's saying that people are happier now than they were in the Middle Ages . . . or at any other period until the last quarter of the nineteenth century ; but the notion that the world had improved within living memory was so novel that, if the sun had not been so pleasantly warm, and the wind on our brows so pleasantly cool, I should have dismissed it with derision. Who that has once been young and now is middleaged can have failed to observe the steady deterioration of the world in so far as men and women have altered it ? I do not wish to indict the present age, but it is an age that has invaded *our* peaceful age with garish petrol pumps, with the odious odours of motor-bicycles, with bungalows, with the dance-music of St. Vitus, with charabancs, with doubts, with psycho-analysis, with high taxation, with standardization of everything from tobacco to opinions, with advertisement and self-advertisement, with paint and powder, with prohibitions more puzzling than the riddle of the Sphinx, with—— But even if I continued the catalogue for a column, it would be impossible to convey to an inhabitant of the present age what an inhabitant of a past age thinks of all the changes that have come over the world since Queen Victoria celebrated her Jubilee.

ROBERT LYND
Happy England (1930)

DESTRUCTION

SILK STOCKINGS

He Richard Corbet was a student . . . of Christ-church in Oxford. He was very facetious, and a good fellowe. One time he and some of his acquaintance being merry at Fryar Bacon's study (where was good liquor sold) they were drinking on the leads of the house, and one of the scholars was asleepe, and had a paire of good silke stockings on. Dr Corbet (then M.A., if not B.D.) gott a paire of cizers and cutt them full of little holes.

JOHN AUBREY
Brief Lives : Richard Corbet (c. 1680)

LIBRARIES

When Oxford was surrendred (24 Junii 1646) the first thing generall Fairfax did was to sett a good guard of soldiers to preserve the Bodleian Library. 'Tis said there was more hurt done by the cavaliers (during their garrison) by way of embezilling and cutting-off chaines of bookes, than there was since. He was a lover of learning, and had he not taken this speciall care, that noble library had been utterly destroyed . . . for there were ignorant senators enough who wouldhave been contented to have had it so.

Ibid.
Brief Lives : Thomas Fairfax (c. 1680)

CUPS

Petronius, late Consull of Rome, when he lay at the point of death, called for a faire broad-mouthed cup of Cassidoine, which had cost him before-time three hundred thousand sesterces, and presently brake it in pieces, in hatred and despight of *Nero*, for feare lest the same prince might have seazed upon it after his desease, and therewith furnished his own boards.

PLINY THE ELDER
Natural History (c. 77)
Trans. Philemon Holland (1601)

CHURCH ORNAMENTS

Sudbury, Jan. 9, 1643. We broke down 10 mighty great Angels in Glass, in all 80.
Haverhill, Jan. 6. We brake down about a hundred superstitious Pictures; and seven Fryars hugging a Nunn; and the picture of God and Christ, and divers others very superstitious.
Clare, Jan. 6. We brake down 1000 Pictures superstitious; I brake down 200; 3 of God the Father, and 3 of Christ, and the Holy Lamb, and 3 of the Holy Ghost like a Dove

with Wings ; and the 12 Apostles were carvd in Wood, on the top of the Roof, which we gave orders to be taken down ; and the Sun and Moon in the East Window, by the King's Arms, to be taken down.

Dunstall, Jan. 23. We broke down 60 superstitious Pictures : and broke in pieces the Rails ; and gave orders to pull down the Steps.

Otley, Feb. 27. A Deputy brake down 50 superstitious Pictures ; a Cross on the Chancel, 2 Brass Inscriptions ; and Moses with a Rod, and Aaron with his Mitre, taken down : and 20 Cherubims to be broke down. etc. etc.

WILLIAM DOWSING
Suffolk Journal (1643–4)

HUSBANDS' MANUSCRIPTS

Her mind was still uneasy about *The Scented Garden*, and she took out the manuscript to examine it. . . . When she opened it, she was perfectly bewildered and horrified. . . . Calming herself, she reflected that the book was written only for scholars and mainly for Oriental students, and that her husband " never wrote a thing from the impure point of view." . . . Then she looked up, and there before her stood her husband, just as he had stood in the flesh. He pointed to the manuscript, and said " Burn it ! " Then he disappeared. As she had for years been a believer in spirits, the apparition did not surprise her, and yet she was tremendously excited. " Burn it ! " she echoed. " This valuable manuscript ? At which he laboured for so many weary hours ? Yet, doubtless, it would be wrong to preserve it . . . What a gentleman, a scholar, and a man of

189

the world, may write when living, he would see very differently as a poor soul standing naked before its God. . . . What would he care for the applause of fifteen hundred men now—for the whole world's praise, and God offended? And yet the book is for students only. . . . "

At this moment the apparition again stood before her, and in a sterner and more authoritative voice said, " Burn it ! " and then again disappeared. In her excitement she scarcely knew where she was, or what she did. . . .

Then for the third time Sir Richard stood before her. Again he sternly bade her burn the manuscript, and, having added threatenings to his command, he again disappeared. By this time her excitement had passed away, and a holy joy irradiated her soul. She took up the manuscript and . . . burnt it, sheet after sheet, until the whole was consumed. As each leaf was licked up by the fire, it seemed to her that "a fresh ray of light and peace" transfused the soul of her beloved husband.

THOMAS WRIGHT
Life of Sir Richard Burton (1906)

HISTORICAL MANUSCRIPTS

It is suspected that our historical antiquary, Speed, owed many obligations to the learned Hugh Broughton, for he possessed a vast number of his MSS. which he burnt. . . . We have had historians who, whenever they met with information which has not suited their historical system, or their inveterate prejudices, have employed interpolations, castrations, and forgeries, and in some cases have annihilated the entire document. . . . Among these suppressors and dilapidators pre-eminently stands the crafty Italian Polydore Vergil . . . who is said to have collected and burnt a greater number of historical MSS. than would have loaded a waggon, to prevent the detection of the numerous fabrications in his History of England, which was composed to gratify Mary and the Catholic cause.

The Harleian MS, 7379, is a collection of state-letters. This MS has four leaves entirely torn out, and is accompanied by this extraordinary memorandum, signed by the principal librarian.

" Upon examination of this book, Nov. 12, 1764, these four last leaves were torn out. C. Morton.

Mem. Nov. 12, sent down to Mrs Macaulay."

. . . This memorandum must involve our female historian in the obloquy of this dilapidation. Such dishonest practices of party feeling, indeed, are not peculiar to any party.

ISAAC DISRAELI
Curiosities of Literature (1792–1817)

HUSBANDS' WORK

Dr Edward Davanant told me that this learned man had a shrew to his wife, who was irreconcileably angrie with him for sitting-up late at night so, compileing his Dictionarie. . . . When he had half-donne it, she had the opportunity to gett into his studie, tooke all his paines out in her lap, and threw it into the fire, and burnt it.

JOHN AUBREY
Brief Lives : Thomas Cooper (c. 1680)

I expressed a wish to know how she came possessed of this book [Volney's *Ruins of Empires*]. She said that a young man, a great Constitutionalist, had given it her . . . and had pressed her much to read it, for that it was one of the best books in the world. I replied, that the author was an emissary of Satan . . . that it was written with the sole aim of bringing all religion into contempt, and that it inculcated the doctrine that there was no future state, nor reward for the righteous, nor punishment for the wicked. She made no reply, but, going into another room, returned with her apron full of dry sticks . . . which she piled upon the fire, and produced a bright blaze. She then took the book from my hand and placed it upon the flaming pile ; then, sitting down, took her rosary out of her pocket, and told her beads till the volume was consumed. This was an *auto-da-fé* in the best sense of the word.

GEORGE BORROW
The Bible in Spain (1843)

CONJURING BOOKS

My old cosen, parson Whitney, told me that in the visitation of Oxon in Edward VI's time, they burned mathematical bookes for conjuring bookes, and if the Greeke professor had not accidentally come along, the Greeke testament had been thrown into the fire for a conjuring booke too.

JOHN AUBREY
Brief Lives : James Whitney (c. 1680)

Strephon, of noble blood and mind,
(For ever shine his name)
As death approch'd, his soul refin'd,
And gave his looser sonnets to the flame.
" Burn, burn," he cried, with sacred rage,
" Hell is the due of ev'ry page :
Hell be its fate "—(But O indulgent Heaven !
So vile the Muse, and yet the man forgiv'n !)
" Burn on, my song ; for not the silver Thames,
Nor Tiber with its yellow streams,
In endless currents rolling to the main,
Can e'er dilute the poison or wash out the stain."

ISAAC WATTS
Repentance of the Earl of Rochester

DETACHMENT

THINKING OF THE FIXED STARS

For my own part, I begin to see the Earth so fearfully little, that I believe from henceforth, I shall never be concern'd at all for any thing : That we so eagerly desire to make our selves great, that we are always designing, always troubling and harassing our selves, is certainly because we are ignorant what these Vortex's are ; but now I hope my new lights will in part justifie my laziness, and when any one reproaches me with my carelessness, I will answer, *Ah, did you but know what the fix'd Stars are !*

B. DE FONTENELLE
A Plurality of Worlds
Trans. John Glanvill (1688)

DOING GEOMETRY

Syracusa being taken, nothinge greved *Marcellus* more then the losse of *Archimedes*, who beinge in his studie when the citie was taken, busily seeking out by him selfe the demonstracion of some Geometricall proposition which he hadde drawen in figure, and so earnestly occupied therein, as he neither sawe nor hearde any noyse of enemies that ranne uppe and downe the citie, and much lesse knewe it was taken : He wondered when he sawe a souldier by him, that bad him go with him to *Marcellus*. Notwithstandynge, he spoke to the souldier, and bad him tary untill he had done his conclusion, and brought it to demonstracion : but the souldier being angry with his aunswer, drew out his sword and killed him. PLUTARCH
Lives (c. 100)
Trans. Sir Thomas North (1572)

AN ISOLATED BEING

I am an isolated Being on the Earth, without a Tie to attach me to life, except a few School-fellows and a *score of females*. LORD BYRON
Letter to Ensign Long (1807)

194

For my part, I never could understand those quarrels of authors with critics, and with one another. " For God's sake, gentlemen, what do they mean ? "

Ibid.
Letter to Thomas Moore (1817)

The man must be enviably happy whom reviews can make miserable. I have neither curiosity, interest, pain, nor pleasure, in anything, good or evil, they can say of me. I feel only a slight disgust, and a sort of wonder that they presume to write my name.

PERCY BYSSHE SHELLEY
Letter to Leigh Hunt (1822)

Sir,

Should you cast your eye on the signature of this letter before you read the contents, you might imagine that they related to a slanderous paper which appeared in your Review some time since. I never notice anonymous attacks. The wretch who wrote it has doubtless the additional reward of a consciousness of his motives, besides the thirty guineas a sheet or whatever it is that you pay him. Of course you cannot be answerable for all the writings that you edit, and I certainly bear you no ill-will for having edited the abuse to which I allude—indeed, I was too much amused by being compared to Pharoah, not readily to forgive editor, printer, publisher, stitcher, or any one, except the despicable writer, connected with something so exquisitely entertaining. Seriously speaking, I am not in the habit of permitting myself to be disturbed by what is said or written of me. . . . But I feel in respect to the writer in question, that " I am there sitting, where he durst not soar."

P. B. SHELLEY
Letter to the Editor of the Quarterly Review (1818)

THE INDIFFERENT INDIAN

Then come some of the *Iroquois* going to eat a Prisoner for their Breakfast, who seems as little concern'd as his Devourers.

BERNARD DE FONTENELLE
A Plurality of Worlds
Trans. John Glanvill (1688)

THE PROCESSION

Dante went one day to a great public procession ; he entered the shop of a bookseller to be a spectator of the passing show. He found a book which greatly interested him ; he devoured it in silence, and plunged into an abyss of thought. On his return, he declared that he had neither seen, nor heard, the slightest occurrence of the public exhibition which had passed before him.

ISAAC DISRAELI
Curiosities of Literature (1792–1823)

But whosoever he be whom fortune hath deprived of his owne native countrey, certes, she hath graunted and allowed him to make choice of that which may please and content him . . . Make choice of the best and most pleasant citie, time will cause it to be thy native countrey, and such a native countrey as shall not distract and trouble thee with any businesse nor impose upon thee these and suchlike exactions : make paiment and contribute to this levie of money : goe in embassage to Rome : receive such a captaine or ruler into thine house, or take such a charge upon thee at thine owne expenses. Now he that calleth these things to remembrance, if he have any wit in his head, and be not over-blind every way in his owne opinion and conceit, will wish and chose, if he be banished out of his owne countrey, to inhabite the verie Isle *Gyaros*, or the rough and barraine Iland *Cinarus*, where trees or plants do hardly grow, without complaining with griefe of hart, without lamenting and breaking out into these plaints and womanly moanes, reported by the Poet *Simonides* in these words,

> The roaring noise of purple sea
> resounding all about,
> Doth fright me much, and so inclose
> that I can not get out.

PLUTARCH

Morals : Of Banishment (c. 100)
Trans. Philemon Holland (1603)

ECCENTRICITY

The Peculiar Crocodile

Most things move th'under-jaw, the Crocodile not ;
Most things sleep lying, th' Elephant leans or stands.

GEORGE HERBERT
Providence (1633)

The Religious Satyr

It is likely there are men also like Satyres inhabiting in
some desert places, for St *Jerom* in the life of *Paul* the
Eremite, reporteth there appeared to S. *Anthony* an *Hippo-
centaure*, such as the Poets describe, and presently he saw
in a rocky valley adjoining, a little man having crooked
nostrils, horns growing out of his forehead, and the neather part of his body had Goats feet : the holy man not dis-
mayed, taking the shield of Faith, and the breastplate of
Righteousness, like a good Souldier of Christ, pressed
towards him, which brought him some fruits of palms as
pledges of his peace, upon which he fed in the journey ;
which St *Antony* perceiving, he asked him who he was,

and received this answer, I am a mortall creature, one of the inhabitants of this Desert, whom the Gentiles (deceived with error) do worship as *Fauni*, Satyres, and *Incubi* : I am come in ambassage from our flock, intreating that thou wouldst pray for us unto the common GOD, who came to save the world ; the which words were no sooner ended, but he ran away as fast as any fowl could flie.

EDWARD TOPSELL
History of Four-Footed Beasts and Serpents (1607)

THE GARDEN PARTY

" Yes, I suppose it is rather a dull Garden Party," I agreed, though my local pride was a little hurt by the disdain of that visiting young woman for our rural society. " Still we have some interesting neighbours, when you get to know them. Now that fat lady over there in purple —do you see her ? Mrs. Turnbull—she believes in Hell, believes in Eternal Torment. And that old gentleman with whiskers and white spats, Colonel Bosco, is convinced that England is tottering on the very brink of the Abyss. And the pie-faced lady he is talking to, Miss Stuart-Jones, was, she says, Mary Queen of Scots in a previous existence. And our Curate—we're proud of our Curate, he's a great cricketer, and a kind of saint as well. They say he goes out in Winter at three o'clock in the morning, and stands up to his neck in a pond, to cool and overcome his appetites."

LOGAN PEARSALL SMITH
More Trivia (1922)

EXERCISE

DAY OUT

" Oh, the wild joys of living ! the leaping from rock up
   to rock,
The strong rending of boughs from the fir-tree, the cool
   silver shock
Of the plunge in a pool's living water, the hunt of the bear,
And the sultriness showing the lion is crouched in his lair.
And the meal, the rich dates yellowed over with gold dust
   divine,
And the locust-flesh steeped in the pitcher, the full
   draught of wine,
And the sleep in the dried river-channel where bulrushes tell
That the water was wont to go warbling so softly and well.
How good is man's life, the mere living ! who fit to employ
All the heart and the soul and the senses for ever in joy !

ROBERT BROWNING
Saul (1842)

LEAPING

Leaping is an exercise very commendable, and healthfull
for the body, especially if you use it in the morning, as

we read *Alexander* and Epaminondas did. Upon a full stomacke or to bedward, it is very dangerous, and in no wise to be exercised.

HENRY PEACHAM
The Compleat Gentleman (1622)

RUNNING

In rennynge the exercise is good also, . . .
Lightly to come and go, rennynge is sure.
Rennynge is also right good at the chase,
And for to lepe a dyke is also good ;

ANON
Of Knyghthode and Batayle (early 15th c.)

FILIAL

LOYALTY

Cicero the younger, who resembled his father in nothing but in name, . . chanced one day to have many strangers at his board, and amongst others saw *Coestius* sitting at the lower end. . . *Cicero* inquired of one of his men what he was. . . It is, said he, the same *Coestius*, of whom some have told you, that in respect of his owne, maketh no account of your father's eloquence. *Cicero* being suddainly mooved, commaunded the said poore *Coestius* to be presently taken from the table, and well whipt in his presence : Lo-heere an uncivill and barbarous host.

MICHEL DE MONTAIGNE
Essays : Of Bookes (1580)
Trans. John Florio (1603)

COMMON SENSE

The Holy Mawle, which they fancy hung behind the church door, which when the father was seaventie, the sonne might fetch to knock his father in the head, as effete and of no more use.

JOHN AUBREY
Remains of Gentilism and Judaism (1687)

A POETICAL SON TO A MUSICAL FATHER

I wish the Pierian springs would turn their water-ways now through my breast, . . . so that, forgetting her feeble strains, my Muse may rise on bold wings to do reverent duty to my father. However her song may be welcomed, it is for you, best of fathers, that she is preparing this inadequate work. I do not know what more fitting gifts from me can answer yours to me, though the greatest possible gifts can not really answer yours ; far less can the meagre thanks returned through empty words, be enough for them. Nevertheless, this page sets forth my assets, and what I have of wealth I have counted out on this paper ; it is nothing beyond what golden Clio has given me, and what slumbers have begotten in me in some secluded cave, and in the shadowed, sacred laurel groves of Parnassus. . . . . .

Do not, I pray you, continue to condemn the holy Muses, nor think them vain and poor, for through their gifts you yourself cunningly compose a thousand strains to apt melodies. . . . Now why is it strange that it has fallen to you to beget me, a poet, that we, so closely joined by dear blood-ties, should pursue allied arts and kindred studies ? Phoebus, wishing to share himself between us, gave these gifts to me, those to my father, so we, father and son, possess the divided god.

But though you pretend to hate the gentle Muses, I think you do not hate them, for, father, you do not command me to go where the broad road opens, where the ground is more favourable for profit, and where the golden hope of amassed wealth steadily shines. You do not drag me to the laws, the ill-kept laws of the nation, nor do you condemn my ears to foolish clamours. But, desiring to enrich my mind further, you withdrew me far from the noise of the city, into deep retirement, and let me walk in the pleasant leisure of the Aeonian banks, a happy companion at Phoebus' side. . . . . .

What greater thing could have been given, by a father, even by Jupiter himself, though he had given all but the heavens ? . . . . But for you, dear father, since I cannot make the return you deserve, . . . let it be enough that I have commemorated your gifts, and told them with a thankful heart.

And you, O youthful songs of mine, trifles of my leisure,

if only you may venture to hope for immortality, . . .
perhaps you will guard these praises, and my father's
name thus sung, as an example to far-off ages.

JOHN MILTON
Ad Patrem (1634?)
(Trans. from Latin)

FLATTERING

THE HOUSES OF PARLIAMENT

If I should thus farre presume upon the meek demeanour
of your civil and gentle greatnesse, Lords and Commons,
as what your publisht Order hath directly said, that to
gainsay, I might defend myselfe with ease, if any should
accuse me of being new or insolent, did they but know
how much better I find ye esteem it to imitate the old and
elegant humanity of Greece, than the barbarick pride of a
Hunnish and *Norwegian* statelines. . . . I know not what
should withhold me from presenting ye with a fit instance
wherein to shew both that love of truth which ye eminently
professe, and that uprightnesse of your judgement which is
not wont to be partiall to yourselves, by judging over
again that Order which ye have ordain'd *to regulate
Printing*.

JOHN MILTON
Areopagitica (1644)

VOLTAIRE

One can never, Sir, be sorry to have been in the wrong when one's errors are pointed out to one in so obliging and masterly a manner. Whatever opinion I may have of Shakespeare, I should think him to blame if he could have seen the letter you have done me the honour to write to me, and yet not conform to the rules you have their laid down. When he lived, there had not been a Voltaire, both to give laws to the stage, and to show on what good sense those laws were founded.

HORACE WALPOLE
Letter to Voltaire (1768)

MRS. MONTAGUE

When Mrs. Montague shewed him some China plates which had once belonged to Queen Elizabeth, he told her, " that they had no reason to be ashamed of their present possessor, who was so little inferior to the first."

HESTHER PIOZZI
Anecdotes of Dr. Johnson (1786)

QUEEN ELIZABETH

See where she sits upon the grassie greene,
  (O seemely sight !)
Yclad in Scarlot, like a mayden Queene,
  And Ermines white :

Upon her head a Cremosin coronet
With Damaske roses and Daffadillies set :
   Bay leaves betweene,
   And Primroses greene,
Embellish the sweete Violet.

Tell me, have ye seene her angelick face
   Like *Phoebe* fayre ?
Her heavenly haveour, her princely grace,
   Can you well compare ?
The Redde rose medled with the White yfere,
In either cheeke depeincten lively chere :
   Her modest eye,
   Her Majestie,
Where have you seene the like but there ? . . .

I see *Calliope* speede her to the place,
   where my Goddesse shines ;
And after her the other Muses trace
   with their Violines.
Bene they not Bay braunches which they doe
   beare,
All for *Elisa* in her hand to weare ?
   So sweetely they play,
   And sing all the way,
That it a heaven is to heare. . . .

Now ryse up, *Elisa*, deckèd as thou art
   in royall aray ;
And now ye daintie Damsells may depart
   Eche one her way.

I feare, I have troubled your troupes to longe :
Let dame *Elisa* thanke you for her song :
   And if you come hether
   When Damsines I gether,
I will part them all you among.

EDMUND SPENSER

The Shepheards Calender (1579)

ADONIS

Even as the sun with purple colour'd face
Had tane his last leave of the weeping morn,
Rose cheekt *Adonis* hied him to the chase ;
Hunting he lov'd, but love he laught to scorne.
Sick-thoughted *Venus* makes amain unto him,
And like a bold fac't suter gins to woe him.

Thrice fairer then my selfe (thus she began)
The fields chiefe flower, sweet above compare,
Staine to all Nymphes, more lovely than a man,
More white and red, than doves or roses are ;
Nature that made thee, with her selfe at strife,
Saith, that the world hath ending with thy life.

Vouchsafe thou wonder to alight thy steed,
And reigne his proud head to the saddle-bowe :
If thou wilt deigne this favour, for thy meed
A thousand hony-secrets shalt thou know :
Here come and sit, where never serpent hisses,
And beeing set, Ile smother thee with kisses.

W. SHAKESPEARE

Venus and Adonis (1593. Edition 1607)

                              Here was he
Put to his wisedome, if her virgin knee,
He should be bold, but kneeling, to embrace ;
Or keepe aloofe, and trie with words of grace,
In humblest suppliance, if he might obtaine
Some cover for his nakedness and gaine
Her grace to shew and guide him to the Towne.
The last he best thought, to be worth his owne,
In weighing both well : to keepe still aloofe,
And give with soft words his desires their
        proofe. . . .
  "Let me beseech (O Queene) this truth of thee ;
Are you of mortal, or the deified race ?
If of the Gods, that th'ample heavens embrace ;
I can resemble you to none above,
So neare as to the chast-borne birth of *Jove*,
The beamie *Cynthia*. Her you full present,
In grace of every God-like lineament :
Her goodly magnitude ; and all the addresse
You promise of her very perfectnesse.
If sprung of humanes, that inhabite earth ;
Thrice blest are both the authors of your birth ;
Thrice blest your brothers, that in your deserts,
Must, even to rapture, beare delighted hearts ;
To see, so like the first trim of a tree,
Your forme adorn a dance. But most blest he
Of all that breathe, that hath the gift t'engage
Your bright necke in the yoke of mariage ;
And decke his house with your commanding
        merit.

I have not seene a man of so much spirit.
Nor man, nor woman, I did ever see,
At all parts equall to the parts in thee.
T' enjoy your sight, doth *Admiration* seise
My eies, and apprehensive faculties.
Lately in *Delos* . . .

                 . . . I beheld
The burthern of a Palme, whose issue sweld
About *Apollos Phane*, and that put on
A grace like thee ; for Earth had never none
Of all her Sylvane issue so adorn'd :
Into amaze my very soule was turnd
To give it observation ; as now thee
To view (O Virgin) a stupiditie
Past admiration strikes me ; joynd with feare
To do a suppliants due, and prease so neare
As to embrace thy knees. . . .
God give you, in requitall, all th'amends
Your heart can wish : . . .
She answerd : " Stranger ! I discerne in thee,
Nor *Sloth*, nor *Folly* raignes ; . . .
Thou shalt not want."

HOMER
Odyssey
Trans. George Chapman (1614)

MRS. KATHERINE PHILLIPS

We allow'd You Beauty, and we did submit
    To all the Tyrannies of it ;
Ah ! Cruel Sex, will you depose us too in Wit ?
    Orinda does in that too raign,

209

Does Man behind her in Proud Triumph draw,
And Cancel great *Apollo's* Salick Law.
  We our old Title plead in vain,
Man may be Head, but Woman's now the Brain.

ABRAHAM COWLEY
On Orinda's Poems (1668)

EVERYBODY

His Art is nothing but delightfull cozenage, whose rules
are smoothing and garded with perjurie ; whose scope is
to make men fooles in teaching them to over-value themselves, and to tickle his friends to death. This man is a Porter of all good tales, and mends them in the carriage ; . . .
When he walks with his friend, hee sweares to him, that
no man els is looked at ; no man talked of ; and that whomsoever he vouchsafes to looke on and nod to, is graced
enough. . . . Sometimes even in absence hee extolleth
his patron, where hee may presume of safe conveiance to
his eares. . . . In short, he is . . . the eare-wig of the
mightie.

JOSEPH HALL
Characters of Vertues and Vices (1608)

FEMALE PLEASURES

HUNTIN'

Thro' the green Oake-wood on a lucent Morn
Turn'd the sweet mazes of a silver Horn :
A Stag rac'd past, and hallowing hard behind,
Dian's young Nymphs ran fleeting down the Wind.
A light-foot Host, green-kirtl'd all they came,
And leapt, and rollickt, as some mountain Streame
Sings cold and ruffling thro' the Forrest Glades ;
So ran, so sang, so hoyted the Moone's Maids.
Light as young Lev'retts skip their buskin'd feet,
Spurning th'enamell'd Sward as they did fleet.
The Wind that buss'd their cheekes was all the Kiss
Was suffer'd by the Girles of *Artemis*,
Whose traffique was in Woods, whom the wing'd Boy
Leauguer'd in vain, whom Man would ne're injoy,
Whose Bed greene Moss beneath the forrest Tree,
Whose jolly Pleasure all in Liberty,
To sport with fellow Maids in maiden cheere,
To swim the Brook, and hollo after Deer.
Thus, the winds wantoning their flying Curles,
So rac'd, so chas'd, those most Delightfull Girles.

ANON
The Chase (c. 1675)

With Horns and with Hounds I waken the Day,
And hye to my Woodland-Walks away;
I tuck up my Robe, and am buskin'd soon,
And tie to my Forehead a wexing Moon;
I course the fleet Stag, unkennel the Fox,
And chase the wild Goats o'er Summits of Rocks,
With shouting and hooting we pierce thro' the Sky;
And Eccho turns Hunter, and doubles the Cry.

JOHN DRYDEN, *The Secular Masque* (1700)

I have very frequently the opportunity of seeing a Rural *Andromache*, who came up to town last Winter, and is one of the greatest Fox-hunters in the Country. She talks of Hounds and Horses, and makes nothing of leaping over a Six-bar Gate. If a man tells her a waggish story, she gives him a Push with her Hand in jest, and calls him an impudent Dog. JOSEPH ADDISON, *Spectator* (1711)

KNITTING

Il faut que les femmes tricotent. NAPOLEON BUONAPARTE

CHICKEN-WINGS

Lord Byron . . . did not like to see women eat, and . . . he had another reason for not liking to dine with them; which was, that they always had the wings of the chicken.

LEIGH HUNT
Lord Byron and Some of his Contemporaries (1828)

UNWHOLESOME FARE

A woman should never be seen eating or drinking, unless it be *lobster salad* and *champagne*, the only truly feminine viands.

LORD BYRON
Letter to Lady Melbourne (1812)

LOOKING OUT OF WINDOWS

Bow Street, where the thieves are examined, is within a few yards of us. Mary had not been here four and twenty hours before she saw a thief. She sits at the window working ; and casually throwing out her eyes, she sees a concourse of people coming this way, with a constable to conduct the solemnity. These little incidents agreeably diversify a female life.

CHARLES LAMB
Letter to Miss Wordsworth (1817)

To see passengers goe by in some great Rode way, or boates in a river, to oversee a Faire, a Market place, or out of a pleasant window into some thorough-fare streete, to behold a continuall concourse, a promiscuous rout, comming and going, or a multitude of spectators at a Theater, a Maske, or some such like shew.

ROBERT BURTON
The Anatomy of Melancholy (1621. Edition 1632)

213

LOOKING INTO WINDOWS

Looking in at the shop windows of Broadway the whole forenoon, flatting the flesh of my nose on the thick plate glass.

WALT WHITMAN
Song of Myself (1855)

GAMBLING

It is generally remarked, that when the odious and corrupting propensity of gambling takes possession of the female mind, its ravages are still more unsparing than upon the characters and feelings of men.

ANON
Edinburgh Review (Jan. 1825)

MEETING GENTLEMEN

The wives and daughters of the Brahmans, . . . go barefooted ; but wear a great many ornaments, which generally consist of three or four bracelets of brass, a necklace of gold or precious stones, and ear-rings of gold or of diamonds. They bind their hair together in a roll on the top of the head, and paint on the forehead some sacred mark. They bear in their hand an umbrella of palm-leaves, which they always hold before their face when they meet any of the male sex. They, however, turn speedily round, in

214

general, when a man has passed them, and seem to cast a wistful look towards him. This is a plain proof that in every country of the globe the daughters of Eve are subject to the like weaknesses.

FRA PAOLINO DA SAN BARTOLOMEO
Voyage to the East Indies (1796)
(Trans. W. Johnson)

BENEVOLENT AFFECTIONS

Nothing, certainly, is so ornamental and delightful in women as the benevolent affections ; but time cannot be filled up, and life employed, with high and impassioned virtues. . . . A scene of distress and anguish is an occasion where the finest qualities of the female mind may be displayed ; but it is a monstrous exaggeration to tell women that they are born only for scenes of distress and anguish. . . . We know women are to be compassionate ; but they cannot be compassionate from eight o'clock in the morning till twelve at night :—and what are they to do in the interval ?

SYDNEY SMITH
Female Education (1809)

LANGUISHING ARDOUR

I know not how to call it, but there is a meltingness of Disposition, and affectionateness of Devotion, an easie Sensibility, an industrious Alacrity, a languishing Ardour in Piety, peculiar to the Sex, which naturally renders them Subjects more pliable, to the Divine Grace, than Men commonly are; So that *Solomon*, had reason to bestow the Epithete *Gracious*, particularly on them.

THOMAS KEN

A Sermon preached at the funeral of the . . . Lady Margaret Mainard. . . . 30th June, 1682

Town Pleasures With Gentlemen

HIPPOLITA : To confine a woman just in her rambling Age ! take away her liberty at the very time she should use it ! O barbarous Aunt ! O unnatural Father ; to shut up a poor girl at fourteen, and hinder her budding ; all things are ripen'd by the Sun : to shut up a poor girl at fourteen !

PRUE : 'Tis true, Miss, two poor young creatures as we are !

HIPPOLITA : Not suffer'd to see a play in a twelve month !

PRUE : Nor to go to *Ponchinello* nor Paradise !

HIP. : Nor to take a Ramble to the Park nor Mulbery-garden !

PRUE : Nor to *Tatnam-Court* nor Islington !

HIP. : Nor to eat a sillybub in new Spring-garden with a Cousin !

PRUE : Nor to drink a Pint of Wine with a Friend at the Prince in the Sun !

HIP. : Nor to hear a Fiddle in good Company !

PRUE : Nor to hear the Organs and Tongs at the Gun in *Moorfields* !

216

HIP. : Nay, not suffer'd to go to Church, because the men are sometimes there ! Little did I think I should ever have long'd to go to Church !

PRUE : Or I either, but between two maids !

HIP. : Nor see a man !

PRUE : Nor come near a man !

HIP. : Nor hear of a man !

PRUE : No, Miss, but to be deny'd a man, and to have no use at all of a man !

WILLIAM WYCHERLEY
The Gentleman Dancing-Master (1672)

BEING LOVED BY ANGELS

Let the Women have the power of their heads, because of the Angels. The reason of the words, *because of the Angels,* is this ; The *Greek* Church held an Opinion that the Angels fell in love with Women.

JOHN SELDEN
Table Talk (1634–54 : pub. 1689)

SPENDING MONEY

A woman who gets the command of money for the first time upon her marriage, has such a gust in spending it, that she throws it away with great profusion.

JAMES BOSWELL
Life of Johnson (1791)

Ceremony keeps up all things ; 'Tis like a Penny-Glass
to a rich Spirit, or some Excellent Water, without it the
water were spilt, the Spirit lost.

Of all people Ladies have no reason to cry down
Ceremonies, for they take themselves slighted without it.
And were they not used with Ceremony, with Comple-
ments and Addresses, with Legs, and Kissing of Hands,
they were the pittyfullest Creatures in the World.

JOHN SELDEN
Table Talk (1634–54 : pub. 1689)

WASHING-DAY

The servants then (commanded) soone obaid ;
Fetcht Coach, and Mules Joynd in it. Then the Maid
Brought from the chamber her rich weeds, and laid
All up in Coach : in which, her mother plac't
A maund of victles, varied well in taste,
And other junkets. Wine she likewise filld
Within a goat-skin bottle, and distilld
Sweete and moist oile into a golden Cruse,
Both for her daughters, and her handmaids use ;
To soften their bright bodies, when they rose
Cleansd from their cold baths. Up to Coach then goes
Th' observed Maid; takes both the scourge and raines ;
And to her side, her handmaid strait attaines,
Nor these alone, but other virgins, grac't
The Nuptiall Chariot. The whole Bevie plac't ;
Nausicaa scourg'd to make the Coach Mules runne

That neigh'd and pac'd their usuall speed : and soone
Both maids and weeds brought to the river side ;
Where Baths for all the yeare, their use supplide.
Whose waters were so pure, they would not staine ;
But still ran faire forth ; and did more remaine.
Apt to purge staines, for that purg'd staine within,
Which, by the waters pure store, was not seene.
These (here arriv'd) the Mules uncoach'd, and drave
Up to the gulphie river's shore, that gave
Sweete grasse to them. The maids from Coach then
    tooke
Thier cloaths, and steept them in the sable brooke.
Then put them into springs, and trod them cleane,
With cleanly feet ; adventring wagers then,
Who should have soonest, and most cleanly done.
    When having throughly cleansd, they spred them on
The flood's shore, all in order. And then, where
The waves the pibbles wash'd, and ground was cleare,
They bath'd themselves ; and all with glittring oile,
Smooth'd their white skins : refreshing then their toile
With pleasant dinner, by the rivers side.
Yet still watcht when the Sunne their cloaths had
    dride.
Till which time (having din'd) *Nausicae*
With other virgins, did at stool-ball play ;
Their shoulder-reaching head-tires laying by.
Nausicae (with wrists of Ivory)
The liking stroke strooke ; singing first a song ;
(As custome orderd) and amidst the throng,
Made such a shew ; and so past all was seene ;
As when the Chast-borne, Arrow-loving Queene,
Along the mountaines gliding ; either over
Spartan Taygetus, whose tops farre discover ;

Or *Eurymanthus* ; in the wilde Bores chace ;
Or swift-hov'd Hart ; and with her, Joves faire race
(The field Nymphs) sporting. Amongst whom, to see
How farre *Diana* had prioritie
(though all were faire) for fairnesse ; yet of all,
(As both by head and forhead being more tall)
Latona triumpht since the dullest sight,
Might easly judge, whom her pains brought to light ;
Nausicaa so (whom never husband tam'd)
Above them all, in all the beauties flam'd.

HOMER
Odyssey. Book VI
Trans. George Chapman (1614)

AT BATH

Hard by the Pump-room, is a coffee-house for the ladies ;
but my aunt says, young girls are not admitted, insomuch
as the conversation turns upon politics, scandal, philosophy, and other subjects above our capacity ; but we
are allowed to accompany them to the booksellers' shops,
which are charming places of resort; where we read novels,
plays, pamphlets, and news-papers . . . and in these offices
of intelligence (as my brother calls them) all the reports
of the day, and all the private transactions of the Bath, are
first entered and discussed. From the booksellers' shop,
we make a tour through the milleners and toymen ; and
commonly stop at Mr. Gill's, the pastry-cook, to take a
jelly, a tart, or a small bason of vermicelli.

TOBIAS SMOLLETT
Humphrey Clinker (1771)

I danced the polka and Cellarius,
Spun glass, stuffed birds, and modelled flowers in wax.

ELIZABETH BARRETT BROWNING
Aurora Leigh (1856)

AN AGREEABLE MAN IN A HACKNEY-COACH

MRS FORESIGHT : I own it, I think there's no Happiness like conversing with an agreeable Man ; I don't quarrel at that, nor I don't think but your Conversation was very innocent ; but the Place is publick, and to be seen with a Man in a Hackney-Coach is scandalous.

WILLIAM CONGREVE
Love for Love (1695)

A HUSBAND

MISS : What, and must not I have e'er a Husband then ? What, must I go to Bed to Nurse again, and be a Child as long as she's an old Woman ? Indeed, but I won't. For now my mind is set upon a Man, I will have a Man some way or other. Oh ! methinks I'm sick when I think of a Man; and if I can't have one, I wou'd go to sleep all my Life : For when I'm awake it makes me wish and long, and I don't know for what—And I'd rather be always asleep, than sick with thinking.

221

FORESIGHT : O fearful ! I think the Girl's influenc'd too,—
Hussy, you shall have a Rod.

MISS : A fiddle of a Rod, I'll have a Husband ! and if
you won't get me one, I'll get one for myself; I'll marry
our Robin the Butler, he says he loves me, and he's a
handsome Man, and shall be my Husband : I warrant he'll
be my Husband, and thank me too, for he told me so.

Ibid.

CHILD-BEARING AND SHUTTLECOCKS

We things cal'd women, only made for shew
And pleasure, created to beare children,
And play at shuttle-cocke.

JOHN MARSTON
The Tragedie of Sophonisba (1606)

JEWELS

This evening my wife did with great pleasure shew me her
stock of jewels, encreased by the ring she hath made lately
as my Valentine's gift this year, a Turky stone set with
diamonds : and, with this and what she had, she reckons
that she hath above £150 worth of jewels, of one kind or
other ; and I am glad of it, for it is fit the wretch should
have something to content herself with.

SAMUEL PEPYS
Diary (Feb. 24, 1668)

Still unaccomplish'd may the Maid be thought,
Who gracefully to Dance was never taught : . . .
To raffle prettily, or slur a Dye,
Implies both Cunning & Dexterity.
Nor is't amiss at Chess to be expert,
For Games, most thoughtful, sometimes most divert.
Learn ev'ry Game, you'll find it prove of use ;
Parties begun at Play, may Love produce.
But, easier 'tis to learn how Bets to lay,
Than how to keep your Temper while you play. . . .
Then, base Desire of Gain, then, Rage appears,
Quarrells and Brawls arise, and anxious Fears ;
Then, Clamours and Revilings reach the Sky,
While losing Gamesters all the Gods defie.
Then horrid Oaths are utter'd ev'ry Cast ;
They grieve, and curse, and storm, may weep at last.
Good *Jove* avert such shameful Faults as these,
Frome ev'ry Nymph whose Heart's inclin'd to please. . . .

Tho' Martial Fields ill sute your tender Frames,
Nor may you swim in *Tiber's* rapid streams ;
Yet when Sol's burning Wheels from Leo drive,
And at the glowing Virgin's Sign arrive,
'Tis both allow'd, and fit, you should repair
To pleasant Walks, and breathe refreshing Air.
To *Pompey's* Gardens, or the shady Groves
Which *Caesar* honours, and which *Phoebus* loves : . . .
To *Isis* Fane, to Theatres resort ;
And in the *Circus* see the noble Sport.
In ev'ry publick Place, by turns, be shown ;
In vain you're Fair, while you remain unknown.

OVID, *Art of Love* (c. 2 B.C.)
Trans. William Congreve (1709)

223

Now they [the Barbarians] say that in their judgment, though it is an act of wrong to carry away women by force, it is a folly to set one's heart on taking vengeance for their rape, and the wise course is to pay no regard when they have been carried away; for it is evident that they would never be carried away if they were not themselves willing to go.

HERODOTUS
History (5th cent. B.C.)
Trans. G. C. Macaulay

FURNISHINGS, CONFECTIONS, PLANTS, MERRY MEETINGS

Now for women instead of laborious studies, they have curious needleworkes, cut-workes, spinning, bone-lace, and many pretty devices of their own making, to adorn their houses, Cushions, Carpets, Chaires, Stooles . . . confections, conserves, distillations, &c. which they shew to strangers. . . . This they have to busie themselves about, houshold offices, &c. neate gardens, full of exotick, versi-colour, diversely varied, sweet smelling flowers, and plants in all kinds, which they are most ambitious to get, curious to preserve and keep, proud to possesse, and much many times bragge of. Their merry meetings and frequent visitations, mutuall invitations in good townes, I voluntarily omit, which are so much in use, gossipping among the meaner sort, &c.

ROBERT BURTON
The Anatomy of Melancholy (1621. Edition 1632)

FRATERNAL

BORN TO FRIENDS

I was much pleased with the tale that you told me of being tutor to your sisters. I, who have no sisters or brothers, look with some degree of innocent envy on those who may be said to be born to friends.

JAMES BOSWELL
Life of Johnson
(1791)

FOND BROTHER

The affection which I bear to you and Hannah is the source of the greatest enjoyment that I have in the world. It is my strongest feeling. It is that which will determine the whole course of my life. It has made me a better man and a far happier man than anything else could have made me. The very regret which I feel for your absence is a more delightful sensation than the pleasure which I take in other people's society. . . . The pleasures of dissipation end in disgust, those in vanity pall with repetition. Ambition itself passes away. But my love for my sweet sisters . . . becomes stronger and stronger from day to day, and from hour to hour. Having been the most restless and aspiring of human creatures, I feel that I would not only without regret but with perfect cheerfulness and satisfaction retire in their society to an obscurity in which my name should never be heard. Wealth, power, fame, become as nothing to me compared with their most sweet and precious affection.

THOMAS BABINGTON MACAULAY
Letter to his sister Margaret
(1831)

ADORING SISTER

Living as I do with a man who will, I fully believe, before long be acknowledged by the world to be the great man I now know him to be, I cannot help regretting that I have never endeavoured to preserve some record of his conversation ; his talents in conversation being equal, if not superior, to any other he possesses. I certainly never listen to any one (and I have listened to some of whom the world thinks highly) who brings into the ordinary intercourse of society, and applies to every subject, the mind, the intellectual power, I have never failed to find in him. . . .

His conversation is often extremely lively and humorous

. . . I do not wonder that he does not like to hide this talent under a bushel, for it is certainly the cleverest nonsense I ever heard. . . . I intend making this a scrap-book about him for my own amusement and that of others in time to come. . . . How sadly shall I, perhaps, in future days, look on these records of the past gay years ! But if my dearest, dearest Tom still loves me, and I am not separated from him, I feel now as if I could bear anything. But the idea of being separated from him is what I cannot support. He has given me tastes which no other person can satisfy, he has for years been the object of my whole heart, every occupation almost has had him for its object and end in some manner, and without him would be void of interest.

I think I was about twelve when I first became very fond of him, and from that time my affection for him has gone on increasing during a period of seven years. I never shall forget my delight and enchantment when I first found that I could talk to him, and that he seemed to like talking to me. His manner indeed was very flattering to such a child as I was, for he always seemed to take as much pains and exert himself as much to amuse and please me, to explain anything I wished to know, or inform me on any subject, as he could have done to the greatest person in the land. . . .

I have been hearing a good deal of speech-making to-day, which has made me wild to hear Tom. . . . It seems to me now as if it would be almost too much for me to witness that mightiest of all triumphs, the triumph of mind over mind, to hear those burning words, those streams of pure and lofty eloquence, to listen to music dearer to my ears than Pasta could ever make, in the enthusiastic applause of all about me, and to feel that he

227

who was exercising this mighty influence prized the happy tears of my proud, triumphant, devoted affection more than the compliments and applause of the first men in his country. And oh ! how almost too happy to feel that in that heart beating so high in the consciousness and the triumph of unrivalled powers—in his very heart of hearts—was reserved a place for me. Dearest, dearest, dearest, I feel as if I could not love him enough. . . .

I have just been looking round our little drawing-room, as if trying to impress every inch of it on my memory, and thinking how in future years it will rise before my mind as the scene of many hours of light-hearted ease and mirth ; how I shall see him again, lolling indolently on the old blue sofa, or strolling round the narrow confines of our room, who was all the world to me. With such a scene will come the remembrance of his beaming, animated countenance, happy, affectionate smile, and joyous laugh . . . grave or gay, making bad puns, rhymes, riddles, and talking all sorts of nonsense, or " more than mortal wise," eloquent and original, pouring out from the stores of his full mind in his own peculiarly beautiful and expressive language. . . . How strange ! I sometimes think, as those enchanting talents which in various ways delight the world are exerted and displayed for my amusement or instruction—how strange that I, of all people, should be so intimately connected with and so dearly love, and above all be loved by him ! But so it is.

MARGARET MACAULAY
Recollections of T.B.M. (1831-2)

GAMES

BOWLS

My Lord Brookes us'd to be much resorted to by those of the preciser sort, who had got a powerful hand over him ; yet they would allow him Christian libertie for his recreations : but being at bowles one day, in much company, and following his cast with much eagernesse, he cryed, " Rubbe, rubbe, rubbe, rubbe, rubbe." His chaplaine (a very strict mann) runns presently to him : and in the hearing of diverse, " O good my Lord, leave that to God—you must leave that to God ! " sayes he.

SIR NICHOLAS LESTRANGE
Merry Passages and Jests (1630–55)

He was the greatest gallant of his time, and the greatest gamester, both for bowling and cards, so that no shopkeeper would trust him for 6*d*, as to-day for instance he might, by winning, be worth £200, the next day he might not be worth half so much, or perhaps be *minus nihile*. He was one of the best bowlers of his time in England. His sisters comeing to the Peccadillo bowling green, crying for the feare he should loose all their portions.

JOHN AUBREY
Brief Lives : Sir John Suckling (c. 1680)

229

FOOTBALL

Football is nothyng but beastely fury and extreme violence, whereof procedeth hurte, and consequently rancour and malice do remayne with thym that be wounded, wherfore it is to be put in perpetuall silence.

SIR THOMAS ELYOT
The Boke Called the Governour (1531)

STOOLBALL

A time there is for all, my mother often sayes,
When she with skirts tuckt very hie, with gyrles at
   stoolball playes.

SIR PHILIP SIDNEY
Dialogue between Two Shepheards (1586)

CHESS

Chesse-play is a good and witty exercise of the minde for some kind of men, and fit for such melancholy . . . as are idle, and have extravagant thoughts impertinent thoughts, or troubled with cares, nothing better to distract their minde and alter their meditations, invented (some say) by the general of an army in a famine, to keep his souldiers from mutiny but . . . it may doe more harme than good ; it is a game too troublesome for some men's braines, too testy full of anxiety, all out as bad as study ; besides, it is a cholericke game, and very offensive to him that looseth the Mate. *William* the Conquerour in his yonger years, playing at Chesse with the Prince of France, . . . losing a Mate, knocked the Chessboard about his pate, which was a cause afterward of much enmity between them. . . . A sport fit for idle Gentlemen, Souldiers in Garrison, and Courtiers that have naught but Love matters to busie themselves about, but not altogether so convenient for such as are students.

ROBERT BURTON
The Anatomy of Melancholy (1621. Edition 1632)

Memorandum : he would say that he look't upon the play at chesse very fitt to be learn't and practiced by young men, because it would make them to have a foresight and be of use to them . . . in their ordering of humane affaires. Quod N.B.

JOHN AUBREY
Brief Lives : Francis Potter (c. 1680)

CRICKET

Cricket of late years is become exceedingly fashionable, being much countenanced by the nobility and gentlemen of fortune, who frequently join in the diversion ; this game, which is played with the bat and the ball, consists of single and double wicket ; the former requires five players on each side, and the latter eleven ; but the number in both instances can be varied at the pleasure of the two parties. At single wicket the striker with his bat is the protector of the wicket, the opponent party stand in the field to catch or stop the ball, and the bowler, who is one of them, takes his place by the side of a small batton or stump set up for that purpose two and twenty yards from the wicket, and thence delivers the ball with the intention of beating it down. If he proves successful the batsman retires from the play, and another of his party succeeds ; if, on the contrary, the ball is struck by the bat and driven into the field beyond the reach of those who stand out to stop it, the striker runs to the stump at the bowler's station, which he touches with his bat and then returns to his wicket. If this be performed before the ball is thrown back, it is called a run, and one notch or score is made upon the tally towards his game ; if, on the contrary, the ball be thrown up and the wicket beaten down with it . . . before the striker is at home . . . he is declared to be out of the play . . . he is also out if he strikes the ball into the air, and if it be caught by any of his antagonists before it reaches the ground. . . . When double wicket is played, two batsmen go in at the same time, one at each wicket. . . . Both parties have two innings, and the side that obtains the most runs in the double contest claims the victory. These are the general outlines of this noble pastime, but . . . those rules are subject to frequent variations, according to the joint determination of the players.

JOSEPH STRUTT
Sports and Pastimes of the People of England (1801)

TRAP-BALL

Trap-ball, when compared with cricket, is but a childish pastime.

Ibid

The ordinary recreations which we have in Winter, and in most solitary times busie our minds with, are *Cardes, Tables,* and *Dice, Shovel-board, Chesse-play,* . . . shuttle-cock, balliarde, musicke, masks, singing, dancing, ule-games, froliks, jests, riddles, catches, purposes, questions and commands, merry tales of Errant Knights, Queenes, Lovers, Lords, Ladies, Giants, Dwarfs, Theeves, Chea-ters, Witches, Fayries, Goblins, Friers, &c. . . and the rest, which some delight to heare, some to tell, all are well pleased with.   ROBERT BURTON
The Anatomy of Melancholy (1621. Edition 1632)

CRIBBAGE

Sir John Suckling . . . invented the game of Cribbidge. He sent his cards to all gameing places in the country, which were marked with private markes of his : he gott £20,000 by this way.   JOHN AUBREY
Brief Lives : Sir John Suckling (c. 1680)

GOLF

Hard by, in the fields called the Links, the citizens of Edinburgh divert themselves at a game called golf, in which they use a curious kind of bats, tipt with horn, and small elastic balls of leather, stuffed with feathers, rather less than tennis balls, but of a much harder consist-ence—— This they strike with such force and dexterity

233

from one hole to another, that they will fly to an incredible distance. Of this diversion the Scots are so fond, that when the weather will permit, you may see a multitude of all ranks, from the senator of justice to the lowest tradesman, mingled together in their shirts, and following the balls with the utmost eagerness—— Among others, I was shewn one particular set of golfers, the youngest, of whom was turned of fourscore—— They were all gentlemen of independent fortunes, who had amused themselves with this pastime for the best part of a century, without having ever felt the least alarm from sickness or disgust ; and they never went to bed, without having each the best part of a gallon of claret in his belly. Such uninterrupted exercise, co-operating with the keen air from the sea, must, without all doubt, keep the appetite always on edge, and steel the constitution against all the common attacks of distemper.

TOBIAS SMOLLETT
Humphry Clinker (1771)

DRAUGHTS

Johnson, I believe, did not play at draughts after leaving College, by which he suffered ; for it would have afforded him an innocent soothing relief from the melancholy which distressed him so often. . . . The game of draughts we know is peculiarly calculated to fix the attention without straining it. There is a composure and gravity in draughts which insensibly tranquillises the mind ; and, accordingly, the Dutch are fond of it.

JAMES BOSWELL
Life of Johnson (1791)

GARDENS

The Turks who past their dayes in Gardens here, will have Gardens also hereafter, and delighting in Flowers on earth, must have Lillies and Roses in Heaven. In Garden Delights 'tis not easie to hold a Mediocritie; that insinuating pleasure is seldome without some extremity. The Antients venially delighted in flourishing Gardens; Many were Florists that knew not the true use of a Flower. ... Some commendably affected Plantations of venemous Vegetables, some confined their delights unto single plants, and Cato seemed to dote upon Cabbadge; While the Ingenuous delight of Tulipists stands saluted with hard language, even by their own Professors.

SIR THOMAS BROWNE
Epistle Dedicatory to The Garden of Cyrus (1658)

FRENCH

I finish'd this day with a walke in the greate garden of the Thuilleries, rarely contriv'd for privacy, shade, or company, by groves, plantations of tall trees, especially that in the middle, being of elmes, the other of mulberys;

235

and that labyrinth of cypresse ; not omitting the noble hedges of pomegranates, fountaines, fishponds, and an aviary ; but above all the artificial echo, redoubling the words so distinctly, and as it is never without some faire nymph singing to its gratefull returns : standing at one of the focus's, which is under a tree, or little cabinet of hedges, the voice seems to descend from the clouds ; at another as if it was underground. This being at the botome of the garden, we were let into another, which was being kept with all imaginable accuratenesse as to the orangery, precious shrubs, and rare fruites, seem'd a paradise.

JOHN EVELYN
Diary (Feb. 8, 1644)

From hence about a league farther we went to see Cardinal Richelieu's villa at Ruell . . . though the house is not of the greatest, the gardens about it are so magnificent that I doubt whether Italy has any exceeding it for all rarities of pleasure. The garden nearest the pavilion is a parterre, having in the middst divers noble brasse statues, perpetually spouting water into an ample bassin, . . . ; but what is most admirable is the vast enclosure, and variety of ground, in the large garden, containing vineyards, cornefields, meadows, groves (whereof one is of perennial greenes), and walkes of vast lengthes, so accurately kept and cultivated, that nothing can be more agreeable. . . . This leads to the Citroniere, which is a noble conserve of all those rarities ; and at the end of it is the Arch of Constantine, painted on a wall in oyle, as large as the real one at Rome, so well don that even a man skill'd in painting may mistake it for stone and sculpture. The skie and hills

which seem to be between the arches are so naturall that
swallows and other birds, thinking to fly through, have
dashed themselves against the wall. I was infinitely taken
with this agreeable cheate.

Ibid. (Feb. 27, 1644)

ITALIAN

Arriv'd at Tivoli, we went first to see the Palace dEste. . . .
In the garden on the right hand are 16 vast conchas of
marble jetting out waters ; . . . Before the ascent of the
palace is the famous fountaine of Leda, and not far from
that, foure sweete and delicious gardens. Descending
thence are two pyramids of water, and in a grove of trees
neere it the fountaines. . . . The grotts are richly pav'd
with pietra-commessa shells, corall, etc.

Towards Roma Triumphans leades a long and spacious
walk, full of fountaines, under which is historized the
whole Ovidian Metamorphosis in rarely sculptur'd *mezzo
relievo*. At the end of this, next the wall, is the cittie of
Rome as it was in its beauty, of small models, representing
that cittie, with its amphiteaters, naumachia, thermae,
temples, arches, aqueducts, streetes, and other magnifi-
cences, with a little streame running thro' it for the Tyber,
gushing out of an urne next the statue of the river. In
another garden is a noble aviarie, the birds artificial and
singing till an owle appeares, on which they suddenly
change their notes. . . . Below this are divers stews and
fish-ponds, in one of which is the statue of Neptune in
his chariot on a sea horse, in another a Triton ; and lastly
a garden of simples.

Ibid. (May 6, 1645)

Indeed, it is the Purest of Human pleasures. It is the greatest Refreshment to the Spirit of Man ; Without which, Buildings and Pallaces are but Grosse Handy-Works : And a Man shall ever see, that when Ages grow to Civility and Elegancie, Men come to build Stately, sooner then to Garden finely : As if Gardening were the Greater Perfection. I doe hold it, in the Royall Ordering of Gardens, there ought to be Gardens for all the Moneths in the Yeare : In which, severally, Things of Beautie may be then in Season. . . .

For Gardens . . . the Contents ought not well to be under Thirty Acres of Ground ; And to be divided into three Parts : A Greene in the Entrance ; A Heath or Desart in the Going Forth ; And the Maine Garden in the midst ; Besides Alleys on both sides. . . . The Greene hath two pleasures ; The one, because nothing is more Pleasant to the Eye then Greene Grasse kept finely shorne ; The other, because it will give you a faire Alley in the midst, by which you may go in front upon a Stately Hedge, which is to inclose the Garden. . . .

As for the Making of Knots, or Figures, with Divers Coloured Earths, that they may lie under the Windowes of the House . . . they be but Toyes : You may see as good Sights, many times, in Tarts. . . . And upon the Upper Hedge, over every Space, between the Arches, a little Turret, with a Belly, enough to receive a Cage of Birds. . . . I, for my part, doe not like Images Cut out in Juniper, or other Garden Stuffe : They be for Children. . . .

For Fountaines, they are a great Beauty, and Refresh-

ment; But Pooles marre all, and make the Garden un-
wholsome, and full of Flies. . . .

For the Heath . . . I wish it to be framed, as much as
may be, to a Naturall wildnesse. . . Thickets, made onely
of Sweet-briar, and Honny-suckl some wilde Vine
amongst; And the Ground set with Violets, Strawberries,
and Prime-Roses. For these are Sweet, and prosper in
the Shade.

FRANCIS BACON
Of Gardens (1625)

GREEK

Without the hall, and close upon the gate,
A goodly orchard ground was situate,
Of neare ten Acres ; about which, was led
A loftie Quickset. In it flourished
High and broad fruit trees, that Pomegranats bore ;
Sweet Figs, Peares, Olives ; and a number more
Most usefull Plants, did there produce their store.
Whose fruits, the hardest Winter could not kill ;
Nor hotest Summer wither. There was still
Fruite in his proper season, all the yeare.
Sweet *Zephire* breath'd upon them, blasts that were
Of varied tempers. These, he made to beare
Ripe fruite ; these blossomes : Peare grew after peare
Apple succeeded apple ; Grape, the Grape ;
Fig after Fig came ; *Time* made never rape,
Of any dainty there. A spritely vine
Spred here his roote ; whose fruite, a hote sunshine
Made ripe betimes. Here grew another greene.

239

Here, some were gathering ; here some pressing
    seene.
A large-allotted severall each fruite had ;
And all th' softn'd grounds their apparance made,
In flowre and fruite, at which the King did aime
To the precisest order he could claime.
        Two Fountaines grac't the garden ; of which, one
Powrd out a winding streame that over-runne
The grounds for their use chiefly : th'other went
Close by the loftie Pallace gate ; and lent
The Citie his sweet benefit ; and thus
The Gods the Court deckt of *Alcinous*.

HOMER
Odyssey. Book VII
Trans. George Chapman (1614)

EDEN

    In this pleasant soile
His farr more pleasant Garden God ordaind ;
Out of the fertil ground he caus'd to grow
All Trees of noblest kind for sight, smell, taste ;
And all amid them stood the Tree of Life,
High, eminent, blooming Ambrosial Fruit
Of vegetable Gold ; and next to Life
Our Death the Tree of Knowledge grew fast by . . .
    Thus was this place,
A happy rural seat of various view :
Groves whose rich Trees wept odorous Gumms and
    Balme,
Others whose fruit burnisht with Golden Rinde

Hung amiable, *Hesperian* Fables true,
If true, here onely, and of delicious taste :
Betwixt them Lawns, or level Downs, and Flocks
Grasing the tender herb, were interpos'd,
Or palmie hilloc, or the flourie lap
Of som irriguous Valley spread her store,
Flours of all hue, and without Thorn the Rose ;
Another side, umbrageous Grots and Caves
Of coole recess, o're which the mantling Vine
Layes forth her purple Grape, and gently creeps ;
Luxuriant ; mean while murmuring waters fall
Down the slope hills, disperst, or in a Lake,
That to the fringed Bank with Myrtle crown'd,
Her chrystall mirror holds, unite thir streams,
The Birds thir quire apply ; aires, vernal aires,
Breathing the smell of field and grove, attune,
The trembling leaves, while Universal *Pan*
Knit with the *Graces* and the *Hours* in dance
Led on th' Eternal Spring.

JOHN MILTON
Paradise Lost. Book IV (1667)

PRUNING

On to thir mornings rural work they haste
Among sweet dewes and flours ; where any row
Of Fruit-trees overwoodie reached too farr
Thir pamperd boughes, and needed hands to check
Fruitless imbraces.

Ibid.
Book V

And now what *Monarch* would not *Gard'ner* be,
My faire Amanda's stately *gate* to see ;
How her feet tempt ! how soft and light she treads,
Fearing to wake the flowers from their beds !
Yet from their sweet green pillowes ev'ry where,
They start and gaze about to see *my Faire* ;
Look at yon flower yonder, how it growes
Sensibly ! how it opes its leaves and blowes,
Puts its best *Easter clothes,* on neat and gay !
Amanda's presence makes it *holy-day* :
Look how on tip-toe that faire *lilie* stands
To look on thee, and court thy whiter hands
To gather it ! I saw in yonder croud
The *Tulip-bed,* of which *Dame-Flora's* proud,
A short dwarfe flower did enlarge its stalk,
And shoot an inch to see *Amanda* walk ; . . .
The broad-leav'd *Sycomore,* and ev'ry tree
Shakes like the trembling *Aspe,* and bends to thee,
And each leaf proudly strives with fresher aire,
To fan the curled tresses of thy hair ;
Nay, and the *Bee* too, with his wealthie thigh,
Mistakes his *hive,* and to thy lips doth flie ;
Willing to treasure up his *honey* there,
Where *honey-combs* so sweet and plenty are :
Look how that pretty modest *Columbine*
Hangs down its head to view those feet of thine !
See the fond motion of the Strawberrie,
Creeping on th'earth, to go along with thee !
The lovely *violet* makes after too,
Unwilling yet, *my dear,* to part with you ;
The *knot-grasse* and the *dazies* catch thy toes

To catch *my faire ones* feet before she goes ;
All court and wish me lay *Amanda* down,
And give *my Dear* a new *green* flower'd *gown*.
Come let me kisse thee falling, kisse at rise,
Thou in the *Garden*, I in *Paradise*.

NICHOLAS HOOKES
To Amanda walking in the Garden (1653)

As Elevating Influences

. . . my abhorrency of those painted and formall projections of our cockney gardens and plotts, which appeare like gardens of past-board and march-pane, and smell more of paynt than of flowers and verdure : our drift is a noble, princely, and universall Elysium, capable of all the amoenities that can naturally be introduced into gardens of pleasure, and such as may stand in competition with all the august designes and stories of this nature, either of antient or moderne times ; . . . We will endeavour to shew how the aire and genius of gardens operat upon humane spirits towards virtue and sanctitie. . . . How caves, grotts, mounts, and irregular ornaments of gardens do contribute to contemplative and philosophicall enthusiasme . . . influence the soule and spirits of man, and prepare them for converse with good angells ; besides which, they contribute to the lesse abstracted pleasures, phylosophy naturall and longevitie : and I would have not onely the elogies and effigies of the antient and famous garden heroes, but a society of the *Paradisi Cultores*. . . . Paradisean and Hortulan saints, to be a society of learned and ingenuous men, such as Dr Browne.

JOHN EVELYN
Letter to Sir Thomas Browne (1658)

243

Chap VII, Lib 3 : Paradise, Elysian fields, Hesperides, Horti Adonidis, Alcinoi, Semyramis, Salomon's, The pensile gardens in Babylon. . . . Democritus's garden, Epicurus's at Athens, *hortorum ille magister*, as Pliny calls him . . . and many others. . . .

Amongst the antient Romanes. . . .

In America. Montezuma's floating garden, and others in Mexico. . . .

In England—Wilton, Dodington, Spensherst . . . my elder brother George Evelyn's in Surrey, far surpassing any else in England, it may be my owne poore garden may for its kind, perpetually greene, not be unworthy mentioning.

The gardens mentioned in Scripture, &c.

Miraculous and extraordinary gardens found upon huge fishes' backs, men over growne with flowers &c.

Romantique and Poeticall gardens out of Sidney, Spencer . . . Homer . . . &c.

JOHN EVELYN

Letter to Sir Thomas Browne (1658)

THE GARDEN OF PLEASURE

The most pleasant and delectable thing for recreation belonging unto our farmes is our flower gardens, . . . It is a commendable and seemely thing to behold out at a window many acres of ground well tilled and husbanded, . . . But yet it is much more to behold faire and comely proportions, handsome and pleasant arboures and as it were closets, delightfull borders of lavender, rosemarie, boxe, and other such like : to heare the ravishing musicke of an infinite number of prettie small birdes, which continually day and night doe chatter and chant their proper and naturall branch songs upon the hedges and trees of the garden : and to smell so sweet a nosegaie so neere at hand : seeing that this so fragrant a smell cannot but refresh the Lord of the farme exceedingly, when going out of his bed-chamber in the morning after the sunne rise, and whiles as yet the cleere and pearlelike dew doth pearch unto the grasse. He giveth himselfe to heare the melodious musicke of the Bees : which busying themselves in gathering of the same, do also fill the aire with a most acceptable, sweet and pleasant harmonie : besides the borders and continued rowes of soveraigne, thyme, balme, rosemarie, marierome, cypers, soothernwood, and other fragrant herbes, the sight and view whereof cannot but give great contentment unto the beholder.

The garden of pleasure must be cast and contrived close to the one side of the kitchin garden, but yet so, as that they be sundred by the intercourse of a great large alleye, as also a hedge of quickset, having three doores. . . . The kitchin garden is to be compassed and set about with lattise worke, and yoong common bordering stuffe to be made up afterward and contrived into arbours, or as it were into small chappels, or oratories and places to make a speech out off, that many standing about and below may heare. In like sort shall the garden of pleasure be set about and compassed in with arbours made of Jesamin, rosemarie, boxe, juniper, cyper-trees savin, cedars, rose-trees, and other dainties first planted and pruned according as the nature of every one doth require, but after brought into some forme and order with willow or juniper poles, such as may serve for the making of arbours. . . .

This garden shall be devided into two equall parts. The one shall containe the herbes and flowres used to make nosegaies and garlands of, . . . and it may be called the nosegaie garden. The other part shall have all other sweet smelling herbes, . . . and this may be called the garden for herbs of a good smell.

CHARLES ESTIENNE

Maison Rustique (1572) Trans. Richard Surflet (1600)

VAUXHALL

By water to Fox-hall, and there walked in Spring Garden. A great deal of company and the weather and garden pleasant : that it is very pleasant and cheap going thither, for a man may go to spend what he will, or nothing, all is one. But to haer the nightinghale and other birds, and here fiddles, and there a harp, and here a Jew's trump, and here laughing, and there fine people walking, is mighty divertising.

SAMUEL PEPYS

Diary (May 28, 1667)

CHIEF HELP AND JOY

When God did Man to his own likenes make, . . .
   He did a garden for him plant
By the quick hand of his omnipotent word.
As the cheif help and joy of human life,
Hee gave him the first gift, first, even before a Wife.

For God, the universale Architect,
  'T had ben as easy to erect
  A Louvre, or Escuriall, or a Tower . . .
But well hee knew what place would best agree
With innocence and with faelicitie ;
And wee elsewhere still seek for them in vain, . . .
God the first garden made, and the first city, Cain.

Oh blessed shades ! oh, gentle cool retreat,
From all th'immoderat heat
In which the frantick world does burn and sweat ! . . .
The birds that dance from bough to bough,
  And sing above in every tree,
  Are not from fears and cares more free
  Then wee who ly, or sit, or walk below,
  And should by right bee singers too.
What princes quire of musick can excel
  That which in this shade does dwel ?
  For which we nothing pay or give,
  They like all other poets live
Without reward or thanks for their obliging pains ; . . .
The whistling winds add their less artfull straines,
And a grave base the murmuring fountains play ;

ABRAHAM COWLEY
The Garden (1666)

EATING FRUIT

That which makes the cares of gardening more necessary,
or at least excuseable, is, that all men eat fruit that can
get it ; so as the choice is only, whether one will eat Good
or Ill. Now whoever will be sure to eat good fruit, must

do it out of a garden of his own; for besides the choice so necessary in the sorts, the soil, and so many other circumstances that go to compose a good garden, or produce good fruits, and there is something very nice in gathering them, and chusing the best even from the same tree. . . . So that for all things out of a garden, either of sallads or fruits, a poor man will eat better, that has one of his own, then a rich man that has none. And this is all I think of, Necessary and Useful to be known upon this subject.

SIR WILLIAM TEMPLE, *Of Gardening* (1685)

GIVING ADVICE

TO LORD BYRON, TO BE MORE RESERVED

Talking one day of his domestic misfortunes, as he always likes to call his separation from Lady Byron, he dwelt in a sort of unmanly strain of lamentation on it, that all present felt to be unworthy of him; and as the evening before I had heard this habititude of his commented on by persons indifferent about his feelings, who even ridiculed his making it a topic of conversation with mere acquaintances, I wrote a few lines in verse expressive of my sentiments and handed it across the table round which we were seated, as he was sitting for his portrait. He read them, became red and pale by turns with anger, and threw them down on the table with an expression of countenance which is not to be forgotten. The following are the lines, which had nothing to offend; but they did offend him deeply, and he did not recover his temper during the rest of his stay.

And canst thou bare thy breast to vulgar eyes ?
And canst thou shew the wounds that rankle there ?
Methought in noble hearts that sorrow lies
Too deep to suffer coarser minds to share.

The wounds inflicted by the hand we love,
(The hand that should have warded off each blow)
Are never heal'd, as aching hearts can prove,
But *sacred* should the stream of sorrow flow.

If *friendship*'s pity quells not real grief,
Can *public* pity soothe thy woes to sleep ?
No ! Byron, spurn such vain, such weak relief,
And if thy tears must fall—in secret weep.

LADY BLESSINGTON
Conversations with Byron (1834)

TO A LADY, FROM ANOTHER, TO BE DISCREET

It is an unruly Age we live in. . . . I understand there is a Gentleman Mr A. B. is extremely prodigal of his pretences to you, in the way of Love and Marriage : my Condition is only this, that you have an eye to your own welfare, build not upon empty promises, for if you once suffer him to please his humour before he is safely yours, you will certainly forfeit your own Honour. Consider, as he is above you in purse, and the portions of this life (Beauty only excepted, for of that Nature hath given you a bountiful proportion) whether his intentions are real or feigned ; make him your own, then . . . he will be bound by the Laws of God and Nature, to bear a part with you in whatsoever happens.

ANON

New Academy of Compliments (1671)

To a Son in France, to Improve his French, Live Religiously, and Keep Insects in a Box

Honest Tom,

. . . . . I wish some Person would direct you a while for the true Pronounsation and writeing of French ; by noe means forget to encrease yr Latin, be Patient Civil and Debonair unto all, be Temperate and stir little in the hot season ; . . . Have the love and fear of God ever before thine eyes, God confirm yr faith in Christ and that you may live accordingly, Je vous recommende A dieu. If you meet with any Pretty insects of any kind keep them in a box.

SIR THOMAS BROWNE

Letter to his son Thomas (1661)

To Cicero, Not to be Disturbed by His Daughter's Death

I have decided to write briefly to you the thoughts that have occurred to my mind on this occasion ; not that I think they escape you, but because perhaps, hampered by grief, you perceive them less clearly.

Why is it that you are so disturbed by a private grief ? Consider how fortune up till now has treated us ; those things have been taken from us which should be no less dear to us than our children—country, reputation, position, all honours. What can this one additional misfortune add to your grief? Or who, trained by these things, ought not to be thick-skinned, and to consider everything else of less importance? . . . .

This, too, if it seems good to you, consider. Lately there perished simultaneously many famous men; the imperial power of the Roman people has been much diminished; all the provinces have been shaken; are you so much moved to trouble because the little life of one little woman has been thrown away? If she had not met her fate now, she would have had to die in a few years, since she was human. You must recall your mind and thoughts from these topics, and remember rather what is worthy of you. . . .

I am ashamed to write more to you about this, lest I should seem to distrust your sense; therefore, when I have mentioned this one thing more, I will stop. We have often seen that you bear good fortune beautifully . . . show us that you can bear adversity equally well, and that you do not consider your burden greater than you should.

When I learn that you are calmer, I shall inform you of the condition of my province.   SERVIUS SULPICIUS RUFUS
Letter to M. T. Cicero (45 B.C.)

To Milton, to Write of Paradise Found

After some common Discourses had passed between us, he called for a Manuscript of his; which being brought, he delivered to me; bidding me, " Take it home with me, and read it at my Leisure; and, when I had so done, return it to him, with my Judgement therupon." When I came home, and had set myself to read it, I found it was that Excellent POEM which he entitled PARADISE LOST. After I had, with the best Attention, read it through : I made him another Visit, and returned him his Book ; with due Acknowledgment of the Favour he had done me in Communicating it to me. He asked me, how I liked it, and what I thought of it ; which I modestly but freely told him. And, after some further Discourse about it, I pleasantly said to him, Thou has said much, here, of PARADISE LOST : but what hast thou to say of PARADISE FOUND ? He made me no answer, but sate some time in a Muse : then brake off that Discourse, and fell upon another Subject. . . .

Afterwards . . . he shewed me his Second Poem, called PARADISE REGAINED : and, in a pleasant tone, said to me, *This is owing to you ! For you put it into my head, by the question you put to me at Chalfont, which, before, I had not thought of.*   THOMAS ELLWOOD
History of his Life (1714)

To The Virgins to Make Much of Time

Gather ye Rose-buds while ye may,
    Old Time is still a flying :
And this same flower that smiles to day
    To morrow will be dying.

The glorious Lamp of Heaven, the Sun,
    The higher he's a getting ;
The sooner will his Race be run,
    And neerer he's to Setting.

That Age is best, which is the first,
    When Youth and Blood are warmer ;
But being spent, the worse, and worst
    Times, still succeed the former.

Then be not coy, but use your time ;
    And while ye may, goe marry :
For having lost but once your prime,
    You may for ever tarry.

                    ROBERT HERRICK
To the Virgins, to make much of time. Hesperides (1648)

To Young Gentlewomen, to Trust No Man

Ye Virgins that from Cupids tents
    do beare away the foyle,
Whose hartes as yet with raginge love
    most paynfully do boyle,

To you I speake ; For you be they
    that good advice do lack ;
Oh ! if I could good counsell give,
    my tongue should not be slacke. . . .

Beware of fayre and painted talke,
    beware of flattering tonges !
The mermaides do pretend no good,
    for all their pleasant Songs. . . .

Trust not a man at the fyrst sight,
    but trye him well before :
I wish all Maids, within their brests,
    to kepe this thing in store ;

For triall shall declare this trueth
and show what he doth think :
Whether he be a Lover true,
or do intend to shrink.

IS. W.

An Admonition to all young Gentlewomen to beware of
Mens flattery (1566)

GOSSIP

CICERO SPURNS IT

What ? Do you consider that this is what I commissioned
you to do, to send me stories about gladiatorial matches,
about adjourned bails, about the robbery of Chrestus, and
such stuff as nobody dares mention to me when I am at
Rome ?

CICERO
Letter to M. Caelius Rufus (B.C. 51)

BUT STILL GETS IT

There is absolutely no news, unless you want me (and I'm
sure you do) to write to you about this kind of thing :
Young Cornificius has promised marriage to Orsetilla's

daughter. Paulla Valeria, Triarius's sister, got a divorce,
without giving a reason, the very day her husband was to
return home from his province. She is to marry D. Brutus.
She has sent back all her ornaments.

A lot of incredible things like this have happened in
your absence. Servius Ocella would never have persuaded
any one that he was an adulterer if he hadn't been caught
at it twice in three days. Where, you will ask? Where
I should least have wished, by Hercules! I leave you
something to find out from others. And I don't mind the
idea of a Commander-in-Chief inquiring of people one
by one who was the lady someone was caught with.

M. CAELIUS RUFUS
Letter to Cicero (B.C. 50)

THE LITTLE NEWS O' THE TOWN

PAGE : Madam, Mr *Medley* has sent to know whether a
Visit will not be Troublesome this Afternoon ?

LADY TOWNLEY : Send him word his visits never are so.

EMILIA : He's a very pleasant man.

LADY TOWN. : He's a very necessary man among us
Women ; he's not scandalous i'the least, perpetually contriving to bring good Company together, and always ready
to stop us a gap at Ombre ; then he knows all the little
news o' the Town.

EMILIA : I love to hear him talk o' the Intrigues, let 'em
be never so dull in themselves, he'l make 'em pleasant
i' the relation.

LADY TOWN. : But he improves things so much one can

take no measure of the Truth from him. Mr *Dorimant* swears a Flea or a Maggot is not made more monstrous by a magnifying Glass, than a story is by his telling it.

EMILIA : Hold, here he comes.

.   .   .   .

EMILIA : Leave your raillery, and tell us, is there any new Wit come forth, Songs or Novels ?

MEDLEY : A very pretty piece of gallantry, by an eminent Author, call'd the *diversions of Bruxells*, ... Then there is the Art of Affectation, written by a late beauty of Quality, teaching you how to draw up your Breasts, stretch up your neck, to thrust out your Breech, to play with your Head, to toss up your Nose, to bite your Lips, to turn up your Eyes, to speak in a silly soft tone of a Voice, and use all the Foolish French Words that will infallibly make your person and conversation charming, with a short apologie at the latter end in the behalf of young Ladies who notoriously wash and paint, though they have naturally good Complexions.

EMILIA : What a deal of stuff you tell us !

MED. : Such as the Town affords, Madam. The *Russians*, hearing the great respect we have for Foreign Dancing, have lately sent over some of their best Ballarins, who are now practicing a famous Ballat which will be suddenly danc'd at the *Bear-Garden*.

LADY TOWN. : Pray forbear your idle stories, and give us an account of the state of Love, as it now stands.

MED. : Truly, there has been some revolutions in those Affairs, great chopping and changing among the old, and some new Lovers, whom malice, indiscretion, and misfortune, have luckily brought into play.

LADY TOWN. : What think you of walking into the next

Room, and sitting down, before you engage in this business ?

MED. : I wait upon you, and I hope, (though Women are commonly unreasonable) by the plenty of Scandal I shall discover, to give you very good Content, Ladies.

SIR GEORGE ETHEREGE
The Man of Mode (1674)

COFFEE HOUSES AT OXFORD

The decay of study, and consequently of learning, are coffy houses, to which most scholars retire and spend much of the day in hearing and speaking of news, in speaking vilely of their superiors.

ANTHONY WOOD
Life and Times (1674)

A PACKET OF IT

I venture to write to you after six Months Neglect. Not that I think you care much for my letters neither ; don't mistake. . . . I know my Lady —— gives you an Account of all material things, Intrigues and new Petticoats. As for *Politicks*, you'd clap them under Minc'd-pies, and well if they fared no worse. In short, I know nothing but *Religion* you care a Farthing for ; and that the Town's so bare of at present, I cou'd as soon send you Money. No-body prays but the Court ; and perhaps they had as good let it alone ; at least No-body sees, by the Effects, what they pray for ; 'tis thought, a general Excise. But Heaven, who knows

IP 257

our wants better, seems to be of Opinion a General Peace will do as well. . . . . .

The first time I shew'd myself, since I came to Town, upon that Theatre of Truth and Good Nature, the *Chocolate-House*, I was immediately regal'd with the old Story (tho' from another Hand) *That now you were gone for certain*. But that worthy Knight-Errant, Mr W——, that Mirrour of *Chivalry* for all wrong'd Ladies, drew his tongue in your Defence ; and I, *Madam*, had the Honour to be his *Sancho Pancho* in your Justification. But how long we shall be able to stand our Ground I can't tell, unless you'll come and lug out too, and then I don't doubt but we shall make our Party good. . . Here's a scoundrel Play come out lately, by which the Author has been pleas'd to bring all the Reverend Ladies of the Town upon his Back, with my Lady —— at the head of 'em. . . But that is not all his Misfortune ; there's a younger Knot, who, having grimac'd themselves into the Faction of Piety, say, '*Tis a wicked Play*, and a *Blasphemous Play*, and a *Beastly, Filthy, Bawdy Play* ; and so never go to it but in a Mask. Dear Mrs S——, come to Town again quickly, and don't put your Country-tricks upon us any longer, for here's a World of Mischief in your Absence : The *V*—— is leaner than ever. I am grown Religious. My Lord *W*—— is going to be Married. Sir *John Fenwick* is going to be Hanged. The *W.L*—— is boarded by a Sea-Officer : The Lady *Sh*—— is Storm'd by a Land one. *Yel*—— has got a high Intrigue ; and the *P*—— has got the Gripes. . . You see all's in Disorder ; nor are things much better in the Country, as I hear : For, 'tis said, the Spirit of Wedlock haunts Folks in *Shropshire*. . . Some-body swore by —— t'other Day, you were Married ; to whom, I have forgot, tho' that was sworn too. But, pray, let's see you here again; and don't tell us a Scripture-story, That you have married a Husband and can't come; the Excuse, you see, was not thought good, even in those Days, when things wou'd pass on Folks that won't now.

My due Respects to the Mayor and Corporation of S——

A PERSON OF HONOUR
Letter to Mrs S—— (1696)

EAGERNESS

The said Mr Aubrey gave Ant. a Wood abundance of other of his informations; and Anthony used to say of him, when he was at the same time in company, "Look, yonder goes such an one, who can tell such and such stories, and I'll warrant Mr Aubrey will break his neck down stairs rather than miss him."

THOMAS HEARNE
Diary (Aug. 5, 1710)

COLLECTING IT

Dear Sir. You desir'd me, when I saw you last, to send you the News of the Town, and to let you see how punctually I have obey'd your Orders, scarce a Day has pass'd over my Head since, but I have been enquiring after the freshest Ghosts and Apparitions for you, Rapes of the newest date, dexterous Murders, and fantastical Marriages, Country Steeples demolish'd by Lightning, Whales stranded in the North, etc, a large Account of all which you may expect when they come in my way.

TOM BROWN
Letter to W. Knight (1690)

NEW ARRIVALS

We have Mr Lampton and his family lately com from London and along with them a figne brisk phesicion and a figne Maid they are Roman Catholics but appear very well at a distance. I suppose we must not converse with them which I am sorry for because they seem well bred people. . . . . .

Mrs Hutton is from us at Present, the death of her father who has left all to his wifes Management will I doubt be injurious to her poor woman she's ill dealt with and wants humer to bear it.

MRS TICKELL
Letter to her son Thomas (1717)

WHO'S TOGETHER

Y'expect to hear, at least, what Love has past
In this lewd Town, since you and I saw last ;
What change has happen'd of Intrigues, and whether
The old ones last, and who and who's together.

JOHN WILMOT, EARL OF ROCHESTER
*Letter from Artemisa in the town to Cloe in the
country* (c. 1670)

BIRTHS, DEATHS AND MARRIAGES

I will be like any gazette, and scrape together all the births, deaths and marriages in the parish. Lady Hartington and Lady Rachel Walpole are brought to bed of sons; Lord Burlington and Lord Gower have had new attacks of palsies: Lord Falkland is to marry the Southwark Lady Suffolk; and Mr Watson, Miss Grace Pelham. Lady Coventry has miscarried of one or two children, and is going on with one or two more, and is gone to France to-day. Lady Townshend and Lady Caroline Petersham have had their anniversary quarrel, and the Duchess of Devonshire has had her secular Assembly, which she keeps once in fifty years; she was more delightfully vulgar at it than you can imagine.... I am ashamed to send you such nonsense, or to tell you how the good women at Hampton Court are scandalized at Princess Emily's coming to chapel last Sunday with a dog under her arm; but I am bid to send news: what can one do at such a dead time of year? I must conclude, as my Lady Gower did very well t'other day in a letter into the country, Since the two Misses were hanged, and the two Misses were married, there is nothing at all talked of. Adieu!

HORACE WALPOLE
Letter to Henry Conway (1732)

THE GOSSIP-MONGER

No newes can stir but by his doore; neither can he know that, which hee must not tell: What everie man ventures in *Guiana* voyage, and what they gained, he knowes to a haire. Whether Holland will have peace hee knowes, and on what conditions; and with what successe, is familiar to him ere it bee concluded. No post can passe him without a question; and rather than he will leese the newes, hee rides backe with him to appose him of tidings; and then to the next man hee meets, hee supplies the wants of his hasty intelligence, and makes up a perfect tale; . . . If hee but see two men talke and reade a letter in the street, hee runnes to them, and asks if he may not be partner of that secret relation; and if they denie it, hee offers to tell, since he may not heare, woonders: and then falles upon the report of the Scotish Mine, or of the great fish taken up at Linne, or of the freezing of the Thames; . . . His tongue like the taile of Sampsons foxes carries fire-brands, and is enough to set the whole field of the world on a flame. Himselfe beginnes table-talke of his neighbour at anothers boord; to whom he beares the first newes, and adjures him to conceale the reporter: whose cholericke answer he returnes to this first host, inlarged with a second edition: so, as it uses to be done in the sight of unwilling mastives, hee claps each on the side apart, and provokes them to an eager conflict; There can no Act passe without his Comment, which is ever far-fetcht, rash, suspicious, delatorie. His eares are long, and his eyes quicke, but most of all to imperfection, which as he easily sees, so he increases with intermedling. Hee harbours another mans servant, and amiddes his entertainment asks what fare is usuall at home, what houres are kept, what talke passeth their meales, what his masters disposition is, what his government, what his guests? And when hee hath by curious enquiries extracted all the juice and spirit of hoped intelligence, turnes him off whence he came, and works on a new.

JOSEPH HALL
Characters of Vertues and Vices
(1608)

Amaranthus, the Philosopher, met *Hermocles*, *Diophantus*, and *Philolaus*, his companions, one day busily discoursing about *Epicurus* and *Democritus* tenents, very solicitous which was most probable and came nearest to truth ; to put them out of that surly controversie and to refresh their spirits, he told them a pleasant tale of *Stratocles* the Physitian's wedding, and of all the particulars, the company, the cheere, the musicke, &c, for he was new come from it, with which relation they were so much delighted, that *Philolaus* wished a blessing to his heart, and many a good wedding, many such merry meetings might he be at, *to please himself with the sight, and others with the narration of it*. Newes are generally welcome to all our eares . . . we long after rumour to heare and listen to it . . . Wee are most part too inquisitive and apt to harken after newes, which *Caesar* . . . observes of the old *Gauls*, they would be enquiring of every Carrier and Passenger, what they had heard or seene, what newes abroad ?   ROBERT BURTON

The Anatomy of Melancholy (1621. Edition 1632)

Above the Clouds

" I do so hate gossip," she murmured.

" How I hate it too ! " I heard myself exclaim.

" There is so much that is good and noble in human nature ; why not talk of that ? "

" Why not indeed ? " I sighed.

" I always feel that it is one's own fault if one dislikes people, or finds them boring."

" How I agree with you ! " I cried sincerely.

" But people are nowadays so cynical—they sneer at everything that makes life worth living—Love, Faith, Friendship——"

" And yet those very names are so lovely that even when used in mockery they shine like stars."

" How beautifully you put it ! I have so enjoyed our talk." I had enjoyed it too, and felt all the better for it, only a little giddy and out of breath, as if I had been up in a balloon.

LOGAN PEARSALL SMITH, *More Trivia* (1922)

GRASPING

MATHEMATICIANS AND LOVERS

In Love and the Mathematicks People reason alike : Allow never so little to a Lover, yet presently after you must grant him more ; nay more and more, which will at last go a great way : In like manner, grant but a Mathematician one little Principle, he immediately draws a consequence from it, to which you must necessarily assent ; and from this consequence another, till he leads you so far (whether you will or no) that you have much ado to believe him. These two sorts of People, Lovers and Mathematicians, will always take more than you give 'em.

B. DE FONTENELLE, *A Plurality of Worlds* (1686)
Trans. John Glanvill (1688)

THE FAULT OF THE DUTCH

In matters of commerce, the fault of the Dutch
Is giving too little and asking too much.

GEORGE CANNING (C. 1822)

USING OPPORTUNITY

Croesus having heard from the Lydians that Alcmaion had done him service, sent for him to Sardia ; and when he came, he offered to give him a gift of as much gold as he could carry away at once upon his own person. With a view to this gift, its nature being such, Alcmaion made preparations and used appliances as follows :—he put on a large tunic leaving a deep fold in the tunic to hang down in front, and he drew on his feet the widest boots which he could find, and so went to the treasury to which they conducted him. Then he fell upon a heap of gold-dust, and first he packed in by the side of his legs so much of the gold as his boots would contain, and then he filled the whole fold of the tunic with the gold, and sprinkled some of the gold-dust on the hair of his head, and took some into his mouth, and having so done he came forth out of the treasury, with difficulty dragging along his boots and resembling anything in the world rather than a man ; for his mouth was stuffed full, and every part of him was swelled out : and upon Croesus came laughter when he saw him, and he not only gave him all that, but also presented him in addition with more not inferior in value to that. Thus this house became exceedingly wealthy, and thus the Alcmaion of whom I speak became a breeder of chariot horses and won a victory at Olympia.   HERODOTUS

History. (5th C B.C.) Trans. G. C. Macaulay

GROTTOES

POPE'S

Twick'nam.

I have put the last Hand to my works of this kind, in happily finishing the subterraneous Way and Grotto : I there found a Spring of the clearest Water, which falls in a perpetual rill, that echoes through the Cavern day and night. From the River *Thames*, you see thro' my Arch up a Walk of the Wilderness, to a kind of open Temple, wholly compos'd of Shells in the Rustic Manner; and from that distance under the Temple you look down thro' a sloping Arcade of Trees, and see the Sails on the River passing suddenly and vanishing, as thro' a Perspective Glass. When you shut the Doors of this Grotto, it becomes on the instant, from a luminous Room a *Camera obscura* ; on the walls of which all the Objects of the River, Hills, Woods and Boats, are forming a moving Picture in their visible Radiations : and when you have a mind to light it up, it affords you a very different Scene ; it is finished with Shells interspersed with Pieces of Looking-glass in angular forms : and in the Ceiling is a Star of the same Material, at which when a lamp (of an orbicular Figure of thin Alabaster) is hung in the Middle, a thousand pointed Rays glitter, and are reflected over the Place. There are connected to this Grotto by a narrower Passage two Porches, with Niches and Seats ; one toward the River ; of smooth Stones, full of light, and open ; the other toward the Arch of Trees, rough with Shells, Flints, and Iron-Ore. The Bottom is paved with simple Pebble, as the adjoining walk up the Wilderness to the Temple, is to be cockle-shells, in the natural Taste, agreeing not ill with the little dripping Murmur, and the Aquatic Idea of the whole Place. It wants nothing to compleat it but a good Statue with an Inscription, like that beautiful antique one which you know I am so fond of,

> *Hujus Nympha loci, sacri custodia fontis,*
> *Dormio, dum blandae sentio murmur aquae,*
> *Parce meum, quisquis tangis cava marmora, somnum*
> *Rumpere ; seu bibas, sive lavare, tace.*

> Nymph of the Grot, these sacred Springs I keep,
> And to the Murmur of these Waters sleep ;
> Ah spare my slumbers, gently tread the cave !
> And drink in silence, or in silence lave !

You'll think I have been very Poetical in this Description, but it is pretty near the Truth. I wish you were here to bear Testimony how little it owes to Art, either the Place itself, or the Image I give of it.

ALEXANDER POPE
Letter to Edward Blount (1725)

(He had greatly inlarged and improved this Grotto not long before his death : and, by incrusting it about with a great number of ores and minerals of the richest and rarest kinds, it was become one of the most elegant and romantic retirements any where to be seen. He has made it the subject of a very pretty poem of a singular cast and composition.) WILLIAM WARBURTON (1751)

Thou who shalt stop, where *Thames'* translucent wave
Shines a broad Mirror thro' the shadowy Cave ;
Where ling'ring drops from min'ral Roofs distill,
And pointed Crystals break the sparkling Rill,
Unpolish'd Gems no ray on Pride bestow,
And latent Metals innocently glow ;
Approach. Great NATURE studiously behold !
And eye the Mine without a wish for Gold.
Approach : But awful ! Lo ! th' Ægerian Grott,
Where, nobly pensive, ST JOHN sate and thought ;
Where *British* sighs from dying WYNDHAM stole,
And the bright flame was shot thro' MARCHMONT'S Soul,
Let such, such only, tread this sacred Floor,
Who dare to love their Country, and be poor.

ALEXANDER POPE
On his GROTTO *at Twickenham, composed of Marbles,*
Spars, Gemms, Ores, and Minerals

The improving and finishing his Grott was the favourite amusement of his declining Years ; and the beauty of his poetic genius, in the disposition and ornaments of this romantic recess, appears to as much advantage as in his best contrived Poems. WILLIAM WARBURTON (1751)

268

Being under the necessity of making a subterraneous passage to a garden on the other side of the road, he adorned it with fossil bodies, and dignified it with the title of a grotto ; a place of silence and retreat, from which he endeavoured to persuade his friends and himself that cares and passions could be excluded.

A grotto is not often the wish or pleasure of an Englishman, who has more frequent need to solicit than exclude the sun ; but Pope's excavation was requisite as an entrance to his garden, and, as some men try to be proud of their defects, he extracted an ornament from an inconvenience, and vanity produced a grotto where necessity enforced a passage. It may be frequently remarked of the studious and speculative ; that they are proud of trifles, and that their amusements seem frivolous and childish ; whether it be that men conscious of great reputation think themselves above the reach of censure, and safe in the admission of negligent indulgences or that mankind expect from elevated genius an uniformity of greatness, and watch its degradation with malicious wonder ; like him who, having followed with his eye an eagle into the clouds, should lament that she ever descended to a perch.

SAMUEL JOHNSON, *Life of Pope* (1781)

POLYPHEMUS'S

My Palace, in the living Rock, is made
By Nature's Hand ; a spacious pleasing Shade :
Which neither Heat can pierce, nor Cold invade.

JOHN DRYDEN, *Acis, Polyphemus and Galatea* (1700)
From Ovid's *Metamorphoses* (C. 5 B.C.)

He did delight to be in the darke, and told me he could then best contemplate. He had a house heretofore at Coombe, in Surrey, a good aire and prospect, where he had caves made in the earth, in which in summer time he delighted to meditate.   JOHN AUBREY

Brief Lives : William Harvey (c. 1680)

A GROTTO PARTY

On Wednesday night a small Vauxhall was acted for us at the grotto in the Elysian fields, which was illuminated with lamps, as were the thicket and the two little barks on the lake. With a little exaggeration, I could make you believe that nothing was ever so delightful. . . The evening was more than cool, and the destined spot anything but dry. There were not half lamps enough, and no music but an ancient militia-man, who played cruelly on a squeaking tabor and pipe. . . . I could not help laughing as I surveyed our troop, which, instead of tripping lightly to such Arcadian entertainment, were hobbling down by the balustrades, wrapped up in cloaks and great-coats, for fear of catching cold. The Earl, you know, is bent double, the Countess very lame, I am a miserable walker, and the Princess, though as strong as a Brunswick lion, makes no figure in going down fifty-stone stairs. Except Lady Ann, and by courtesy Lady Mary, we were none of us young enough for a pastoral. We supped in the grotto, which is as proper to this climate as a sea-coal fire would be in the dog-days at Tivoli.

HORACE WALPOLE, *Letter to George Montagu* (1770)

The Lincolnshire lady who shewed him a grotto she had been making came off no better . . . Would it not be a pretty cool habitation in summer ? said she, Mr Johnson ? " I think it would, Madam (replied he)—for a toad."

HESTHER PIOZZI, *Anecdotes of Dr. Johnson* (1786)

GROTTOES ON THE CONTINENT
(a) Brussels

From hence we walked into the Park . . . nor is it less plesant than if in the most solitary recesses, so naturally is it furnish't with whatever may render it agreable, melancholy and country-like. Here is a stately heronry, divers springe of water, artificiall cascads, rocks, grotts ; one whereof is compos'd of the extravagant roots of trees, cunninly built and hung together with wires . . .

From hence we were led into the Menag, and out of that into a most sweete and delicious garden, where was another grott of more neate and costly materials, full of noble statues, and entertaining us with artificial musiq ; but the hedge of water, in form of lattice-worke, which the fontanier caused to ascend out of the earth by degrees, exceedinly pleased and surpris'd me.

JOHN EVELYN, *Diary* (Oct. 8, 1641)

(b) Cardinal Richelieu's Villa at Ruell

We then saw a large and very rare grotto of shell-worke, in the shape of satyres and other wild fancys : in the middle stands a marble table, on which a fountaine playes in divers formes of glasses, cupps, crosses, fanns, crownes, etc. Thene the fountainiere represented a showre of rayne from the topp, mett by small jetts from below. At going out, two extravagant musqueteeres shot us with a streme of water from their musket barrells. Before this grotto is a long poole into which ran divers spouts of water from leaden escalop basins. The viewing this paradise made us late at St Germains.

Ibid. (Feb. 27, 1644)

(c) *St Germains*

Subterranean grotts and rocks, where are represented severall objects in the manner of sceanes and other motions, by force of water, shewn by the light of torches onely; amongst these is Orpheus with his musiq; and the animalls, which dance after his harp ; in the second is the King and Dolphin ; in the third, is Neptune sounding his trumpet, his charriot drawne by seā-horses ; in the fourth, the story of Perseus and Andromeda ; mills, hermitages ; men fishing ; birds chirping ; and many other devices. There is also a dry grott to refresh in ; all having a fine prospect towards the river, and the goodly country about it, especially the forrest.

Ibid. (Feb. 27, 1644)

(d) *Villa Borghese*

The grotto is very rare, and represents, among other devices, artificial raine, and sundry shapes of vessells, flowers, etc., which is effected by changing the heads of the fountains.

Ibid. (Nov. 17, 1644)

(e) *Lago d'Agnano*

We tried the old experiment on a dog in the Grotto del
Cane, or Charon's Cave. Whatever having life enters it,
presently expires. Of this we made trial with two doggs,
one of which we bound to a short pole to guide him the
more directly into the further part of the den, where he
was no sooner enter'd but, without the least noyse, or so
much as a struggle . . . we drew him out dead to all
appearance ; but immediately plunging him into the
adjoining lake, within lesse than halfe an hour he
recover'd, and swimming to shore, ran away from us. We
tried the same on another dogg, without the application
of the water, and left him quite dead. The experiment has
been made on men, as on that poore creature whom Peter
of Toledo caus'd to go in ; likewise on some Turkish
slaves ; two souldiers, and other foolehardy persons, who
all perished, and could never be recover'd by the water of
the lake, as are doggs ; for which many learned reasons
have been offer'd.

Ibid. (Feb. 8, 1645)

(f) *Grand Duke's Villa, Pratolino*

In another grotto is Vulcan and his family, the walls richly compos'd of coralls, shells, copper, and marble figures,
with the hunting of severall beasts, moving by the force
of water. Here, having been well wash'd for our curiosity,
we went down a large walk.

Ibid. (May 1645)

273

He maried . . . and lived at Enston, Oxon ; where having some land lyeing on the hanging of a hill faceing the south, at the foot whereof runnes a fine cleare streame which petrifies, and where is a pleasant solitude, he spake to his servant Jack Sydenham to gett a labourer to cleare some boscage which grew on the side of the hill, and also to dig a cavity in the hill to sitt, and read or contemplate. . . .

Here in fine weather he would walke all night. . . .

He did not encumber him selfe with his wife, but here enjoyed himselfe thus in this paradise till the war broke out. . . .

Memorandum:—the grotto below lookes just south ; so that when it artificially raineth, upon the turning of a cock, you are enterteined with a rainebow. In a very little pond (no bigger than a basin) opposite to the rock, and hard by, stood (1643, Aug. 8) a Neptune, neatly cutt in wood, holding his trident in his hand, and ayming with it at a duck which perpetually turned round with him, and a spaniel swimming after her—which was very pretty.

JOHN AUBREY
Brief Lives : Thomas Bushell (1680)

GROTTO OF NAIADS

The Grot he enter'd, Pumice built the Hall,
And Tophi made the Rustick of the Wall ;
The Floor, soft Moss, an humid Carpet spread,
And various shells the chequer'd Roof inlaid.

'Twas now the Hour when the declining Sun
Two Thirds had of his daily Journey run;
At the spread Table Theseus took his Place,
Next his Companions in the daring Chace; . . . .
The Nymphs were Waiters, and with naked Feet
In order serv'd the Courses of the Meat.
The Banquet done, delicious Wine they brought,
Of one transparent Gem the Cup was wrought.

OVID
Metamorphoses (c. 5 B.C.)
Trans. Mr. Vernon (1713)

At the head of the port there is a large-leafed olive; and
near it a delightful cave, shaded, sacred to the Nymphs,
who are called Naiads. And there are stone cups and
casks in it; and there then the bees stow away their
honey. And in it there are stone distaffs of a great length,
and there the Nymphs weave their sea-purple robes, a
marvel to behold. And in it there are perpetual flowing
waters; and it has two doors: these to the North to be
descended by men, but those on the other hand, to the
South, are more sacred; nor do men enter at all by that
way; but it is the way of the immortals.

HOMER
Odyssey, Book XIII
Trans. T. A. Buckley (1860)

275

HANDICRAFTS

GRINDING, SPINNING, AND WEAVING

To encounter feast with houswifry,
In one roome fiftie women did apply
Their severall tasks. Some, apple-colourd corne
Ground in faire quernes, and some did spindles
    turne,
Some worke in loomes ; no hand, least rest receives ;
But all had motion, apt as Aspen leaves,
And from the weeds they wove, (so fast they laid,
And so thicke thrust together, thred by thred)
That th'oile (of which the wooll had drunke his fill)
Did with his moisture, in light dewes distill.
As much as the *Phaeacian* men exceld
All other countrimen, in art to build
A swift-saild ship ; so much the women there,
For worke of webs, past other women were.
Past meane, by *Pallas* meanes, they understood
The grace of good works ; and had wits as good.

HOMER
Odyssey. Book VII
Trans. George Chapman (1614)

I know no happier-looking woman of the *tranquilly* happy sort than Mrs. J. since she took to making Dresden china of leather for the *Roman Catholic bazaars*.

JANE WELSH
Letter to William Dods (Unpublished. No date)

HANDSOME PERSONS

WHAT HUMAN BEAUTY IS

Touching corporall beautie, before I goe any further, it were necessarie I knew whether we are yet agreed about her description. It is very likely that we know not well, what beautie either in nature or in generall is, since we give so many, and attribute so diverse formes to humane beautie. . . . Of which if there were any naturall or lively description, we should generally know it, as we doe the heat of fire. We imagine and faine her formes, as our fantaisies lead us. . . . The Indians describe it blacke and swarthy, with blabbered-thick lips, with a broad and flat nose, the inward gristle whereof they loade with great gold-rings, hanging downe to their mouth, and their neather lips with great circlets beset with precious stones, which cover all their chins, deeming it an especiall grace to shew their teeth to the roots. In *Peru*, the greatest eares ar ever esteemed the fairest. . . . There are other Nations who endevour to make there teeth as blacke as Jeat, and skorne to have them white, and in other places they die them red. Not onely in the province of *Baske*, but in other places, women are accounted fairest when their heads are shaven ; and which is strange, in some of the Northerly frozen-countries, as *Plinie* affirmeth. Those of *Mexico*, esteeme the littlenesse of their foreheads, as one of the chiefest beauties. . . . Amongst us, one would have her white, another browne, one soft and delicate, another strong and lustie : some desire wantonnesse and blithnesse, and othersome sturdinesse and majestie to be joyned with it. Even as the preheminence in beautie, which *Plato* ascribeth unto the sphericall figure, the Epicurians refer the same into the Piramidall or Squat. . . . We are excelled in comelinesse by many living creatures. . . . Concerning those of the Sea . . . both in colour, in neatnesse, in smoothnesse, and in disposition, we must give place unto them : which in all qualities we must likewise do to the ayrie ones.

MICHEL DE MONTAIGNE

Essays (1580). Trans. John Florio (1603)

LA BEL PUCEL

And first of all, my hart gan to learne
Right well to regester, in remembraunce
Howe that her beauty I might then discerne
From toppe to tooe, endued with pleasaunce,
Whiche I shall shewe, withouten variaunce.
Her shining heere so properly she dresses
Aloft her foreheade, with fayre golden tresses.

Her forheade stepe, with fayre browes ybent,
Her eyen gray, her nose straight and fayre,
In her white cheekes the faire bloude it went
As among the wite, the redde to repayre.
Her mouthe right small, her breathe swete of ayre,
Her lippes soft, and ruddy as a rose.
No hart on live, but it would him appose.

With a little pitte in her well favoured chynne,
Her neck long, as white as any lilly,
With vaynes blewe, in which the bloude ranne in,
Her pappes rounde, and therto right prettye,
Her armes slender, and of goodly bodye,
Her fingers small and therto right long,
White as the milke with blewe vaynes among.

Her fete proper, she gartred well her hose.
I never saw so fayre a creature.
Nothing she lacketh, as I do suppose,
That is longyng to faire dame Nature.
Yet more over, her countenaunce so pure
So swete, so lovely, would any hart enspire
With fervent love, to attayne his desire.

STEPHEN HAWES
The Passetyme of Pleasure (1509)

SHE SMILED LIKE A HOLIDAY

Sweet she was, as kind a love
    As ever fetter'd swayne ;
Never such a daynty one
    Shall man enjoy again

Sett a thousand on a rowe
  I forbid that any showe
Ever the like of her
  Hey nonny nonny noe.

Face she had of filberd hue,
  And bosm'd like a swan ;
Back she had of bended ewe,
  And wasted by a span.
Haire she had as black as crowe
  From the head unto the toe,
Downe, downe, all over her
  Hye nonny nonny noe.

She smiled like a Holy-day
  And simpred like the Spring,
She pranck't it like a popingaie
  And like a swallow sing,
She trip't it like a barren doe,
  She strutted like a gor-crowe,
Which made the men so fond of her
  Hye nonny nonny noe.

ANON (c. 1640)

SIR PHILIP SIDNEY

When he descended downe the mount,
His personage seemed most divine,
A thousand graces one might count,
Upon his lovely cheereful eine,
  To heare him speake and sweetely smile,
  You were in Paradise the while.

A sweete attractive kinde of grace,
A full assurance given by lookes,
Continuall comfort in a face,
The lineaments of Gospell books,
    I trowe that countenaunce cannot lie,
    Whose thoughts are legible in the eie

Was never eie, did see that face,
Was never eare, did heare that tong,
Was never minde, did minde his grace,
That ever thought the travell long,
    But eies, and eares, and every thought
    Were with his sweete perfections caught.

MATTHEW ROYDON

An Elegie, or friends passion for his Astrophill
The Phoenix Nest (1593)

ADONIS

To see his face, the Lyon walkt along,
Behind some hedge, because he wold not fear him :
To recreate himself, when he hath song,
The Tiger would be tame, and gently heare him ;
If he had spoke, the Wolfe would leave his pray,
And never fright the silly lamb that day.

When he beheld his shadow in a brooke,
The fishes spred on it their golden gils :
When he was by, the birds such pleasure tooke,
That some would sing, some other in their bils
Would bring him mulberries, and ripe red chereries,
He fed them with his sight, they him with berries.

W. SHAKESPEARE

Venus and Adonis (1593. Edition 1607)

He was a tall, handsome, and bold man. . . . His beard turned up naturally. . . . He had a most remarkeable aspect, an exceeding high forehead, long-faced, and sour eie-lidded, a kind of pigge-eie.

JOHN AUBREY, Brief Lives (c. 1680)

RICHARD LOVELACE

Richard Lovelace, esq : he was a most beautifull gentle-man.

> Geminum, seu lumina, sydus,
> Et dignos Baccho digitos, et Apolline crines,
> Impubesque genas, et eburnea colla, decusque
> Oris, et in niveo mustum candore ruborem.

Obiit in a cellar in Long Acre, a little before the restauration of his majestie. . . . One of the handsomest men of England. *Ibid.*

VENETIA DIGBY

She was a most beautiful desireable creature ; . . . She had a most lovely and sweet-turn'd face, delicate darke-browne haire. She had a perfect healthy constitution ; strong ; good skin ; well-proportioned ; much enclining to a *Bona Roba*. . . Her face, a short oval ; darke-browne eie-browe, about which much sweetness, as also in the opening of her eie-lidds. The colour of her cheekes was just that of the damaske rose, which is neither too hott nor too pale. She was of a just stature, not very tall. *Ibid.*

COMMONLY A FOOL

If she be faire, as the saying is, she is commonly a foole.

ROBERT BURTON
The Anatomy of Melancholy (1621. Edition 1632)

OUT-FLOURISHING MAY

I Beheld her on a Day,
When her looke out-flourisht May;
And her dressing did out-brave
All the Pride, the fields than have : . . .

BEN JONSON
A Celebration of Charis : How he saw her (*published* 1640)

LOVE'S STAR WHEN IT RISETH

See the Chariot at hand here of love
 Wherein my Lady rideth !
Each that drawes is a Swan, or a Dove
 And well the Carre Love guideth
As she goes, all hearts doe duty
 Unto her beauty ;
And enamour'd, doe wish, so they might
But enjoy such a sight,
That they still were, to run by her side,
Through Swords, through Seas, whether she
  would ride.

Doe but looke, on her eyes ! They doe light
 All that Loves World compriseth !
Doe but looke on her Haire, it is bright
 As Loves starre, when it riseth !

Doe but marke her forhead's smoother
Then words that soothe her !
And from her arched browes, such a grace
  Sheds it selfe through the face,
As alone there triumphs to the life
All the Gaine, all the Good, of the Elements
  strife.

Have you seene but a bright Lillie grow,
  Before rude hands have touch'd it ?
Ha'you mark'd but the fall o'the Snow
  Before the soyle hath smutch'd it ?
Ha'you felt the wooll of Bever ?
  Or Swans Downe ever ?
Or have smelt o'the bud o'the Brier ?
  Or tasted the Nard in the fire ?
Or have tasted the bag of the Bee ?
O so white ! O so soft ! O so sweet is she !
                    Ibid. Her Triumph

WENCHES WITH GREAT EYES

Because great eyes in *Turkey* are esteemed an excellencie,
therefore *Mahomet*, well knowing their desire, promiseth
them in his Paradise, wenches with great eyes like saucers.
                                      JOHN BULWER
Anthropometamorphosis, or The Artificial Changeling
                                          (1650)

NECESSITY OF A NOSE

That face must needs be plain that wants a nose.   *Ibid.*

A Man shall see Faces, that if you examine them Part
by Part, you shall finde never a good ; And yet all together
doe well.

FRANCIS BACON
Essayes : Of Beauty (1625)

JANE WELSH

As a child she was remarkable for her large black eyes
with their long curved lashes. As a girl, she was extremely
pretty—a graceful and beautifully formed figure, upright
and supple, a delicate complexion of creamy white with a
pale rose tint in the cheeks, lovely eyes full of fire and soft-
ness, and with great depths of meaning. Her head was
finely formed, with a noble arch and a broad forehead.
Her other features were not regular ; but they did not
prevent her conveying all the impression of being beautiful. . . . She danced with much grace.

GERALDINE JEWSBURY
In Memoriam Jane Welsh Carlyle (1866)

AN EVANESCENT CHILD

My first dash into poetry was as early as 1800. It was the
ebullition of a passion for my first Cousin Margaret
Parker . . . one of the most beautiful of evanescent beings. . . . Her dark eyes ! her long eye-lashes ! her com-
pletely Greek cast of face and figure ! I was then about
twelve—She rather older, perhaps a year. . . . I do

not recollect scarcely anything equal to the *transparent* beauty of my cousin. . . . She looked as if she had been made out of a rainbow—all beauty and peace.

LORD BYRON
Detached Thoughts (1821–2)

LORD BYRON

In external appearance Byron realised that ideal standard with which imagination adorns genius. He was in the prime of life, thirty-five ; of middle height, five feet eight and a half inches; regular features, without a stain or furrow on his pallid skin, his shoulders broad, chest open, body and limbs finely proportioned. His small, highly finished head and curly hair had an airy and graceful appearance from the massiveness and length of his throat; you saw his genius in his eyes and lips. In short, Nature could do little more than she had done for him. . . . There was no peculiarity in his dress, it was adapted to the climate ; a tartan jacket braided—he said it was the Gordon pattern, and that his mother was of that ilk. A blue velvet cap with a gold band, and very loose nankeen trousers, strapped down so as to cover his feet : his throat was not bare, as represented in drawings.

E. J. TRELAWNEY
Recollections of the Last Days of Shelley and Byron (1858)

His appearance at that time was the finest I ever saw it, a great deal finer than it was afterwards, when he was abroad. He was fatter than before his marriage, but only

just enough so to complete the manliness of his person ;
and the turn of his head and countenance had a spirit and
elevation in it, which though not unmixed with disquiet,
gave him altogether a nobler look than I ever knew him to
have, before or since. His dress, which was black, with
white trowsers, and which he wore buttoned close over the
body, completed the succinctness and gentlemanliness of
his appearance.

LEIGH HUNT
Lord Byron and some of his Contemporaries (1828)

THE HANDSOME COLONEL

He was of a middle stature, of a slender and exactly
well-proportion'd shape in all parts, his complexion faire,
his hayre of light browne, very thick sett in his youth,
softer than the finest silke, and curling into loose greate
rings att the ends ; his eies of a lively grey, well-shaped
and full of life and vigour, graced with many becoming
motions ; his visage thinne, his mouth well made, and his
lipps very ruddy and gracefull, allthough the nether chap
shut over the upper, yett it was in such a manner as was
not unbecoming ; his teeth were even and white as the
purest ivory, his chin was something long, and the mold
of his face, his forehead was not very high ; his nose was
rays'd and sharp, but withall he had a most amiable
countenance, which carried in it something of magnani-
mity and majesty mixt with sweetenesse, that at the same
time bespoke love and awe in all that saw him ; his skin
was smooth and white, his legs and feete excellently well-
made, he was quick in his pace and turnes, nimble and

active and gracefull in all his motions, he was apt for any bodily exercise, and any that he did became him ; . . . he was wonderful neate, cleanly, and gentile in his habitt, and had a very good fancy in it, but he left off very early the wearing of aniething that was costly, yett in his plainest negligent habitt appear'd very much a gentleman.

LUCY HUTCHINSON
To her Children concerning their Father (c. 1665)

CHINESE BEAUTIES

Europeans have a quite different idea of beauty from us. When I reflect on the small-footed perfections of an Eastern beauty, how is it possible I should have eyes for a woman whose feet are ten inches long ? I shall never forget the beauties of my native city of Nanfew. How very broad their faces ! how very short their noses ! how very little their eyes ! how very thin their lips ! how very black their teeth ! the snow on the tops of Bao is not fairer than their cheeks ; and their eyebrows as small as the line by the pencil of Quamsi. Here a lady with such perfections would be frightful; Dutch and Chinese beauties, indeed, have some resemblance, but English women are entirely different; red cheeks, big eyes, and teeth of a most odious whiteness, are not only seen here, but wished for ; and then they have such masculine feet, as actually serve *some* for walking !

OLIVER GOLDSMITH
Letters from a Citizen of the World to his Friends in the East (1762)

This amazing, confounding, admirable, amiable Beauty, *than which in all Natures treasure,* (saith Isocrates), *there is nothing so majesticall and sacred, nothing so divine, lovely, pretious, 'tis natures Crown, gold and glory;* ... speak *Alcibaides,* though drunk, we will willingly hear thee as thou art. Faults in such are no faults. For when the said *Alcibiades* had stoln *Anytus* his gold and silver plate, he was so far from prosecuting so foul a fact (though every man else condemned his imprudence and insolvency) that he wished it had been more, and much better (he loved him dearly) for his sweet sake. No worth is eminent in such lovely persons, all imperfection hid; ... for hearing, sight, touch, etc., our mind and all our senses are captivated. ... *O vis superba formae,* a Goddess beauty is, whom the very Gods adore, ... she is *Amoris domina,* loves harbinger, loves loadstone, a witch, a charm, etc. Beauty is a dowre of it self, a sufficient patrimony, an ample commendation, an accurate epistle. Beauty deserves a Kingdome, and *more have got this honour and eternity for their beauty than for all other vertues besides :* and *such as are fair are worthy to be honoured of God and men.* That *Idalian Ganymedes* was therefore fetched by *Jupiter* into Heaven, *Hephestion* dear to *Alexander, Antinous* to *Adrian. Plato* calls beauty, for that cause, natures master-piece. ... They will adore, cringe, complement, and bow to a common wench (if she be fair) as if she were a noble woman, a Countess, a Queen, or a goddess. Those intemperate young men of *Greece* erected at *Delphi* a golden Image, with infinite cost, to the eternal memory of *Phryne* the curtizan, as *Ælian* relates, for she was a most beautiful woman. Thus yong men will adore and honour beauty; nay Kings themselves I say will . . . voluntarily submit their soveraignty to a lovely woman. . . . *When they have got gold and silver, they submit all to a beautiful woman, give themselves wholly to Her, gape and gaze on her, and all men desire her more than gold or silver, or any pretious thing : they will leave father and mother, and venture their lives for her.* . . . When as *Troy* was taken, and the wars ended . . . angry *Menelaus,* with rage and fury armed, came with his sword drawn to have killed *Helena* with his own hands, as being the sole cause of all those wars and miseries : but when he saw her fair face, as one amazed at her divine beauty, he let his weapon fall, and embraced her besides, he had no power to strike so sweet a creature. . . . *Hiperides* the orator, when *Phryne* his client was accused at *Athens* for her lewdness, used no other defence in her cause, but tearing her upper garment, disclosed her naked breast to the Judges, with which comeliness of her body, and amiable gesture, they were so moved and astonished, that they did acquit her forthwith, and let her go. O noble piece of Justice, mine author exclaims, and who is he that would not rather lose his seat and robes, forfeit his office, than give sentence against the majesty of beauty ? Such prerogatives have fair persons, and they alone are free from danger. *Parthenopaeus* was so lively and fair, that when he fought in the *Theban* wars, if his face had been by chance bare, no enemy would offer to strike at, or hurt him. Such immunities hath beauty ; beasts themselves are moved with it. *Sinalda* was a woman of such excellent feature, and a Queen, that when she was to be trodden on by wild horses for a punishment, *the wild beasts stood in admiration of her person . . . and would not hurt her.* . . . I could tell you such another story of a spindle that was fired by a fair ladies looks, or fingers, some say, I know not well whether, but fired it was by report, and of a cold bath that suddenly smoaked, and was very hot, when naked *Caelia* came into it . . . men are mad, stupifyed many times at the first sight of beauty, amazed, as that fisherman in *Aristaenetus*, that espied a maid bathing herself by the Sea side. . . . *Charmides* in *Plato* was a proper young man, . . . *whensoever fair* Charmides *came abroad, they seem'd all to be in love with him.* . . . the *Athenian* Lasses stared on *Alcibiades*; *Sapho* and the *Mitilean* women on *Phaon* the fair. Such lovely sights do not onely please, entise, but ravish and amaze. *Cleonimus*, a delicate and tender youth, present at a feast which *Androcles* his uncle made in *Piraeos* at *Athens*, when he sacrificed to *Mercury*, so stupified the guests, . . . that they could not eat their meat, they sate all supper time gazing, glancing at him, stealing looks, and admiring of his beauty. Many will condemn these men that are so enamoured, for fools; but some again commend them for it. . . . Beauty is to be preferred. . . . Great *Alexander* married *Roxane*, a poor mans child, onely for her person. 'Twas well done of *Alexander*, and heroically done, I admire him for it.

ROBERT BURTON
Anatomy of Melancholy (1621. Edition 1652)

HELEN'S FRIENDS SING

In Sparta, long agoe, where Menelaus wore the crowne,
Twelve noble Virgins, daughters to the greatest in the
   towne . . .
Danst at the chamber doore of Helena the Queene,
What time this Menelay, the younger son of Atreus,

Did marry with this lovely daughter of Prince Tyndarus ;
And therwithal, at eve, a wedding song they jointly sung,
With such a shuffling of their feete that all the palace rung.

Fair Bridegroome do you sleep ? Hath slumber all your
lims possesst.
What, are you drousie, or hath wine your bodie so oppresst
That you are gone to bed ? For if you needes would take
your rest,
You should have tane a season meete. Mean time, till it
be daie,
Suffer the Bride with us, and with her mother deere to
plaie. . . .

For we, her peers in age, whose course of life is evne the
same,
Who at Eurotas streames like men are oiled to the game :
And foure times sixtie maides, of all the weemen youth
we are ;
Of these none wants a fault, if her with Hellen we compare,
Like as the rising Morning shewes a gratefull lightening,
When sacred night is past, and winter nowe lets loose the
spring,
So glittering Hellen shinde among the maides, lustie and tal,
As is the furrowe in a field that far outstretcheth al ;
Or in a garden is a Cypres tree ; or in a trace
A steede of Thessalie ; so shee to Sparta was a grace. . . .

O faire, O lovely Maide, a matrone now is made of thee !
But wee wil everie spring, unto the leaves in meadowes goe
To gather Garlands sweete, and there, not with a little
woe,
Will often think of thee. . . .   ANON
Sixe Idillia from Theocritus translated into English
verse (1588)

HAPPY DEATHS

Of Laughter

Philemon, a Comick Poet, died with extreme laughter at
the conceit of seeing an asse eate figs.   THOMAS NASHE
The Unfortunate Traveller (1594)

Of a Grape-Stone

The manner of his [Anacreon's] death is said to have been
very extraordinary, for they tell us he was choaked with
a grape-stone, which he swallowed as he was regaling on
some new wine. Mr Cowley, who has so happily imitated
the style and manner of Anacreon, has honoured him
with an elegy in his own strain, which concludes in this
manner:

> It grieves me when I see what Fate
> Does on the best of *Mankind* wait.
> *Poets* or *Lovers* let them be,
> 'Tis neither *Love* nor *Poesie*
> Can arm against *Deaths* smallest dart
> The *Poets Head,* or *Lovers Heart.*

But when their *Life* in its decline,
Touches th' *Inevitable Line*,
All the *Worlds Mortal* to 'em then,
And *Wine* is *Aconite* to men.
Nay in *Deaths Hand* the *Grape-stone* proves
As strong as *Thunder* is in *Joves*.

WILLIAM OWEN AND WILLIAM JOHNSTON
Biographical Dictionary (1755)

OF MILK

Or, as *Fabius* a Senator of Rome, and Lord chiefe Justice
besides, who in a draught of milk fortuned to swallow a
small haire, which strangled him.

PLINY, *Natural History* (c. 77)
Trans. Philemon Holland (1601)

A DAINTY DEATH

Heliogabalus, the most dissolute man of the world,
amidst his riotous sensualities, intended, whensoever
occasion should force him to it, to have a daintie death.
Which, that it might not degenerate from the rest of his
life, he had purposely caused a stately towre to be built,
the nether part and fore-court whereof was floored with
boardes richly set and enchased with gold and precious
stones, from-off which he might headlong throwe himselfe
downe : He had also caused cordes to be made of gold
and crimson silke therewith to strangle himselfe: and a rich

golden rapier, to thrust himselfe through: and kept poison in boxes of Emeraldes and Topases, to poison himselfe with, according to the humor he might have, to chuse which of these deaths should please him.

MICHEL DE MONTAIGNE
Essays : Of judging of others death (1580)
Trans. John Florio (1603)

A HIPERBOREAN NATION

Plinie reporteth of a certaine *Hiperborean* nation, wherin, by reason of the mild temperature of the aire, the inhabitants thereof commonly never dye, but when they please to make themselves away, and that being weary and tired with living, they are accustomed at the end of a long-long age, having first made merry and good cheare with their friends, from the top of a high-steepy rocke, appointed for that purpose, to cast themselves headlong into the sea.

MICHEL DE MONTAIGNE
Essays : A Custom of the Isle of Cea (1580)
Trans. John Florio (1603)

AN ASTRONOMER

Caius Gallus . . . in a good old Age, as he was sitting in his Study, with his Head and his Hands full of his *Astronomy*, went away as peaceably as an Infant; and as it happen'd, while I was in the Room with him.

CICERO, *De Senectute* (45 B.C.)
Trans. Samuel Parker (1704)

295

For either Death puts the Soul out of being, and there's an end of the matter; or else it translates it to a State of indefeasible Security, and then we cannot wish for a happier Change. . . . Can any Thing be more natural than for a Man to die in his Old Age ? . . . An Old Man's *Trunk* wastes kindly, takes its own Time, and glimmers off into Ashes. So agen, 'tis harsh and violent to pluck an Apple from the Tree before 'tis ripe ; let it hang till the Sun has fully completed its Maturation, and then 'twil soon fall of its own Accord. . . . As I advance nearer and nearer to the finishing *Crisis*, I look upon myself as *making to Shore*, and upon the Point of sliding into Harbour after a tedious Voyage. . . . How fortunate is the Man that retains all the Powers of his Soul and the Use of his Senses unimpair'd till Nature's full Time is up, and she comes to take her own Work to Pieces in her own Way. . . . 'Twas *Solon's* Ambition and a celebrated Wish of his, *That whenever he dy'd, his Friends would take it to Heart, and put on a Pomp of Sorrow for him ;* . . . I declare for *Ennius* against him, *Nemo me lacrymis*, etc.

> *Kind Heaven ! Whene're it comes to be my Turn,*
> *Avert wry Funeral Faces from my Urn.*

'Tis very unaccountable (thought he) that People should make such a Rout about dying, when 'tis the ready Road to a State of Immortality. As for Agonies and Convulsions in the Article of expiring, they are over in a trice. . . . And then comes on either a final Cessation of all Perceptions, or else the most refin'd or improv'd ones. . . . Besides, as far as I can find by myself, a Man may be cloy'd and surfeited with one Thing after another in this World; till it comes to that pass with him that *Life its self* shall lie upon his Hands. . . . *Living* becomes perfectly fulsome, and we grow impatient to receive our Discharge.

And this is not all neither. For I must be so free with my Friends (and I hope no Offence) as to discover the secret and serious Persuasion of my Soul to them, with regard to the State of the Dead : . . . At present we are all close Prisoners, immured with Flesh and Bones, and ty'd to the Toil and Tendence of a miserable but indispensable Servitude ; the Soul being of a Divine or Celestial Nature . . . plunged into a Tenement of *Dirt*, a Situation and Residence disagreeable enough to a Being of an Immortal and Heavenly kind. . . . I have held out the Race, and I don't desire to be brought agen to the *Starting-Post* ; and if Heaven should graciously make me this overture, *If you have a Mind to't, you shall be remanded to a State of Infancy and go to Nurse again*, I should humbly and earnestly pray to be excused. . . . My Foot is already in the Stirrup ; and I leave this World, not as a Man would leave his *Mansion-House*, but his *Inn*. How long art thou coming, Auspicious Hour ! When I'm to be releas'd out of these Territories of Dirt and Distraction, and incorporated into the sacred Society of the great Souls above. . . . Perhaps I may be too confident and overweaned in the Point of the Soul's Immortality ; if so, 'tis at least a very obliging Error, and I am so heartily in love with it, that I would not be disabus'd, methinks, for the World.

Ibid.

Let it be remember'd only . . . how often our own Legions have thrown themselves with an incredible Transport and Ardour upon such hot and desperate Services, that they could not suppose a single Man of them should come off again alive : Not to look up so high as our Heros of the first Order ; *Lucius Brutus* that dropt in the Prosecution of his Country's Deliverance ; the *Decii* that gallop'd full speed to a Death that they might have avoided ; *Marcus Attilius*, that rather than he would not be true to Articles, re-committed himself to the Malice and Indignation of the Enemy ; the two *Scipios*, that planted themselves as a Breast-Work, against the Impressions of the whole *Carthaginian* Army, either to make an effectual Stand, or be cut in Pieces, in the Cause of the Commonwealth. . . . *Marcus Marcellus*, the noble circumstances of whose Death had such an Effect upon the savage *Carthaginians* themselves that they took Care he should be handsomely interr'd.

Ibid.

AN EARNEST PURSUIT

He that dies in an earnest Pursuit, is like one that is wounded in hot *Bloud* ; who, for the time, scarce feeles the Hurt ; And therefore, a Minde fixt, and bent upon somewhat that is good, doth avert the Dolors of *Death* ; But, above all, beleeve it, the sweetest Canticle, is *Nunc dimittis* ; when a Man hath obtained worthy Ends, and Expectations. *Death* hath this also ; That it openeth the

Gate to good Fame, and extinguisheth Envye—*Extinctus amabitur idem.*

FRANCIS BACON, *Essayes : Of Death* (1625)

DYING IN AN INN

He [Archbishop Leighton] used often to say, that if he were to choose a Place to die in, it should be an Inn ; it look'd like a Pilgrim's going Home. . . . He added, that the officious Tenderness, and care of Friends, was an Entanglement to a dying man, and that the unconcern'd Attendance of those that could be procur'd in such a place, would give less disturbance : and he obtain'd what he desir'd ; for he died at the *Bell Inn,* in *Warwick Lane.*

GILBERT BURNET
History of his own Time (Pub. 1723–34)

A MERRY SYMPOSIAQUE

He was a very handsome man, a gracefull speaker, facetious, and well-beloved. I thinke he dyed of a merry symposiaque. JOHN AUBREY
Brief Lives : Richard Martin (c. 1680)

DEATHBED OF A HEROINE

You may be glad to know the particulars of her happy exit. . . .

I approached the bed. . . . " Oh ! Mr Bedford," said

299

she, in broken periods . . . " A few—a very few moments —will end this strife—And I shall be happy ! Comfort here, Sir "—turning her head to the Colonel—Comfort my cousin—See !—the blameable kindness—He would not wish me to be happy—so *soon* ! "

. . Then, resuming, . . . " I am all blessed hope—Hope itself."

She *looked* what she said, a sweet smile beaming over her countenance.

After a short silence, " Once more, my dear cousin," said she . . . " commend me most dutifully to my Father and Mother "—There she stopt. And then proceeding— " To my Sister, To my Brother, To my Uncles—And tell them, I bless them with my parting breath—for all their goodness to me—Even for their displeasure, I bless them —Most happy has been to me my punishment here !— Happy indeed ! "

. . . Then, " *O death !* " said she, " *where is thy sting !* " (The words I remember to have heard in the Burial- service read over my Uncle and poor Belton.) And after a pause, " *It is good for me that I was afflicted !* "—Words of Scripture, I suppose.

Then, turning towards us, who were lost in speechless sorrow—" O dear, *dear* gentlemen," said she, " you know not what *foretastes*, what *assurances*." And there she again stopt, and looked up, as if in a thankful rapture, sweetly smiling.

Then turning her head towards me—" Do *you*, Sir, tell your friend, that I forgive him ! And I pray to God to forgive him ! " Again pausing, and lifting up her eyes, as if praying that He would—" Let him know how happily I die.—And that such as my own, I wish to be his last hour. . . .

My sight fails me ! Your voices only "—(for we both applauded her christian, her divine frame, tho' in accents as broken as her own) . . . " Is not this Mr Morden's hand ? " pressing one of his . . . " Which is Mr Bedford's ? " . . . I gave her mine. " God Almighty bless you both," said she, " and make you both—in your last hour —for you *must* come to this—happy as I am." . . .

She paused again, her breath growing shorter ; and after a few minutes . . . " And tell my dear Miss Howe— and vouchsafe to see, and to tell my worthy Mrs Norton —She will be one day, I fear not, tho' now lowly in her fortunes, a Saint in Heaven—Tell them both, that I remember them with thankful blessings in my last moments ! " . . .

Her sweet voice and broken periods methinks fill my ears, and never will be out of my memory.

After a short silence . . . " And you, Mr Bedford, pressing my hand, may God preserve you, and make you sensible of all your errors—You see, in me, how All ends —May *you* be——" And down sunk her head upon her pillow, she fainting away. . . .

We thought she was then gone ; and each gave way to a violent burst of grief.

But soon showing signs of returning life, our attention was again engaged ; and I besought her, when a little recovered, to complete in my favour her half-pronounced blessing. She waved her hand to us both, and bowed her head six several times, as we have since recollected, as if distinguishing every person present ; not forgetting the nurse and the maid-servant . . . and she spoke falteringly and inwardly,—" Bless—bless—bless—you All—And now —And now——" (holding up her almost lifeless hands for the last time) " Come—O come—Blessed Lord—JESUS ! "

And with these words, the last but half-pronounced, expired : Such a smile, such a charming serenity overspreading her sweet face at the instant as seemed to manifest her eternal happiness already begun.

O Lovelace !—But I can write no more !

SAMUEL RICHARDSON
Clarissa. (Letter from Mr Bedford to Robert
Lovelace Esq.) (1749)

PROOFS

He [Bayle] died as he had lived, in the same uninterrupted habits of composition; for with his dying hand, and nearly speechless, he sent a fresh proof to the printer.

ISAAC DISRAELI
Curiosities of Literature (1791–1823)

RISING TO THE OCCASION

He [Sir Richard Grenville] was borne into the ship called the Saint Paule, wherin was the Admirall of the fleet, Don Alonso de Barsan. There his woundes were drest by the Spanish surgeons ; . . . the Captaines and Gentlemen went to visite him . . . wondering at his courage and stout heart, for that he shewed not any signe of faintness, nor changing of colour : but feeling the hower of death to approach, hee spake these wordes in Spanish, and said, Here die I, *Richard Greenfield*, with a joyfull and quiet mind, for I have ended my life as a true soldier ought to do, that hath fought for his countrey, Queene, religion, and honour : whereby my soule most joyfull departeth out of this bodie, and shall leave alwaies behind it an everlasting fame of a valiant and true soldier, that hath done his dutie, as he was bound to doe.

When hee had finished these, or such other like wordes, he gave up the ghost, with great and stout courage; and no man could perceive any true signe of heavinesse in him.

J. H. VAN LINSCHOTEN
Discourse of Voyages to East and *West Indies*
Trans. from Dutch (1598)

THE ENEMY RUN

When no longer able to stand, his [Wolfe's] only concern was lest the men should be disheartened by his fall. " Support me," he whispered to an officer near him ; " let not my brave soldiers see me drop. The day is ours—keep it." . . .

The cry was heard, " They run—they run ! " Like one suddenly aroused from heavy sleep, Wolfe demanded, with great earnestness, " Who run ? " " The enemy, Sir . . . they give way everywhere." Thereupon the expiring hero . . . rejoined, " Go, one of you . . . to Colonel Burton : tell him to march Webb's regiment with all speed down to Charles river, and cut off the retreat." . . . He then turned upon his side, and his last words were, " Now God be praised ; I die in peace ! "

CAPTAIN KNOX, *Journal of Campaigns* (1769)

[But the surgeon present reported his dying words to be " Lay me down, I am suffocating." One can take one's choice.]

" Is the wound a mortal one ? " asked Montcalm.

" Yes," replied Arnoux. . . .

" I am content," replied Montcalm ; " how much longer have I to live ?

" Not twenty-four hours."

" So much the better," returned the dying man. " I shall not live to see the English masters of Quebec."

ABBÉ CASGRAIN, Wolfe and Montcalm (1905)

A BUTT OF MALMESEY

1ST MURDERER : . . . and then throwe him into the Malmesey-Butte in the next roome.

2ND MURD. : O excellent device ; and make a sop of him.

1ST MURD. : Soft, he wakes. . . .

CLARENCE : Where art thou Keeper ? Give me a cup of wine.

2ND MURD. : You shall have Wine enough my Lord anon.

WILLIAM SHAKESPEARE
Richard III (1597. Edition 1623 folio)

ANOTHER VERSION

Attainted was hee by parliament and judged to the death, and thereupon hastely drouned in a Butt of Malmesey.

SIR THOMAS MORE, History of Richard III (1513)

LAMPREYS

When therefore the King [Henry I] returned from hunting, at St Denis in the forest of Lyons, he ate the flesh of
lampreys, which always disagreed with him, and he always loved them. But when his doctor forbade this food,
the king did not acquiesce in this counsel of health.

HENRY OF HUNTINGDON
Historia Anglorum (1154) (Trans.)

Ranulphe says, he [Henry I] tooke a surfet by etynge
of a lamprey, and therof dyed.

ROBERT FABYAN, *Concordance of Histories* (1516)

[This seems an inferior version; one would prefer to believe that
poor Henry had more than one of his favourite fish before he died.]

PEACHES AND NEW CIDER

He King John passed the next night at a convent
called Swineshead, where . . . he surfeited himself with
peaches and drinking new cider. . . . He rode to Newark ;
there his sickness increased, and he confessed himself and
received the sacrament from the abbot of Croxton.

ROGER OF WENDOVER, *Flores Historiarum* (1235)

TAKING ONE'S TIME

Petronius . . . did not rashly kill himselfe, but cutting his
vaines, and binding them up, as pleased him, opened them

305

againe, and talked with his friends, though not of any serious matter, . . . nothing of the immortality of the soul, or opinions of wise men ; but of light verses, and easie songs. On some of his slaves he bestowed gifts, and on some stripes. He went sometimes abroade, and gave himselfe to sleepe, that although his death was constrained, yet it should be like a casuall death.

TACITUS
Annales (c. 100)
Trans. Richard Grenewey (1598)

MY HAPPY TOMB

When timely death my life and fortune ends,
Let not my hearse be vext with mourning friends,
But let all lovers rich in triumph come,
And with sweet pastimes grace my happie tombe.
And, Lesbia, close up thou my little light,
And crowne with love my ever-during night.

THOMAS CAMPION
Book of Ayres (1601)

A GOOD HANGING

The parliament intended to have hanged him ; and he expected no lesse, but resolved to be hangd with the Bible under one arme and Magna Charta under the other.

JOHN AUBREY
Brief Lives : David Jenkins (c. 1680)

I feele no more perturbation within mee to departe this worlde, than I have done in my best health to aryse from table, when I have well dyned, and thence to retire to a pleasant walke. I have had my parte in this worlde, and now I must give place to fresh gamesters. Farewell.

SIR ANTHONY BEND
His *Will* (1618)
(Pub. Thomas Hearne, *Diary*, 1707)

RESURRECTION

The *Phoenix* faire which rich *Arabia* breedes,
When wasting time expires hir tragedy
No more on *Phoebus* radiant raise she feedes,
But heapeth up great store of spicery
And on a loftie towring Cedar tree,
With heavenly substance, she hir selfe consumes.
From whence she yoong againe appeeres to bee,
Out of the Cinders of hir peerelesse plumes.

WILLIAM SMITH
Chloris (1596)

A HAPPY LOT

The Most Temperate Planet

I am sure, *says the Countess*, we have one great convenience
in the situation of our World ; it is not so hot as *Mercury*
or *Venus*, or so cold as *Jupiter* or *Saturn* ; and our Country
is so justly plac'd, that we have no excess either of Heat or
Cold. I have heard of a Philosopher, who gave thanks to
Nature that he was born a Man, and not a Beast, a *Greek*,
and not a *Barbarian* ; and for my part, I render thanks that
I am seated in the most temperate Planet of the Universe,
and in one of the most temperate Regions of that Planet.
You have more reason, *said I*, to give thanks that you are
Young, and not Old ; that you are Young and Handsome,
and not Young and Ugly ; that you are Young, Handsome,
and an *English* Woman, and not Young, Handsome, and a
Spaniard, or an *Italian* ; these are other guess Subjects for
your thanks, than the Situation of your Vortex, or the
Temperature of your Countrey. Pray Sir, *says she*, let me
give thanks for all things, to the very Vortex in which I am
planted : Our proportion of Happiness is so very small,
that we should lose none, but improve continually what
we have, and be grateful for every thing, tho' never so
common or inconsiderable. If nothing but exquisite pleasure will serve us, we must wait a long time, and be sure
to pay too dear for it at last.   B. DE FONTENELLE

A Plurality of Worlds (1686). Trans. John Glanvill (1688)

When I contemplate the common lot of mortality, I must acknowledge that I have drawn a high prize in the lottery of life. The far greater part of the globe is over-spread with barbarism or slavery; in the civilised world the most numerous class is condemned to ignorance and poverty, and the double fortune of my birth in a free and enlightened country, in an honourable and wealthy family, is the lucky chance of an unit against millions. The general probability is about three to one—that a new-born infant will not live to compleat his fiftieth year. I have now passed that age. . . .

1. The first indispensable requisite of happiness is a clear conscience, unsullied by the reproach or remembrance of an unworthy action.

> Hic murus aheneus esto
> Nil conscire sibi, nulla palescere culpa.

I am endowed with a cheerful temper, a moderate sensibility, and a natural disposition to repose rather than to action : some mischievous appetites and habits have perhaps been corrected by philosophy or time. The love of study, a passion which derives fresh vigour from enjoyment, supplies each day, each hour, with a perpetual source of independent and rational pleasure, and I am not sensible of any decay of the mental faculties. The original soil has been highly improved by labour and manure ; but it may be questioned whether some flowers of fancy, some grateful errors, have not been eradicated with the weeds of prejudice.

2. Since I have escaped from the long perils of my childhood, the serious advice of a physician has seldom

been requisite. " The madness of superfluous health "
I have never known ; but my tender constitution has been
fortified by time. . . .

3. . . . The oeconomy of my house is settled without
avarice or profusion ; at stated periods all my bills are
regularly paid, and in the course of my life I have never
been reduced to appear, either as plaintiff or defendant,
in a court of Justice.

Should I add that, since the failure of my first wishes, I
have never entertained any serious thoughts of a matri-
monial connection ?

EDWARD GIBBON, *Autobiography* (1789)

LITERARY BREAKFASTS

It is not possible for anything on earth to be more agreeable to my taste than my present manner of living. I am
so much at my ease ; have a great many hours at my own
disposal : read my own books, and see my own friends ;
and, whenever I please, may join the most polished and
delightful society in the world ! Our breakfasts are little
literary societies.

HANNAH MORE, *Letter to her sister* (1776)

TWO GARDENERS EXCHANGE COMPLIMENTS

O the sweet evenings and mornings, and all the day
besides which are yours !

.... while Cowley's made
The happy tenant of the shade !

310

And the sun in his garden gives him all he desires, and all that he would enjoy ; the purity of visible objects and of true Nature, before she was vitiated by imposture or luxury !

> Books, wise discourse, gardens and fields,
> And all the joys that unmixt Nature yields.

You gather the first roses of the spring, and apples of autumn ; and as the philosopher in Seneca desir'd only bread and herbs to dispute felicity with Jupiter, you vie happiness in a thousand easy and sweet diversions ; not forgetting the innocent toils which you cultivate, the leisure and the liberty, the books, the meditations, and above all, the learned and choice friendships that you enjoy. Who would not, like you, *cacher sa vie* ? . . . I assure you, Sir, it is what in the world I most inwardly breathe after and pursue, not to say that I envy your felicity, deliver'd from the gilded impertinences of life, to enjoy the moments of a solid and pure contentment ; since those who know how usefully you employ this glorious recess, must needs be forced either to imitate, or, as I do, to celebrate your example.

JOHN EVELYN
Kalendarium Hortense : Dedication to A. Cowley
(1664. Edition 1776)

I know no body that possesses more private happines than you do in your Garden, and yet no man who makes his happines more publique by a free communication of the art and knowledg of it to others.

ABRAHAM COWLEY
The Garden : Dedication (1666)

Thus, then, I live ; something read or written every day ; after that, not to be lacking in courtesy to my friends, I feast with them.

CICERO
Letter to Paetus (46 B.C.)

THE ANGLER

No life, my honest Scholer, no life so happie and so pleasant, as the life of a well-governed *Angler* ; for when the *Lawyer* is swallowed up with businesse, and the *Statesman* is preventing or contriving plots, we sit on Cowslip banks, hear the Birds sing, and possesse our selves in as much quietnesse as these silver streames, which we now see glide by us.

IZAAK WALTON
The Compleat Angler (1653)

ENJOYING THINGS

" Life," said a gaunt widow, with a reputation for being clever,—" life is a perpetual toothache."

In this vein the conversation went on : the familiar topics were discussed of labour troubles, epidemics, cancer, tuberculosis, and taxation.

Next me there sat a little old lady who was placidly drinking her tea, and taking no part in the melancholy

312

chorus. " Well, I must say," she remarked, turning to me and speaking in an undertone, " I must say I enjoy life."

" So do I," I whispered.

" When I enjoy things," she went on, " I know it. Eating, for instance, the sunshine, my hot-water bottle at night. Other people are always thinking of unpleasant things. It makes a difference," she added, as she got up to go with the others.

" All the difference in the world," I answered.

LOGAN PEARSALL SMITH
More Trivia (1922)

HOT BATHS

ARCHIMEDES DOES GEOMETRY IN THEM

Often times his servants got him agaunst his will to the bathes, to washe and annoynt him : and yet being there he would ever be drawing out of the Geometricall figures, even in the very imbers of the chimney. And while they were annointing of him with oyles and swete savors, with his fingers he did draw lines upon his naked body : so farre was he taken from himself, and brought into an extasy or trauns, with the delite he had in the study of Geometry, and truely ravished with the love of the Muses.

PLUTARCH, *Lives* (c. 100)
Trans. Sir Thos. North (1579)

Both our hosts had baths in their houses, but in neither did they happen to be available; so I set my own servants to work. . . . I made them dig a pit . . . either near a spring or by the river; into this a heap of red-hot stones was thrown, and the glowing cavity then covered over with an arched roof of wattled hazel. . . . Water was thrown on the hot stones . . . In these vapour baths we passed whole hours, with lively talk and repartee, all the time the cloud of hissing steam enveloping us induced the healthiest perspiration. When we had perspired enough, we bathed in hot water; the treatment removed the feeling of repletion, but left us languid; we therefore finished off with a bracing douche from the fountain, well, or river.

SIDONIUS APOLLINARIS
Letter to Donidius (461–7). Trans. T. Hodgkin (1892)

BATHING DE LUXE

Christ. Ærerus, in a consultation of his, hold once or twice a week sufficient to bathe, the water to be warme, not hot, for feare of sweating. *Felix Plater* . . . for a Melancholy Lawyer, will have lotions of the head still joyned to these bathes, with a lee wherein capitall herbs have been boyled. *Laurentius* speaks of bathes of milke, which I find approved by many others. And still, after bath, the body to be annointed with oyle of bitter Almonds, of violets, new or fresh butter, Capons grease, especially the backe bone. . . . The *Romans* had their publike Bathes, very sumptuous and stupend, as those of *Antoninus* and

Dioclesian. . . . Some bathed seven times a day, as Commodus the Emperor is reported to have done, usually twice a-day, and they were after annoynted with most costly oyntments : rich women bathed themselves in milke, some in the milke of 500 she-asses at once. . . .

Of cold Bathes I finde little or no mention in any Physitian ; some speake against them. ROBERT BURTON

Anatomy of Melancholy (1621. Edition 1632)

FOR HEALTH

At eight in the morning, we go in dishabille to the Pump-room, which is crowded like a Welsh fair; and there you see the highest quality and the lowest trade folks, jostling each other, without ceremony, hail-fellow well met. The noise of the music playing in the gallery, the heat and flavour of such a crowd, and the hum and buz of their conversation, gave me the head-ach and vertigo the first day; but, afterwards, all these things became familiar, and even agreeable. Right under the Pump-room windows is the King's Bath ; a huge cistern, where you see the patients up to their necks in hot water. The ladies wear jackets and petticoats of brown linen, with chip hats, in which they fix their handkerchiefs to wipe the sweat from their faces ; but truly, whether it is owing to the steam that surrounds them, or the heat of the water, or the nature of the dress, or to all these causes together, they look so flushed and so frightful, that I always turn my eyes another way. My aunt, who says every person of fashion should make her appearance in the bath, as well as in the abbey church, contrived a cap with cherry-coloured ribbons to suit her complexion, and obliged Win to attend her yesterday morning in the water. But really, her eyes were so red, that they made mine water as I viewed her from the Pump-room; and as for poor Win, who wore a hat trimmed with blue, what betwixt her wan complexion and her fear, she looked like the ghost of some pale maiden, who had drowned herself for love. When she came out of the bath, she took assafoetida drops, and was fluttered all day; so that we could hardly keep her from going into hysterics: but her mistress says it will do her good; and poor Win curtsies, with the tears in her eyes.

TOBIAS SMOLLETT
Humphrey Clinker (1771)

HOUSES

A ROMAN MERCHANT'S HOUSE

Why, you should not come into anie mannes house of account, but hee hadde fish-pondes and little orchardes on the toppe of his leads. If by raine or any other meanes those ponds were so full that they need to be slust or let out, even of their superfluities they made melodious use, for they had greate winde instruments in stead of leaden spoutes, that went duly on consort, onely with this waters rumbling discent. I sawe a summer banketting house belonging to a merchaunt, that was the mervaile of the world, and could not be macht except God should make

316

another paradise. It was builte round of greene marble, like a Theater with-out; within there was a heaven and earth comprehended both under one roofe, the heaven was a cleere overhanging vault of christall, wherein the Sunne and Moone, and each visible Starre had his true similitude, shine, scituation, and motion, and by what enwrapped arte I cannot conceive, these spheares in their proper orbes observed their circular wheelinges and turnings, making a certaine kinde of soft angelical murmering musicke in their often windings and going about, which musick the philosophers say in the true heaven by reason of the grosenes of our senses we are not capable of. For the earth, it was counterfeited in that liknes that Adam lorded it out before his fall. . . . The flore was painted with the beautifullest flouers that ever mans eie admired which so linealy were delineated, that he that viewd them a farre off and had not directly stood pouringly over them, would have sworne they had lived in deede. The wals round about were hedgde with Olives and palme trees, and all other odoriferous fruit-bearing plants, which at anie solemn entertainment dropt mirrhe and frankensence. Other trees that bare no fruit were set in just order one against another, and divided the roome into a number of shadie lanes, leaving but one over-spreading pine tree arbor, where wee sate and banketted. On the wel clothed boughs of this conspiracie of pine trees against the resembled Sun beames, were pearcht as many sortes of shrill breasted birdes as the Summer hath allowed for singing men in her silvane chappels. Who though there were bodies without soules, and sweete resembled substances without sense, yet by the mathematicall experimentes of long silver pipes secretlye inrinded in the intrailes of the boughs wheron they sate, and undiscerneablie convaid under their bellies into their small throats sloaping, they whistled and freely carold theyr naturall field note. Neyther went those silver pipes straight, but by many edged unsundred writhings, and crankled wanderinges aside, strayed from bough to bough into an hundred throats. . . . But so closely were all those organizing implements obscured in the corpulent trunks of the trees, that everie man there present renounst conjectures of art, and sayd it was done by inchantment.

One tree for his fruit bare nothing but inchained chirping birdes, whose throates beeing conduit pipt . . . and charged siring-wise with searching sweet water, . . . made a spirting sound, such as chirping is, in bubling upwards through the rough crannies of their closed bills. Under tuition of the shade of everie tree that I have signified to be in this round hedge, on delightful levie cloisters lay a wylde tyranous beast asleepe all prostrate : under some, two together, as the Dogge nusling his nose under the necke of the Deare, the Wolfe glad to let the Lambe lye upon hym to keepe him warme, the Lyon suffering the Asse to cast hys legge over him. . . . No poysonous beast there reposed (poyson was not before our parent *Adam* transgressed). There were no sweete-breathing Panthers, that would hyde their terrifying heads to betray : no men imitating *Hyoenaes*, that chaunged their sexe to seeke after bloud. Wolves as now when they are hungrie eate earth, so then did they feed on earth only, and abstained from innocent flesh. The Unicorne did not put his horne into the streame to chase awaye venome before hee dronke, for then there was no suche thing extant in the water or on the earth. Serpents were as harmlesse to mankinde, as they are still one to another : the rose had no cankers, the leves no caterpillers, the sea no *Syrens*, the earth no usurers. Goats then bare wooll, as it is recorded in *Sicily* they doo yet. The torride Zone was habitable : only Jayes loved to steale gold and silver to build their nests withall, and none cared for covetous clientrie, or runing to the Indies. As the Elephant understands his countrey speach, so everie beast understood what man spoke. The ant did not hoord up against winter, for there was no winter but a perpetuall spring, as *Ovid* saith. No frosts to make the greene almound tree counted rash and improvident, in budding soonest of all other : or the mulberie tree a strange polititian, in blooming late and ripening early. . . . Young plants for their sap had balme, for their yellow gumme glistering amber. The evening dewed not water on flowers, but honnie. Such a golden age, such a good age, such an honest age was set forth in this banketting house. O *Rome*, if thou hast in thee such soul exalting objects, what a thing is heaven in comparison of thee ? THOMAS NASHE

The Unfortunate Traveller (1594)

A GAUDY PALACE

Like heavens two maine lights,
The roomes illustrated, both daies and nights.
On every side stood firme a wall of brasse,
Even from the threshold to the inmost passe ;
Which bore a roofe up that all Saphire was ;
The brazen thresholds both sides, did enfold
Silver Pilasters, hung with gates of gold ;
Whose Portall was of silver ; over which
A golden Cornish did the front enrich.
On each side, Dogs, of gold and silver fram'd,
The houses Guard stood ; which the Deitie (lam'd)   Vulcan.

319

With knowing inwards had inspir'd ; and made,
That *Death* nor *Age,* should their estates invade,
   Along the wall, stood every way a throne ;
From th'entry to the Lobbie : every one,
Cast over with a rich-wrought cloth of state.
Beneath which, the *Phæacian* Princes sate
At wine and food ; and feasted all the yeare.
Youths forg'd of gold, at every table there,
Stood holding flaming torches ; that, in night
Gave through the house, each honourd Guest, his
     light.

HOMER
Odyssey. Book VII
Trans. George Chapman (1614)

A FINE HALL

   A goodly hall
Of jaspar stones, it was wonderflye wrought
The windowes cleare, depured all of christal
And in the roufe, on hye over all
Of golde was made, a right crafty vyne,
In stede of grapes, the Rubies there did shyne.
The flore was paved with berall clarified
With pillars made of stones precious
Like a place of pleasure, so gayely glorified
It might be called, a palaice glorious
So muche delectable, and solacious.
The hall was hanged, bye and circuler
With clothe of arras, in the richest maner.

STEPHEN HAWES
The Passetyme of Pleasure (1509)

HOUSE-PRIDE

I have nothing more to send you but a new ballad, which
my Lord Bath has made on this place ; you remember the
old burden of it, and the last lines allude to Billy Bristow's
having fallen in love with it.

> Some talk of Gunnersbury,
>   For Sion some declare ;
> And some say that with Chiswick House
>   No villa can compare ;
> But all the beaux of Middlesex,
>   Who know that country well,
> Say that Strawberry Hill, that Strawberry
>   Doth bear away the bell.
>
> Though Surrey boasts its Oatlands,
>   And Claremont kept so gim ;
> And though they talk of Southcote's,
>   It's but a dainty whim ;
> For ask the gallant Bristow,
>   Who does in taste excel,
> If Strawberry Hill, if Strawberry
>   Don't bear away the bell.

I am a little pleased to send you this, to show you that
in summer we are a little pretty.   HORACE WALPOLE
                          Letter to George Montagu (1755)

ICE

YOUNG MEN PLAY ON IT

When the great fenn, or Moore, which watereth the walles of the citie on the North side, is frozen, many young men play upon the ice; some stryding as wide as they may, doe slide swiftly; others make themselves seates of ice, as great as milstones; one sits downe, many hand in hand do drawe him, and one slipping down on a sudden, all fall together; some tye bones to their feete and under their heeles; and shoving themselves by a little picked staffe, do slide as swiftly as a bird flyeth in the aire, ar an arrow out of a crossebow. Sometime two runn together with poles, and hitting one the other, either one or both doe fall, not without hurt; some break their armes, some their legs, but youth desirous of glorie, in this sort exerciseth it selfe against the time of warre.   WILLIAM FITZSTEPHEN

Vita Sancti Thomae (c. 1180). Trans. John Stow (1598)

SLIDING AND SKATING

Having seene the strange and wonderful dexterity of the sliders on the new canal in St James's Park, perform'd before their Maties by divers gentlemen and others with scheets, after the manner of the Hollanders, with what swiftness they passe, how suddainely they stop in full carriere upon the ice, I went home by water, but not without exceeding difficultie the Thames being frozen, greate flakes of ice encompassing our boate.

JOHN EVELYN, *Diary* (Dec. 1, 1662)

ICICLES

The Hautboys who playd to us last night had their breath froze in their instruments till it dropt of the ends of 'em in icicles by god this is true.

WILLIAM CONGREVE
Letter to Edward Porter (Jan. 1st, 1700 ?)

CARNIVAL

London enjoyed a carnival of the utmost brilliancy. . . . Frozen roses fell in showers when the Queen and her ladies walked abroad. Coloured balloons hovered motionless in the air. Here and there burnt vast bonfires of cedar and oak wood, lavishly salted, so that the flames were of green, orange, and purple fire. But however fiercely they burnt, the heat was not enough to melt the ice which, though of singular transparency, was yet of the hardness of steel. So clear indeed was it that there could be seen, congealed at a depth of several feet, here a porpoise, there a flounder. Shoals of eels lay motionless in a trance, but whether their state was one of death or merely of suspended animation which the warmth would revive puzzled the philosophers Near London Bridge, where the river had frozen to a depth of some twenty fathoms, a wrecked wherry boat was plainly visible, lying on the bed of the river where it had sunk last autumn, overladen with apples. The old bumboat woman, who was carrying her fruit to market on the Surrey side, sat there in her plaids and farthinghales with her lap full, of apples, for all the world as if she were about to serve a customer, though a certain blueness about the lips hinted the truth. 'Twas a sight King James specially liked to look upon, and he would bring a troupe of courtiers to gaze with him. In short nothing could exceed the brilliancy and gaiety of the scene by day. But it was at night that the carnival was at its merriest. For the frost continued unbroken ; the nights were of perfect stillness ; the moon and stars blazed with the hard fixity of diamonds, and to the fine music of flute and trumpet the courtiers danced.

VIRGINIA WOOLF, *Orlando* (1928)

IGNORANCE

INNOCENCE

A learned and a happy Ignorance
   Divided me
  From all the Vanity,
From all the Sloth, Care, Sorrow, that advance
   The Madness and the Misery
Of Men. No Error, no Distraction, I
Saw cloud the Earth, or over-cast the Sky.

324

I knew not that there was a Serpent's Sting,
    Whose Poyson shed
  On Men, did overspread
The World : Nor did I dream of such a thing
As Sin, in which Mankind lay dead.
They all were brisk and living Things to me,
Yea, pure and full of immortality.

Unwelcom Penitence I then thought not on ;
    Vain costly Toys,
  Swearing and roaring boys,
Shops, Markets, Taverns, Coaches, were unknown,
    So all things were that drown my Joys :
No thorns choakt-up my Path, nor hid the face
Of Bliss and Glory, nor eclypt my place.

Only what Adam in his first Estate
    Did I behold ;
  Hard silver and dry Gold
As yet lay underground : My happy Fate
    Was more acquainted with the old
And innocent Delights which he did see
    In his Original Simplicity.

THOMAS TRAHERNE
Eden : Poems of Felicity (? 1656–66)

Pleasant Gentlemen

The Ancients were pleasant Gentlemen, to imagine that
the celestial Bodies were in their own nature unchange-
able, because they observed no change in them.

B. DE FONTENELLE
A Plurality of Worlds (1686). Trans. John Glanvill (1688)

. . . As Knowledge cast Adam out of Paradise, so it do's all those who apply themselves to it, for the more they understand, they do but more plainly perceive, their own wants and Nakedness, as he did, which before in the State of Ignorance were hidden from him, untill the eies of his understanding were opened, only to let him see his losses, and the Miseries which he had betrayed himself unto. For the world appeares a much finer thing to those that understand it not then to those who do, and Fooles injoy their Pleasures with greater Appetite and Gust then those who are more sensible of their vanity and unwholesomnes.

SAMUEL BUTLER
Miscellaneous Observations (c. 1660–70)

NOT READING THE MAGAZINES

I have been thinking over our late correspondence, and wish to propose to you the following articles for our future :—

. . . 4thly, That you send me *no periodical works* whatsoever—no *Edinburgh*, *Quarterly*, *Monthly*, nor any Review, Magazine, Newspaper, English or foreign, of any description. 5thly, That you send me *no* opinions whatsoever, either *good*, *bad*, or *indifferent*, of yourself, or your friends, or others, concerning my work, or works of mine past, present, or to come. . . . Reviews and Magazines are at the best but ephemeral and superficial reading : *who thinks* of the *grand article* of *last year*, in any given review ? in the next place, if they regard myself, they tend to increase *Egotism* ; if favourable, I do not deny that the praise *elates*, and if unfavourable, that the abuse irritates—the latter may conduct me to inflict a species of Satire, which would neither do good to you nor to your friends : they may smile *now*, and so may *you*, but if I took you all in hand, it would not be difficult to cut you up like gourds . . . Therefore let me hear none of your provocations. If any thing occurs so very *gross* as to require my notice, I shall hear of it from my personal friends. For the rest, I merely request to be left in ignorance. The same applies to opinions, *good*, *bad*, or *indifferent*, of persons in conversation or correspondence : . . . they *soil the current* of my *Mind*. I am sensitive enough, but *not* till I am *touched* ; and *here* I am beyond the touch of the short arms of literary England. . . . All these precautions in England would be useless : the libeller or the flatterer would there reach me in spite of all ; but in Italy we know little of literary England and think less, except what reaches us through some garbled and brief extract in some miserable Gazette.

LORD BYRON
Letter to John Murray (1821)

SANCTA SIMPLICITAS

Yon cottager, who weaves at her own door,
Pillow and bobbins all her little store,
Content, though mean ; and cheerful, if not gay ;
Shuffling her threads about the live-long day,
Just earns a scanty pittance ; and at night
Lies down secure, her heart and pocket light :
She, for her humble sphere by nature fit,
Has little understanding, and no wit,

Recieves no praise ; but, though her lot be such,
(Toilsome and indigent) she renders much ;
Just knows, and knows no more, her Bible true—
A truth the brilliant Frenchman never knew ;
And in that charter reads, with sparkling eyes,
Her title to a treasure in the skies.
  O happy peasant ! Oh, unhappy bard !
His the mere tinsel, hers the rich reward ;
He prais'd, perhaps, for ages yet to come ;
She never heard of half a mile from home :
He, lost in errors, his vain heart prefers ;
She, safe in the simplicity of hers.
  Not many wise, rich, noble, or profound
In science, win one inch of heav'nly ground.
And is it not a mortifying thought
The poor should gain it, and the rich should not ?

WILLIAM COWPER
Truth (1782)

RESULTS OF CENSORSHIP

Another sort there be who when they hear that all things
shall be order'd, all things regulated and setl'd ; nothing
writt'n but what passes through the custom-house of
certain Publicans that have the tunaging and poundaging
of all free spok'n truth, will strait give themselvs up into
your hands, mak'em and cut'em out what religion ye
please ; there be delights, there be recreations and jolly
pastimes that will fetch the day about from sun to sun, and
rock the tedious year as in a delightfull dream. What need
they torture their heads with that which others have tak'n

so strictly, and so unalterably into their own pourveying. These are the fruits which a dull ease and cessation of our knowledge will bring forth among the people. How goodly, and how to be wisht were such an obedient unanimity as this, what a fine conformity would it starch us all into !

JOHN MILTON
Areopagitica (1643)

IN BED

Singing

At night, when he was abed, and the dores made fast, and was sure nobody heard him, he sang aloud (not that he had a very good voice) but for his health's sake : he did beleeve it did his lunges good, and conduced much to prolong his life.

JOHN AUBREY
Brief Lives : Thomas Hobbes (c. 1680)

Mathematics

I have heard Mr Hobbes say that he was wont to draw lines on his thigh and on the sheetes, abed, and also multiply and divide.

Ibid.

Let sleep creep over you while you hold a book, and let the ... page support your falling face.

ST JEROME, *Letter to Eustochium* (384)

COMFORT

Rode easily to Welling, where we supped well, and had two beds in the room and so lay single, and still remember it that of all the nights that ever I slept in my life I never did pass a night with more epicurism of sleep ; there being now and then a noise of people stirring that waked me, and then it was a very rainy night, and then I was a little weary, that what between waking and then sleeping again, one after another, I never had so much content in all my life, and so my wife says it was with her.

SAMUEL PEPYS, *Diary* (Sept. 23, 1660)

THINKING OF WIT

Dr Swift lies a-bed till eleven o'clock, and thinks of wit for the day.

JOSEPH SPENCE, *Anecdotes* (c. 1734)

FLOODS OF DOWN

And to your more bewitching, see, the proud
Plumpe Bed beare up, and swelling like a cloud,
Tempting the two too modest ; can
Yee see it brusle like a Swan,

           And you be cold
Too meet it, when it woo's and seemes to fold
    The Armes to hugge it ? throw, throw
Your selves into the mighty over-flow
    Of that white Pride, and Drowne
The night, with you, in floods of Downe.

                              ROBERT HERRICK
*A Nuptiall Song, or Epithalamie, on Sir Clipseby Crew
                      and his Lady. Hesperides* (1648)

THE FLEA ASLEEP

My Bed was such, as Down nor Feather can
Make one more soft, though *Jove* againe turn swan ;
No fear-distracted thoughts my slumbers broke,
I heard no screech owl shreek, nor Raven croak ;
Sleep's foe, the Flea, that proud insulting Elfe,
Is now at truce, and is asleep it selfe.

                          SIR JOHN MENNIS
                              *The Nightinghale
                      Musarum Deliciae* (1655)

CARDS

He played at cards rarely well, and did use to practise by
himselfe a bed, and there studyed how the best way of
managing the cards could be.

                              JOHN AUBREY
          Brief Lives : Sir John Suckling (c. 1680)

Another time, as he [Thomas Traherne] was in bed,
he saw a basket come sailing in the air, along by the
valence of his bed ; I think he said there was fruit in the
basket : it was a Phantom.

JOHN AUBREY
Apparitions (*Miscellanies*) (1696)

LYING LATE

O Thou that sleep'st like *Pigg* in Straw,
Thou Lady dear, arise ;
Open (to keep the *Sun* in awe)
Thy pretty pinking eyes :
And, having stretcht each Leg and Arme,
Put on your cleane white Smock,
And then I pray, to keep you warme,
A *Petticote* on *Dock*.

Arise, arise ! Why should you sleep,
When you have slept enough ?
Long since, French Boyes cry'd Chimney-sweep,
And Damsels Kitching-stuffe.
The Shops were open'd long before,
And youngest Prentice goes
To lay at's Mrs. Chamber-doore.
His Masters shining Shooes.

Arise, arise ; your Breakfast stayes,
Good Water-grewell warme,
Or Sugar-sops, which *Galen* sayes
With Mace, will doe no harme.

Arise, arise ; when you are up,
You'l find more to your cost,
For Mornings-draught with Caudle-cup,
Good Nutbrown-Ale, and Tost.

SIR WILLIAM DAVENANT
News from Plimouth (1635)

LYING LATE

'Tis the voice of the Sluggard; I hear him complain,
" You have wak'd me too soon, I must slumber again."
As the Door on its Hinges, so he on his Bed,
Turns his Sides, and his Shoulders, and his heavy Head.

" A little more Sleep and a little more Slumber " ;
Thus he wastes half his Days and his Hours without
   number ;
And when he gets up, he sits folding his Hands,
Or walks about sauntering, or trifling he stands.

ISAAC WATTS
The Sluggard. Moral Songs (pub. 1743)

JOHNSON : " I have, all my life long, been lying till noon ;
yet I tell all young men, and tell them with great sincerity,
that nobody who does not rise early will ever do any
good."

JAMES BOSWELL
Tour to the Hebrides with Samuel Johnson (1785)

I purpose to rise at eight, because, though I shall not yet
rise early, it will be much earlier than I now rise, for I
often lie till two.

SAMUEL JOHNSON
Prayers and Meditations (1765)

Thus talking hand in hand alone they pass'd
On to thir blissful Bower ; it was a place
Chos'n by the sovran Planter, when he fram'd
All things to mans delightful use ; the roofe
Of thickest covert was inwoven shade
Laurel and Mirtle, and what higher grew
Of firm and fragrant leaf ; on either side
Acanthus, and each odorous bushie shrub
Fenc'd up the verdant wall ; each beauteous flour,
Iris all hues, Roses, and Gessamin
Rear'd high thir flourisht heads between, and
   wrought
Mosaic ; underfoot the Violet,
Crocus, and Hyacinth with rich inlay
Broiderd the ground, more colour'd then with
   stone
Of costliest Emblem : other Creature here
Beast, Bird, Insect, or Worm durst enter none ;
Such was thir awe of man. In shadier Bower
More sacred and sequesterd though but feignd,
Pan and *Silvanus* never slept, nor Nymph,
Nor *Faunus* haunted. Here in close recess
With Flowers, Garlands, and sweet-smelling Herbs
Espoused *Eve* deckt first her Nuptial Bed,
And heav'nly Quires the Hymenaean sung. . . .
These lulld by Nightinghales imbraceing slept,
And on thir naked limbs the flourie roof
Showrd Roses, which the Morn repair'd. Sleep on,
Blest Pair.
                        JOHN MILTON
               Paradise Lost, Book IV (1667)

Theis are the spels which to kind sleep invite, . . .
  Who would not choos to bee awake,
While hee's encompasst round with such delight,
To th'ear, the nose, the touch, the tast, and sight ?
When *Venus* would her dear *Ascanius* keep
A pris'ner in the downy bands of sleep,
She odorous herbs and flowers about him spred,
  As the most soft and sweetest bed ;
Not her own lap would more have charm'd his head.
  Who that has Reason, and his smel,
Would not amoungst roses and jasmin dwell,
  Rather then all his spirits choak
With exhalations of dirt and smoak ?

ABRAHAM COWLEY
The Garden (1666)

MUSIC AND VIRTUOUS THOUGHTS

Happy are they that go to bed with grave musick like
Pythagoras, or have wayes to compose the phantasticall
spirit, whose unrulie wandrings takes of inward sleepe,
filling our heads with St. Anthonies visions, and the
dreames of Lipara in the sober chambers of rest.

Virtuous thoughts of the day laye up good treasors for
the night . . . hereby Solomons sleepe was happy.

SIR THOMAS BROWNE
On Dreams (?)

LOVE

Busie old foole, unruly Sunne,
　　Why dost thou thus,
Through windowes, and through curtaines call on us ?
Must to thy motions lovers seasons run ?
　　Sawcy pendantique wretch, goe chide
　　Late schoole boyes, and sowre prentices,
Goe tell Court-huntsmen, that the King will ride,
Call countrey ants to harvest offices ;
Love, all alike, no season knowes, nor clyme,
Nor houres, dayes, moneths, which are the rags of
　　　　time. . . .

　　If her eyes have not blinded thine,
　　Looke, and to morrow late, tell mee,
Whether both the India's of spice and Myne
Be where thou leftst them, or lie here with mee.
Aske for those Kings whom thou saw'st yesterday,
And thou shalt heare, All here in one bed lay.

　　She is all States, and all Princes, I,
　　Nothing else is.
Princes doe but play us ; compar'd to this,
All honor's mimique ; All wealth alchemie.
　　Thou sunne art halfe as happy as wee,
　　In that the world's contracted thus ;
Thine age askes ease, and since they duties bee
To warme the world, that's done in warming us.
Shine here to us, and thou art every where ;
This bed thy center is, these walls, thy spheare.

JOHN DONNE
The Sunne rising (Songs and Sonnets 1590–1601)

Safety

From noise of Scare-fires rest ye free,
From Murders *Benedicitie*.
From all mischances, they may fright
Your pleasing slumbers in the night :
Mercie secure ye all, and keep
The Goblin from ye, while ye sleep.
Past one aclock, and almost two,
My Masters all, *Good day to you*.

ROBERT HERRICK
The Bell-man. Hesperides (1648)

Sleep

Come sleepe, o sleepe, the certaine knot of peace,
  The baiting place of wit, the balme of woe,
  The poore mans wealth, the prisoners release,
  Th' indifferent Judge betweene the high and low ;

With shield of proofe shield me from out the prease
  Of those fierce darts, dispaire at me doth throw :
  O make in me those civill warres to cease ;
  I will good tribute pay if thou wilt do so.

Take thou of me smooth pillowes, sweetest bed,
  A chamber deafe to noise, and blind to light :
  A rosie garland, and a wearie hed :

And if these things, as being thine in right,
  Move not thy heavy grace, thou shalt in me,
  Livelier than else-where *Stellas* image see.

SIR PHILIP SIDNEY
Astrophel and Stella (1591)

But the phantasmes of sleepe do commonly walk in the great roade of naturall and animal dreames ; wherein the thoughts or actions of the day are acted over and echoed in the night. Who can therefore wonder that Chrysostome should dreame of St Paul who dayly read his Epistles ; or that Cardan whose head was so taken up about the starres should dreame that his soule was in the moone ! Pious persons whose thoughts are dayly buisied about heaven and the blessed state thereof, can hardly escape the nightly phantasmes of it . . .

Physitians will tell us that some food makes turbulent, some gives quiet dreames. Cato who doated upon cabbadge might find the crude effects thereof in his sleepe ; wherin the Ægyptians might find some advantage by their superstitious abstinence from onyons. Pythagoras might have more calmer sleepes if hee totally abstained from beanes. . . .

To adde unto the delusion of dreames, the phantasticall objects seeme greater then they are . . . whereby it may prove more easie to dreame of Gyants then pygmies. Democritus might seldome dreame of Atomes, who so often thought of them. . . . .

That some have never dreamed is as improbable as that some have never laughed, That children dreame not the first half yeare, that men dreame not ins some countries, with many more, are unto mee sick mens dreames, dreames out of the Ivorie gate, and visions before midnight.

SIR THOMAS BROWNE
On Dreams (undated)

Thou only canst each absent Blessing grant,
Which, but asleep, we languish for and want.
Thou'rt the chast Comfort of the Widow's Bed,
That kindly do'st restore the Husband dead ;
And O, thou full Refreshment to the Maid,
Who do'st, in Dreams, her feav'rish Passion aid . . .
No man's undone, who seems apprest by Thee ;
Debtors are under thy Arrest made free ;
Thou cansy poor Slaves from Chains awhile release,
In Durance give them Freedom, Health, and Ease.
By Thee, our Cares in diff'rent Lights are rang'd,
And black Despair for Cheerful Hopes exchang'd.
Distance and Time thou canst at Will oe'rleap,
And compremise whole Years in one short Sleep.
By Thee divided Freinds embrace in Thought,
And absent Lovers are together brought.

WILLIAM WYCHERLEY
Sleep and Death (? 1729)

Awake, awake, my little boy !
Thou wast thy mother's only joy ;
Why dost thou weep in thy gentle sleep ?
Awake ! thy father does thee keep.

" O, what land is the Land of Dreams ?
What are its mountains, and what are its streams ?
O father ! I saw my mother there,
Among the lilies by waters fair.

Among the lambs, clothèd in white,
She walk'd with her Thomas in sweet delight.
I wept for joy, like a dove I mourn ;
O ! when shall I again return ? "

Dear child, I also by pleasant streams
Have wander'd all night in the Land of Dreams ;
But tho' calm and warm the waters wide,
I could not get to the other side.

" Father, O father ! what do we here
In this land of unbelief and fear ?
The Land of Dreams is better far,
Above the light of the morning Star."

WILLIAM BLAKE
The Land of Dreams (c. 1802)

My Lady Seymour dreamt, that shee found a nest, with
nine finches in it. And so many children shee had by the
Earl of Winchelsea, whose name is Finch.

When Sir Christopher Wren was at Paris, about 1671
. . . he dreamt, that he was in a place where Palm-trees
grew (suppose Eygpt) and that a woman in a romantick
habit, reach'd him dates.

JOHN AUBREY
Dreams (*Miscellanies*) (1696)

Methought I saw my late espousèd Saint
Brought to me like *Alcestis* from the grave,
Whom *Joves* great Son to her glad Husband gave,
Rescu'd from death by force though pale and faint.
Mine as whom washt from spot of child-bed taint,
Purification in the old Law did save,
And such, as yet once more I trust to have
Full sight of her in Heaven without restraint,

Came vested all in white, pure as her mind :
Her face was vail'd, yet to my fancied sight,
Love, sweetness, goodness, in her person shin'd
So clear, as in no face with more delight.
But O as to embrace me she enclin'd
I wak'd, she fled, and day brought back my night.

JOHN MILTON
Sonnet XIX (c. 1657)

AN INTELLIGENT PHYSICIAN

When a sad and sicke patient was brought to him [Epicurus]
to be cured, *Hee laid him on a downe bed, crowned him*
with a garland of sweet-smelling flowres, in a faire perfumed
closet delicately set out, and, after a potion or two of good
drink, which he administred, he brought in a beautifull young
wench that could play upon a Lute, sing and dance, &c. . . .
Most of our looser Physitians in some cases . . . allow of
this, and all of them will have a melancholy, sad, and
discontented Person, make frequent use of honest sportes,
companies, and recreations.

ROBERT BURTON
The Anatomy of Melancholy
(1621. Edition 1632)

INDUSTRY

A DILIGENT YOUTH

Before I was sixteen, I had exhausted all that could be learned in English of the Arabs and Persians, the Tartars and Turks ; and the same ardour urged me to guess at the French of d'Herbelot, and to construe the barbarous Latin of Pocock's Abulpharagius. . . . The maps of Cellarius and Wells imprinted in my mind the picture of ancient Geography ; from Strauchius I imbibed the elements of Chronology ; the tables of Helvicus and Anderson, the annals of Usher and Prideaux, distinguished the connection of events, and I engraved the multitude of names and dates in a clear and indelible series. But in the discussion of the first ages I overleaped the bounds of modesty and use. In my childish balance I presumed to weight the systems of Scaliger and Petavius, of Marsham and Newton which I could seldom study in the originals ; the Dynasties of Assyria and Egypt were my top and cricket-ball ; and my sleep has been disturbed by the difficulty of reconciling the Septuagint with the Hebrew commutation. . . .

At the conclusion of this first period of my life, I am tempted to utter a protest against the trite and lavish praise of the happiness of our boyish years, which is echoed with so much affectation in the World. That happiness I have never known, that time I have never regretted ; and were my poor aunt still alive, she would bear testimony to the early and constant uniformity of my sentiments. . . . My name, it is most true, could never be enrolled among the sprightly race, the idle progeny of Eton or Westminster, who delight to cleave the water with pliant arm, to urge the flying ball, and to chace the speed of the rolling circle. . . . A state of happiness arising only from the want of foresight and reflection shall never provoke my envy; such degenerate taste would tend to sink us in the scale of beings from a man to a child, a dog, and an oyster, till we had reached the confines of brute matter, which cannot suffer because it cannot feel.

EDWARD GIBBON
Autobiography (1792)

MIDNIGHT STUDY

This man whom about mid-night, when others take their rest, thou seeest come out of his study meagre-looking, with eyes-trilling, flegmatique, squalide, and spauling, doest thou thinke, that plodding on his books he doth seek how he shall become an honester man ; or more wise, or more content ? There is no such matter. He will either die in his pursuit, or teach posteritie the measure of Plautus verse, and the true orthography of a Latine word.

MICHEL DE MONTAIGNE
Essays : Of Solitarinesse (1580)
Trans. John Florio (1603)

343

A person of great temperance, and deepe thought, and a working head, never idle. From 14 he had a candle burning by him all night, with pen, inke, and paper, to write downe thoughts as they came into his head ; that so he might not loose a thought. Was ever a great lover of Naturall Philosophie. His whole life has been perplext in lawe-suits . . . in which he alwaies over-came . . . one lasted 18 yeares.

JOHN AUBREY
Brief Lives : James Bovey (c. 1680)

BUILDING A TOWN

Thebes being at that time inhabited by a barbarous unpolished People, was nothing but a confused Heap of Huts, scattered here and there ; and the Town, if yet it deserved the Name, had no Walls capable to defend it against any Attacks from without. *Amphion*, relying on the Assistance of the *Muses*, proposed to render his new Conquest an impregnable Fort, and to give it an Air of Magnificence worthy of the Residence of Kings. He invokes those Goddesses who had always made him their peculiar Care, and no sooner does he begin to tune his Voice and touch the Lyre, than the Stones, animated by his inchanting Strains, leap from the Rocks, and raise themselves into regular Buildings, as if they had been placed by the Hand of a skilful Architect : Walls and Towers rise round *Thebes*, and its mean Cottages are changed into lofty Palaces.

ANON
The Temple of the Muses (1738)
(From the French of Michel de Marolles)

Nor was his age onely so industrious, but in his most unsetled youth he was (being in health) never knowne to be in bed after foure of the clock in the morning, nor usually out of his chamber till ten, and imployed that time constantly (if not more) in his Studie. Which, if it seeme strange, may gain beliefe by the visible fruits of his labours : some of which remaine to testifie what is here written : for he left the resultance of 1400 Authors, most of them analyzed with his owne hand ; He left also six score Sermons, also, all writ with his owne hand ; a large and laborious Treatise concerning Selfe-murther, called *Biathanatose*, wherein all the Lawes violated by that act, are diligently survayed, and judiciously censured ; A Treatise written in his youth, which alone might declare him then, not onely perfect in the Civil and Canon Law, but in many other such studies and arguments as enter not into the consideration of many profest Scholars, that labour to be thought learned Clerks, and to know all things.

Nor were these onely found in his Studie, but all businesses that past of any publique consequence in this or any of our neighbour Kingdoms, he abbreviated either in Latine, or in the Language of the Nation, and kept them by him for a memoriall. So he did the Copies of divers Letters and Cases of Conscience that had concerned his friends, (with his solutions) and divers other businesses of importance, all particularly and methodically digested by himselfe.

· IZAAK WALTON
Life and Death of Dr. Donne (1640)

INSULT

He related to me a short dialogue that passed between himself and a writer of the first eminence in the world, when he was in Scotland . . . Dr. —— asked me (said he) why I did not join in their public worship when among them ? for (said he) I went to your churches often when in England. " So (replied Johnson) I have read that the Siamese sent ambassadors to Louis Quatorze, but I never heard that the king of France thought it worth his while to send ambassadors from his court to that of *Siam*." . . . . When I one day lamented the loss of a first cousin killed in America—" Prithee, my dear (said he) have done with canting : how would the world be worse for it, I may ask, if all your relations were at once spitted like larks and roasted for Presto's supper ? " Presto was the dog that lay under the table. . . . One day at dinner I meant to please Mr Johnson particularly with a dish of very young peas. Are not they charming ? said I to him, while he was eating them.—" Perhaps (said he) they would be so—to a *pig*."

HESTHER PIOZZI
Anecdotes of Dr. Johnson (1786)

An essay . . . maintaining the future life of brutes . . . was mentioned, and the doctrine insisted on by a gentleman who seemed fond of curious speculation. Johnson, who did not like to hear of any thing concerning a future state which was not authorised by the regular canons of orthodoxy, discouraged this talk ; and being offended by its continuation, he watched an opportunity to give the gentleman a blow of reprehension. So, when the poor speculatist, with a serious metaphysical face, addressed him, " But really, Sir, when we see a very sensible dog, we don't know what to think of him," Johnson, rolling with joy at the thought which beamed in his eye, turned quickly round and replied, " True, Sir : and when we see a very foolish *fellow*, we don't know what to think of *him*." He then rose up, strided to the fire, and stood for some time laughing and exulting.

JAMES BOSWELL, *Life of Johnson* (1792)

SOME OF MILTON'S

His very first page notoriously bewraies him an illiterat and arrogant presumer . . . bearing us in hand as if hee knew both Greek and Ebrew, and is not able to spell it . . . I shall yet continue to think that man full of other secret injustice and deceitfull pride, who shall offer in public to assume the skill, though it bee but of a tongue which hee hath not . . . Nor did I finde this his want of the pretended Languages alone, but accompanied with such a low and home-spun expression of his Mother *English* all along, without joynt or frame, as made mee, ere I knew furder of him, often stop, and conclude, that this Author could for certain bee no other then some Mechanick . . . a gross

347

and sluggish, yet a contentious and overweening pretender
. . . since ratifi'd to bee no other, if any can hold laughter,
then an actual Serving-man. This creature . . . tūrn'd
Solliciter . . . a Servingman by nature and by practice, an
Idiot by breeding, and a Solliciter by presumption. . . .
Observe now the arrogance of a groom, how it will mount
. . . jesting and frisking in the luxury of his non-sense to
cog a laughter from us . . . this odious fool, who thus ever
when hee meets with ought above the cogitation of his
breeding, leavs the noysom stench of his rude slot behind
him . . . . the filth and venom of this gourmand . . . not a
golden but a brazen ass. Since my fate extorts from mee
a talent of sport, which I had thought to hide in a napkin,
hee shall bee my *Batrachomuomachia*, my *Bavius*, my
Calandrino, the common adagy of ignorance and overweening. . . .

Thus much to this *Nuisance*.   JOHN MILTON
                                       Colasterion (1645)

KNOWLEDGE

ECSTASY

The discovery of the two actively opposite tartaric acids
was a momentous one, effecting a revolution in the views
of chemists regarding molecular structure; and we can well
understand the feeling of happiness and the nervous excitement by which Pasteur was overcome on making his discovery. Rushing from his laboratory and meeting a curator

he embraced him, exclaiming, " I have just made a great discovery ! I have separated the sodium ammonium paro-tartrate with two salts of opposite action on the plane of polarisation of light. The dextro-salt is in all respects identical with the dextro-tartrate. I am so happy and over-come by such nervous excitement that I am unable to place my eye again to the polarisation apparatus."

ALEXANDER FINDLAY
Chemistry in the Service of Man (1916)

TEASING THE ASSEMBLY OF DIVINES

He was one of the Assembly of Divines in those days . . . . and was like a Thorne in their sides; for he did baffle and vex them ; for he was able to runne them all downe with his Greeke and antiquities. JOHN AUBREY
Brief Lives : John Selden (c. 1680)

WISDOM REWARDED

And the Quene of Saba hearde of the fame of Salomon and came to prove him with ryddelles at Jerusalem, with a very great companye, and with camelles that bare swete odoures and plentye of golde and preciouse stone. And when she was come to Salomon, she communed with him of all that was in her herte. And Salomon foyled her all her questions, that there was nothing hid from Salomon which he tolde her not. And when the quene of Saba had sene the wisdom of Salomon and the house that he had built, and the meat of hys table, and the syttinge of hys servantes, and the standynge of hys wayters and their apparell, and hys buttelars with their apparell, and his parlour out of which he went into the house of the Lord, she was so astonyed that there was no moare herte in her. And then she sayde to the kynge . . . . the one halfe of thy wysdome was not tolde me : thou exceedest the fame that I hearde, happye are thy men, and happye are these thy servauntes which stande before thee allwaye and heare thy wisdome. . . . And she gave the Kyng an hundred and twenty talentes of gould, and of swete odoures exceedynge great abounddance with preciouse stones, and there was no soche swete odoures as the quene of Saba gave kynge Salomon.

Chronicles ii
Trans. by William Tyndale. *Matthew's Bible* (1537)

LIBERTY

OF THE ENGLISH

I look upon Humour to be almost of English Growth ; at least, it does not seem to have found such encrease on any other Soil. And what appears to me to be the reason of it, is the great Freedom, Privilege and Liberty which the Common People of *England* enjoy. Any Man that has a Humour is under no restraint, or fear of giving it Vent ; They have a proverb among them, which, may be, will shew the Bent and Genius of the People, as well as a longer

Discourse *He that will have a May-Pole, shall have a May-Pole*. This is a Maxim with them, and their Practice is agreeable to it. I believe something Considerable too may be ascribed to their feeding so much on Flesh, and the Grossness of their Diet in general. But I have done, let the Physicians agree that.

WILLIAM CONGREVE, *Letter to John Dennis* (1695)

OF DRUNKARDS

It must be confess'd that the notion of *Liberty* is deeply imprinted in our hearts, there being certainly nothing more advantagious, nothing more beneficial, more pleasing, and more agreeable to human Reason. 'Tis *Liberty* that by its origin and excellence imparts to us a great resemblance, and, as it were, unites us with the Divine Nature itself: for the Gods, tho' they injoy immense Pleasures, yet their highest excellency consists in having their Will unlimited by any superior Power. You that are enemies to Drunkenness, consider seriously the course of all sublunary things : consider whether 'Tis not the Drunkard that, before all Others, can boast of this *Liberty*, and acts as uncontroulable as the Gods themselves.

TOM BROWN, *Oration in Praise of Drunkenness* (169–)

OF CONVERSING WHERE WE LIKE

MRS FRAIL : Lord, where's the Comfort of this Life, if we can't have the Happiness of conversing where we like ?

WILLIAM CONGREVE, *Love for Love* (1695)

In short, Sir, I have got no further than this : every man has a right to utter what he thinks truth, and every other man has a right to knock him down for it.

JAMES BOSWELL
Life of Johnson (1791)

OF THE PRESS

The Multiplicity of *Religious Sects* tolerated among us . . . is another Source of unexhaustible Publication, almost peculiar to ourselves ; for *Controversies* cannot be long continued . . . where an *Inquisitor* has a Right to shut up the Disputants in dungeons ; or where Silence can be imposed on either Party, by the Refusal of a *License*.

Not that it should be inferred from hence, that *Political* or *Religious* Controversies are the *only* Products of the *Liberty* of the *British Press* ; the Mind once let loose to Enquiry, and suffered to operate without Restraint, necessarily deviates into peculiar Opinions, and wanders in new Tracks, where she is indeed sometimes lost in a Labyrinth . . . yet sometimes makes useful Discoveries, or finds out nearer Paths to Knowledge. . . .

All these and many other Causes, too tedious to be enumerated, have contributed to make Pamphlets and *small Tracts* a very *important* Part of an *English* Library.

SAMUEL JOHNSON
Origin and Importance of small tracts (1744)

LUNATIC

New Moon

For in the new moone they [elephants] come together in
great companies, and bath and wash them in a river, and
lowte each to other, and turne so againe to their own places.

BARTHOLOMEW ANGLICUS
De Proprietatibus Rerum (c. 1240)
Trans. John Trevisa (1398, modernised 1582)

Mutianus saith . . . that when the moon is in the wain,
the monkies and marmosets . . . are sad and heavy, but the
new moone they adore and joy at, which they testifie by
hopping and dancing.   PLINY THE ELDER
Natural History (c. 77). Trans. Philemon Holland (1601)

The Moon's Men

FALSTAFF : Now, *Hal*, what time of day is it Lad ?
PRINCE : . . . . What a divell hast thou to do with the
time of the day ? unlesse houres were cups of Sacke,
and minutes Capons, and clockes the tongues of Bawdes,

and dialls the signes of Leaping-Houses, and the blessed Sunne himselfe a faire hot Wench in Flame-coloured Taffata; I see no reason, why thou shouldest bee so superfluous, to demaund the time of the day.

FAL. : Indeed you come neere me now *Hal*, for we that take Purses, go by the Moone and seven Starres, and not by Phoebus hee, that wand'ring Knight so faire. And I prithee sweet Wagge, when thou art King . . . let not us that are Squires of the Nights bodie, bee call'd Theeves of the Dayes beautie. Let us be *Dianaes* Forresters, Gentlemen of the Shade, Minions of the Moone ; and let men say, we be men of good Government, being governed as the Sea is, by our noble and chast mistris the Moone, under whose countenance we steale.

PRINCE : Thou say'st well, and it holds well too : for the fortune of us that are the Moones men, doeth ebbe and flow like the Sea, being governed as the Sea is, by the Moone : as for proofe. Now a Purse of Gold most resolutely snatch'd on Monday night, and most dissolutely spent on Tuesday Morning ; got with swearing, Lay by, and spent with crying, Bring in : now, in as low an ebbe as the foot of the Ladder, and by and by in as high a flow as the ridge of the Gallowes.

WILLIAM SHAKESPEARE
Henry IV, Part I (1596)
(Edition 1623)

HONEY

Take hony at the chaungyng of the moon.

Book of St. Albans (1486)

354

I am surpriz'd, *said the Countess*, that there should be so little mystery in Eclipses and that the whole World should not know the Cause of 'em. Nor ever will, *said I*, as some People go about it. In the East Indies, when the Sun and Moon are in Eclipse . . . the Rivers are cover'd with the Heads of *Indians*, who are up to the Neck in Water, because they esteem it a very devout Posture, to implore the Sun and the Moon to defend themselves against the Devil. In *America* they are persuaded that the Sun and the Moon, when eclipsed, are angry, and what is it they will not do to be reconciled with them? The *Greeks*, who were so refin'd, did they not believe the Moon was enchanted, and that the Magicians forc'd her to descend from Heaven, and shed a dangerous juice on the Plants ? . . .

But what do you think, *said she*, of the People in the Moon, are they as afraid of an Eclipse as we are ? It would be very burlesque for the *Indians* there to be up to the Neck in Water ; that the *Americans* should believe the Earth angry with them ; the *Greeks* fancy we were bewitch'd, and would destroy their Plants ; in short, that we should cause the same Consternation among them, as they do here. And why not, *said I* ? I do not doubt it at all ; for why should the People of the Moon have more Wit than we ? For my part, I believe that since a prodigious company of Men have been and still are such Fools to adore the Moon, there are People in the Moon that worship the Earth, and that we are upon our knees the one to the other. . . .

I am going to tell you one of the agreeable Follies of *Ariosto*, and I am confident you will be well pleas'd to hear it : I must confess he had better have let alone St *John*, whose Name is so worthy of Respect, but 'tis a Poetical License, and must be allow'd. . . . *Astolfo* a Knight Errant, finding himself one day in the terrestrial Paradise, which was on the top of a very high Mountain, whereto he was carry'd by his flying Horse, meets St *John* there, who tells him . . . he must make a Voyage with him into the Moon. *Astolfo,* who had a great mind to see Countrys, did not stand much upon entreaty, and immediately there came a fiery Chariot, which carry'd the Apostle and the Knight up into the Air ; *Astolfo* being no great Philosopher, was surpriz'd to find the Moon so much bigger than it appear'd to him when he was upon the Earth ; to see Rivers, Seas, Mountains, Cities, Forrests, nay, what would have surpriz'd me too, Nymphs hunting in those Forrests ; but that which was most remarkable, was a Valley where you might find any thing that was lost in our World, of what Nature so ever ; Crowns, Riches, Fame, and an infinity of Hopes, the time we spend in Play, and in searching for the Philosophers stone, the Alms we give after our Death, the Verses we present to great Men and Princes, and the Sighs of Lovers . . . I assure you the Moon keeps all safe that is lost here below . . . everything is there, even to the donation of *Constantine,* i.e. the Popes have pretended to be Masters of *Rome* and *Italy* by Virtue of a Donation which the Emperour *Constantine* made Sylvester ; and the truth is, no body knows what is become of it ; but what do you think is not to be found in the Moon ? Folly, all that ever was upon the Earth is kept there still, but in lieu of it, it is not to be imagin'd how many Wits (if I may so call 'em) that are lost here, are got up into the Moon, they are so many Vials full of a very subtile Liquor, . . . and upon every one of these Vials the Names are written to whom the Wits belong'd. . . .

One of these days there may be a Communication between the Earth and the Moon, and who knows what great Advantages we may procure by it ? Do but consider *America* before it was discover'd by *Columbus*, how profoundly ignorant were those People, they knew nothing at all of Arts or Sciences, they went naked, had no other Arms but a Bow and Arrows, and did not conceive they might be carry'd by Animals. . . . The unheard of and most surprizing Sight appears, vast great Bodies, with white Wings, are seen to fly upon the Sea, to vomit Fire from all Parts, and to cast upon their Shoars an unknown People, all scaled with Iron, who dispose and govern Monsters as they please ; carry Thunder in their Hands, and destroy whoever resists 'em. . . . Do but consider, Madam, the surprize of the *Americans*, there can be nothing greater ; and after this, shall any one say there shall never be a Communication between the Moon and the Earth. . . .

Since then there are no Vapours thick enough, nor no Clouds of Rain about the Moon, farewell Dawn, adieu Rainbow ! What must Lovers do for Similies in that Countrey, when such an inexhaustible Magazine of Comparisons is taken from them ?

I doubt not, *said the Countess*, but there are those in the Moon as good at Simily as the greatest Beau in *Covent-Garden*; and had they neither Sun nor Stars, Pearls nor Rubies, Roses nor Lillies, yet could say as many fine things to a Visor-Mask, as the pertest Wit at the Puppet Show. . . . How glorious are their days, the Sun continually shining ! How pleasant their Nights, not the least Star is hid from them ! . . . You are describing the Moon, *I reply'd*, like an enchanted Palace ; but do you think it is so pleasant to have a scorching Sun always over our

Heads, and not the least Cloud to moderate its Heat? Tho'
I fancy 'tis for this reason that Nature hath made great
Cavities in the Moon; . . . what do we know but the
Inhabitants of the Moon, being continually broil'd by the
excessive heat of the Sun, do retire into those great Wells;
perhaps they live no where else, and 'tis there they build
'em Cities; . . . 'Tis no matter, *said the Countess*, I can
never suffer the Inhabitants of the Moon to live in perpetual darkness. You will be more concern'd for 'em,
I reply'd, when I tell you that one of the ancient Philosophers did long since discover the Moon to be the
abode of the blessed Souls departed out of this Life, and
that all their Happiness consisted in hearing the Harmony
of the Spheres; that is the Musick (I had like to have said
Noise) which is made by the motion of the Celestial
Bodies; if you have seen a *Raree Show*, you will easily
comprehend it. . . . He tells you, that when the Moon is
obscur'd by the shadow of the Earth, they no longer hear
the Heavenly Musick, but howl like so many Souls in
Purgatory; so that the Moon taking pity of 'em, makes all
the haste she can to get into the Light again.

BERNARD DE FONTENELLE
A Plurality of Worlds (1686)
Trans. John Glanvill (1688)

Well, Madam, *said I*, I have great News for you; that
which I told you last Night, of the Moon's being inhabited, may not be so now: There is a new Fancy got
into my Head, which puts those People in great Danger.
I cannot suffer it, *said she*; yesterday you were preparing
me to receive a Visit from 'em, and now there are no such
People in Nature: Once you would have me believe the

Moon was inhabited ; I surmounted the Difficulty I had, and will now believe it. . . . Methinks I have a strange inclination for 'em, and would not have 'em destroyed, if it were possible to save 'em. You know, Madam, *said I*, I can deny you nothing ; the Moon shall no longer be a Desart, but to do you service, we will repeople her. . . .

Ibid.

DREAMS AT THE NEW MOON

Another way is, to Charm the Moon thus ; At the first appearance of the new Moon after New-year's Day, go out in the Evening, and stand over the Sparrs of a Gate, or Stile, looking on the Moon and say,

> *All Hail to the Moon, all Hail to thee,*
> *I prithee good Moon reveal to me,*
> *This Night, who my Husband (wife) must be,*

You must presently after go to Bed.

I knew two Gentlewomen that did this when they were young Maids, and they had Dreams of those that Married them.

JOHN AUBREY, *Miscellanies* (1696)

THE MOON SINGS

> The Moon, in her pride, once glanced aside
> Her eyes and espied the day ;
> As unto his bed, in wastcoat of red,
> Faire *Phoebus* him led the way ;

Such changes of thought, in her chastitie wrought,
That thus she besought the boy,
O tarry, and marry the Starry *Diana*,
That will be thy Jem and Joy.

I will be as bright at noon as at night,
If that may delight the day;
Come hither and joine thy glories with mine,
Together we'el shine for aye.
The night shall be noon, and every moon
As pleasant as *June* or *May*;
O tarry, and marry the Starry *Diana*,
That will be thy Jem and Joy.

Enamour'd of none, I live chast and alone,
Though courted of one, some say;
And true if it were so frivolous feare
Let never my dear dismay;
I'le change my opinion, and turne my old Minion,
The Sleepy *Endimion* away,
O tarry, and Marry the Starry *Diana*,
That will be thy Jem and Joy.

And but that the night, should have wanted her
    light,
Or lovers in sight should play,
Or *Phoebus* should shame to bestow such a dame
(With a dow'r of his flame) on a Boy,
Or day should appear, eternally here,
And night otherwhere, the day
Had tarry'd and marry'd the starry'd *Diana*,
And she been his Jem and Joy.

ANON

The Moons Love. (Westminster Drollery, 1672)

I saw new Worlds beneath the Water lye,
  New Peeple ; yea, another Sky . . .
    Just such another
    Of late my Brother
Did in his Travel see, and saw by Night,
  A much more strange and wondrous Sight :
Nor could the World exhibit such another
  So Great a Sight, but in a Brother. . . .

As he went tripping o'r the King's high-way,
  A little pearly River lay
    O'r which, without a Wing
    Or Oar, he dar'd to swim,
      Swim throu the Air
      On Body fair ;
He would not, use nor trust *Icarian* wings
  Lest they should prov deceitful things ;
For had he faln, it had been wondrous high,
  Not from but from abov, the Sky ;
He might have dropt throu that thin Element
  Into a fathomless Descent ;
    Unto the nether Sky
    That did beneath him ly,
      And there might tell
      What wonders dwell,
On Earth abov. Yet doth he briskly run,
  And bold the Danger overcom ;
Who, as he leapt, with Joy related soon
  How *happy* he o'r-leapt the Moon. . . .

361

As much as others thought themselvs to ly
 Beneath the Moon, so much more high
  Himself he thought to fly
  Abov the starry Sky,
   As *that* he spy'd
   Below the Tide . . .
Thus did he yield me in the shady Night
 A wondrous and instructiv Light,
Which taught me that under our Feet there is,
 As o'r our Heads, a Place of Bliss.
To the same purpos ; he, not long before
 Brought home from Nurse, going to the door
  To do som little thing
  He must not do within,
   With Wonder cries,
   As in the Skies
He saw the Moon, *O yonder is the Moon*
 Newly com after me to Town,
That shin'd at Lugwardin but yesternight,
Where I enjoy'd the self-same Light.

THOMAS TRAHERNE
On Leaping over the Moon : Poems of Felicity
(? 1656–66)

.

THE MAN IN THE MOON

For this man affirmeth that the thing, which we call the
face in the Moone, are the images and figures of the great
ocean, represented in the Moone as in a mirrour. . . .

And the full Moone her selfe is, for evennesse, smooth-nesse, and lustre, the most beautifull and purest mirrour in the world. . . .

> The figure of the Ocean
> is just resembled here
> In flaming mirrour, when great waves
> it doth against it reare. . . .

As to that dull and slowe course of hers, that weake and feeble heat. . . . unto what shall we attribute the same, if not to her imbecilitie, in case an eternall and heavenly body can be subject unto any such passion.

PLUTARCH
Morals : Of the Face appearing in the Roundle of the Moone
Trans. Philemon Holland (1603)

STRANGE EFFECT ON WOMEN

In Yorkeshire the country woemen doe still *hailst the new mewne*, . . . they kneel with their bare knees on a *grownd-fast stene* and say *all haile* etc. The moon hath a greater influence on woemen than on men.

JOHN AUBREY
Remaines of Gentilisme and Judaisme (1687)

MAKING A FUSS

A LADY RISES

LADY : Hoe ! who is in the inner Chamber ? how now, Maidens, heere you not ? are you deafe ?

PRUDENCE : I am heere Madam.

LADY : Why do you suffer me to sleepe so long ? I am ashamed of myself truely.

PRUDENCE : I came heather soft and faire, once or twice, to see if you were awaked, and seeing you a sleepe I durst not awake you, but it is not so late as you thinke.

LADY : What is it a clocke ?

PRUDENCE : It is but halfe an houre past seaven.

LADY : What is it so farre day ? Oh God ! I went to bed yesternight so timely, thinking to rise this morning, at the farthest at 6 a clock : now I verifie in me the grave speeches of that great Philosopher, the Emperor Marc. Aur. speaking of the unsatiableness of mankinde, when he said (among other things) the more I sleep, the more I would sleep. Go too go too, draw the windowe Curtaines : call my page, let him bring some wood to my Chamber doore, make a fier quickly, that I may rise . . .

LADY : God ! how long you make me tarrye ! Kindle the fire

364

quickly, warme my smocke and give it to me. Where is Joly ? Call her :

PRUDENCE : She commeth Madame. Mistress Jolye, My Ladye calleth you in great hast : . . .

LADY : Will you keepe me heere all the day ? Where be all my thinges ? Goe fetch my cloathes : bring my petty-coate bodyes : I meane my damask quilt bodies with whale bones, what lace doe you give me heere ? this lace is too shorte, the tagges are broken, I cannot lace myselfe with it, take it away, I will have that of greene silke : when shall I have my undercoate ? Give me my peticoate of wroughte Crimson velvet with silver fringe : why doe you not give me my nightgowne ? For I take colde : where be my stockens ? Give me some cleane sockes, I will have no woorsted hosen, showe me my Carnation silk stockins : where laid you last night my garters ? Take away these slippers, give me my velvet pantofles ; send for the shoo-maker that he may have again these turn-over shooes, for they be too high. Put on my white pumpes ; set them up I will have none of them : Give me rather my Spanish leather shooes, for I will walke to-day. . . . Tye the strings with a strong double knot, for feare they untye them-selves : Jolye, come dresse my head, set the Table further from the fire, it is too neere. Put my chayre in his plaçe. Why doe you not set my great looking glasse on the table ? It is too high, set the supporter lower. Undoe my night attire : Why doe you not call the Page to warme the rubbers ? let him be called : heere sirra warme that, and take heede you burne it not. I praye you Jolye rubbe well my head, for it is very full of dandrife, are not my combes in the case ? Combe me with the boxen combe : Give me first my combing cloth, otherwise you will fill me full of haires, the haires will fall upon my cloathes, Combe backeward, O God! you combe too harde, you scratch me, you pull out my hayres, can you not untangle them softly with your handes before you put the combe to it?

JOLYE : Will it please you to rise up a little Madame? For your haires are so long, that they trayle on the ground.

LADY : My daughter Fleurimonde is like me in that, hath she not fayre haires, what say you of it?

JOLYE : Truly Madame she hath the fayrest, the longest flaxen-couler haires that one can see, there needeth no curling of them, for they are curled of themselves. In truth she hath the fayrest head of haires that ever I sawe.

LADY : I like her the better for it, it is a thing verye comely for a woman, and as *Saint Paul* saith, It is an Ornament unto her, but whilst we prattle, we forget that the time goeth away : go too, I am combed enough. Page take the combe-brushes, and make cleane my combes, take heed you doe not make them cleane with those that I use to my head : take a quill to take away the filth from them, and then put them in the case, that none be missing : go too, make an end of dressing my head.

JOLYE : What doth it please you to weare to-day Madame? Will it please you to weare your haires onely, or els to have your French whood? . . .

LADY : Set up then my French whood and my Border of Rubies, give me an other head attyre : take the key of my closet, and goe fetch my long boxe where I set my Jewels (for to have them out) that I use to weare on my head, what is become of my wyer? Where is the haire-cap? Have you any ribans to make knots? Where be the laces for to bind my haires? Go too Page, give me some water to wash, where's my muske ball? Give me rather my paste of Almonds, for it scoureth better : where is my

366

piece of Scarlet to wipe my face ? Give me that napkin :
now set on my Carkenet of precious stones : call my
Taylor to bring my gowne, not the close one, but my
open gowne of white Sattin layd on with buttons of
Pearle. Prudence, give me my bracelets of Aggathes :
Shall I have no vardingale ? You remember nothing, you
have a Coneyes memorye, you lose it in running, go too
you head-braine fellowe, Page hear you ? You doe but
playe the foole, doe you not see that I want my buske ?
what is become of the buske-poyne ?

JOLYE : What dooth it please you to have Madame, a ruffe
band or a Rebato ?

LADY : Let me see that ruffe, How is it that the supporter
is so soyled ? I knowe not for what you are fit, that you
cannot so much as to keep my cloathes cleane : I beleeve
that the meanest woman in this towne, hath her apparel
in better order then I have : take it away give me my
Rebato of cut-worke edged, is not the wyer after the same
sorte as the other ? It is a great wonder if it be any thing
better, Me think it is now time that you should know
how to serve. Is there no small pinnes for my Cuffes ?
Looke in the pinne-cushen. Pinne that with a blacke pinne,
give me my girdle and see that all the furniture be at it :
looke if my Cizers, the pincers, the pen-knife, the knife
to close Letters, with the bodkin, the ear-picker, and my
Seale be in the case : where is my pursse to weare upon
my gowne ? And see that my silver Comfet box be full
of Comfets : have I a cleane handkercher ? I will have no
Muffe, for it is not colde, but shall I have no gloves ?
Bring my maske and my fanne, Help me to put on my
Chayne of pearles. Page come hether, goe to my Ladye
of Beau-Sejour, have me most humblye commended unto
her, and tell her that if she have not greater busines, if it

pleaseth her to take the paines to come and dyne with us, and bring with her, her sister, Mistresse Du-Pont-Gailliard, they shall be most hartilie welcome, and whome so ever it shall please them to bring with them, and we will do something this afternoone for to recreate us and passe the time : goe your wayes, bring me an answer forthwith : and you Prudence set up all my night-geare, put them in the cushen cloath, dresse my chamber, and then goe aske Mistresse Clemence (my Daughters Mistresse) if they be readye ? Bid her bring with her to me in the galleris, Fleurimonde and Charlot with their worke. Jolye come with me, carye with you my prayer-booke and my Psalter, first goe to the boyes chamber, see if they be readie : come againe by and by, to the end that I be not alone, you shall finde me in the gallerie.

PIERRE ERONDELL
The French Garden (1605)

MAKING MERRY

DRINK AND BE MERRY

Let us *drink* and be *merry, dance, Joke* and *Rejoice*,
With *Claret* and *Sherry, Theorbo* and *Voice*,
The changeable *World* to our *Joy* is unjust,
All *Treasure* uncertain, then down with your dust.
 In Frollicks dispose your pounds, shillings, and pence,
 For we shall be nothing a hundred year hence.

Wee'l kiss and be free with *Nan*, *Betty* and *Philly*,
Have *Oysters*, and *Lobsters*, to cure *Maids Belly* ;
Fish-Dinners will make a *Lass* spring like a *Flea*,
Dame Venus (Love's Godess) was born of the *sea*.
With her and with Bacchus *wee'll tickle the sense*,
For we shall be past it a hundred year hence.

THOMAS JORDAN
The Epicure. Sung by one in the habits of a Town
Gallant (1675)

AT VAUXHALL

But Lord ! to see how my nature could not refrain from
the temptation ; but I must invite them to Foxhall, to
Spring Gardens, though I had freshly received minutes
of a great deal of extraordinary business. However, I
could not help it. . . . So here I spent 20s. upon them,
and were pretty merry. Among other things, had a fellow
that imitated all manner of birds, and dogs, and hogs, with
his voice, which was mighty pleasant. Staid here till night.

SAMUEL PEPYS
Diary (May 29, 1666)

IN THE WINE-CELLAR

His chaplain, Dr Lushington, was a very learned and ingeniose man, and they loved one another. The bishop sometimes would take the key of the wine-cellar, and he and his
chaplaine would goe and lock themselves in and be merry.

Then first he layes downe his episcopall hat,—" *There
lyes the Dr.*" Then he putts of his gowne,—" *There lyes
the Bishop.*" Then 'twas,—" *Here's to thee, Corbet,*" and
" *Here's to thee, Lushington.*"

JOHN AUBREY
Brief Lives : Richard Corbet (c. 1680)

AT OXFORD

Allsouls day, soldiers and trumpeters with Leopold Finch,
warden of Allsouls, in the dining roome next to the street
all the afternoon till about 9 at night, drinking healths
and every health they sounded—the English church then
languishing. What ! Are the Oxonian scholars mad ? to
revel it; drink and eat; frequent taverns, alehouses, coffee-
houses ; be debonare—when the church layes languishing.

ANTHONY WOOD, *Life and Times* (Nov. 2, 1679)

AT BRIGHTHELMSTONE

At Brighthelmstone . . . in the year 1808, Hobhouse,
Scrope Davies, Major Cooper and myself, having dined
together with Lord Delvin, Count (I forget the french
Emigrant nomenclature) and others, did about the middle
of the night (we four) proceed to a house of Gambling,
being then amongst us possest of about twenty guineas
of ready cash. . . . We lost them, returning home in bad
humour. Cooper went home, Scrope and Hobhouse and I
(it being high Summer) did firstly strip and plunge into
the sea, whence after half an hour's swimming . . . we

emerged in our dressing-gowns to discuss a bottle or two
of Champaigne and Hock (according to choice) at our
quarters. In course of this discussion, words arose;
Scrope seized H. by the throat; H. seized a knife in self-
defence, and stabbed Scrope in the shoulder to avoid being
throttled. Scrope fell bathed in blood and wine—for the
bottle fell with him—being infinitely intoxicated with
Gaming, Sea-bathing at two in the morning, and Supple-
mentary Champaigne. . . . At length, with many oaths and
some difficulty, he was gotten to bed.

LORD BYRON, Detached Thoughts (1821–2)

MAY-GAMES

SPUDEUS : But what ? Be there any abuses in their Maie-
games like unto these :

PHILOPONUS : As many as in the other. The order of them
is thus : Against Maie, Whitsondaie, or some other tyme
of the yeare, every Parishe, Towne, and Village, assemble
themselves together, bothe men, women, and children,
olde and yong, even all indifferently; and either goyng
all together, or devidyng themselves into companies, they
goe some to the woodes and groves, some to the hilles
and Mountaines, some to one place, some to an other,
where they spende all the night in pleasant pastymes, and
in the mornyng they returne, bringing with them Birch,
Bowes, and braunches of Trees, to deck their assemblies
withall: And no marvaile, for there is a great lord present
amongst them, as superintendent and Lorde over their
pastymes and sportes : namely, Sathan, Prince of Hell.
But their cheefest jewell they bring from thence is their

Maie poole, which they bring home with greate veneration, as thus : They have twentie or fourtie yoke of Oxen, every Oxe havyng a sweete Nosegaie of flowers tyed on the tippe of his hornes, and these Oxen drawe home this Maie poole (this stinckyng Idoll rather), which is covered all over with Flowers and Hearbes, bounde rounde aboute with stringes, from the top to the bottome, and sometyme painted with variable colours, with twoo or three hundred men, women, and children followyng it, with greate devotion. And thus beyng reared up, with handkercheifes and flagges streamyng on the toppe, they strawe the grounde aboute, binde greene boughes about it, sett up Sommer Haules, Bowers, and Arbours hard by it; and then fall they to banquet and feast, to leape and daunce aboute it, as the Heathen people did at the dedication of their Idolles, whereof this is a perfect patterne, or rather the thyng it self. . . .

Assuredly, I thinke neither Jewes nor Turkes, Sarasins, nor Pagans, nor any other people, how wicked or barbarous soever, have ever used such devilish exercises as these ; naie, they would have been ashamed, once to have named them, muche lesse to have used them : yet wee that would bee Christians thinke them not amisse. The Lorde forgive us, and remove them from us !

PHILIP STUBBES
The Anatomie of Abuses (1583)

AUGUST

It is now August . . . now beginne the Gleaners to follow the Corne Cart, and a little bread to a great deale of drinke makes the Travailers dinner : the Melowne and the Cucumber is now in request: and Oyle and vinegar give attendance on the Sallet hearbes : the Alehouse is more frequented then the Taverne . . . and in the fayre Rivers, swimming is a sweet exercise: the Bow and the Bowle pick many a purse, and the Cockes with their heeles spurne away many a mans wealth : The Pipe and the Taber is now lustily at worke, and the Lad and the Lasse will have no lead on their heeles : the new Wheat makes the Gossips Cake, and the Bride Cup is carried above the heads of the whole Parish : the Furmenty pot welcomes home the Harvest Cart, and the Garland of flowers crownes the Captaine of the Reapers. Oh, tis the merry time, wherein honest Neighbours make good cheere, and God is glorified in his blessings on the earth. In summe, for that I find, I thus conclude, I hold it the worlds welfare, and the earths warming-pan.

NICHOLAS BRETON
Fantasticks (1626)

HARVEST HOME

Come Sons of Summer, by whose toile,
We are the Lords of Wine and Oile :
By whose tough labours, and rough hands,
We rip up first, then reap our lands.
Crown'd with the eares of corne, now come.
And, to the Pipe, sing Harvest home ;
Come forth, my lord, and see the Cart
Drest up with all the Country Art . . .

373

The Horses, Mares, and frisking Fillies,
(Clad, all, in Linnen, white as Lillies)
The Harvest Swaines, and Wenches bound
For joy, to see the *Hock-cart* crown'd.
About the Cart, heare, how the Rout
Of Rurall Younglings raise the shout ;
Pressing before, some coming after,
Those with a shout, and these with laughter.
Some blesse the Cart ; some kisse the sheaves ;
Some prank them up with Oaken leaves : . . .
Well, on, brave boyes, to your Lords Hearth,
Glitt'ring with fire ; where, for your mirth,
Ye shall see first the large and cheefe
Foundation of your Feast, Fat Beefe : . . .
With Sev'rall dishes standing by,
As here a Custard, there a Pie,
And here all tempting Frumentie.
And for to make the merry cheere,
If smirking Wine be wanting here,
There's that, which drowns all care, stout
    Beere : . . .
To the rough Sickle, and crookt Sythe,
Drink frollick boyes, till all be blythe. . . .
And, you must know, your Lords word's true,
Feed him ye must, whose food fils you,
And that this pleasure is like raine,
Not sent ye for to drowne your paine,
But for to make it spring againe.

ROBERT HERRICK
The Hock-Cart, or Harvest Home. Hesperides (1648)

MALE PLEASURES

RUNNING AND RAMBLING

GATTY : How I envy that Sex ! well ! we cannot plague
'em enough when we have it in our power for those
privileges which custom has allow'd 'em above us.

ARIANA : The truth is, they can run and ramble here, and
there, and every where, and we poor Fools rather think
the better of 'em.

GATTY : From one Play-house to the other Play-house,
and if they like neither the Play nor the Women, they seldom
stay any longer than the combing of their Perriwigs, or a
whisper or two with a Friend ; and then they cock their
Caps, and out they strut again.   SIR GEORGE ETHEREGE
She wou'd if she cou'd (1668)

FEMALES

Women, while untainted by affectation, have a natural
cheerfulness of mind, tenderness, and benignity of heart,
which justly endears them to us, either to animate our
joys, or soothe our sorrows.   LORD CHESTERFIELD
On Female Coxcombs (1737)

The spontaneous grace, the melting voice, and the soothing looks of a female.

ISAAC DISRAELI, *Curiosities of Literature* (1791–1823)

BUSY WIVES

They have all many wives, and the Lordes five fold to the
common sort : their wives never eate with their husbands,
nor among the men, but serve their husbandes at meales,
and afterwardes feede by themselves. Those that are past
their yonger yeares, make all their breade and drinke, and
worke their cotton beddes, and doe all else of service and
labour, for the men doe nothing but hunte, fish, play and
drinke, when they are out of the wars.

SIR WALTER RALEIGH, *The Discoverie of Guiana* (1596)

The Women of the Land of *Jesso*, who spend all their
time in dressing their Husbands Dinners and Suppers, and
painting their Lips and Eye-brows blue, only to please the
greatest Villains in the World.

B. DE FONTENELLE, *A Plurality of Worlds* (1686)
Trans. John Glanvill (1688)

HOUNDS

He makes mortal War with the Fox for committing Acts
of Hostility against his Poultry. He is very solicitous to

have his Dogs well descended of worshipfull Families, and understands their Pedigree as learnedly as if he were a Herald. . . . He is both Cook and Physician to his Hounds. . . . Nor is he less skilfull in Physiognomy, and from the Aspects of their Faces, Shape of their Snouts, falling of their Ears and Lips, and Make of their Barrells, will give a shrewd Guess at their Inclinations, Partes, and Abilities, and what Parents they are lineally descended from. . . . He believes no Musick in the World is comparable to a Chorus of their Voices, and that when they are well match'd they will hunt their Partes as true at first Scent, as the best Singers of Catches, that ever open'd in a Tavern, that they understand the Scale as well as the best Scholler . . . and that when he windes his Horn to them, 'tis the very same thing with a Cornet in a quire. . . . Let the Hare take which Way she will, she selldom fails to lead him at long running to the Alehouse, where he meets with an Aftergame of Delight, in making up a Narrative, how every Dog behav'd himself; which is never done without long Dispute . . . and if there be any Thing remarkable, to his Thinking, in it, he preserves it to please himself, and, as he believes, all People els with, during his naturall Life, and after leaves it to his Heirs Male entail'd upon the Family, with his Bugle-Horn and Seal-Ring.

SAMUEL BUTLER

Characters : A Hunter (1667–69)

BAR ROOM

A glimpse through an interstice caught
Of a crowd of workmen and drivers in a bar-room around

the stove late of a winter night, and I unremark'd seated in a corner,

Of a youth who loves me and whom I love, silently approaching and seating himself near, that he may hold me by the hand,

A long while amid the noises of coming and going, of drinking and oath and smutty jest,

There we two content, happy in being together, speaking little, perhaps not a word.
WALT WHITMAN
A Glimpse (1855)

STAG-PARTIES

He-festivals, with blackguard gibes, ironical license, bull-dances, drinking, laughter.
WALT WHITMAN
Song of Myself (1855)

AT THE DRAGON AND THE LION

Thence we went to the Green Dragon, on Lambeth Hill ... and there we sang of all sorts of things ... and after that I played on my flageolet, and staid there till nine o'clock, very merry and drawn on with one song after another till it came to be so late. After that Sheply, Harrison and myself, we went towards Westminster on foot, and at the Golden Lion, near Charing Cross, we went in and drank a pint of wine, and so parted, and thence home, where I found my wife and maid a-washing. I staid up till the bell-man came by with his bell just under my window

as I was writing of this very line, and cried, " Past one of
the clock, and a cold, frosty, windy morning." I then went
to bed, and left my wife and the maid a-washing still.

SAMUEL PEPYS, Diary (Jan. 16, 1660)

A Post-Chaise with a Pretty Woman

In our way, Johnson strongly expressed his love of
driving fast in a post-chaise. " If [said he] I had no duties,
and no reference to futurity, I would spend my life in
driving briskly in a post-chaise with a pretty woman ;
but she should be one who could understand me, and
would add something to the conversation."

JAMES BOSWELL, Life of Johnson (1791)

A Tavern with a Well-Dressed One

A well-dressed man may lead in a well-dressed woman to
any tavern in London.
Ibid.

Rougher Sports

Soft Recreations fit the Female-kind ;
Nature, for Man, has rougher Sports design'd
To wield the Sword, and hurl the pointed Spear ;
To stop, or turn the Steed, in full Career.

OVID, Art of Love (C. 2 B.C.)
Trans. William Congreve (1709)

Madame,

I have heard . . . that you are safely delivered of a daughter. I am extreamly glad . . . that you have a daughter, for my opinion hath ever bin that I would have handsome Woemen have none but daughters, and I hope you will have as many as your Mother hath had and will have. . . .

LORD CONWAY

Letter to Countess of Devonshire (1640)

MALICE

BAITING GIBBON

You will be diverted to hear that Mr Gibbon has quarrelled with me. He lent me his second volume in the middle of November. I returne it with a most civil panegyric. He came for more incense; I gave it, but alas! with too much sincerity; I added, " Mr Gibbon, I am sorry *you* should have pitched on so disgusting a subject as the Constantinopolitan History. There is so much of the Arians and Eunomians and semi-Pelagians; and there is such a strange contrast between Roman and Gothic manners, and so little harmony between a Consul Sabinus and a Ricimer, Duke of the Palace, that, though you have written the story as well as it could be written, I fear few will have patience to read it." He coloured ; all his round features squeezed themselves into sharp angles ; he screwed up his button-mouth, and rapping his snuff-box, said, " It had never been put together before "—*so well*, he meant to add—but gulped it. He meant *so well*, certainly, for Tillement, whom he quotes on every page, has done the very thing. I well knew his vanity, even about his ridiculous face and person, but thought he had too much sense to avow it so palpably.

HORACE WALPOLE
Letter to William Mason (1781)

LIBELLING POETS

For the libel you speak of, upon that most unwitty Generation, the present *Poets*, I rejoyce in it with all my Heart, and shall take it for a Favour if you will send me a copy. He cannot want Wit utterly, that has a Spleen to those Rogues, tho' never so dully express'd.

JOHN WILMOT, Earl of Rochester
Letter to Henry Savile (1678)

RIDICULING POETS

Byron always became gay when any subject afforded him an opportunity of ridiculing poets ; he entered into it *con amore*.

LADY BLESSINGTON
Journal of Conversation with Lord Byron (1834)

Poor Fielding! I could not help telling his sister that I was equally surprised at and concerned for his continued lowness. Had your brother, said I, been born in a stable, or been a runner at a sponging-house, we should have thought him a genius, and wished he had had the advantage of a liberal education, and of being admitted into good company.

SAMUEL RICHARDSON
Letter to Mrs Balfour (1754)

ANNOYING ENVIOUS MEN

Will. Prosper . . . makes it his business to join in Conversation with Envious Men. He points to such an handsom Young Fellow, and whispers that he is secretly married to a Great Fortune : When they doubt, he adds Circumstances to prove it ; and never fails to aggravate their Distress by assuring 'em that to his knowledge he has an Uncle will leave him some Thousands. *Will.* has many Arts of this kind to torture this sort of Temper, and delights in it. When he finds them change colour, and say faintly They wish such a Piece of News is true, he has the Malice to speak, some good or other of every Man of their Acquaintance.

The Reliefs of the Envious Man are those little Blemishes and Imperfections, that discover themselves in an Illustrious Character. It is matter of great Consolation to an Envious Person, when a Man of Known Honour does

a thing Unworthy himself : . . . . . You see an Envious
Man clear up his Countenance, if in the Relation of any
Man's Great Happiness in one Point, you mention his
Uneasiness in another. When he hears such a one is very
rich he turns Pale, but recovers when you add that he has
many Children.

RICHARD STEELE
Spectator (1711)

CHARMED WITH SCANDAL

To your Business hereafter, but first lets have a Dance,
as Mr *Bays* says . . . I found your three Letters full of
Wit and Humour. I was charm'd with the scandal you writ
in the first and enclosed in the last, *viz.* A—'s poem . . .
Certainly, since the Devil was Dumb, there never was
such a Poet.

WALTER MOYLE
Letter to John Dennis (1695)

HATING ONE'S COLLEAGUES

Grr— there go, my heart's abhorrence !
Water your damned flower-pots, do !
If hate killed men, Brother Lawrence,
God's blood, would not mine kill you ! . . .
At the meal we sit together :
Salve tibi ! I must hear
Wise talk of the kind of weather,
Sort of season, time of year : . . . .

Whew! We'll have our platter burnished,
Laid with care on our own shelf!
With a fire-new spoon we're furnished,
And a goblet for ourself,
Rinsed like something sacrificial
Ere 'tis fit to touch our chaps—
Marked with L. for our initial!
(He, he! There his lily snaps!) . . .

There's a great text in Galatians,
Once you trip on it, entails
Twenty-nine distinct damnations,
One sure, if another fails,
If I trip him just a-dying,
Sure of Heaven as sure can be,
Spin him round and send him flying
Off to Hell, a Manichee?

ROBERT BROWNING
Soliloquy of the Spanish Cloister (1842)

SCORING OFF MAGICIANS

Simon Magus . . . having challenged St. *Peter* to doe
miracles with him, attempted to fly from the Capitoll to
the Aventine Hill. But when he was in the midst of the
way, St. *Peters* prayers did overcome his sorceries, and
violently bring him to the ground, in which fall having
broke his thigh, within a while after he died.

JOHN WILKINS
Mathematickall Magick (1648)

MARINE

NEPTUNE'S KINGDOM

Neptune sate in his Chariot High
Drawn by Six *Hippopotami* ; . . .
On tunefull Shells the *Tritons* playd,
The Winds and Storms to sleep were laid,
And a profound Peace o'r the Deep was spread.
Mermaids in melting streins their Voices try'd,
And Sea-Nymphs in soft Airs reply'd ;
That even rude Rocks and surly Seas took in the
Musick Pride.

Mountainous *Whales* before the Court were sent,
That mov'd all Lets out of the way ;
And, where the Road thro' Creeks or Inlets lay,
Shuffled up Isles into a Continent. . . .

Near these their Place did take
Sea-*Elephants* that on the Rocks do sleep,
That overlook the Deep ; . . .
The *Sea-Mors*, that's kill'd for his sovereign Horn,
And thought by some the onely *Unicorn*. . . .
The *Dolphin*, that in Musick doth delight,
And all surpasses in a speedy flight. . . .

The *Remora*, the Wonder of the Sea,
  That Ships even under sail can stay :
Small in his Bulk, but hoisting round their Keels,
No Waves or Tydes the Captive force away :
Whom *Neptune* did forbid to touch his Chariot-
      Wheels. . . .

    Within and round are shown
  The Tombs of the *Atlantian* Kings :
    Which of themselves are Stately things,
But by accession of Sea-Treasure Nobler gown.
    Each common Stone
A *Jaspis* or a *Hyacinth* doth grow :
Mother of *Pearl* the common roads doth strow,
And ev'n *Plebean* Tombs do *Sapphires* show.. . .

A Band of *Tritons* upon *Neptune* wait,
    And guard his Palace Gate,
And yet keep up the old *Atlantian State*.
    The Castles and the Towns remain,
The Citties yet their Privileges retain :
Tritons do in the Nobles Houses stay,
And Sea-Nymphs in the Groves and Meadows
    play. . . .

    Hence Curiosity me led
    To view the Neighbouring Sea :
    Where 'tis with Green *Sargossa* spread,
    And imitates a Flowry Mead ;
Doth the unwearied Eye to rove invite,
And every where gives Prospects of Delight :
  Under whose Shade the harmless Fry,
    No Fear nor Danger nigh,
    Their Innocent Revels keep,
And deck with sparkling Pearly scales the Deep. . . .

Nor could I miss *Cape Comori*,
Where mounts of Fruitfull Shell-fish ly,
That *Orient* Pearls do in their womb contain.
Where the bold *Indian* jumps into the Main,
Doth down into the Shining Bottom Dive,
That needs no Light, but what the Pearls do
give. . . .

THOMAS HEYRICK
The Submarine Voyage (1691)

THE MUSICAL AND AFFECTIONATE DOLPHIN

The swiftest of al other living creatures whatsoever, and not of sea-fish only, is the Dolphin, quicker than the flying fowle, swifter than the arrow shot out of a bow. . . . The Dolphin is a creature that carries a loving affection not only unto man, but also to musicke : delighted he is with harmony in song, but especially with the sound of the water instrument, or such kind of pipes. Of a man he is nothing affraid, neither avoides from him as a stranger : but of himselfe meeteth their ships, plaieth and disportes himselfe, and fetcheth a thousand friskes and gamboles before them. He will swim along by the mariners, as it were for a wager, who should make way most speedily, and alwaies outgoeth them, saile they with never so good a fore-wind.

In the daies of *Augustus Ceasar* the Emperour, there was a Dolphin entred the gulfe or poole Lucrinus, which loved wondrous well a certain boy a poore mans son ; who using to goe every day to schoole from Baianum to Puteoli, was woont also about noone-tide to stay at the water side, and to call unto the Dolphin, *Simo, Simo*, and many times would give him fragements of bread, which of purpose he ever brought with him, and by this meanes allured the Dolphin to come ordinarily unto him at his call. (I would make scruple and bash to insert this tale in my storie and to tell it out, but that *Mecenas Fabianus*, *Flavius Alfius*, and many others have set it downe for a truth in their chronicles.) Well in processe of time, at what houre soever of the day this boy lured for him and called *Simo*, were the Dolphin never so close hidden in any secret or blind corner, out he would and come abroad, yea and skud amaine to this lad ; and taking bread and other victuals at his hand, would gently offer him his back to mount upon, and then downe went the sharp pointed prickles of his fins, which he would put up as it were within a sheath for fear of hurting the boy. Thus when he had him once on his back, he would carry him over the broad arme of the sea as farre as Puteoli to schoole ; and in like manner convey him back again home : and thus he continued for many yeeres together, so long as the child live. But when the boy was fallen sicke and dead, yet the Dolphin gave not over his haunt, but usually came to the wonted place, and missing the lad, seemed to be heavie and mourne again, until for very griefe and sorrow (as it doubtles to be presumed) he also was found dead upon the shore. . . . .

But there is no end of examples in this kinde : for the Amphilochians and Tarentines testifie as much, as touching Dolphins which have bin enamoored of little boies : which induceth me the rather to beleeve the tale that goes of *Arion*. This *Arion* being a notable musitian and plaier of the harpe, chanced to fall into the hands of certain mariners in the ship where he was, who supposing that he had good store of money about him, which he had gotten with his instrument, were in hand to kill him and cast him over boord for the said monie . . . he, seeing himselfe at their devotion and mercie, besought them in the best manner that he could devise to suffer him yet before he died, to play one fit of mirth with his harpe ; which they granted : (at his musicke and sound of harpe, a number of Dolphins came flocking about him :) which done, they turne him over shipbord into the sea ; where one of the Dolphins tooke him upon his backe, and carried him safe to the bay of Taenarus.

PLINY THE ELDER
Natural History (c. 77)
Trans. Philemon Holland (1601)

TURTLE-SHELL BOATS

The *Tyrian* Merchant, or the *Portuguese*,
Can hardly build one Ship of many Trees :
But of one *Tortoise*, when he list to float,
Th' Arabian Fisher-man can make a boat.

JOSHUA SYLVESTER
Divine Weekes and Workes (1592)
Trans. from Guillaume Du Bartas

SUBMARINE PALACE

As large, as bright, as coloured as the bow
Of Iris, when unfading it doth show
Beyond a silvery shower, was the arch
Through which this Pathian army took its march
Into the outer courts of Neptune's state :
Whence could be seen, direct, a golden gate. . . .

389

Far as the mariner on highest mast
Can see all round upon the calmed vast
So wide was Neptune's hall : and as the blue
Doth vault the waters, so the waters drew
Their doming curtains, high, magnificent,
Awed from the throne aloof ;—and when storm-rent
Disclosed the thunder-gloomings in Jove's air ;
But, soothed as now, flash'd sudden everywhere
Noiseless sub-marine cloudlets, glittering
Death to a human eye : for there did spring
From natural west, and east, and south and north,
A light as of four sunsets, blazing forth
A gold-green zenith 'bove the Sea-God's head.
Of lucid depth the floor, and far outspread
As breezeless lake, on which the slim canoe
Of feather'd Indian darts about, as through
The delicatest air. . . .

         They stood in dreams
Till Triton blew his horn. The palace rang
The Nereids danced ; the Syrens faintly sang. . . .

JOHN KEATS
Endymion (1818)

THE SEASON OF SAILING

This is the season for sailing. For already the twittering
swallow has come, and the pleasant west wind ; the meadows are in flower, and the sea, broken lately by waves and
the rough gale, has become silent. Take up the anchors,
sailor, and let loose the ropes, and set sail, giving out the

whole canvas. This I, Priapus of the harbour, command,
that you, O man may set sail for all kinds of traffic.

Leonidas of Tarentum (3rd cent. B.C.)
Trans. George Burges

SATISFACTION TO SAILORS

This morning the King's Proclamation against drinking,
swearing, and debauchery, was read to our ships' companies in the fleet, and indeed it gives great satisfaction to all.

SAMUEL PEPYS, *Diary* (June 4, 1660)

MERMAIDS

Then, looking on the waters, I was ware
Of something drifting through delighted air,
—An isle of roses—and another near ;—
And more, on each hand, thicken, and appear
In shoals of bloom ; as in unpeopled skies
Save by two stars, more crowding lights arise,
And planets bud where'er we turn our mazed eyes.
I gaz'd unhinder'd : Mermaids six or seven,
Ris'n from the deeps to gaze on sun and heaven,
Cluster'd in troops and halo'd by the light,
Those Cyclads made that thicken'd on my sight....
    Soon—as when Summer of his sister Spring
Crushes and tears the rare enjewelling,
And boasting " I have fairer things than these "
Plashes amidst the billowy apple-trees
His lusty hands, in gusts of scented wind

Swirling out bloom till all the air is blind
With rosy foam and pelting blossom and mists
Of driving vermeil-rain ; and, as he lists,
The dainty onyx-coronals deflowers,
A glorious wanton ;—all the wrecks in showers
Crowd down upon a stream, and jostling thick
With bubbles bugle-eyed, struggle and stick
On tangled shoals that bar the brook—a crowd
Of filmy globes and rosy floating cloud :
So those Mermaidens crowded to my rock,
And thicken'd, like that drifted bloom, the flock
Sun-flush'd, until it seem'd their father Sea
Had gotten him a wreath of sweet Spring-broidery.
    Careless of me they sported : some would plash
The languent smooth with dimpling drops, and flash
Their filmy tails. . . . .
Some, diving merrily, downward drove, and gleam'd
With arm and fin ; the argent bubbles stream'd
Airwards, disturb'd ; and the scarce troubled sea
Gurgled, where they had sunk, melodiously.
Others with fingers white would comb among
The drenched hair of slabby weeds that swung
Swimming, and languish'd green upon the deep
Down that dank rock o'er which their lush long
        tresses weep.
But most in a half-circle watch'd the sun ;
And a sweet sadness dwelt on everyone ;
I knew not why,—but know that sadness dwells
On Mermaids, whether that they ring the knells
Of seamen whelm'd in chasms of the mid-main,
As poets sing ; or that it is a pain
To know the dusk depths of the ponderous sea,
The miles profound of solid green, and be

With loath'd cold fishes, far from man—or what ;—
I know the sadness but the cause know not.
Then they, thus rang'd, 'gan make full plaintively
A piteous Siren sweetness on the sea,
Withouten instrument, or conch, or bell,
Or stretch'd cords tunable on turtle's shell ;
Only with utterance of sweet breath they sung
An antique chaunt and in unknown tongue.
Now melting upward through the sloping scale
Swell'd the sweet strain to a melodious wail ;
Now ringing clarion-clear to whence it rose
Slumber'd at last in one sweet, deep, heart-broken close.
　　But when the sun had lapsed to Ocean, lo
A stealthy wind crept round seeking to blow,
Linger'd, then raised the washing waves and drench'd
The floating blooms and with tide flowing quench'd
The rosy isles : so that I stole away
And gain'd thro' growing dusk the stirless bay ;
White loom'd my rock, the water gurgling o'er,
Whence oft I watch but see those Mermaids now
　　no more.

GERALD MANLEY HOPKINS
A Vision of the Mermaids (1862)

MERMAIDS AND MERMEN

But above all, the *Mermaids* and *Men-fish* seem to me the
most strange fish in the waters. Some have supposed them
to be devils or spirits in regard of their whooping noise
that they make. For (as if they had power to raise extraordinarie storms and tempests) the winds blow, seas rage,

and clouds drop, presently after they seem to call. Questionlesse natures instinct works in them a quicker insight, and more sudden feeling and foresight of these things, then is in man ; upon which we see even in other creatures upon earth, as in fowls, who feeling the alteration of the aire in their feathers and quills, do plainly prognosticate a change of weather before it appeareth to us. And of these not onely the poets, but others also have written. The poets fein there were three *Mermaids* or *Sirens* ; in their upper parts like maidens, and in their lower parts fishes : which dwelling in the sea of Sicilie would allure sailors to them, and afterwards devoure them ; being first brought asleep with hearkening to their sweet singing. Their names (they say) were *Parthenope*, *Lygia*, and *Leucasia* ; wherefore sometime alluring women are said to be *Sirens*.

JOHN SWAN
Speculum Mundi (1635)

SEA NYMPHS

The delicacies of the Sea

These Nymphs trick'd up in tyers, the Sea-gods to delight :
Of Corral of each kind, the blacke, the red, the white ;
With many sundry shels, the Scallop large and faire ;
The Cockle small and round, the Periwinkle spare,
The Oyster, wherein oft the pearle is found to breed,
The Mussell, which retaines that daintie Orient seed :
In Chaines and Bracelets made, with linkes of sundry
      twists,
Some worne about their wasts, their necks, some on the
      wrists.
Great store of Amber there, and Jeat they did not misse ;

394

Their lips they sweetned had with costly Ambergris. . . . .
Now thus together com'n, they friendly doe devise,
Some of light toyes, and some of matters grave and wise.
But to breake off their speech, her reed when *Syrinx* sounds,
Some cast themselves in Rings, and fell to Hornepipe
      rounds :
They ceasing, as againe to others turnes it falls,
They lustie Galiards tread, some other Jiggs, and Braules.
This done, upon the Banke together being set,
Proceeding in the cause, for which they first were met,
In mightie *Neptunes* praise, these Sea-borne Virgins
      sing : . . .
Where is there one to him that may compared be,

The Song
of the Sea-
Nymphs in
praise of
Neptune

That both the Poles at once continually doth see ;
And Gyant-like with heaven as often maketh warres ;
The Ilands (in his power) as numberlesse as Starres,
He washeth at his will, and with his mightie hands
He makes the even shores oft mountainous with Sands :
Whose creatures, which observe his wide Emperiall seat,
Like his immeasured selfe, are infinite and greate.
    Thus ended they their Song, and off th'Assembly
    brake.

    MICHAEL DRAYTON, *Poly-Olbion*. Song XX (1622)

SAILING TO THE GUITAR

I have a boat here . . . it is swift and beautiful, and
appears quite a vessel. Williams is captain, and we drive
along in this delightful bay in the evening wind under the
summer moon until earth appears another world. Jane
brings her guitar, and if the past and future could be

obliterated, the present would content me so well that I could say with Faust to the passing moment, " Remain, thou art so beautiful."

P. B. SHELLEY
Letter to John Gisborne (Lerici, 1822)

HAPPINESS OF SAILORS

BOSWELL : " Yet sailors are happy." JOHNSON : " They are happy as brutes are happy, with a piece of fresh meat, —with the grossest sensuality."

JAMES BOSWELL
Life of Johnson (1791)

FORESTS OF THE SEA

The world below the brine,
Forests at the bottom of the sea, the branches and leaves,
Sea-lettuce, vast lichens, strange flowers and seeds, the
    thick tangle, openings, and pink turf,
Different colors, pale gray and green, purple, white, and
    gold, the play of light through the water,
Dumb swimmers there among the rocks, coral, gluten,
    grass, rushes, and the aliment of the swimmers,
Sluggish existences grazing there suspended, or slowly
    crawling close to the bottom,
The sperm-whale at the surface blowing air and spray,
    or disporting with his flukes,
The leaden-eyed shark, the walrus, the turtle, the hairy
    sea-leopard, and the sting-ray. . . .

WALT WHITMAN
The World below the Brine. Sea-Drift (1860)

MATHEMATICAL

A Thousand Advantages

Whereas *Mathematicks* improves all our Faculties, makes the Judgment stronger, and the Memory take in more. The Dull it teaches to perceive, and the Giddy to Attend. It distinguishes between *True* and *False*, and enures us to Difficulties : Besides, it gives us a thousand Advantages in Life. By this the *Miser* counts his Bags, and the *Countryman* knows his Times and Seasons. This gives our Cannon aim in War, and in Peace furnishes every Workman with his Tools. How many noble Engines has it invented ? In one the Wind labours for us, and another turns Bogs and Pools into firm Land. This builds us Houses, defends our Towns, and makes the Sea useful. Nor are its effects less wonderful than advantagious. The *Mathematicks* can do more things than any Poet e'er yet conceiv'd. He in a Map can contract *Asia* to a Span, and in a Glass shew a City from a Single House, and an Army from a Man. He can set the Heavens a thousand years forward, and call all the Stars by their Names. There is scarce anything without his reach ; He can gauge the Channel of the Sea, and weigh *Saturn*. He sees farthest into the Art and Skill of the *Creator*, and can write the best Comment on the Six Days Work.

Be advis'd therefore to employ yourself rather in the improving of your Understandings than debauching of your Passions . . . To my mind, to make a *Dial* is harder than to find a *Motto* to it, and a Prospect drawn in Lines pleasanter than one in Words. Instead of descriptions of cool Groves and flowry Gardens, you may inform yourself of the Situation and Extent of Empires, and while others are wandring in *Elysian*-fields and fancy'd Shades below, you may raise your Thoughts to the Infinity of *Space* above, and visit all those Worlds that shine upon us here . . . and mind little in *Venus* but her periodic Motion.

F. G. DE QUEVEDO
Trans. John Savage (1696)

ARCHIMEDES AND HIS SIREN

Archimedes had such a great minde, and was so profoundly learned, having hidden in him the onely treasure and secrets of Geometricall inventions : as he would never set forth any booke how to make all these warlicke engynes, which wanne him at that time the fame and glory, not of mans knowledge, but rather of divine wisedom. But he esteminge all kinde of handy craft and invention to make engines, and generally all maner of sciences bringing common commodity by the use of them, to be but vyle, beggarly, and mercenary drosse : employed his witte and study onely to write thinges, the beawty and subtiltie whereof were not mingled any thinge at all with necessitie. For all that he hath written, are geometricall proposicions, which are without comparison of any other writings whatsoever : bicause the subject whereof they treate, doth appeare by demonstracion, the matter giving them the grace and the greatnes, and the demonstracion proving it so exquisitely, with wonderfull reason and facilitie ... And therefore that me thinks is like enough to be true, which they write of him ; that he was so ravished and dronke with the swete intysements of this Sirene, which as it were lay continually with him.

PLUTARCH
Lives (c. 100)
Trans. Sir Thomas North (1572)

In Love with Geometry

He [Hobbes] was 40 yeares old before he looked on geometry ; which happened accidentally. Being in a gentleman's library ... Euclid's Elements lay open, and 'twas the 47 El. libri I. He read the proposition. " By G——" sayd he, " this is impossible ! " So he reads the demonstration of it, which referred him back to such a proposition ; which proposition he read. That referred him back to another, which he also read. Et sic deinceps, that at last he was demonstratively convinced of that trueth. This made him in love with geometry.

JOHN AUBREY
Brief Lives : Thomas Hobbes (c. 1680)

MATRIMONY

HAPPY NUPTIAL LEAGUE

So hand in hand they passd, the lovliest pair
That ever since in loves imbraces met,
Adam the goodliest man of men since born
His Sons, the fairest of her Daughters *Eve.*
Under a tuft of shade that on a green
Stood whispering soft, by a fresh Fountain side
They sat them down, and after no more toil
Of thir sweet Gardning labour then suffic'd
To recommend coole *Zephyr*, and made ease
More easie, wholsom thirst and appetite
More grateful, to thir Supper Fruits they fell,
Nectarine Fruits, which the compliant boughes
Yeilded them, side-long as they sat recline
On the soft downie Bank damaskt with flours :
The savourie pulp they chew, and in the rinde
Still as they thirsted scoop the brimming stream
Nor gentle purpose, nor endearing smiles
Wanted, nor youthful dalliance as beseems
Fair couple, linkt in happie nuptial League,
Alone as they. About them frisking playd
All Beasts of th'Earth, since wilde, and of all chase
In Wood or Wilderness, Forrest or Den ;

Sporting the Lion rampd, and in his paw
Dandl'd the Kid ; Bears, Tygers, Ounces, Pards
Gambold before them, th'unwieldy Elephant
To make them mirth us'd all his might, and
  wreathd
His lithe Proboscis

JOHN MILTON
Paradise Lost, Book IV (1667)

PROLOGUE AND PLAY

BELINDA : Yes : You fluttering Men of the Mode have
made Marriage a meer *French* dish. . . . You are so curious
in the Preparation, that is, your Courtship, one wou'd
think you meant a noble Entertainment—But when we
come to feed, 'tis all Froth, and poor, but in show Nay,
often, only Remains, which have been I know not how
many times warm'd for other Company, and at last serv'd
up cold to the Wife.

BELLMOUR : But you timorous Virgins form a dreadful
Chimaera of a Husband, as of a Creature contrary to that
soft, pliant, easie thing, a Lover ; so guess at Plagues in
Matromony, in Opposition to the Pleasures of Courtship.
Alas ! Courtship to Marriage is but as the Musick in the
Play-House, 'till the Curtain's drawn ; but that once up,
then opens the Scene of Pleasure.

BELINDA : Oh, foh—no : Rather, Courtship to Marriage,
as a very witty Prologue to a very dull Play.

WILLIAM CONGREVE
The Old Batchelor (1693)

At noon I home to dinner with my poor wife, with whom now-a-days I enjoy great pleasure in her company and learning of Arithmetique.

SAMUEL PEPYS

Diary (Dec. 1, 1663)

QUALIFYING FOR THE FLITCH

At last an hospitable House they found,
A homely Shed ; the Roof, not far from Ground,
Was thatch'd with Reeds and Straw, together bound.
There *Baucis* and *Philemon* liv'd, and there
Had liv'd long marry'd, and a happy Pair :
Now old in Love, though little was their Store, . . .
Command was none, where equal Love was paid,
Or rather both commanded, both obey'd . . .

    .   .   .   .

Then thus the Sire of Gods, with Looks serene :
Speak thy Desire, thou only Just of Men ;
And thou, O Woman, only worthy found
To be with such a Man in Marriage bound.
  A-while they whisper ; then, to *Jove* address'd,
Philemon thus prefers their joint Request : . . .
And since not any Action of our Life
Has been polluted with Domestick Strife ;
We beg one Hour of Death, that neither she
With Widow's Tears may live to bury me,
Nor weeping I, with wither'd Arms, may bear
My breathless *Baucis* to the Sepulcher.
  The Godheads sign their Suit. They run the Race

In the same Tenour all th' appointed Space :
Then, when their Hour was come, while they relate
These past Adventures at the Temple Gate,
Old *Baucis* is by old *Philemon* seen
Sprouting with sudden Leaves of spritely green :
Old *Baucis* look'd where old *Philemon* stood,
And saw his lengthen'd Arms a sprouting Wood :
New Roots their fasten'd Feet begin to bind,
Their Bodies stiffen in a rising Rind :
Then, ere the Bark above their Shoulders grew,
They give and take at once their last Adieu.
At once, Farewell, O faithful Spouse, they said :
At once th' incroaching Rinds their closing Lips invade.
Ev'n yet, an ancient *Tyranean* shows
A spreading Oak, that near a Linden grows ;
The Neighbourhood confirm the Prodigy,
Grave Men, nor vain of Tongue, nor like to lye.
I saw myself the Garlands on their Boughs,
And Tablets hung for Gifts of granted Vows.
And, off'ring fresher up, with pious Pray'r,
The Good, said I, are God's peculiar Care,
And such as honour Heav'n, shall heav'nly Honour
    share.

OVID, *Metamorphoses* (C. 5 B.C.)
Trans. John Dryden (1700)

HARMONY

There is no happy life
But in a wife
The Comforts are so sweete
When they doe meete

403

Tis plenty Peace a Calme
Like Droping Balme
Loves wether is so fayre
Perfumed Aire
Each work such pleasure brings
Like soft toucht strings
Loves Passion moves the harte
On Eyther parte
Such harmony together
So pleasd in Eyther
No discords, Concords still
Seald with one will
By love, God, man, made one
Yett not alone
Like Stamps of Kinge, and Queene
Itt may be seene
Two figures but one Coyne
So they doe Joyne
Onely they not Imbrase
We face to face.

DUKE OF NEWCASTLE
The Phanseys : Loves Matremony (c. 1645)

'TIS HONOURABLE

I shou'd have persuaded you to Marriage, but to deal
ingeniously, I am a little out of Arguments that way at
present : 'Tis honourable, there's no question on't ; but
what more, in good Faith, I cannot readily tell.

SIR JOHN SUCKLING
Letter to a Cousin (1638)

Which if it were so needfull before the fall, when man was much more perfect in himselfe, how much more is it needfull now against all the sorrows and casualties of life to have an intimate and speaking help, a ready and reviving associate in marriage : whereof who misses by chancing on a mute and spiritles mate, remains more alone than before.... But this pure and more inbred desire of joyning to it selfe in conjugall fellowship a fit conversing soul (which desire is properly call'd love) *is stronger than death*, as the spouse of Christ thought, *many waters cannot quench it, neither can the floods drown it*. This is that rationall burning that marriage is to remedy, . . . which how can he asswage who by mis-hap hath met the most unmeetest and unsutable mind ? . . .

If he be such as hath spent his youth unblamably, and layd up his chiefest earthly comforts in the enjoyment of a contented marriage, . . . when he shall find himselfe bound fast to an uncomplying discord of nature, or, as it oft happens, to an image of earth and fleam, with whom he lookt to be the co-partner of a sweet and gladsome society, and sees withall that his bondage is now inevitable, though he be almost the strongest Christian, he will be ready to despair in vertue, and mutin against divine providence : and this doubtless is the reason of those lapses and that melancholy despair which we see in many wedded persons, though they understand it not, or pretend other causes....

Did he open so to us this hazardous and accidental doore of mariage to shut upon us like the gate of death without retracting or returning, without permitting to change the worst, most insupportable, most unchristian mischance of mariage for all the mischiefes and sorrows that can ensue, being an ordinance which was especially giv'n as a cordiall and exhilarating cup of solace the better to beare our other crosses and afflictions ? . . . .

So likewise the Apostle witnesseth, . . . that in mariage *God hath call'd us to peace*. The rest whom either disproportion or deadnesse of spirit, or something distastefull and averse in the immutable bent of nature, renders unconjugall, error may have joyn'd, but God never joyn'd. . . .

For what kind of matrimony can that remain to be, what one dutie between such can be perform'd as it should be from the heart, when their thoughts and spirits flie asunder as farre as heaven from hell : . . .

The same may be said touching those persons who being of a pensive nature and cours of life, have sum'd up all their solace in that free and lightsome conversation which God and man intends in marriage : whereof when they see themselves depriv'd by meeting an unsociable consort, they oft-times resent one anothers mistake so deeply, that long it is not ere griefe end one of them. . . .

JOHN MILTON
Doctrine and Discipline of Divorce (1643)

AUSTIN MISTAKEN

Austin contends that manly friendship in all other regards had bin a more becoming solace for Adam, than to spend so many secret years in an empty world with one woman. But our Writers deservedly reject this crabbed opinion ; and defend that there is a peculiar comfort in the maried state besides the genial bed, which no other society affords. . . . We cannot alwayes be contemplative, or pragmaticall abroad, but have need of som delightfull intermissions, wherin the enlarg'd soul may leav off a while her severe schooling ; and like a glad youth in wand-ring vacancy, may keep her holidaies to joy and harmles pastime : which as she cannot well doe without company, so in no company so well as where the different sexe in most resembling unlikeness, and most unlike resemblance cannot but please best. . . . Wisest *Salomon* among his gravest Proverbs countenances a kinde of ravishment and erring fondnes in the entertainment of wedded leisures ; and in the Song of Songs, which is generally beleev'd, even in the jolliest expressions to figure the spousals of the Church with Christ, sings of a thousand raptures between those two lovely ones farre on the hither side of carnall enjoyment. By these instances and more which might be brought we may imagine how indulgently God provided against man's loneliness. . . . But God is no deceitfull giver, to bestow that on us for a remedy of loneliness, which if it bring not a sociable minde as well as a con-junctive body, leavs us no lesse alone than before ; and if it bring a minde perpetually avers and disagreeable, betraies us to a wors condition than the most deserted lonelines. . . .

Therefore shall a man leav his father and his mother, and shall cleav unto his wife ; and they shall be one flesh.

This vers, . . . is the great knot tier, . . . this that greisly Porter, who having drawn men and wisest men by subtle allurement within the train of an unhappy matrimony, claps the dungeon gate upon them, as irrecoverable as the grave. But if we view him well, and hear him with not too hasty and prejudicant ears, we shall finde no such terror in him. . . . *Cleav to a wife,* but let her bee a wife, let her be a meet help, a solace, not a nothing, not an adversary, not a desertrice ; . . . Wee know that flesh can neither joyn, nor keep together two bodies of it self; what is it then, must make them one flesh, but likenes, but fitnes of mind and disposition, which may breed the Spirit of concord, and union between them? If that be not in the nature of either, and that there has bin a remediles mistake, as vain wee goe about to compell them into one flesh, as if wee undertook to weav a garment of drie sand. . . .

JOHN MILTON, Tetrachordon (1645)

A Moving Thing

DORINDA : Mine offer'd Marriage.
MRS SULLEN : O lard! D'ye call that a moving thing?
DOR. : The sharpest Arrow in his Quiver, my dear Sister.
. . . If I marry my Lord *Aimwell*, there will be Title, Place and Precedence, the Park, the Play, and the drawing-room, Splendor, Equipage, Noise, and Flambeaux.—Hey, my Lady *Aimwell's* Servants there—Lights, Lights to the Stairs—My Lady *Aimwell's* Coach put forward—Stand by, make room for her Ladyship—Are not these things moving?

GEORGE FARQUHAR, The Beaux' Stratagem (1707)

Incompatibility

MRS. SULLEN : Pray, Spouse, what did you marry for?
SULLEN : To get an Heir to my Estate.
SIR CHARLES : And have you succeeded?
SUL. : No.

ARCHER : The Condition fails of his side.—Pray, Madam, what did you marry for ?

MRS SUL. : To support the Weakness of my Sex by the Strength of his, and to enjoy the Pleasures of an agreeable Society.

SIR CH. : Are your Expectations answer'd ?

MRS SUL. : No.

SIR CH. : What are the Bars to your mutual Contentment ?

MRS SUL. : In the first place, I can't drink Ale with him.

SUL. : Nor can I drink Tea with her.

MRS SUL. : I can't hunt with you.

SUL. : Nor can I dance with you.

MRS SUL. : I hate Cocking and Racing.

SUL. : And I abhor Ombre and Piquet.

MRS SUL. : Your Silence is intollerable.

SUL. : Your Prating is worse.

MRS SUL. : Have we not been a perpetual Offence to each other—A gnawing Vulture at the Heart ?

SUL. : A frightful Goblin to the Sight.

MRS SUL. : A Porcupine to the Feeling.

SUL. : Perpetual Wormwood to the Taste.

MRS. SUL. : Is there on Earth a thing we cou'd agree in ?

SUL. : Yes—To part.

MRS. SUL. : With all my Heart.   *Ibid.*

FOR BETTER, FOR WORSE

SIR OLIVER : Well, a pox of this tying man and woman together, for better, for worse !   SIR GEORGE ETHEREGE
She wou'd if she cou'd (1668)

LYDIA : But if I cou'd be desperate, now, and give you up my liberty, cou'd you find in your heart to quit all other engagements, and voluntrarily turn your self over to one woman, and she a Wife too ? Cou'd you away with the insufferable bondage of Matrimony ?

RANGER : You talk of Matrimony as irreverently as my Lady *Flippant*. The bondage of Matrimony, no——

> *The end of Marriage now is Liberty,*
> *And two are bound—to set each other free.*

WILLIAM WYCHERLEY
Love in a Wood (1671)

A FATHER'S CHOICE

PRUE : By that time, he'll be your Husband, if your Father come to-night.

HIPPOLITA : Or if I provide no not myself with another in the meantime ! For Fathers seldom chuse well, and I will no more take my Father's choice in a Husband than I would in a Gown or a Suit of Knots : so that if that Cousin of mine were not an ill-contrived Frekeish-fool, in being my Father's choice, I shou'd hate him.

WILLIAM WYCHERLEY
The Gentleman Dancing-Master (1672)

NOTHING VIOLENT

Lord L. bowed, delighted ; and if *he* did, his good Lady, you may be sure, partook of her Lord's delight. They are a happy pair ! They want not sense ; they have both fine understandings ! But, O ! my Lucy, they are not the striking, dazzling qualities in men and women, that make happy. Good sense, and solid judgment, a natural complacency of temper, a desire of obliging, and an easiness to be obliged, procure the silent, the serene happiness, to which the fluttering, tumultuous, impetuous fervors of passion can never contribute. Nothing violent can be lasting.

SAMUEL RICHARDSON
Sir Charles Grandison (1754)

HUMAN NATURE

SIR CHARLES : My friend Beauchamp deserves the best of women. *You* are excellent in my eyes ; but I have known two very worthy persons, who, taken separately, have been admired by every one who knew them, and who admired each other before marriage, yet not happy in it.

MISS GRANDISON : Is it possible ? To what could their unhappiness be owing ?—Both, I suppose, *continuing* good ?

SIR C. : To a hundred almost nameless reasons—Too little consideration on one side ; too much on the other : Diversions different : Too much abroad the man—Too much at home will sometimes have the same effect : Acquaintances approved by the one—Disapproved by the other : One liking the town ; the other the country : Or either preferring town or country in different humours, or at different times of the year. Human nature, Charlotte.

MISS G. : No more, I beseech you, Brother—Why this

human nature, I believe, is a very vile thing ! I think, Lady L., I won't marry at all.

SIR C. : Some such trifles, as these I have enumerated, will be likely to make you, Charlotte, with all your excellencies, not so happy as I wish you to be. If you cannot have a man of whose understanding you have a higher opinion than you have of your own, you should think of one who is likely to allow to yours a superiority. . . . And now the question recurs, What shall I say to Lord G. ? What to Sir Walter ?

MISS G. : Why, I think you must make my compliments to Sir Walter, if you will be so good ; and, after the example of my Sister Harriet to the men she sends a grazing, very civilly tell him, he may break his heart as soon as he pleases ; for that I cannot be his.

SIR C. : Strange girl ! But I wish not to lower this lively spirit—You will put your determination into English.

MISS G. : In plain English, then, I can by no means think of encouraging the address of Sir Walter Watkins.

SIR C. : Well, and what shall I say to Lord G. ? . . . Can you, do you think, love Lord G. ?

MISS G. : Love him ! love Lord G. ? what a question is that ! Why no, I verily believe, that I can't say that.

SIR C. : Can you esteem him ?

MISS G. : Esteem ! Why that's a quaint word, tho' a *female* one. I believe if I were to marry the honest man, I could be civil to him, if he would be very complaisant, very observant, and all that. . . .

SIR C. : . . . But if *you* cannot be *more* than civil, and if *he* is to be very observant, you'll make it your agreement with him, before you meet him at the altar, that he shall subscribe to the woman's part of the vow, and that you shall answer to the man's.

MISS G. : A good thought, I believe ! I'll consider of it. If I find, in courtship, the man will bear it, I may make the proposal.—Yet I don't know, but it will be as well to *suppose* the vow changed, without *conditioning* for it, as other good women do ; and act accordingly. One would not begin with a singularity, for fear of putting the parson out. I heard an excellent Lady once advice a good wife, who, however, very little wanted it, to give the man a hearing, and never do anything that he would wish to be done, except she chose to do it. If the man loves quiet, he'll be glad to compound.

SAMUEL RICHARDSON
Sir Charles Grandison (1754)

THE PERFECT HUSBAND

Never man had a greater passion for a woman, nor a more honourable esteeme of a wife, yet he was not uxurious, nor remitted not that just rule which it was her honor to obey, but manag'd th' reines of governement with such prudence and affection that she who would not delight in such an honourable and advantageable subjection, must have wanted a reasonable soule : he govern'd by perswasion, which he never employ'd but to things honorable and profitable for herself : He lov'd her soule and her honor more than her outside, and yet he had even for her person a constant indulgence, exceeding the common temporary passions of the most uxurious fooles : if he esteem'd her att a higher rate than she in herselfe could

-have deserv'd, he was the author of that vertue he doated on, while she only reflected his own glories upon him ; all that she was, was *him*, while he was here, and all that she is now at best is but his pale shade. So liberall was he to her, and of so generous a temper, that he hated the mention of sever'd purses ; his estate being so much at her dispose, that he never would receive an account of aniething she expended ; so constant was he in his love, that when she ceas'd to be young and lovely, he began to shew most fondnesse ; he lov'd her at such a kind and generous rate as words cannot expresse ; yet even this, which was the highest love he or anie man could have, was yet bounded by a superior, he lov'd her in the Lord as his fellow creature, not his idoll, but in such a manner as show'd that an affection, bounded in the just rules of duty, far exceeds every way all the irregular passions in the world. He lov'd God above her, and all the other dear pledges of his heart, and at his command, and for his glorie chearefully resign'd them. He was as kinde a father, as deare a brother, as good a master, and as faithful a friend as the world had.

LUCY HUTCHINSON
To her Children concerning their Father (c. 1665)

TRAPPED

SILVIA : But do you intend to marry me ?

HEARTWELL : That a Fool should ask such a malicious question ! Death, I shall be drawn in, before I know where I am— . . . Marry you ? no, no, I'll love you.

SILVIA : Nay, but if you love me, you must marry me ;

414

what don't I know my Father lov'd my Mother, and was married to her ?

HEART. : Ay, ay, in old Days, People married where they lov'd ; but that Fashion is chang'd, Child.

SIL. : Never tell me that, for I know it is not chang'd by my self ; for I love you, and would marry you. . . .

HEART. : Damn her, let her go, and a good riddance—Yet so much Tenderness and Beauty and Honesty together is a Jewel—Stay, *Silvia*— But then to marry—Why every Man plays the Fool once in his Life : But to marry is playing the Fool all one's Life long. . . . Well, farewel then—if I can get out of Sight I may get the better of myself.

SIL. : Well—good buy. (*Turns and Weeps.*)

HEART. : Ha ! Nay come, we'll kiss at parting . . . By Heav'n, her kiss is sweeter than Liberty—I will marry thee—There thou hast don't. All my Resolves melted in that Kiss—one more.

SIL. : But when ?

HEART. : I'm impatient till it be done ; I will not give myself Liberty to think, lest I should cool—I will about a Licence straight. . . . One Kiss more to confirm me mad ; so.

WILLIAM CONGREVE
The Old Batchelor (1693)

IMPROVING THE MIND

But the Grand affair of your life will be to gain and pre-serve the Freindship and Esteem of your Husband. You are married to a Man of good education and learning, of an excellent understanding, and an exact taste. It is true, and it is happy for you, that these Qualities in him are adorned with great Modesty, a most amiable Sweetness of Temper, and an unusual disposition to Sobriety and Virtue: But neither Good-Nature nor Virtue will suffer him to esteem you against his Judgment; and although he is not capable of using you ill, yet you will in time grow a thing indifferent, and perhaps contemptible; unless you can supply the loss of Youth and Beauty with more durable Qualities. You have but a very few years to be young and handsome in the eyes of the World; and as few months to be so, in the eyes of a Husband, who is not a Fool; for I hope you do not still dream of Charms and Raptures, which Marriage ever did, and ever will, put a sudden end to. Besides, yours was a match of Prudence and common good-liking, without any mixture of that ridiculous Passion which has no Being but in Play-Books and Romances.

You must therefore use all endeavours to attain to some degree of those Accomplishments which your Husband most values in other People, and for which he is most valued himself. You must improven your Mind. . . . You must get a collection of History and Travels which I will recommend to you, and spend some hours every day in reading them, and making extracts from them if your Memory be weak. You must invite Persons of knowledge and understanding to an acquaintance with you, by whose Conversation you may learn to correct your Taste and Judgement; and when you can bring yourself to comprehend and relish the good Sense of others, you will arrive in time to think rightly yourself, and to become a Reasonable and Agreeable Companion. This must produce in your Husband a true Rational Love and Esteem for you, which old Age will not diminish. He will have a regard for your

416

Judgment and Opinion in matters of the greatest Weight ; you will be able to entertain each other without a Third Person to releive you by finding Discourse. The endowments of your Mind will even make your Person more agreeable to him ; and when you are alone, your Time will not lie heavy upon your hands for want of some trifling Amusement. . . .

I desire you will keep this Letter in your Cabinet, and often examine impartially your whole Conduct by it: And so God bless you, and make you a fair Example to your Sex, and a perpetual Comfort to your Husband and your Parents.

JONATHAN SWIFT
A Letter to a Very Young Lady (1727)

THE MOST REFINED PLEASURE

How delightful it is when the mind of the female is so happily disposed, and so richly cultivated, as to participate in the literary avocations of her husband ! It is then truly that the intercourse of the sexes becomes the most refined pleasure. What delight, for instance, must the great Budaeus have tasted. . . . His wife left him nothing to desire . . . she brought him the books he required to his desk ; she collated passages, and transcribed quotations ; the same . . . ardour for literature eminently appeared in these two fortunate persons. . . . She was sedulous to animate him when he languished. Ever at his side, and ever assiduous ; ever with some useful book in her hand. . . . Yet she did not neglect the education of eleven children.

ISAAC DISRAELI
Curiosities of Literature (1791–1823)

Faithful Fish

The constant *Cantharus*,
Who, ever faithful to his dearest Spouse,
In Nuptiall Duties spending all his life,
Loves never other than his onely wife.
But, for her love, the *Mullet* hath no Peer ;
For, if the Fisher have surpriz'd her Pheer,
As mad with wo to shore she followeth,
Prest to consort him both in life and death.
As yerst those famous, loving *Thracian Dames*
That leapt alive into the funerall flames
Of their dead Husbands ; who deceast and gone,
Those loyall Wives hated to live alone.

JOSHUA SYLVESTER
Divine Weekes and Workes (1592)
Trans. from Guillaume Du Bartas

A Rash Venture

I knew your new brother-in-law at school, but have not seen him since. But your sister was in love, and must consequently be happy to have him. Yet I own, I cannot much felicitate anybody that marries for love. It is bad enough to marry ; but to marry where one loves is ten times worse. It is so charming at first, that the decay of inclination renders it infinitely more disagreeable afterwards. Your sister has a thousand merits ; but they don't count : but then she has good sense enough to make her happy, if her merit cannot make him so.

HORACE WALPOLE, *Letter to Horace Mann* (1743)

Marriage is not commonly unhappy, otherwise than as life is unhappy.   SAMUEL JOHNSON, *Rambler* (1750–52)

REMEDY FOR THE SPLEEN

MR SOLUS : Now I think marriage is an excellent remedy for the spleen. I have known a Gentleman at a feast receive an affront, disguise his rage, step home, vent it all upon his wife, return to his companions, and be as good company as if nothing had happened.

          MRS INCHBALD, *Every one has his fault* (1793)

METROPOLITAN

HERRICK BACK IN LONDON

From the dull confines of the drooping West,
To see the day spring from the pregnant East,
Ravisht in spirit, I come, nay more, I flie
To thee, blest place of my Nativitie !
Thus, thus with hallowed foot I touch the ground,
O fruitfull Genius ! that bestowest here
An everlasting plenty, yeere by yeere.

O *Place* ! O *People* ! Manners ! fram'd to please
All *Nations, Customes, Kindreds, Languages* !
I am a free-born *Roman* ; suffer then,
That I amongst you live a Citizen.
London my home is ; though by hard fate sent
Into a long and irksome banishment ;
Yet since cal'd back ; henceforward let me be,
O native countrye, repossest by thee !
For, rather than I'le to the West return,
I'le beg of thee first here to have mine Urn.
Weak I am grown, and must in short time fall ;
Give thou my sacred Reliques Buriall.

ROBERT HERRICK
His returne to London. Hesperides (1648)

CICERO PRAISES ROME

The City, the City, my Rufus—stay in it and live in its light ! Sojourning elsewhere, is, as I have declared from my youth up, obscure and paltry to those whose activities can make them illustrious in Rome.   CICERO

Letter to M. Caelius Rufus (50 B.C.)

STILL THE CAPITAL OF THE WORLD

Come to Rome. It is a scene by which expression is overpowered ; which words cannot convey. . . .

What shall I say of the modern city? Rome is yet the capital of the world. It is a city of palaces and temples more glorious than those which any other city contains, and of

ruins more glorious than they. Seen from any of the emin-
ences that surround it, it exhibits domes beyond domes,
and palaces, and colonnades interminably, even to the
horizon ; interspersed with patches of desert, and mighty
ruins which stand girt by their own desolation, in the
midst of the fanes of living religions, and the habitations
of living men, in sublime loneliness.   P. B. SHELLEY
Letter to T. L. Peacock (1819)

OVID IS ROME-SICK

In that place, there is leisure now, and the garrulous wars
of the wordy forum give place to the games, in rapid
succession. Now there is sport with horses, now play with
light arms, now with the ball, now with the round hoop
that swiftly turns ; now the young men, stained with the
slippery oil, lave tired limbs in the water of Virgo. The
stage is lively, applause is hot with zeal and partisanship,
and three theatres resound instead of three fora. O four
times happy, happy more times than one may count, is
he to whom is permitted the enjoyment of the unforbidden
city ! . . .   OVID
Tristia. III. 12 (9–10 A.D.)

BEAUTY OF ROME

Since I have been absent from you, thrust away to the
Scythian shores, the rising of the Pleiades has brought
four autumns. Do not think it is the conveniences of city

life which Naso seeks—and yet nevertheless he does seek
them. For sometimes I recall you to my mind, my sweet
friends, at other times my dear wife and daughter : and
from my house I go out once more to the places of the
lovely city, and my mind beholds them all with its own
eyes. Now the fora, now the temples, now the marble-
cased theatres, now every colonnade with its levelled
ground, come into my thoughts ; now the grass of the
Campus that looks on the beautiful gardens, and the
pools, and the moats, and the stream Virgo.

OVID, *Ex Ponto*. I. 8 (12–13 A.D.)

PRETTY WENCHES OF ROME

Behold the populous City in her pride
Yeelds thee more choice than all the world beside :
More eares of ripe Corne grows not in the fields,
Nor half so many boughs the Forrest yeelds ;
So many greene leaves grow not in the Woods,
Nor swimme so many fish in the salt floods,
So many Starres in heaven you cannot see,
As here be pretty wenches, *Rome*, in thee.

OVID, *Ars Amatoria* (C. 2 B.C.)
Trans. Wye Saltonstall (1639)

PARIS

MASCARILLE : Well, ladies, what do you say of Paris ?
MADELON : Alas ! what can we say of it ? It would be
against all reason not to confess that Paris is the great

422

bureau of marvels, the centre of good taste, of wit, and of gallantry.

MASCARILLE : As for me, I hold that outside Paris there is no well-being for genteel people.

CATHOS : It's an incontestable truth.

MADELON : It's rather dirty, but we have the chair.

JEAN BAPTISTE MOLIÈRE
Les Précieuses Ridicules (1659)

ELEGANCE OF PARIS

My Dearest Friend,

And do I really address you from Paris ? Am I at this moment a denizen of the far-famed queen of arts and arms —the centre of all that is refined and estimable ?—

> The glass of fashion and the mould of form,
> The observed of all observers !—

I am dizzy with the thought ! . . .

Only think how charming the way of life here ! For every meal, separate establishments, and all fitted up with that united elegance and splendour which none but Parisians understand. Here is the *Café des Milles Colonnes*, with its flashing radiance of gold and glass !—its host of waiters, swift and silent as attendant spirits ! . . . and then the company !— . . . Of these enchanted spots there are many hundreds, and also of *Restaurateurs*, where luxury assumes her most seductive form, and eating is no longer a *vulgar* appetite. Fancy your friend choosing her dinner from a *carte* of two hundred and fifty dishes ! And then their names so different from your low plough-boy English ones—

"boiled beef and greens"! "roast goose and apple sauce"! horrid! I am sure after *poulet nouveau en fricassée— pigeons de volière aux points d'asperges—omelette soufflée* and *beignets d'abricot*, I shall never bear to pronounce, much less partake of, the gross aliments of our own country.

But the *Louvre*, my dear creature, with its "Parian stairs" and names imperial—the "Hall of the Emperors"; the "Hall of the Seasons"; the "Hall of the Romans." Don't you feel your mind elevated while pronouncing them? And then the interminable gallery itself, with its imperishable records of artists now in the cold grave! I am bewildered like Eve among the flowers of Paradise. . . .

But to return to Paris, *chère, chère Paris!* I have been here but a fortnight, but I already feel my mind prodigiously expanded. . . . What, my dear friend, can that person know of elegance, who has never seen the Palais Royal with its *boutiques* and *bijouterie*?

MARIA JANE JEWSBURY
Phantasmagoria (1825)

FLORENCE

I have crept on upon time from day to day here; fond of Florence to a degree: 'tis infinitely the most agreeable of all the places I have seen since London: that you know one loves, right or wrong, as one does one's nurse. Our little Arno is not boated and swelling like the Thames, but 'tis vastly pretty, and, I don't know how, being Italian, has something visionary and poetical in its stream. Then One's unwilling to leave the gallery, and—but—in short,

one's unwilling to get into a post-chaise. I am as surfeited
with mountains and inns, as if I had eat them.

HORACE WALPOLE, Letter to Henry Conway (1740)

MANHATTAN

City of orgies, walks and joys,
City whom I that have lived and sung in your midst will
    one day make you illustrious,
Not the pageants of you, not your shifting tableaux, your
    spectacles, repay me,
Not the interminable rows of your houses, nor the ships
    at the wharves,
Nor the processions in the street, nor the bright windows
    with goods in them,
Nor to converse with learn'd persons, or bear my share in
    the soirée or feast ;
Not those, but as I pass, O Manhattan, your frequent
    and swift flash of eyes offering me love,
Offering response to my own—these repay me,
Lovers, continual lovers, only repay me.

WALT WHITMAN, City of Orgies (1855)

BOSTON

I come from the city of Boston,
    The home of the bean and the cod,
Where Cabots speak only to Lowells,
    And Lowells speak only to God.

SAMUEL C. BUSHNELL (19th cent.)

MRS SULLEN : *London*, dear *London*, is the place for managing and breaking a Husband.

DORINDA : And has not a Husband the same opportunities there for humbling a Wife ?

MRS SUL : No, no, Child, 'tis a standing Maxim in Conjugal Discipline, that when a Man wou'd enslave his Wife, he hurries her into the Country; and when a Lady wou'd be arbitrary with her Husband, she wheedles her Booby up to Town.—A Man dare not play the Tyrant in *London*, because there are so many Examples to encourage the Subject to rebel. O *Dorinda, Dorinda* ! a fine Woman may do any thing in *London* : O' my Conscience, she may raise an Army of Forty thousand Men.

GEORGE FARQUHAR
The Beaux' Stratagem (1707)

RETURN TO TOWN

COURTALL : Only my joy to see you, Sir *Oliver*, and to welcome you to Town.

SIR OLIVER : Methinks, indeed, I have been an age absent, but I intend to redeem the time : and how and how stand Affairs, prithee now ? is the Wine good ? are the Women kind ? Well, faith, a man had better be a vagabond in this Town, than a Justice of Peace in the Country : I was e'ne grown a Sot for want of Gentlemanlike recreations.

SIR GEORGE ETHEREGE
She wou'd if she cou'd (1668)

GOODLY LONDON

O more than mortall man, that did this Towne begin !
Whose knowledge found the plot, so fit to set it in.
What God, or heavenly power was harbourd in thy
    breast,
From whom with such successe thy labours should be
    blest ?
Built on a rising Bank, within a Vale to stand, The goodly situation of
And for thy healthfull soyle, chose gravell mixt with London.
    sand. . . .
And to the North and South, upon an equall reach,
Two Hils their even Banks do somewhat seeme to stretch,
Those two extreamer Winds from hurting it to let ;
And only levell lies, upon the Rise and Set.
Of all this goodly *Ile*, where breathes most cheerefull
    aire,
And every way there-to the wayes most smooth and faire ;
As in the fittest place, by man that could be thought,
To which by Land, or Sea, provision might be brought.
And such a Road for Ships scarce all the world commands,
As is the goodly *Tames*, neer where *Brute's* City stands.
Nor any Haven lies to which is more resort,
Commodities to bring, as also to transport.

MICHAEL DRAYTON
Poly-Olbion. Song XVI (1613)

STREETS AND LIFE

Streets, streets, streets, markets, theatres, churches,
Covent Gardens, shops sparkling with pretty faces of

industrious milliners, neat sempstresses, ladies cheapening, gentlemen behind counters lying, authors in the street with spectacles, George Dyers (you may know them by their gait), lamps lit at night, pastrycooks' and silversmiths' shops, beautiful Quakers of Pentonville, noise of coaches, drowsy cry of watchmen at night, with bucks reeling home drunk; if you happen to wake at midnight, cries of " Fire ! " and " Stop thief ! " inns of court, with their learned air, and halls, and butteries, just like Cambridge colleges; old book-stalls, " Jeremy Taylors," " Burtons on Melancholy," and " Religio Medicis " on every stall. These are thy pleasures, O London, with thy many sins. O City, abounding in w . . . , for these may Keswick and her giant brood go hang !

CHARLES LAMB
Letter to Thomas Manning (1800)

ITALIAN CITY

Had I but plenty of money, money enough and to spare,
The house for me, no doubt, were a house in the city-
squib;
Ah, such a life, such a life, as one leads at the window
there ;

Something to see, by Bacchus, something to hear, at
least !
There, the whole day long, one's life is a perfect feast ;
While up at a villa one lives, I maintain it, no more than a
beast. . . .

But the city, oh the city—the square with the houses !
    Why ? . . .
You watch who crosses and gossips, who saunters, who
    hurries by ;
Green blinds, as a matter of course, to draw when the sun
    gets high ;
And the shops with fanciful signs which are painted
    properly. . . .

Is it ever hot in the square ? There's a fountain to spout
    and splash !
In the shade it sings and springs ; in the shine such foam-
    bows flash
On the horses with curling fish-tails, that prance and
    paddle and pash
Round the lady atop in her conch—fifty gazers do not
    abash,
Though all that she wears is some weeds round her waist
    in a sort of sash. . . .

Ere you open your eyes in the city, the blessed church-
    bells begin :
No sooner the bells leave off than the diligence rattles in :
You get the pick of the news, and it costs you never a
    pin.
By and by there's the travelling doctor gives pills, lets
    blood, draws teeth ;

Or the Pulcinello-trumpet breaks up the market beneath.
At the post-office such a scene-picture—the new play,
    piping hot !
And a notice how, only this morning, three liberal thieves
    were shot.

Above it, behold the Archbishop's most fatherly of
rebukes,
And beneath, with his crown and his lion, some little
new law of the Duke's ! . . .

Noon strikes,—here sweeps the procession ! Our Lady
borne smiling and smart
With a pink gauze gown all spangles, and seven swords
stuck in her heart !
Bang-whang-whang goes the drum, *tootle-te-tootle* the
fife ;
No keeping one's haunches still : it's the greatest pleasure
in life. . . .

Look, two and two go the priests, then the monks with
cowls and sandals,
And the penitents dressed in white shirts, a-holding the
yellow candles ;
One, he carries a flag up straight, and another a cross
with handles,
And the Duke's guard brings up the rear, for the better
prevention of scandals :
Bang-whang-whang goes the drum, *tootle-te-tootle* the fife.
Oh, a day in the city-square, there is no such pleasure in
life !

ROBERT BROWNING
Up at a Villa—Down in the City (1842)

ODIUM THEOLOGICUM

DISLIKING PRELATES

Now I appeale to all wise men, what an excessive wast
of Treasury hath beene within these few yeares in this
Land . . . in the Idolatrous erection of Temples beautified
exquisitely to out-vie the Papists, the costly and deare-
bought Scandals, and snares of Images, Pictures, rich
coaps, gorgeous Altar-clothes. . . . What can we suppose
this will come to ? What other materials then these have
built up the spirituall BABEL to the heighth of her Abomin-
ations ? . . . The soure levin of humane Tradition mixt in
one putrified Masse with the poisonous dregs of hypoc-
risie in the hearts of *Prelates* that lye basking in the Sunny
warmth of Wealth and promotion, is the Serpents Egge
that will hatch an *Antichrist* wheresoever, and ingender
the same Monster as big, or as little as the Lump is which
breeds him. If the splendor of *Gold* and *Silver* begin to
Lord it once againe in the Church of England, wee shall
see *Antichrist* shortly wallow here, though his cheife
Kennell be at *Rome*. If they had one thought upon *God's
glory* and the advancement of Christian Faith, they would
be a meanes that with these expences thus profusely
throwne away in trash, rather *Churches* and *Schools* might
be built, where they cry out for want . . . a moderate
maintenance distributed to every painfull Minister, that

now scarse sustaines his Family with Bread, while the *Prelats* revell like Belshazzar with their full carouses in *Goblets*, and *vessels* of *gold* snacht from *God's Temple*. . . .

These devout *Prelates*, spight of our great Charter, and the soules of our Progenitors that wrested their liberties out of the *Norman* gripe with their dearest blood and highest prowesse, for these many years have not ceas't in their Pulpits wrinching and spraining the text, to set at nought and trample under foot all the most sacred and life blood Lawes, Statutes and Acts of *Parliament* . . . by proscribing and confiscating from us all the right we have to our owne bodies, goods and liberties. What is this, but to blow a trumpet, and proclaime a hereditary and perpetuall civill warre. . . .

Most certaine it is (as all our *Stories* beare witnesse) that ever since their coming to the See of *Canterbury* for neere twelve hundred yeares, to speak of them [the bishops] in generall, they have beene in *England* to our Soules a sad and dolefull succession of illiterate and blind guides : to our purposes and goods a wastfull band of robbers, a perpetuall havock and rapine : To our state a continuall *Hydra* of mischiefe and molestation, the forge of discord and rebellion . . .

O let them not bring about their damned *designes* that stand now at the entrance of the bottomlesse pit expecting the Watch-word to open and let out those dreadfull *Locusts* and *Scorpions*, to *re-involve* us in that pitchy *Cloud* of infernall darknes, where we shall never more see the *Sunne* of the *Truth* againe, never hope for the cheerfull dawne, never more heare the *Bird* of *Morning* sing. . . .

But they contrary . . . after a shamefull end in this *Life* (which *God* grant them) shall be throwne eternally into the *darkest* and *deepest Gulfe* of HELL, where under

432

the *despightfull controule*, the trample and spurne of all
the other *Damned*, that in the anguish of their *Torture*
shall have no other ease then to exercise a *Raving* and
Bestiall Tyranny over them as their *Slaves* and *Negro's*,
they shall remaine in that plight for ever, the *basest*, the
lowermost, the *most dejected*, most *underfoot and downe-
trodden Vassals of Perdition*.

JOHN MILTON, *Of Reformation in England* (1641)

DISLIKING THE FATHERS

Whatsoever time, or the heedlesse hand of blind chance,
hath drawne down from of old to this present, in her huge
dragnet, whether Fish, or Sea-Weed, Shells, or Shrubbs,
unpickt, unchosen, those are the Fathers.

JOHN MILTON, *Of Prelatical Episcopacy* (1641)

DISLIKING BISHOPS

She [Katherine Philips] was when a child much against
the bishops, and prayd to God to take them to him.

JOHN AUBREY, *Brief Lives : Katherine Philips* (c. 1680)

THEOLOGIANS DISLIKING ONE ANOTHER

Then he went into his owne country, to Beaudley (a
market-towne) at which time Mr Baxter (his antagonist)
preacht at Kidderminster, the next market-towne, two

433

miles distant. They preacht against one another's doctrines, and printed against each other. Mr Tombes was the Coryphaeus of the Anabaptists : both had great audience ; they went severall miles on foot to each doctor. Once (I thinke oftner) they disputed face to face, and the followers were like two armies, about 1500 of a party; and truly at last they fell by the eares, hurt was donne, and the civill magistrate had much adoe to quiet them.

Ibid.

John Tombes (c. 1680)

DISLIKING JESUIT MATHEMATICAL BOOKS

In Sir Charles Scarborough's time (he was of Caius College) Dr Batchcroft (the head of that house) would visit the boyes chambers, and see what they were studying ; and Charles Scarborough's genius let him to the mathematics, and he was wont to be reading of Clavius upon Euclid. The old Dr. had found in the title " *e Societate Jesu*," and was much scandalized at it. Sayd he, "By all meanes leave-off this author, and read Protestant mathematicall bookes."

Ibid.

Thomas Batchcroft

DISLIKING ROMAN CATHOLICISM

The retaining of this Romish Liturgy is a provocation to God and a dishonour to our Church. . . . If we have indeed given a Bill of Divorce to Popery and Superstition, why do wee not say, as to a divors't wife, those things which are yours take them all with you, and they shall sweepe after you? Why were we not thus wise at our parting from Rome? Ah! like a crafty adulteresse, she forgot nor all her smooth looks and inticing words at her parting: Yet keep these letters, these tokens, and these few ornaments. . . . Thus did those tenderhearted reformers dotingly suffer themselves to be overcome with harlot's language. . . . For we are deepe in dotage.

JOHN MILTON
An Apology for Smectymnuus (1642)

From an Usurping Vice-Christ, whose ambition is so boundless as to extend to the Prophetical, Priestly, and Kingly Headship, over all the Earth. . . . From a Leprous Sect, which Condemneth the far greatest part of all Christ's Church on Earth, and calleth itself the *whole* and *only Church* : From that Church that decreeth Destruction, to all that renounce not humane Sense . . . and that decreeth the Excommunication, Deposition, and Damnation, of all Princes that will not exterminate all such: and absolveth their Subjects from their Oaths of Allegiance : From that Beast whose Mark is *Perjury, Perfidiousness, and Persecution,* and that think they do God acceptable Service by killing his Servants, or tormenting them. . . . From the infernal Dragon, the Father of Lies, Malice and Murder, and all their Ministers and Kingdom of Darkness, Good Lord make haste to deliver thy Flock.

RICHARD BAXTER
The Protestant Religion Truely Stated and Justified
(Pub. 1692)

As to Popery . . . which for a thousand years past hath been introducing and multiplying corruptions both in doctrine and discipline, I look upon it to be the most absurd system of Christianity professed by any nation. But I cannot apprehend this kingdom to be in much danger from it. . . . Their common people are sunk in poverty, ignorance and cowardice, and of as little consequence as women and children.

JONATHAN SWIFT
The Presbyterians' Plea of Merit in order to take off the Test impartially examined (1733)

DISLIKING PROTESTANTS

If we give any credit to this picture of Anne Boleyn, she was a lady of neither spirit nor beauty. Yet she had both. I am apt to think it is a burlesque upon her. It may be, 'twas done at the expence and by the direction of a Roman Catholic. We know Roman Catholics hate her mortally, and therefore it is no wonder that she should be represented as a woman of no beauty or accomplishments.

THOMAS HEARNE, *Diary* (June 10, 1718)

DISLIKING DISSENTERS

J.C.

Honred Old friend,

I must not omitt giveing you an accompt of Mr. Baxter's tryall, lately at Guild-Hall before Sr George Jeffery's our now Lord Chief Justice, where you'l find him declaimeing violently, upon the common theam of his

436

owne ignorance, and putrid mallice, against that most excelent saint, and grave minister of Christ, Mr. Baxter. When I saw the meeke man stand before the flameing eyes, and feirce look's of this Biggott, I thought of Paul standing before Nero . . . you'l see him driveing on furiously, like the Great Hanebal makeing his way Over the alps with fire and vinegar, pouring all the contempt and scorn upon him, as if he had bin a link boy, or rake kennel, . . .

LORD C. J.: Oy is not this now an old knave. . . . Lord, we are thy people, thy peculiar people, thy Dear people, etc.,—and then he snorts and speaks thro' the nose, and clenches his hands, and lifts up his gogle eyes, in a mimicall way, runing on furiously as he saith they use to pray: But old Pollixfin [Baxter's counsel] gave him a bite now and then, tho' he could hardly crowd in a word.

POLL.: Why some tel you my lord tis hard measure to stop up these mens mouths and yet not suffer them to speak thro' the nose.

LORD C. J.: Pollixfin I know you well enough, and Ile set a mark upon you, for you are the patron for the faction, this is an old Rogue and hath poyson'd the world with his Kederminster Doctrine : . . . an old sismaticall knave, an hipocritticall villain.

POLL : I beseech your lordship suffer me a word for my Clyent : tis well known to all intelligable men of age of this Nation, that these things agree not at all to the carracter of Mr Baxter, . . . and, my lords, Mr. Baxter's loyall and peaceable spirit King Charles the 2d woud have rewarded with a Bishoprick, when he came in, if he could have conformed,

LORD C. J.: Oy oy we know that but what ail'd the old

stockcole unthankfull villain, that he could not conforme
—was he better or wiser then other men ? He hath been
ever since the spring of the faction, I am sure he hath
poyson'd the world with his lincee-wolsie doctrin : . . .
a conceited, stuborn, fanaticall dog, that did not conforme
when he might have been prefer'd, hang him this one
old fellow, hath cast more reproch upon the constitution
and excelent discipline of our Church, then will be wip'd
of this hundred years, but Ile handle him for it, for by
God he deserves to be whipt thro the city.

POLL : My lord, I am sure these things are not ad rem : . . .

LORD C. J. : But Ile handle him well enough, I'le warrant
you. . . . Come you, what do you say for your self, you
old knave, come speak up : what doth he say : I am not
afraid of you for all the sniveling calves that are got about
you.

MR. BAXTER : Your lordship need not, for I will not hurt
you.

[Calamy]   Mr. Rotherham urg'd . . . that Baxter . . . had
spoken very moderately and honourably of the Bishops
of the Church of *England*. . . .

BAXTER *for Bishops*, says JEFFREYS, *that's a merry
conceit indeed . . . Ay, This is your* Presbyterian *Cant;
truly call'd to be Bishops*, that is himself and such Rascals,
call'd to be Bishops of *Kidderminster*, and other such
Places. *Bishops set apart by such Factious*, *Sniveling*
Presbyterians *as himself ;* a Kidderminster *Bishop he
means*.

[Morrice]   Baxter himselfe desired leave to speake, the Lord Chief
Justice said Richard, Richard, dost thou think wee will
incur the danger of being at a Conventicle to heare
thee preach, thou hast infected the kingdome and now

438

wouldst infect this Court, with thy Kederminster stuff.
. . . *Richard* thou art an old Fellow, an Old Knave ;[Calamy]
thou hast written Books eno' to Load a Cart, every one
as full of Sedition (I might say Treason) as in Egg is full
of Meat. Hadst thou been whipp'd out of thy Writing
Trade, Forty Years ago, it had been happy . . . but by
the Grace of God I'll look after thee . . . by the Grace of
Almighty God I'll *Crush you all*.

> *Richard Baxter's Trial. Letter* from J. C. (1685)
> *Entring Book* of J. Morrice (30th May, 1685) and
> *Life of Baxter* by Edmund Calamy (1702)

We have an account from Whitechurch, in Shropshire,
that the dissenters there having prepared a great quantity
of bricks to erect a capacious conventicle, a destroying Angel came by night and spoyled them all, and confounded
their Babel in the beginning, to their great mortification.

> THOMAS HEARNE, *Diary* (Aug. 6, 1706)

Almost every evening during the latter part of this
winter [1792] there were riotous assemblages, and the
windows of many of the Dissenters were broken. A very
numerous mob collected one evening, who after breaking
several windows, did great injury to the Meeting-House.
. . . The Rev. George Whitmore, Tutor of the above
College [St John's] thought more favourably of the conduct of the mob. Addressing his pupils next morning
. . . he expressed a hope that none of them had joined in
the disturbance, which he was pleased to designate " A
LAUDABLE EBULLITION OF JUSTIFIABLE ZEAL ! " . . .

Sir Busick Harwood . . . made the following remark :
" In general, every man ought to be considered honest
until he has proved himself a rogue ; but with Dissenters,
the maxim should be reversed, and every Dissenter should
be considered a rogue, until he had proved himself an
honest man.

HENRY GUNNING
Reminiscences of Cambridge (1852)

Lord Eldon has the following reminiscence of this visit:
" I had a walk in New Inn Hall Garden with Dr Johnson and Sir Robert Chambers. Sir Robert was gathering
snails, and throwing them over the wall into his neighbour's
garden. The Doctor reproached him very roughly, and
stated to him that this was unmannerly and unneighbourly.
" Sir," said Sir Robert, " my neighbour is a Dissenter."
" Oh ! " said the Doctor ; " if so, Chambers, toss away,
toss away, as hard as you can."

GEORGE BIRKBECK HILL
Note to Boswell's Life of Johnson (1887)

DISLIKING METHODISTS

I talked of the recent expulsion of six students from the
University of Oxford, who were Methodists, and would
not desist from publickly praying and exhorting. JOHN-
SON: " Sir, that expulsion was extremely right and proper.
What have they to do at an University who are not willing
to be taught, but will presume to teach ? Where is religion
to be learnt but at an University ? Sir, they were examined, and found to be mighty ignorant fellows." Bos-
WELL : " But was it not hard, Sir, to expel them, for I

440

am told they were good beings?" JOHNSON: "I believe they might be good beings; but they were not fit to be in the University of Oxford. A cow is a very good animal in the field; but we turn her out of a garden." Lord Elibank used to repeat this as an illustration uncommonly happy.

JAMES BOSWELL
Life of Johnson (1791)

DISLIKING PRESBYTERIANS

That diabolical fanatick Sect which then destroyed Church and State.

JONATHAN SWIFT
Note written in Heylin's History of Presbyterians (1728)

Characteristics of the Presbyterians and Independents 1659: Manners; factious, saucy, and some impudent and conceited, morose,...false, factious in college, and delighting in petty plots...

They would avoid a taverne and ale-house, but yet send for their commodities to their respective chambers and tiple and smoake till they were over-taken with the creature.... Some I confess did venture, but then if overtaken would in their way home counterfeit a lameness or that some suddaine paine came upon them. ... Many also of them that were the sons of upstart gentlemen, such as that had got the good places into their hands belonging to the lawcourts and had bought the lands of the clergy and gentry, were generally very proud, saucy, impudent.

ANTHONY WOOD
Life and Times

An age given over to all vice—whores and harlots, pimps and panders, bauds and buffoons, lechery and treachery, atheists and papists, rogues and rascalls, reason and treason, playmakers and stage players, officers debauched and corrupters . . . aggravated and promoted by presbytery.

Ibid. (1667)

Covenanters and presbyterians have been the ruine of many families, the authour of bloodshed, the causes of decay of common honesty ; and from their base dealings wee see how the former pietie and plaine dealing of this nation is turned into cruelty and cunning. IZAAK WALTON
Life of Bishop Sanderson (1678)

DONATISTS DISLIKING CATHOLICS

Is it not so that at Hippo, where I am, there are those who remember that your Faustinus, in the time of his authority, ordered that, since there were very few Catholics here, no-one should bake their bread for them, so that a baker, who was the lodger of one of our deacons, threw away his landlord's bread unbaked ? ST. AUGUSTINE
Scripta contra Donatistas. (Part II. Book II. c. 83)

DISLIKING THE ENGLISH PRAYER-BOOK

To contend that it is fantasticall, if not senselesse in some places, were a copious argument. . . . The like, or worse, may be said of the Litany, wherin neither priest nor people speak any intire sense of them selves throughout the whole... they keep life between them in piece of gasping sense, and keep down the saucinesse of a continuall rebounding non-sense . . . we all know it hath bin obvious to be the pattern of many a jig. And he who hath but read in good books of devotion . . . will presently perceave this Liturgy all over in conception leane and dry, of affections empty and unmoving ; of passion, or any heighth wherto the soule might soar upon the wings of zeale, destitute and barren besides errors, *tautologies*, impertinencies, as those thanks in woman's churching in her delivery from sun-burning and moon-blasting, as if she had bin travailing not in her bed, but in the deserts of *Arabia*.

So that while some men cease not to admire the incomparable frame of our Liturgy, I cannot but admire as fast what they think is become of judgment and tast in other men, that they can hope to be heard without laughter. . . . But when we remember this our Liturgy, where we found it, whence we had it . . . it may be wondered how we can demurre whether it should be done away or no, and not rather fear we have highly offended in using it so long. It hath indeed bin pretended to be more ancient then the Masse . . . but so little proved that . . . having receav'd it from the Papall Church as an originall creature, for aught can be shewn to the contrary, form'd and fashion'd by work-maisters ill to be trusted, we may be assur'd that if God loathe the best of an idolater's prayer, much more the conceited fangle of his prayer. . . . Are we stronger than hee, to brook that which his heart cannot brook ? It is not surely because we think that prayers are no where to be had but at Rome !

JOHN MILTON, *Apology for Smectymnuus* (1642)

The Common-Prayer-Book was sent down into Scotland, where the King had no more Right to send it, than into the *Mogul's* country; but it was under a pretence of *Uniformity*, . . . But the old Herb-woman at Edinburgh put an end to that Game, for hearing the Arch-bishop who watch'd the Rubrick, directing him to read in the Book the Collect for the Day, she . . . cry'd, *The Dieul Collick in the wemb of thee*, and withal threw her Cricket-stool at his Head, which gave a beginning to the War of Scotland.

SAMUEL JOHNSON
Notes upon the Phenix edition of the Pastoral Letter (1694)

DISLIKING QUAKERS

The Quakers unmasked, and clearly detected to be but the Spawn of *Romish Frogs*, *Jesuites*, and *Franciscan Freeres*; sent from *Rome* to seduce the intoxicated *Giddy-headed English Nation*.

WILLIAM PRYNNE
Title of a *Tract* (1654)

DISLIKING LATITUDINARIANS

They push hard at the Latitude men as they call them, some in their pulpitts call them sons of Belial, others make the Devill a latitudinarian, which things are as pleasant to me as the raillery of a jack-pudding at one end of a dancing-rope. For I understand not the sottishness of their language nor whom they mean, nor what they would have.

HENRY MORE
Letter to Lady Conway (1665)

444

The settled aversion Dr Johnson felt towards an infidel he expressed to all ranks and at all times, without the smallest reserve. . . . We talked of a dead wit one evening, and somebody praised him. " Let us never praise talents so ill employed, Sir ; we foul our mouths by commending such infidels " (said he). The Abbé Reynal probably remembers that, being at the house of a common friend in London, the master of it approached Johnson with that gentleman so much celebrated in his hand, and this speech in his mouth : " Will you permit me, Sir, to present to you the Abbé Reynal ? " " *No, Sir,*" (replied the Doctor very loud) and suddenly turned away from them both.

HESTHER PIOZZI, *Anecdotes of Dr Johnson* (1786)

A gentleman . . . said, that in his opinion the character of an infidel was more detestable than that of a man notoriously guilty of an atrocious crime. I differed from him. . . . JOHNSON : Sir, I agree with him, for the infidel would be guilty of any crime if he were inclined to it.

JAMES BOSWELL, *Life of Johnson* (1791)

SANS RANCUNE

Mons. Voltaire remained in the drawing-room, with a great Bible before us, and if ever two mortal men disputed with vehemence, we did.

JAMES BOSWELL, *Letter to William Temple* (Ferney, 1764)

OLD AGE

THE SEAS ARE QUIET

The Seas are quiet, when the Winds give o're ;
So calm are we, when Passions are no more :
For then we know how vain it was to boast
Of fleeting Things, so certain to be lost.
Clouds of Affection from our younger Eyes
Conceal that emptiness, which Age descries.

The Soul's dark Cottage, batter'd and decay'd,
Lets in new Light thrô chinks that time has made
Stronger by weakness, wiser Men become
As they draw near to their Eternal home :
Leaving the Old, both Worlds at once they view
That stand upon the Threshold of the New.

EDMUND WALLER
Of the last Verses in the Book (1686)
(Poems, ed. 5)

PIOUS EJACULATIONS

I remember before the Civill Warrs, ancient people,
when they heard the clock strike, were wont to say,
" Lord, grant that my last houre may be my best houre."

They had some pious ejaculation too, when the cock did crow, which did put them in mind of the trumpet at the Resurrection.

JOHN AUBREY
Remains of Gentilism and Judaism (1687)

A CHEERFUL PROSPECT

If I live to be Old, for I find I go down,
Let this be my Fate. In a Country Town,
May I have a warm house, with a Stone at the Gate,
And a cleanly young Girl, to rub my bald Pate.

    Chorus
      May I govern my Passion with absolute Sway,
      And grow Wiser, and Better, as my Strength wears
        away.
      Without Gout, or Stone, by a gentle decay.

Near a shady Grove, and a murmuring Brook,
With the Ocean at Distance, whereupon I may look,
With a spacious Plain, without Hedge or Stile,
And an easy Pad-Nag, to ride out a Mile.
      May I govern, etc.

With *Horace* and *Petrarch*, and Two or Three more
Of the best Wits that reign'd in the Ages before,
With roast Mutton, rather than Ven'son or Veal,
And clean, tho' coarse Linnen at every Meal.
      May I govern, etc.

With a Pudding on Sundays, with stout humming Liquor,
And Remnants of Latin to welcome the Vicar,
With *Monte-Fiascone* or *Burgundy* Wine
To drink the Kings Health as oft as I dine.
      May I govern, etc.

With a Courage undaunted, may I face my last Day,
And when I am dead may the better sort say,
In the Morning, when sober, in the Evening, when
  Mellow,
He's gone and left not behind him his Fellow.
    May I govern my Passion, etc.

WALTER POPE, *The Wish* (1697)

TELLING STORIES AND BEADS

Or when three or foure good companions meet, tell old
stories by the fier side, or in the Sunne, as old folkes
usually doe . . . remembering afresh and with pleasure
auncient matters, and such like accidents, which happnd
in their younger yeares. . . .

Old folks have their beades, an excellent invention to
keepe them from idlenesse that are by nature melancholy,
and past all affaires, to say so many *Paternosters, Ave-
maries, Creedes,* if it were not prophane and superstitious.

ROBERT BURTON
The Anatomy of Melancholy (1621. Edition 1632)

WIT IMPROVES WITH YEARS

As you *Apollo's* Eldest Off-Spring are
You of his Spirit claim a double share . . .
True Wit, like Wine, thro' Age does riper grow,
Brisker and clearer, nay and stronger too . . .
Thus your old Laurels flourish to this Day
Like full-grown Trees, themselves to Heav'n display,

448

And see young Suckers under them decay ...
So *Phoebus*, after all his Course, appears
Bright as at first, and as unchang'd by Years :
Does nothing of his Fire or Lustre lose,
But sets at last, as glorious as he rose !

WILLIAM WYCHERLEY
To that Incomparable Poet, Mr Waller, in his Old Age
(before 1687)

DOWAGERS, CARDS, MIRTH, AND MEMORY

I thought you would at least come and while away the
remainder of life on the banks of the Thames in gaiety
and old tales. . . . We shall neither of us ever be grave :
dowagers roost all around us, and you could never want
cards or mirth. . . . We should get together and comfort
ourselves with reflecting on the brave days we have known
—not that I think people were a jot more clever or wise
in our youth than they are now ; but as my system is
always to live in a vision as much as I can, and as visions
don't increase with years, there is nothing so natural as
to think one remembers what one does not remember.

HORACE WALPOLE, *Letter to George Montagu* (1768)

LADIES AT SIXTY

I have known Ladies at Sixty, to whom all the polite part
of the Court and Town paid their addresses, without any
further view than that of enjoying the pleasure of their
Conversation.
JONATHAN SWIFT
A Letter to a Very Young Lady (1727)

Why shou'd Old Age to most so dreadful be ?
Which, there are none but wish and pray to see ;
What we, by that, lose in our Apetites,
It, in our Sense and Temperance, requites ;
Age, with our Body's Imbecility,
But best our Sense and Soul does fortifie ;
Weak'ning the Body, strengthens more the Mind,
Which, as more Weak the Body grows, (we find)
Is to resist strong Passions more inclin'd. . . .
Tho' Death's afar off Grim, 'tis Tame when near,
So keeps our Huffing Youth but most in fear. . .
Then Death to Men sated with Life is Ease,
Rest to the Tir'd, to th' Bed-rid a Release ;
To the Long-Liv'd, the sole Variety,
Who have done all they cou'd before, but Die,
And Repetition is worst Drudgery ;
The best of Life is but the same thing still,
The Feast is loath'd, when we have had our Fill . . .
Thus Age what Virtue ne'er cou'd compass does,
Makes the Soul, in the Jail the Body loose. . . .

WILLIAM WYCHERLEY
In the Praise and Defence of Old Age : To a Vain
Young Man, who said, There was nothing to be said for
it, and that it was more dreadful than Death (c. 1704 ?)

GAIETY CONTEMPTIBLE

A fondness for the amusements and gaieties of fashionable
life in an advanced age, seems to me not only contemptible but miserable, though I have often heard people
envied for it.

MRS. DONNELLAN, *Letter to Samuel Richardson* (1752)

You'll tell me that Age is apt to impair the *Memory* :
. . . I'll say that for my self, I can give a very particular
and competent Account of the present Generation, and of
their *Fathers* and *Grandfathers* before them too. . . . Was
it ever known in this world that a doting *Volpone* forgot
where he bury'd his Money ? Misers can remember
what they have a mind to, as well as other People. . . .
Sophocles wrote for the Stage as long as he liv'd. . . .
Solon in his Verses values himself upon reflecting, that
his Understanding improv'd as fast as his Days multiplyed.
. . . *Socrates* toward the latter End of his Life became
a Practitioner in *Musick* ; a very creditable Accomplishment in the Opinion of the Ancients ; and I could wish I
had try'd it my self. However, I have minded my Book,
and lost no Time in my Closet. . . .

In the second Place, as to any Decrease of Strength and
Vigour (which was the second Hardship objected) in
earnest, I find my self, upon the Experiment, altogether
as insensible of the Loss, as in my Prime I was of the want
of a Bull's or an Elephant's Muscles. . . .

No Man is under a Necessity to play the Fool in his
Old Age ; but every Man may if he pleases. *Appius* was
quite dark some Time before he died, and yet capable of
managing and disciplining four Sons (full grown) five
Daughters, and a large Dependence of Relations and In-
feriours. He minded his Business, and kept his Understanding brac'd ; and when his Vigour had fail'd him,
'twas more than his Age could do to foil him. . . . In a
word, he modell'd his Family like a primitive *Roman*,
and follow'd the good old Way ; . . . .

And (in Truth) let a Man follow his Business diligently,

and always keep himself thus honestly and usefully employ'd, and he will have no leisure to perceive the Encroachments of Old Age. 'Twill slide along with him by very gentle and insensible Degrees, till at last he sails (as 'twere) into Port, before he has had Occasion to take Notice of his Voyage. . . .

If we must bid adieu to the *Carnival* of Life, to the Relish of large Glasses and the Delicacies of the Board the best on't is, we take our leave at the same Time of Giddiness, Headach, Indigestion, Qualms, Fumes, Broken-sleeps, and Distracting Dreams. . . . And if an Old Man at an Entertainment cannot swallow as liberally, he may refresh himself as comfortably as the rest of the Company. There was old *Caius Duilius*, *Marcus's* Son, he that gave the first Blow to the Pride of *Carthage* by Sea. Many a Time when I was a Youngster, have I stood to look upon him as he was marching home after Supper, with a wax-taper to light him, and a *Violin* playing before him. . . .

I am sure as to my self, all the Pleasure that I am affected with at a Repast in Season, is the Opportunity it gives me of conferring Notes now and then with some or other of those few *Cavaliers* remaining, that have seen as much of the world as my self; but much more frequently with those that have not known it so long, as particularly, Gentlemen, your selves. My Years, I must tell you, have oblig'd me extreamly by diverting the Forwardness of my Appetite and the Curiosity of my Palat, from *Diet* to *Discourse*. . . . And this has been my Way of living in the Country; a Day never passes but I get my good Neighbours about me, bid them welcome to what the House affords, and so we set round, talking of this Thing and t'other, till ten, eleven, perhaps twelve a Clock at Night.

To return, I shall be told, perhaps, that as a Man grows in Years, he loses all the lively Flavour and Briskness of his Pleasures. No matter, so long as he does not *miss* it. . . . An old Dotard was pleas'd to examine *Socrates, whether he had no private Concerns, now and then, upon Occasion, with t'other Sex ? Bless me, what do you mean, Sir ?* (say'd the Philosopher like himself), *I were in a fine condition indeed, if I had not in all this Time broke the Tyranny of that insolent unruly Passion.* . . .

In short, what can we desire more than a fair and full Discharge from the Service of our own Appetites and Frenzies, our Lusts, Animositie, Ambition, etc., and to have our Souls and Senses, as we say, to our selves? And then if there's a Foundation of Learning withal, and Leisure and Opportunity to work upon it, O ! how deliciously does an old Man enjoy himself ! *Caius Gallus* . . . took a Pride and Satisfaction in nothing so much as his Knowledge of Eclipses. . . . *Noevius* the Poet, how happily he pass'd the Time, while he was composing his Performance about the *Punick War* ! And so *Plautus*, when his *Truculentus* and *Pseudolus* were upon the Stocks. And old *Livy* was as fortunate as either of them. . . . Now what comparison is there between such significant Recreations as these, and the *Beau's Paradise*, the *Taverns*, the *Stage*, and the *Masks* ? . . .

Next let us turn our Thoughts towards the Country, and the Scene of those agreeable Cares and Concerns which belong to it. These, I must own, are my beloved *Employments*, as well they deserve to be. For when we are grown too old for other Things, we may still be fit enough to manage these matters. . . .

Be it so ; yet aged People are strangely Sour, Sollicitous, Passionate, Peevish ; and 'tis odds but their Constitution's over-run with Avarice too. Possibly : But then take Notice these Imperfections are owing not to the number of our Years, but to the Error of our Conduct. . . . The Difference is the same in Men, as in Wines : There are some so well Body'd and Generous that Age cannot *turn* them. . . .

By this Time, Gentleman, I suppose the Wonder's over, and you may be sufficiently instructed to account for that Easiness and Serenity, nay that Delight and Pleasure, which crown these hoary Temples. . . . In a Word, 'tis with *Life*, as with other Things, a moderate Measure and Quantity does best ; and whether there's another Life in Reversion or not, he that is much troubled about putrefying, when 'tis Time, is his own Enemy. Old Age is the last Result, the clinching Scene of the Play ; and if we don't grow Sick on't by that Time, we should be glad, however, if we could fairly get out of the House betimes, and escape the Hurry.

CICERO, *De Senectute* (45 B.C.)
Trans. Samuel Parker (1704)

GAY OLD MEN

1. Ah *Posthumus* ! Our yeares hence flye,
   And leave no sound ; nor piety,
       Or prayers, or vow
   Can keepe the wrinkle from the brow :
       But we must on,
   As Fate do's lead or draw us ; none,
   None, *Posthumus*, co'd ere decline
   The doome of cruell *Proserpine*. . . .

454

3. W'ave seen the past-best Times, and these
   Will nere return, we see the Seas,
     And Moons to wain ;
   But they fill up their Ebbs again :
     But vanisht man,
   Like to a Lilly-lost, nere can,
   Nere can repullulate, or bring
   His dayes to see a second Spring.

4. But on we must, and thither tend,
   Where *Anchus* and rich *Tullus* blend
     Their sacred seed ;
   Thus has *Infernall Jove* decreed ;
     We must be made,
   Ere long, a song, ere long, a shade,
   Why then, since life to us is short,
   Lets make it full up, by our sport. . . .

7. If we can meet, and so conferre,
   Both by a shining Salt-seller ;
     And have our Roofe,
   Although not archt, yet weather proofe,
     And seeling free,
   From that cheape *Candle baudery* :
   We'le eate our Beane with that full mirth,
   As we were Lords of all the earth. . . .

12. . . . . . I'le call my young
    Julus to sing such a song
    I made upon my *Julia's* brest ;
    And of her blush at such a feast. . . .

13.   For to beget
    In me a more transcendant heate,
    Then that insinuating fire,
    Which crept into each aged Sire.

14. When the faire *Hellen,* from her eyes,
Shot forth her loving Sorceries :
    At which I'le reare
Mine aged limbs above my chaire :
    And hearing it,
Flutter and crow, as in a fit
Of fresh concupiscence, and cry,
No lust theres like to Poetry.

15. Thus frantick crazie man (God wot)
Ile call to mind things half forgot :
    And oft between,
Repeat the Times that I have seen ! . . .

16. Then next I'le cause my hopefull Lad
(If a wild Apple can be had)
    To crown the Hearth,
(*Larr* thus conspiring with our mirth)
    Then to infuse
Our browner Ale into the cruse :
Which sweetly spic't, we'l first carouse
Unto the *Genius* of the house. . . .

18. To those, and then agen to thee
We'l drink, my *Wickes,* untill we be
    Plump as the cherry,
Though not so fresh, yet full as merry
    As the crickit ;
The untam'd Heifer, or the Pricket,
Untill our tongues shall tell our ears,
W'are younger by a score of years.

19. This, till we see the fire lesse shine
From th' embers, than the kitlings eyne,
    We'l still sit up,
Sphering about the wassail cup,

To all those times,
Which gave me honour for my Rhimes,
The cole once spent, we'l then to bed,
Farre more than night bewearied.

ROBERT HERRICK

His Age, dedicated to his peculiar friend, Mr. John
Wickes. Hesperides (1648)

REMEMBERING ONE'S AGE

It is my felicity to have remember how ridiculous I have
formerly thought old people who forgot their own age
when everybody else did not ; and it is lucky too that I
feel no disposition that can lead me into absurdities. The
present world might be my grandchildren ; as they are
not, I have nothing to do with them. I am glad they are
amused, but neither envy nor wish to partake of their
pleasures or their business. When one preserve one's
senses and faculties and suffers no pain, old age would
be no grievance but for one ; yet oh ! that one is a heavy
calamity—the surviving one's friends : nay, even the loss
of one's contemporaries is something ! at least I cannot
feel interested in a generation that I do not know.

HORACE WALPOLE, *Letter to Sir Horace Mann* (1784)

A FULL LIFE

I have seen a mistress of James the Second, the Duke of
Marlborough's burial, three or four wars, the whole
career, victories and death of Lord Chatham, the loss of

America, the second conflagration of London by Lord George Gordon—and yet I am not so old as Methusalem by four or five centuries ! In short, I can sit and amuse myself with my own memory, and yet find new stores at every audience that I give to it. Then, for private episodes, varieties of characters, political intrigues, literary anecdotes, etc., the profusion that I remember is endless ; in short, when I reflect on all I have seen, heard, read, written, the many idle hours I have passed, the nights I have wasted playing at faro, the weeks, nay months, I have spent in pain, you will not wonder that I almost think I have, like Pythagoras, been Panthoides Euphorbus, and have retained one memory in at least two bodies.

Ibid. (1785)

A Comfortable Doctrine

I shall soon enter the period which, as the most agreeable of his long life, was selected by the judgement and experience of the sage Fontenelle. . . . I am far more inclined to embrace than to dispute this comfortable doctrine : I will not suppose any premature decay of the mind or body ; but I must reluctantly observe that two causes, the abbreviation of time and the failure of hope, will always tinge with a browner shade the evening of life. . . . In old age, the consolation of hope is reserved for the tenderness of parents, who commence a new life in their children ; the faith of enthusiasts who sing Hallelujahs above the clouds, and the vanity of authors who presume the immortality of their name and writings.

EDWARD GIBBON, *Autobiography* (1791)

Old Age brings along with its uglinesses the comfort that you will soon be out of it. . . . To be out of the war, out of debt, out of the drouht, out of the blues, out of the dentist's hands, out of the second thoughts, mortifications, and remorses that inflict such twinges and shotting pains,—out of the next winter, the high prices, and company below your ambition,—surely these are soothing hints. And, harbinger of this, what an alleviator is sleep, which muzzles all these dogs for me every day.

RALPH WALDO EMERSON, *Journal* (1864)

ORCHARDS

POMONA'S

In this kings reigne *Pomona* lived. There was not too bee
found
Among the woodnymphes any one in all the *Latian*
ground
That was so conning for too keepe an Ortyard as was shee,
Nor none so paynefull to preserve the frute of every tree.
And theruppon she had her name. Shee past not for the
woodes
Nor rivers, but the villages and boughes that bare both
buddes

And plentuous frute. In sted of dart a shredding hooke
   shee bare,
With which the overlusty boughes shee eft away did
   pare
That spreaded out too farre, and eft did make therwith
   a rift
To greffe another imp uppon the stocke within the
   clift.
And lest her trees should die through drought, with water
   of the springs.
Shee moysteth of theyr sucking roots the little crumpled
   strings.
This was her love and whole delyght. And as for Venus
   deedes
Shee had no mynd at all for them. And forbycause shee
   dreedes
Enforcement by the countrye folke, shee walld her yards
   about,
Not suffring any man at all to enter in or out.

OVID

Metamorphoses (c. 5 B.C.)
Trans. Arthur Golding (1567)

POLYPHEMUS'S

My Garden fill'd with Fruits you may behold,
And Grapes in Clusters, imitating Gold ;
Some blushing Bunches of a Purple Hue,
And these, and those, are all reserv'd for you
Red Strawberries, in Shades, expecting stand,
Proud to be gather'd by so white a Hand.

Autumnal Cornels later Fruit provide,
And Plumbs, to tempt you, turn their glossy Side:
Not those of common Kinds; but such alone,
As in *Phracian* Orchards might have grown:
Nor Chestnuts shall be wanting to your Food,
Nor Garden-Fruits, nor Wildings of the Wood;
The laden Boughs for you alone shall bear;
And yours shall be the Product of the Year.

JOHN DRYDEN
Acis, Polyphemus and Galatea (1700)
From Ovid, *Metamorphoses* (c. 5 B.C.)

AT THE CROSSROADS

I, Hermes, stand here by the windy orchard at the crossroads near the grey sea-shore, resting tired men on their
way; and the spring wells out cold pure water.

ANYTE OF TEGEA (3rd C. B.C.)

A FEAST

Up thou north wynde, come thou south wynde, and blowe
upon my garden, that the smel therof may be caried on
every syde. yee that my beloved may come into my garden,
and eate of the frutes and apples that growe therein.

Come in to my garden, O my syster, my Spouse: I have
gathered my Myrre with my spyce. I will eate my hony and
my honycombe, I wyll dryncke my wyne and my mylcke.

SALAMONS BALLET
Trans. Miles Coverdale. *Matthew's Bible* (1537)

Wassail the Trees, that they may beare
You many a Plum, and many a Peare :
For more or lesse fruits they will bring.
As you doe give them Wassailing.

ROBERT HERRICK, *Hesperides* (1648)

KENTISH

Saluting the deare soyle, O famous *Kent*, quoth shee,
What Country hath this Ile that can compare with
thee, ...
Where *Thames*-ward to the shore, which shoots upon the
rise,
Rich *Renham* undertakes thy Closets to suffize
With Cherries, which wee say, the Sommer in doth bring,
Wherewith *Pomona* crowns the plump and lustfull Spring;
From whose deepe ruddy cheeke, sweet *Zephyrs* kisses
steales,
With their delicious touch his love-sicke hart that heales.
Whose golden gardens seeme th'*Hesperides* to mock :
Nor there the Damzon wants, nor daintie Abricock,
Nor Pippin, which we hold of kernell-fruits the King,
The Apple-Orendge ; then the savory Russetting :
The Peare-maine, which to *France* long ere to us was
knowne,
Which carefull Frut'rers now have denizend our owne.
The Renat : which though first it from the Pippin came,
Growne through his pureness nice, assumes that curious
name,

Upon the Pippin stock, the Pippin beeing set ;
Aso on the Gentle, when the Gentle doth beget
(Both by the Sire and Dame beeing anciently descended)
The issue borne of them, his blood hath much amended.
The Sweeting, for whose sake the Plow-boyes oft make
    warre :
The Wilding, Costard, then the wel-known Pomwater,
And sundry other fruits, of good, yet severall taste,
That have their sundry names in sundry Countries plac't.

MICHAEL DRAYTON
Poly-Olbion. Song XVIII (1612)

AT NUN APPLETON

When we have run our Passions heat,
Love hither makes his best retreat.
The *Gods*, that mortal Beauty chase,
Still in a Tree did end their race.
Apollo hunted *Daphne* so,
Only that she might Laurel grow.
And *Pan* did after *Syrinx* speed,
Not as a Nymph, but for a Reed.

What wond'rous Life in this I lead
Ripe Apples drop about my head ;
The Luscious Clusters of the Vine
Upon my Mouth do crush their Wine ;
The Nectaren and curious Peach,
Into my hands themselves do reach ;
Stumbling on Melons, as I pass,
Insnar'd with Flowers, I fall on Grass.

463

Mean while the Mind, from pleasure less,
Withdraws into its happiness:
The Mind, that Ocean where each kind
Does streight its own resemblance find;
Yet it creates, transcending these,
Far other Worlds, and other Seas;
Annihilating all that's made
To a green Thought in a green Shade.

Here at the Fountains sliding foot,
Or at some Fruit-tree's mossy root,
Casting the Bodies Vest aside,
My Soul into the boughs does glide:
There like a Bird it sits, and sings,
Then whets, and combs its silver Wings;
And, till prepar'd for longer flight,
Waves in its Plumes the various Light.

Such was that happy Garden-state,
While Man there walk'd without a Mate:
After a Place so pure, and sweet,
What other Help could yet be meet!
But 'twas beyond a Mortal's share
To wander solitary there:
Two Paradises 'twere in one
To live in Paradise alone.

ANDREW MARVELL, *The Garden* (c. 1653: pub. 1681)

When to Transplant Orange Trees

Now forasmuch as Gentlemen are very inquisitive when
were the best and securest season for exposing their
Orange-trees, and more tender curiosities, I give them

this for a rule the most infallible : that they observe the Mulberry-tree, when it begins to put forth and open the leaves (be it earlier or later) bring your Oranges &c. boldly out of the Conservatory ; 'tis your onely season to transplant and remove them.

JOHN EVELYN
Kalendarium Hortense (1664)

MASTERING THE FRUIT-TREES

Who would not joy to see his conquering hand
Oe'r all the vegetable world command ?
And the wild gyants of the wood receive
    What law hee's pleas'd to give ?
Hee bids th'ill-natur'd crab produce
The gentler apples winy juice ;
The golden fruit that worthy is
of Galatea's purple kiss ;
Hee does the savage hawthorn teach
To bear the Medlar and the Pear ;
Hee bids the rustique Plum to rear
A nobler trunck, and bee a Peach,
Even Daphnes coyness hee does mock,
And weds the Cherry to her stock ;
Though shee refus'd Apollos suit ;
Ev'n she, the chast, and virgin tree,
Now wonders at her self, to see
That shee's a mother made, and blushes in her
    fruit.

ABRAHAM COWLEY
The Garden (1666)

PARENTAL

Indiscriminate Love of Infants

I cannot receive this passion, wherewith some embrace children scarsly borne, having neither motion in the soule, nor forme well to be distinguished in the body, whereby they might make themselves lovely or amiable. And I could never well endure to have them brought up or nursed neere about me. A true and well ordred affection ought to be borne and augmented with the knowledge they give us of themselves; and then, if they deserve it (naturall inclination marching hand in hand with reason) to cherish and make much of them, with a perfect fatherly love and loving friendship, and conformably to judje of them if they be otherwise, always yeelding our selves into reason . . . For the most part, it goeth clean contrary, and commonly we feele our selves more moved with the sports, idlenesse, wantonnesse, and infant-trifles of our children, then afterward we do with all their actions, when they be men : As if we had loved them for our pastimes, as we do apes, monkies, or perokitoes, and not as man. And some that liberally furnish them with sporting bables while they be children, will miserably pinch it in the least expence for necessaries when they grow men. Nay, it seemeth that the jelousie we have to see them appeare into and injoy the world, when we are ready to leave them, makes us more sparing and close-handed toward them.

> MICHEL DE MONTAIGNE
> *Essays : Of the affection of fathers to their*
> *Children* (1580)
> Trans. John Florio (1603)

THE NAKED INDIAN'S QUESTION

None could answer the naked *Indian*, Why one Man should take Pains, and run Hazards by Sea and Land all his Life, that his Children might be safe and lazy all theirs.

> SIR WILLIAM TEMPLE
> *Of Gardening* (1685)

EATING JACKS

When Arch Bishop's Abbot's mother . . . was with child of him, she did long for a jack, and she dreamt that if shee should eat a jack, her son in her belly should be a great man. She arose early the next morning, and went with her payle to the river side . . . to take up some water, and in the water in her payle shee found a good jack, which she dresst, and eat it all, or very near. Severall of the best inhabitants of Guildford were invited (or invited themselves)

467

to the Christening of the child ; it was bred up a Scholar in the town, and by degrees, came to be Arch Bishop of Canterbury.

JOHN AUBREY, *Miscellanies* (1696)

TOO HEAVY

There was a feast of Hera among the Argives, and it was by all means necessary that their mother should be borne in a car to the temple. But, since their oxen were not brought up in time from the field, the young men, barred from all else from lack of time, submitted themselves to the yoke and drew the wain, their mother being borne by them upon it ; and so they brought it on for five and forty furlongs, and came to the temple. Then after they had done this and been seen by the assembled crowd, there came to their life a most excellent ending ; and in this the deity declared that it was better for man to die than to continue to live. For the Argive men were standing round and extolling the strength of the young men, while the argive women were extolling the mother to whose lot it had fallen to have such sons ; and the mother, being exceedingly rejoiced both by the deed itself and by the report made of it, took her stand in front of the image of the goddess and prayed that she would give to Cleobis and Biton her sons, who had honoured her greatly, that gift which is best for man to receive : and after this prayer, when they had sacrificed and feasted, the young men lay down to sleep within the temple itself, and never rose again.

HERODOTUS, *History* (5th cent. B.C.)
Trans. G. C. Macaulay

Jan. 27th, 1658. After six fits of a quartan ague with which it pleased God to visite him, died my deare Son Richard, to our inexpressible griefe and affliction, 5 yeares and 3 days old onely, but at that tender age a prodigy for witt and understanding; for beauty of body a very angel; for endowment of mind of incredible and rare hopes. To give onely a little taste of them, and thereby glory to God, sense of God he had learn'd all his catechisme who out of the mouths of babes and infants does sometimes perfect his praises: at 2 years and a halfe old he could perfectly reade any of the English, Latine, French, or Gottic letters, pronouncing the three first languages exactly. He had before the 5th yeare, or in that yeare, not onely skill to reade most written hands, but to decline all the nouns, conjugate the verbs regular, and most of the irregular; learn'd out " Puerilis," got by heart almost the entire vocabularie of Latine and French primitives and words, could make congruous syntax, turne English into Latine, and *vice versâ,* construe and prove what he read, and did the government and use of relatives, verbs, substantives, elipses, and many figures and tropes, and made a considerable progress in Comenius's Janua; began himselfe to write legibly, and had a strong passion for Greeke. The number of verses he could recite was prodigious, and what he remember'd of the parts of playes, which he would also act; and when seeing a Plautus in one's hand, he ask'd what booke it was, and being told it was comedy, and too difficult for him, he wept for sorrow. Strange was his apt and ingenious application of fables and morals, for he had read Æsop; he had a wonderful disposition to mathematics, having by heart divers propositions of Euclid that were read to him in play, and he would make lines and demonstrate them. As to his piety, astonishing were his applications of Scripture upon occasion, and his early, and understood the historical part of the Bible and New Testament to a wonder, how Christ came to redeeme mankind, and how, comprehending these necessarys himselfe, his godfathers were discharg'd of their promise. These and the like illuminations, far exceeding his age and experience, considering the prettinesse of his addresse and behaviour, cannot but leave impressions in me at the memory of him. When one told him how many dayes a Quaker had fasted, he replied that was no wonder, for Christ had said that man should not live by bread alone, but by the Word of God. He would of himselfe select the most pathetic psalms, and chapters out of Job, to reade to his mayde during his sicknesse, telling her when she pitied him, that all God's children must suffer affliction. He declaim'd against the vanities of the world before he had seene any. Often he would desire those who came to see him to pray by him, and a yeare before he fell sick, to kneel and pray with him alone in some corner. How thankfully would he receive admonition, how soone be reconciled ! how indifferent, yet continualy cherefull ! He would give grave advice to his Brother John, beare with his impertinencies, and say he was but a child. If he heard of or saw any new thing, he was unquiet till he was told how it was made ; he brought to us all such difficulties as he found in books, to be expounded. He had learn'd by heart divers sentences in Latin and Greeke, which on occasion he would produce even to wonder. He was all life, all prettinesse, far from morose, sullen, or childish in any thing he said or did. The last time he had been

470

at church (which was at Greenewich), I ask'd him, according to costome, what he remembered of the sermon; two good things, Father, said he, *bonum gratiæ* and *bonum gloriæ*, with a just account of what the preacher said.

JOHN EVELYN, Diary

An Excellent Daughter

March 10*th*, 1685. . . . The justnesse of her stature, person, comeliness of countenance, gracefullnesse of motion, unaffected th' more than ordinary beautifull, were the least of her ornaments compared with those of her mind. Of early piety, singularly religious, spending a part of every day in private devotion, reading, and other vertuous exercises, she had collected and written out many of the most usefull and judicious periods of the books she read in a kind of commonplace, She had read and digested a considerable deale of history and of places. The French tongue was as familiar to her as English; she understood Italian, . . . and she did make very prudent and discrete reflexions upon what she had observ'd of the conversations among which she had at any time ben, . . . She had an excellent voice, to which she play'd a thorough-bass on the harpsichord, the sweetnesse of her voice and management of it added such an agreeablenesse to her countenance, without any constraint or concerne, that when she sung, it was as charming to the eye as to the eare; What shall I say, ... of the cheerefullness and agreeablenesse of her humour? condescending to the meanest servant in the family. . . . She would often reade to them, examine, instruct, and pray with them if they were sick, so as she was exceedingly beloved of every body. Piety was so prevalent an ingredient of her constitution (as I may say), that even amongst equals and superiors she no sooner became intimately acquainted, but she would endeavour to improve them, by insinuating something of religious, . . . she had one or two confidents with whom she used to passe whole dayes in fasting, reading, and prayers, especialy before the monethly communion and other solemn occasions. She abhorr'd flattery, and tho' she had aboundance of witt, the raillery was so innocent and ingenuous that it was most agreeable ; she sometimes would see a play, but since the stage grew licentious, express'd herselfe weary of them, She never play'd at cards without extreame importunity and for the company, but this was so very seldome that I cannot number it among any thing she could name a fault. No one could read prose or verse better or with more judgment ; and as she read, so she writ, not only most correct orthography, with that maturitie of judgment and exactnesse of the periods, choice of expressions, and familiarity of stile, that some letters of hers have astonish'd me and others to whom she has occasionally written. She had a talent of rehersing any comical part or poeme, as to them she might be decently free with ; she daunc'd with the greatest grace I had ever seene. . . . Nothing affected, but natural and easy as well in her deportment as in her discourse, which was always materiall, not trifling, and to which the extraordinary sweetnesse of her tone, even in familiar speaking, was very charming. Nothing was so pretty as her descending to play with little children, whom she would caresse and humour with greate delight. But she most affected to be with grave and sober men, of whom she might learne something, and improve herselfe. . . .

472

comprehensive of uncommon notions, curious of knowing every thing to some excesse, had I not sometimes repressed it. Nothing was so delightful to her as to go into my study, where she would willingly have spent whole dayes, for as I sayd she had read aboundance of history and all the best poets, even Terence, Plautus, Homer, Vergil, Ovid ; all the best romances and modern poemes ; . . . but all these are vaine trifles to the virtues which adorn'd her soule ; . . .

. . . There were foure gentlemen of quality offering to treate with me about marriage, and I freely gave her her owne choice, knowing her discretion. She showed greate indifference to marrying at all, for truly, says she to her mother (the other day), were I assured of your life and my deare father's, never would I part from you ; I love you and this home, where we serve God, above all things, nor ever shall I be so happy ; I know and consider the vicissitudes of the world, I have some experience of its vanities, and but for decency more than inclination, and that you judge it expedient for me, I would not change my condition, but rather add the fortune you designe me to my sisters, . . . This was so discreetly and sincerely utter'd that it could not but proceede from an extraordinary child, . . .

. . . Divers noble persons honour'd her funeral, some in person, others sending their coaches, of which there were six or seven with six horses, viz. the Countesse of Sunderland, Earle of Clarendon, Lord Godolphin, Sir Stephen Fox, Sir Wm. Godolphin, Viscount Falkland and others. There were distributed amongst her friends about 60 rings.   *Ibid.*

LADY : It seemeth unto me, that . . . parents and masters ought to search diligently, if their Children be adicted to any vice, to free them from the same, even from their youth, before they be over much rooted in them. I pray you to tell me the truth (for I am not any of those foolish mothers, which will never beleeve any imperfections of children, but like the Ape, It seems unto them that they be above al other faire and perfect) doe you finde any bad inclination in mine ? . . .

MASTER : . . . your sonne Guy is somwhat slowe to rise in the morning, for one must call him three or foure times before he come out of his bed, I have thought good to tell it you before his face, specially at this time, to the end it may please you to take the paine to tell him his lesson, as well as to his yonger brother.

LADY : Is it true ? Truly M. Champorte-advis, the greatest faulte is in you, it is but a benumming of the limbes that he hath, which you ought to supply, in annointing him with the juice of Birch, which is excellent for such a cure, and if you apply it but twise or thrice, You shall see a mervailous operation, But if your medicine be not of force, let me knowe it, and I will make him such a morning song that it wil awake him in all diligence and hasten him more then a good pace. Come hether freind, I am ashamd to hear that what I hear of you, . . . You have attayned to the age of nyne yeeres, at least to eight and a halfe, and seeing that you knowe your dutie, if you neglect it you deserve greater punishment than he which through ignorance doth it not. Think not that the nobilite of your Ancesters doth free you to doe all that you list, contrary-wise, it bindeth you more to followe vertue. . . .

PIERRE ERONDELL, *The French Garden* (1605)

The Joyes of *Parents* are Secret ; And so are their Griefes, and Feares : They cannot utter the one ; Nor they will not utter the other. *Children* sweeten Labours ; but they make Misfortunes more bitter : They increase the Cares of Life ; but they mitigate the Remembrance of Death. . . .

The Difference in Affection, of *Parents*, towards their severall *Children*, is many Times unequall ; And sometimes unworthy ; Especially in the *Mother* ; as Salomon saith ; *A wise Sonne rejoyceth the Father ; but an ungracious Sonne shames the Mother.* A Man shall see, where there is a house full of *Children*, one or two, of the eldest, respected, and the youngest made Wantons ; But in the middest, some that are, as it were forgotten, who, many times, neverthelesse, prove the best.   FRANCIS BACON
Essayes : Of Parents and Children (1625)

BYRON'S DAUGHTER

I shall be glad to hear from you, and of your children and mine. By the way, it seems that I have got another—a *daughter*, by that same lady, whom you will recognise by what I said of her in former letters.—I mean *her* who returned to England to become a Mamma incog., and who I pray the Gods to keep there. I am a little puzzled how to dispose of this new production (which is two or three months old, though I did not receive the accounts till at Rome) but shall probably send for and place it in a Venetian convent, to become a good Catholic, and (it may be) a *Nun*, being a character somewhat wanted in our family.

They tell me it is very pretty, with blue eyes and *dark* hair ; and, although I never was attached nor pretended attachment to the mother, still in case of the eternal war and alienation which I foresee about my legitimate daughter, Ada, it may be as well to have something to repose a hope upon. I must love something in my old age, and probably circumstances will render this poor little creature a great, and perhaps my only, comfort.

LORD BYRON
Letter to the Hon. Augusta Leigh (1817)

My little girl, Allegra, (the child I spoke to you of) has been with me these three months : she is very pretty, remarkably intelligent and a great favourite with everybody ; . . . She has very blue eyes, and that singular forehead, fair curly hair, and a devil of a Spirit—but that is Papa's.
Ibid. (1818)

About Allegra, I can only say to Claire, that I so totally disapprove of the mode of children's treatment in their [the Shelley's] family, that I should look upon the Child as going into a hospital. Is it not so ? Have they *reared* one ? Her health here has hitherto been *excellent*, and her temper not bad ; she is sometimes vain and obstinate, but always clean and cheerful, and as in a year or two I shall either send her to England or put her in a Convent for education, these defects will be remedied as far as they can in human nature. But the Child shall not quit me again to perish of Starvation and green fruit, or be taught to believe that there is no Deity. . . .

476

The Girl is not so well off as with you, but far better than with them; the fact is she is spoilt, being a great favourite with every body on account of the fairness of her skin, which shines among their dusky children like the milky way. . . . She has grown considerably, is very clean and lively. She has plenty of air and exercise at home, and she goes out daily with Me Guiccioli in her carriage to the Corso.

Ibid.
Letter to R. B. Hoppner (1820)

Clare writes me the most insolent letters about Allegra; see what a man gets by taking care of natural children. Were it not for the poor little child's sake, I am almost tempted to send her back to her atheistical mother, but that would be too bad. You cannot conceive the excess of her insolence, and I know not why, for I have been at great care and expense, taking a house in the country on purpose for her [Allegra]. She has *two* maids, and every possible attention. If Clare thinks she shall ever interfere with the child's morals or education, she mistakes; she never shall. The girl shall be a Christian, and a married woman, if possible. . . . She may see her, under proper restrictions; but she is not to throw everything into confusion with her Bedlam behaviour. To express it delicately, I think Madame Clare is a damned bitch. What think you?

Ibid. (1820)

I have neither spared trouble nor expense in the care of the child; and as she was now four years old complete, and quite above the control of the servants,—and as a *man*

477

living without any woman at the head of his house cannot much attend to a nursery—I had no resource but to place her for a time (at a high pension too) in the convent of Bagna-Cavalli, (twelve miles off) where the air is good, and where she will, at least, have her learning advanced and her morals and religion inculcated. . . . Abroad, with a fair foreign education and a portion of five or six thousand pounds, she might and may marry very respectably.   *Ibid.* (1821)

I am no enemy to religion, but the contrary. As a proof, I am educating my natural daughter a strict Catholic in a convent of Romagna ; for I think people can never have *enough* of religion, if they are to have any.   *Ibid.*
Letter to Thomas Moore (1822)

AFFECTIONATE APES

The she Apes of all sorts are wondrous fond of their little ones : and such as are made tame within house will carry them in their armes all about so soon as they have brought them into the world, keepe a shewing of them to every bodie, and they take pleasure to have them dandled by others, as if thereby they tooke knowledge that folke joyed for their safe deliverance : but such a culling and hugging of them they keep, that in the end with very clasping and clipping they kill them many times.   PLINY THE ELDER
Natural History (c. 77)
Trans. Philemon Holland (1601)

The old Lord *Gray* (our English *Achilles*) when hee was Deputie of *Ireland*, to inure his sonnes for the warre, would usually in the depths of Winter, in frost, snow, raine, and what weather soever fell, cause them at midnight to be raised out of their beds, and carried abroad on hunting till the next morning, then perhaps come wet and cold home, having for a breakefast, a browne loafe and a mouldie Cheese, or (which is ten times worse) a dish of Irish butter: and in this manner the *Spartans* and *Laconians* dieted and brought up their children, till they come into mans estate.

HENRY PEACHAM
The Compleat Gentleman (1622)

COCKERING THEM

Fond and foolish Parents . . . whose cockering and apish indulgence (to the corrupting of the minds of their Children, disabling their wits, effeminating their bodies) how bitterly doth *Plato* taxe and abhorre !

Ibid.

Branchus the son of *Apollo*, whom he begot of *Jance*, *Succrons daughter* (saith *Lactantius*) when he kept King *Admetus'* heards in *Thessaly*, now grown a man, was an earnest suitor to his mother to know his father ; the Nymph denied him, because *Apollo* had conjured her to the contrary ; yet overcome by his importunity, at last

479

she sent him to his father; when he came into *Apollo's* presence, . . . he carried himself so well, and was so fair a yong man, that *Apollo* was infinitely taken with the beauty of his person, he could scarce look off him and said he was worthy of such parents, gave him a crown of gold, the spirit of Divination, and in conclusion made him a Demi-god.

ROBERT BURTON
Anatomie of Melancholy (1621. Edition 1652)

PARTIES

Going Out to Dinner

I am vexed that you have given up going out to dinner, for you have deprived yourself of much pleasure and delight. Then too, I am afraid (for I may speak the truth to you) that you will unlearn and forget your habit of giving little dinners yourself. . . .

But by Hercules, Paetus, joking apart, I advise you to do what I believe belongs to a happy life, and associate with good, and agreeable men who are fond of you. Nothing is better suited to happy living. And I don't refer to the pleasures of appetite, but to good fellowship, and that relaxation of mind which is effected most by familiar conversation, and which is most delightful at convivial banquets, as our nation, wiser than the Greeks, call them ;

for the latter call them symposia, or syndeipna, that is, drinkings together, or dining together, but we call them "livings together," for then do our lives most meet. You see how I am trying to recall you to dinners by philosophy? Take care to keep well. The easiest way to do this is to dine out.

CICERO
Letter to Papirius Paetus (43 B.C.)

SUPPER WITH THE WARDEN OF WADHAM

I sup'd with the warden of Wadham at his lodgings, Mr. Lloyd being with me. He desir'd Mr Lloyd to bring me with him. He gave me roast meat and beat me with the spit. He told me that my book was full of contumelies, falsities, contradictions, and full of frivolous stuff. . . . He had the book there and read it scornfully.

ANTHONY WOOD
Life and Times (1674)

CAROUSING IN GUIANA

Those *Guianians* and also the borderers, and all others in that tract which I have seen are marveylous great drunkardes, in which vice I think no nation can compare with them: and at the times of their solemne feasts when the Emperor carowseth with his Captayns, tributories, and governours, the manner is thus. All those that pledge him are first stripped naked, and their bodies annoynted al over with a kinde of white *Balsamum* (by them called *Curcai*) of which

there is great plenty and yet very deare amongst them, and it is of all other the most pretious, whereof we have had good experience: when they are annointed all over, certaine servants of the Emperor having prepared gold made into fine powder blow it thorow hollow canes upon their naked bodies, until they be al shining from the foote to the head, and in this sort they sit drinking by twenties and hundreds and continue in drunkennes sometimes sixe or seven daies togither: the same is also confirmed by a letter written into *Spaine* which was intercepted, which master *Robert Dudley* told me he had seen.   SIR WALTER RALEIGH
The Discoverie of Guiana (1596)

MR. PEPYS ENTERTAINS

April 28, 1667. We had, with my wife and I, twelve at table, and very good and pleasant company, and a most neat and excellent but dear dinner; but Lord! to see with what envy they looked upon all my fine plate was pleasant; for I made the best shew I could, to let them understand me and my condition, to take down the pride of Mrs Clerke, who thinks herself very great. We sat long, and very merry, and all things agreeable; and, after dinner, went out by coaches . . . but I thought all the charge ought not to be mine, and therefore I endeavoured to part the company.

Jan. 6, 1668. By and by to my house, to a very good supper, and mighty merry, and good musick playing; and after supper to dancing and singing till about twelve at night; and then we had a good sack posset for them, and an excellent cake, cost me near 20s., of our Jane's making, which was

482

cut into twenty pieces, there being by this time so many of our company, by the coming in of . . . some others of our neighbours, young men that could dance, hearing of our dancing ; . . . And so to dancing again, and singing, with extraordinary great pleasure, till about two in the morning, and then broke up. . . . They being gone, I paid the fiddlers £3 among the four, and so away to bed, weary and mightily pleased, and have the happiness to reflect upon it as I do sometimes on other things, as going to a play or the like, to be the greatest real comfort that I am to expect in the world, and that it is that that we do really labour in the hopes of; and so I do really enjoy myself, and understand that if I do not do it now I shall not hereafter, it may be, be able to pay for it, or have health to take pleasure in it, and so fill myself up with vain expectations of pleasure and go without it.

March 1. 1669. Did resolve to go on with our feast and dancing to-morrow ; and so, after supper, left the maids to make clean the house, and to lay the cloth, and other things against to-morrow, and we to bed.

March 2. Up and at the office till noon, when home, and there I find my company come . . . I had a noble dinner for them as I almost ever had, and mighty merry, and particularly pleased with looking on Betty Turner, who is mighty pretty. We fell to dancing, and continued, only with intermission for a good supper, till two in the morning, the musick being Greeting, and another most excellent violin, and theorbo, the best in town. And so with a mighty mirth, and pleased with their dancing of jigs . . . and lastly W. Batelier's " Blackmore and Blackmore Mad," and then to a country-dance again, and so broke up with extraordinary pleasure, as being one of the days and nights of my life spent with the greatest content; and that which I can but hope to repeat again a few times in my whole life.

March 6. This day my wife made it appear to me that my late entertainment this week cost me above £12, an expence which I am almost ashamed of, though it is but once in a great while, and is the end for which, in the most part, we live, to have such a merry day once or twice in a man's life.

SAMUEL PEPYS
Diary

BALLS

Twice a week there is a ball. . . . I was there Friday last with my aunt. . . . The place was so hot, and the smell so different from what we are used to in the country, that I was quite feverish when we came away. Aunt says it is the effect of a vulgar constitution, reared among woods and mountains, and that as I become accustomed to genteel company, it will wear off.

TOBIAS SMOLLETT
Humphrey Clinker (1771)

AL FRESCO

. . . The other evening we happened to be got together in a company of eighteen people, men and women of the best fashion here, at a garden in the town to walk; when one of the ladies bethought herself of asking. Why should we not sup here ? Immediately the cloth was laid by the side of a fountain under the trees, and a very elegant supper served up ; after which another said, Come, let us sing ; and directly began herself : From singing we insensibly fell to dancing, and singing in a round ; when somebody mentioned the violins, and immediately a company of them was ordered : Minuets were held in the open air, and then came country dances, which held till four o'clock next morning, at which hour the gayest lady there proposed that such as were weary should get into their coaches, and the rest of them should dance before them, with the music in the van ; and in this manner we paraded through all the principal streets of the city, and waked every body in it. Mr Walpole had a mind to make a custom of the thing. . . .

THOMAS GRAY
Letter to his mother (Rheims, 1739)

AT MR. CONOLLY'S

The ball at Mr. Conolly's was by no means delightful—the house is small, it was hot, and was composed of young Irish.

HORACE WALPOLE
Letter to George Montagu (1759)

A THÉ

. . . and came home in the evening to a *Thé* at Mrs Montagu's. Perhaps you do not know that a *Thé* is among the stupid new follies of the winter. You are to invite fifty

to a hundred people to come at eight o'clock : there is to
be a long table, or little parties at small ones ; the cloth is
to be laid, as at breakfast ; the table is covered with rolls,
wafers, bread and butter ; and what constitutes the very
essence of a *Thé*, an immense load of hot buttered rolls
and muffins, all admirably contrived to create a nausea in
persons fresh from the dinner table. Now, of all nations
under the sun, as I take it, the English are the greatest
fools :—because the Duke of Dorset in Paris, where
people dine at two, thought this would be a pretty fashion
to introduce, we, who dine at six, must adopt this French
translation of an English fashion. . . . This will be a short
folly.

HANNAH MORE
Letter to her Sister (1788)

A Late Party

LADY : What is it a clocke ? I beleeve it is verie late.

MISTRIS : It is halfe an houre past ten Madam, almost
eleven.

LADY : We have been long at supper, then afterward we
have had dauncing . . . then came a Maske which made a
faire shewe. They played at Cardes, at Cent, at Primeroe,
at trompe, at dice, at Tables, at lurch, at Draughts, at
perforce, at pleasant, at blowing, at Queenes game, at
Chesses : The Maydens did play at purposes, at sales, to
thinke, at wonders, at states, at vertues, at answers, so
that we could not come sooner, but it is all one. We will
sleepe the longer to-morrow for amends.

PIERRE ERONDELL
The French Garden (1605)

We talked of an evening society for conversation at a house in town . . . of which Johnson said, " It will never do, Sir. There is nothing served about there, neither tea, nor coffee, nor lemonade, nor anything whatever ; and depend upon it, Sir, a man does not love to go to a place from which he comes out exactly as he went in. . . . I told Mrs Thrale once, that as she did not choose to have card tables, she should have a profusion of the best sweet-meats, and she would be sure to have company enough come to her."

JAMES BOSWELL
Life of Johnson (1791)

SOCIAL SUCCESS

The servant gave me my coat and hat, and in a glow of self-satisfaction I walked out into the night. " A delightful evening," I reflected, " the nicest kind of people. What I said about finance and French philosophy impressed them ; and how they laughed when I imitated a pig squealing."

But soon after, " God, it's awful," I muttered, " I wish I were dead.".

LOGAN PEARSALL SMITH
Trivia (1918)

PATRIOTISM

BRITISH

England as Good as Italy

I find no cause nor judge I reason why
My Countrey should give place to *Lumbardy*.
As goodly flow'rs on *Thamesis* doe growe
As beautifies the Bankes of wanton *Po* ;
As many Nymphs as haunt rich *Arnus'* strand
By silver *Severne* tripping hand in hand
Our shade's as sweet, though not to us so deere,
Because the Sunne hath greater power there.

MICHAEL DRAYTON, *England's Heroicall Epistles* (1597)

And the English as Witty as any People

Be it spoken to the honour of the English, our nation can
never want in any age such who are able to dispute the
Empire of Wit with any People in the Universe.

JOHN DRYDEN, *Dramatick Poesy* (1668)

In Fact, God's Chosen Nation

What does he then but reveal Himself to his servants, and
as his manner is, first to his Englishmen. . . . Behold now

this vast City ; a City of refuge, the mansion house of liberty, encompast and surrounded with his protection ; . . . there be pens and hands there, sitting by their studious lamps, musing, searching, revolving new notions, and idea's . . . others as fast reading, trying all things, assenting to the force of reason and convincement. What could a man require more from a Nation so pliant and so prone to seek after knowledge. What wants there to such a towardly and pregnant soile, but wise and faithfull labourers, to make a knowing people, a Nation of Prophets, of Sages, and of Worthies.

JOHN MILTON
Areopagitica (1643)

The Best Patron Saint

Henry the Fifth, he conquered all *France*,
He quartered their Arms, his Honour to advance,
He rac'd their Walls, and pull'd their Cities down,
And he garnished his Head with a double tripple Crown,
He thumped the *French*, and after home he came ;
But St. *George*, St. *George* he made the Dragon tame :
  St. George *he was for* England, *St*. Dennis *was for* France,
  Sing, Honi soit qui maly pence.

St. *David* you know loves Leeks and toasted Cheese,
And *Jason* was the Man brought home the Golden Fleece,
And *Patrick* you know he was St. *George's* Boy,
Seven Years he kept his Horse, and then stole him away,
For which Knavish Act, a Slave he doth remain ;
St. *George*, St. *George* he hath the Dragon slain :
  St. George *he was for England*, etc. . . .

Poldragon and *Cadwallader* of British Blood did boast ;
Tho' *John* of *Gaunt* his Foes did daunt, St *George* shall
    rule the Roast ;
Agamemnon, and *Clemedon,* at *Macedon* did Feats,
But compared to our Champion, they are but meerly
    Cheats ;
Brave *Malta* Knights in *Turkish* Fights, their brandish'd
    Swords outdrew ;
But St. *George,* St. *George* met the Dragon, and run him
    thro' and thro'.
   St. George *he was for England,* etc.   ANON

A New Ballad of St. George and the Dragon
(late 17th c.)

The Only Peaceful Country

Now warre is all the world about,
And every where *Erynnis* raignes,
Or else the Torch so late put out
The stench remaines.
Holland for many yeares hath beene
Of Christian tragedies the stage,
Yet seldome hath she play'd a Scene
Of bloudyer rage.
And *France* that was not long compos'd
With civill Drummes againe resounds,
And ere the old one fully clos'd
Receives new wounds.
The great *Gustavus* in the west
Plucks the Imperiall Eagles wing,
Than whom the earth did ne're invest
A fiercer King. . . .
What should I tell of *Polish* Bands,

And the blouds boyling in the North?
Gainst whom the furied *Russians*
Their troops bring forth. . . .
Only the Island which wee sowe,
(A world within the world) so farre
From present wounds, it cannot showe
An ancient skarre.
White Peace (the beautiful'st of things)
Seemes here her everlasting rest
To fix, and spreads her downy wings
Over the nest.
As when great *Jove* usurping Reigne
From the plagu'd world did her exile,
And ty'd her with a golden chaine
To one blest Isle.
Which in a sea of plenty swamme,
And Turtles sang on every bough,
A safe retreat to all that came,
As ours is now.

SIR RICHARD FANSHAWE
Ode (1630)

Writing in English

I apply'd myselfe to that resolution which *Ariosto* follow'd
against the perswasions of *Bembo*, to fix all the industry
and art I could unite to the adorning of my native tongue;
not to make verbal curosities the end, that were a toylsom
vanity, but to be an interpreter and relater of the best and
sagest things among mine own Citizens throughout this
Iland in the mother dialect. That which the greatest and
choycest wits of *Athens*, *Rome*, or modern *Italy*, and those
Hebrews of old did for their country, I in my proportion
with this over and above of being a Christian, might doe

for mine : not caring to be once nam'd abroad, though perhaps I could attaine to that, but content with these British Ilands as my world, whose fortune hath hitherto bin, that if the Athenians, as some say, made their small deeds great and renowned by their eloquent writers, *England* hath had her noble achievments made small by the unskilfull handling of monks and mechanicks.

JOHN MILTON

The Reason of Church-government urg'd against
Prelaty (1641)

British Trade

291.

The utmost Malice of their Stars is past,
    And two dire Comets which have scourg'd the Town,
In their own Plague and Fire have breath'd their last :
    Or, dimly, in their sinking sockets frown.

293.

Me-thinks already, from this Chymick flame,
    I see a City of more precious mold :
Rich as the Town which gives the *Indies* name,
    With Silver pav'd, and all divine with Gold.

295.

More great than human, now, and more *August*,
    New deified she from her Fires does rise :
Her widening Streets, on new Foundations trust,
    And, opening, into larger parts she flies.

297.

Now, like a Maiden Queen, she will behold,
    From her high Turrets, hourly Sutors come :
The East with Incense, and the West with Gold,
    Will stand, like Suppliants, to receive her Doom.

298.

The silver *Thames*, her own domestick Floud,
    Shall bear her Vessels, like a sweeping Train ;
And often wind (as of his Mistress proud)
    With longing eyes to meet her Face again

299.

The wealthy *Tagus*, and the wealthier *Rhine*,
    The glory of their Towns no more shall boast :
And *Sein*, that would with *Belgian* Rivers join,
    Shall find her Lustre stain'd, and Traffick lost.

300.

The vent'rous Merchant, who design'd more far,
    And touches on our hospitable Shore,
Charm'd with the Spendour of this Northern Star,
    Shall here unlade him, and depart no more.

301.

Our pow'rful Navy shall no longer meet,
    The wealth of *France* or *Holland* to invade :
The beauty of this Town without a Fleet,
    From all the world shall vindicate her Trade.

302.

And while this fam'd Emporium we prepare,
    The *British* Ocean shall such Triumphs boast,
That those who now disdain our Trade to share,
    Shall rob like Pyrats on our wealthy Coast.

303.

Already we have conquer'd half the War,
    And the less dang'rous part is left behind :
Our Trouble now is but to make them dare,
    And not so great to Vanquish as to Find

Thus to the Eastern wealth through Storms we go,
    But now, the Cape once doubled, fear no more :
A constant Trade-wind will securely blow,
    And gently lay us on the Spicy shore.

JOHN DRYDEN, Annus Mirabilis (1666)

A Fond Hope

When *Britain* first at heaven's command,
Arose from out the azure main ;
This was the charter of the land,
And guardian Angels sung this strain :
" Rule, *Britannia*, rule the waves ;
Britons never will be slaves."

The nations, not so blest as thee,
Must, in their turn, to tryants fall :
Whilst thou shalt flourish great and free,
The dread and envy of them all.

Still more majestic shalt thou rise,
More dreadful, from each foreign stroke :
As the loud blast that tears the skies,
Serves but to root thy native oak.

Thee haughty tyrants ne'er shall tame :
All their attempts to bend thee down,
Will but arouse thy generous flame ;
And work their woe, and thy renown.

To thee belongs the rural reign ;
Thy cities shall with commerce shine :
All thine shall be the subject main,
And every shore it circles thine.

The muses, still with freedom found,
Shall to thy happy coast repair :
Blest isle, with matchless beauty crown'd,
And manly hearts to guard the fair.
" Rule, *Britannia*, rule the waves ;
Britons never will be slaves."

JAMES THOMSON
Alfred (1740)

ROMAN

Caring for the Republic

Mind you do not suspect me of having given up my care
for the republic. Be sure of this, Paetus, that, day and
night, I have no other motive or anxiety but that my fellow
citizens should be safe and free. On no occasion do I omit
to advise, act, and look ahead. In short, I am of such a
mind that, if in this charge and administration, my life
should be taken, I shall consider myself to have done
nobly.

CICERO
Letter to Paetus (43 B.C.)

Rome shall rule

stet Capitolium
Fulgens triumphaatisque possit
Roma ferox dare jura Medis.

Horrenda late nomen in ultimas
Extendat oras, qua medius liquor
Secernit Europen ab Afro,
Qua tumidus rigat arva Nilus. . . .

Quicumque mundo terminus obstitit,
Hunc tanget armis, visere gestiens,
Qua parte debacchantur ignes,
Qua nebulae pluviique rores.

[Let the Capitol stand in glory, and let brave Rome be
able to dictate laws to the conquered Medes. Feared far
and wide, let her spread her name to the farthest shores,
where the middle sea divides Europe from the African,
where the swelling Nile waters the field. . . . Whatever
boundary is set to the world, this she shall touch with her
armies, rejoicing to visit both the regions where fires
rave, and those where there are mists and rainy dews.]

HORACE
De Roma Troiaque. Carmina, Bk. III (c. 20 B.C.)

ATHENIAN

We laugh at the simplicity of him who said that the moon
at Athens was better than the moon at Corinth.

PLUTARCH, *Morals* (c. 100)

SPARTAN

Sparta is fallen to thy lot (saith the proverbe); adorne and
honour it, for so thou are bound to doe ; be it that it is
of small or no account ; say that it is seated in an unwhole-
some aire, and subject to many diseases ; or plagued with
civill dissensions, or otherwise troubled. . . .

Ibid.
Trans. Philemon Holland (1601)
496

I have passed the world by, and I have taken history for my life. Now it is over. I regret nothing. I demand nothing. Ah, what should I demand, dear France, with whom I have lived, whom I leave with so much regret ! With what close companionship I have passed with you forty years (ten centuries). What passionate, noble, austere hours we have had together before dawn, even in winter ! What days of toil and study deep in the archives ! For you I worked, came and went, searched, wrote. Each day I gave the whole of myself, perhaps even more. Each new morning, finding you on my table, I felt myself one with you, strong with your powerful life and with your eternal youth.

But how is it that, having had the singular happiness of such a society, having lived for long years with your great soul, I have not profted more in myself ? Ah ! it is because, in order to re-create all that for you, I have had to re-tread the long road of misery, of cruel experiences, of a hundred morbid and deadly things. I have drunk too much bitterness. I have swallowed too many calamities, too many vipers, too many kings.

Well, my great France, if it has been necessary, in order to find again your life, that one man should give himself, should pass and re-pass so many times the river of the dead, he consoles himself for it ; more, he thanks you. And his greatest grief is that he must leave you here.

J. MICHELET
Preface to L'Histoire de France (1869)
(Trans.)

497

Land of coal and iron! Land of gold! land of cotton,
    sugar, rice!
Land of wheat, beef, pork! land of wool and hemp!
    land of the apple and the grape!
Land of the pastoral plains, the grass-fields of the world!
    land of those sweet-air'd interminable plateaus!
Land of the herd, the garden, the healthy house of
    adobe! . . .
Land of the eastern Chesapeake! land of the Delaware!
Land of Ontario, Erie, Huron, Michigan!
Land of the Old Thirteen! Massachusetts land! Land of
    Vermont and Connecticut!
Land of the ocean shores! land of sierras and peaks!
Land of boatmen and sailors! fishermen's land! . . .
Far breath'd land! Arctic braced! Mexican breez'd! the
    diverse! the compact!
The Pennsylvanian! the Virginian! the double Carolin-
    ian!
O all and each well-loved by me! my intrepid nations! O
    I at any rate include you all with perfect love! . . .
Here for you! and here for America!
Still the present I raise aloft, still the future of the States
    I harbinge glad and sublime,
And for the past I pronounce what the air holds of the
    red aborigines.   WALT WHITMAN
                        Starting from Paumanok (1860)

And I will report of all heroism from an American point
of view.   *Ibid.*

I was glad when they said unto me : We wil go into the house of the Lord.

Our feet shàl stand in thy gates : O Hierusalem.

Hierusalem is builded as a citie : that is a unitie in it selfe.

For thither the tribes goe up, even the tribes of the Lord ; to testifie unto Israel, to give thankes unto the Name of the Lord.

For there is the seate of judgement ; even the seate of the house of David.

O pray for the peace of Hierusalem : they shall prosper that love thee.

Peace be within thy walles : and plenteousnesse within thy palaces.

For my brethren and companions sakes : I will wish thee prosperitie.

Yea, because of the house of the Lord our God : I will seek to doe thee good.

Psalm 122
Trans. Miles Coverdale (1611 edition)

By the waters of Babylon we sate downe and wept : when wee remembred thee O Sion.

As for our harpes, we hanged them up : upon the trees that are there in.

For they that led us away captive required of us then a song and melodie, in our heavinesse : sing us one of the songs of Sion.

How shal we sing the Lords song : in a strange land.

If I forget thee, O Hierusalem : let my right hand forget
her cunning.
If I do not remember thee, let my tongue cleave to the
roofe of my mouth : yea, if I preferre not Hierusalem
in my mirth.

Ibid. Psalm 137

GERMAN

Deutschland, Deutschland, über alles,
Über alles in der Welt.

H. V. FALLERSLEBEN, Das Lied der Deutschen

Deutsche Worte hor ich wieder—
Sei begrüsst mit Herz und Hand !
Land der Freude, Land der Lieder,
Schönes heitres Vaterland !

Ibid. Heimkehr

ITALIAN

Bella Italia, amate sponde,
Pur vi torno a riveder !
Trema in petto, e si confonde
L'alma oppressa dal piacer,
Tua bellezza, che di pianti
Fonte amara ognor ti fu,
Di stranieri e crudi amanti
T'avea posta in servitù.

Ma bugiarda e mal sicura
La speranza fia de' re ;
Il giardino di natura
No, pei barbari non è.

VINCENZO MONTI, Marengo (1802)

PORTUGUESE

Gentlemen, remember that you are Portuguese.
> *Address to troops before battle by a Portuguese*
> *General during Peninsular War*

PET ANIMALS

OSTRICHES

I beleeve you must be carefull of your Ostridge this returne of cold wether, least it perish by being bredd in so hot a countrey and perhaps not seen snowe before or very seldome, so that I beleeve it must bee kept under covert and have strawe to sitt upon and water sett by it to take of both day and night ; must have it observed how it sleepeth and whether not with the head under the wing, especially in cold wether : whether it bee a wachfull and quick hearing bird like a goose, for it seemes to bee like a goose in many circumstances. It seemes to eat anything

501

that a goose will feed on, and like a goose to love the same
green hearbes and to delight in Lettuce, endive, sorrell,
&c. . . . To geese they give oates &c moystnd with beere,
butt sometimes they are inebriated with it. If you give
any Iron, it may be wrapped up in dowe or past : perhaps
it will not take it up alone. You may trie whether it will
eat a worme or a very small eele ; whether it will drinck
milk, and observe in what manner it drincks water. . . . You
may lay a bay leafe by the oestridge and observe whether it
will take it up. . . . When it is Anatomized, I suppose the
sceleton will bee made and you may stuffe the skinne with
the fethers on. . . . If it delights not in salt things you
may trie it with an olive.

SIR THOMAS BROWNE
Letter to his son Edward (1681)

LAMPREYS

Caius Hirtius was the man by himselfe, that before all
others devised a pond to keep Lampreys in. . . . In processe of time folk grew to have a love and cast a fancy to
some one severall fish above the rest. For the excellent
Orator *Hortensius* had an house at Bauli, upon the side
that lieth to Baiae, and a fish-pond to it belonging : and
he took such an affection to one Lamprey in that poole,
that when it was dead (by report) he could not hold but
weep for love of it. Within the same poole belonging to
the said house, *Antonia* the wife of *Drusus* (unto whom
they fell by inheritance) had so great a liking to another
Lamprey, that she could find in heart to decke it, and to
hang a paire of golden earings about the guils thereof.

And surely for the novelty of this strange sight, and the
name that went thereof, many folke had a desire to see
Bauli, and for nothing else.

PLINY THE ELDER, *Natural History* (c. 77)
Trans. Philemon Holland (1601)

SPARROWS

Sparrow, the darling of my girl, with whom she plays,
whom she holds in her lap, or gives you her finger to
peck, and incites you to bite sharply. . . .

My girl's sparrow is dead, my girl's pet, whom she
loved more than her own eyes : for he was as sweet as
honey, and knew her as well as a girl knows her own
mother. Nor would he move from her lap, but hopping
about now here now there, chirped continuously to his
mistress only. Now he goes along the dark road to the
place whence, they say, none returns.

CATULLUS, *Carmina* (c. 60 B.C.)

And prytily he wolde pant
When he saw an ant.
Lord, how he wolde prye
After a buterflye !
Lord, how he wolde hoppe
After the grassoppe !
And when I said Phip, Phip !
Than he wolde lepe and skyppe,
And take me by the lyppe. JOHN SKELTON
The Boke of Philipp Sparrowe (c. 1500)

503

And so home and to dinner with my father and sister and family, mighty pleasant all of us; and, among other things, with a sparrow that our Mercer hath brought up now for three weeks, which is so tame that it flies up and down, and upon the table, and eats and pecks, and do every thing so pleasantly, that we are mightily pleased with it.

SAMUEL PEPYS
Diary (May 31, 1666)

DRAGONS

There was a little Dragon-whelp bred in *Arcadia*, and brought up familiarly with a little boy from his infancy, until the Boy became a young Man, and the Dragon also became of great stature, so that one of them loved another so well as Man and beast could love together, or rather two play-fellows from the Cradle. At last the friends of the Boy seeing the Dragon grow so great in so short a space, began to be suspicious of him ; whereupon they took the bed wherein the Boy and the Dragon were lodged, and carryed the same into a far remote place of Woods and Wildernesse, and there set down the bed with the Boy and the Dragon together. The boy after a little while returned, and came home again to his friends ; the Dragon wandered up and down in the Woods, feeding upon herbs and poyson, according to his nature, and never more cared for the habitation of men, but rested content with a solitary life. In the length of time it came to passe that the boy grew to be a perfect man, and the Dragon also remained in the Wood, and although absent one from the other, yet mutually loving as well as ever. It hapned that this young man travelled through that place where the Dragon was lodged, and fell among theeves, when the young man saw their swords about his ears, he cryed out, and the Dragons den being not far off, his cry came to the Dragons ears, who instantly knowing the voice of his play-fellow, answered the same with another, at whose hissing the theeves grew afraid, and began to run away, but their legs could not carry them so fast as to escape the Dragons teeth and claws ; for he came speedily to release his friend, and all the theeves that he could find, he put to cruel death, then did he accompany his friend out of the place of peril, and returned back again to his den, neither remembering wrath, that he was exposed to the Wildernesse, and there left by his play-fellow nor yet like perverse men, forsaking their old friends in danger.

PLINY THE ELDER
Natural History (c. 77)
Trans. Philemon Holland (1601)

HORSES

Caligula . . . loved *Prasinus* the Cochman so wel, that for good wil to the master, he bid his horse to supper, gave him wine to drink in cups of estate, set barly graines of golde before him to eate, and swore by no bugs, that hee would make him a Consul : which thing (saith *Dion*) had bin performed, had hee not bin prevented by suddain death.

STEPHEN GOSSON
The Schoole of Abuse (1579)

Among those domesticall creatures that converse with us, there be many things worth the knowledge : and namely, as touching dogges . . . and also horses. I have heard it credibly reported of a dogge, that in defence of his master fought hard against theeves . . . and albeit he were sore wounded even to death, yet would he not abandon the dead body of his master, but drave away both wild foule and savage beast, from seizing of his carkasse. Also of another in Epirus, who in a great assembly of people knowing the man that had murdered his Mr. flew upon him with open mouth, barking and snapping at him so furiously . . . until he at length confessed the fact. . . . *Duris* makes mention of another dogge, which he named *Hircanus*, that so soone as the funerall fire of king *Lysimachus* his master was set a-burning, leapt into the flame. . . . A dog that *Nicomedes* king of Numidia kept flew upon the queene Consingis his wife, and al to mangled and worried her, for toying and dallying overwantonly with the king her husband. . . . They be the only beasts of all others that know their masters, and let a stranger unknown be come never so suddenly, they are ware of his coming and give warning. They alone know their own names, and all those of the house by their speech. Be the way never so long, and the place from whene they came never so far, they remember it, and can go thither againe. . . . As furious and raging as they be otherwhiles, yet appeased they wil be and quieted, by a man sitting downe upon the ground. . . . The longer we live, the more things we observe and marke still in these dogges. . . .

PLINY THE ELDER, *Natural History* (c. 77)

Trans. Philemon Holland (1601)

Of the Delicate, Neate, and Pretty Kind of Dogges called the Spaniel Gentle, or the Comforter, in Latine Melitoeus or Fotor

These dogges are litle, pretty, proper and fyne, and sought for to satisfie the delicatenesse of daintie dames, and wanton womens wills, instrumentes of folly for them to play and dally withall, to tryfle away the treasure of time, to withdraw their mindes from more commendable exercises, and to content their corrupted concupiscencees with vaine disport (a selly shift to shunne yrcksome ydlenesse). These puppies the smaller they bee, the more pleasure they provoke, as more meete play fellowes for minsing mistresses to beare in their bosoms, to keepe company withal in their chambers, to succour with sleepe in bed, and nowrishe with meate at bourde, to lay in their lappes, and licke their lippes as they ryde in their waggons. . . . That plausible proverbe verifie upon a Tyraunt, namely that he loved his sowe better then his sonne, may well be applyed to these kinde of people who delight more in dogges that are deprived of all possibility of reason, then they doe in children that be capable of wisedome and judgement.

> JOHN CAIUS, *Treatise of English Dogges* (1570)
> Trans. from Latin by Abraham Fleming (1576)

Of the Mastive or Bandogge . . . called in Latine Canis Lunarius, in Englishe the Mooner

Because he doth nothing else but watch and warde . . . wasting the wearisome night season without slombering or sleeping, bawing and yawing at the Moone . . . a qualitie in mine opinion strange to consider. *Ibid.*

. . . They meet their Master with reverence and joy, crouching or bending a little, (like shamefast and modest persons) and although they know none but their Masters and familiars, yet will they help any man against another Wilde beast. . . .

There was a Dog in *Venice* which had been three years from his Master, yet knew him again in the Market place ; discerning him from thousands of people present. He remembreth any man which giveth him meat ; when he fauneth upon a man he wringeth his skin in the forehead. . . . *Ælianus* thinketh that Dogs have reason. . . . There was a Dog in *Africa* in a ship, which in the absence of the Mariners came to a pitcher of oil to eat some of it, and the mouth of the pot being too narrow for his head to enter in (because the pot was not full) he devised to cast flint stones into the vessel, whereby the Oil rose to the top of the Pitcher, and so he eat therof his fill, giving evident testimony thereby, that he discerned by nature, that heavy things will sink down and light things will rise up and flie aloft. . . .

When a Dragon was setting upon *Orpheus*, as he was occupied in hawking, by his Dogs his life was saved, and the Dragon devoured. . . .

There was never anything more strange in the nature of Dogs, to then that which happened at *Rhodes* besieged by the *Turks*, for the Dogs did there discern between Christians and *Turks* ; for towards the *Turks* they were most eager, furious and unappeasable, but towards Christians, although unknown, most easie, peaceable, and placidious.

Of the Mimick, or Getulian-Dog, and the little Melitaean-Dogs of Gentlewomen

There is also in England two other sorts of Dogs, . . . being apt to imitate all things it seeeth, for which cause some have thought that it was conceived by an Ape ; for in wit and disposition it resembleth an Ape, but in face sharpe and blacke like a Hedge-hog, having a short recurved body, very long legs, shaggie hair, and a short tail ; . . . these being brought up with Apes in their youth learn very admirable and strange feats, whereof there were great plenty in *Egypt* in the time of King *Ptolemy*, which were taught to leap and play, and dance, at the hearing of musick, and in many poor mens houses they served in stead of servants for divers uses.

These are also used by Players and Puppet-Mimicks to work strange tricks, for the sight whereof they get much money : such an one was the Mimicks dog, of which *Plutarch* writeth that he saw in a publick spectacle at *Rome* before the Emperor *Vespasian*. The Dog was taught to act a play, wherein were contained many persons parts . . . at last there was given him a piece of bread, wherein, as wass said, was poison, having virtue to procure a dead sleep, which he received and swallowed: and presently after the eating thereof he began to reel and stagger to and fro like a drunken man, and fell down to the ground as if he had been dead, and so lay a good space not stirring foor nor limb, . . . but when he percived by the time and other signes that it was requisite to arise, he first opened his eyes, and lift up his head a little, then stretched forth himself like as one doth when he riseth from sleep ; at the last, up he getteth and turneth to him to whom that part belonged, not without the joy and good content of *Caesar* and all other the beholders. . . .

There is a Town in *Pachynus*, a Promontory of *Sicily* (called *Melita*) from whence are transported many fine little dogs they were accounted the Jewels of Women, but now the said Town is possessed by Fisher-men, and there is no such reckoning made of those tender little Dogs, for these are not bigger than common Ferrets, or Weasils, yet are they not small in understanding, nor mutable in their love to men : for which cause they are also nourished tenderly for pleasure. . . .

Now a dayes they have found another breed of little Dogs in all Nations. . . . They are not above a foot, or half a foot long, and alway the lesser, the more delicate and precious. . . . They are of pleasant disposition and will leap and bite without pinching, and bark prettily, and some of them are taught to stand upright holding up their fore legs like hands ; other to fetch and carry in their mouths, that which is cast unto them. . . .

Publius had a little dog (called *Issa*) having about the neck two silver bels, upon a silken Collar, which for the neatness thereof, seems to be rather a picture than a creature ; whereof *Martial* made an elegant epigram.

EDWARD TOPSELL
History of Four-Footed Beasts and Serpents (1607)

Beloved little Bitch

Issa is more wicked than Catullus's sparrow, Issa is cleaner than a dove's kiss, Issa is more caressing than any girl, Issa is more precious than Indian gems, Issa is Publius's beloved little bitch. You think she is speaking if she whines ; she feels joy and grief. She lies resting on his neck, and sleeps so that her breathing is not heard ; and when impelled by the requirements of her inside, she never by one drop betrays the coverlet, but with coaxing paw she rouses and warns you to put her down from the bed, and asks to be taken up again. Such is the modesty of this chaste little dog that she knows nothing of love, nor can we find a husband worthy of so tender a maid. In order that death may not take her from his sight altogether, Publius has expressed her in a picture, in which you will see so similar an Issa that not even she herself is so like herself.

MARTIAL, Epigrams (c. 84)

A little Cur-Dog

This William (the founder of this family) had a little cur-dog which loved him, and the earl loved the dog. When the earle dyed the dog would not goe from his master's dead body, but pined away, and dyed under the hearse ; the picture of which dog is under his picture, in the Gallery at Wilton. Which putts me in mind of a parallell storie in Appian (Syrian Warr) :—Lysimachus being slaine, a dog that loved him stayed a long time by the body and defended it from birds and beasts till such time as Thorax, king of Pharsalia, finding it out gave it buriall.

JOHN AUBREY
Brief Lives : William Herbert, 1st Earl of Pembroke

CATS

He is a full lecherous beast in youth, swift, pliant, and merrie, and leapeth and reseth on althing that is to fore him : and is led by a straw, and playeth therewith : and is a right heavie beast in age and full sleepy, and lieth slily in wait for mice : and is ware they be, more by smell than by sight, and hunteth and reseth on them in privy

places : and when he taketh a mouse, he plaieth therewith, and eateth him after the play. . . . And they maketh
a ruthful noise and gastful, when one proffereth to fight
with another.

BARTHOLOMEW ANGLICUS, *De Proprietatibus Rerum*
Trans. John Trevisa (1398, modernized 1582)

Turkie Gentlewomen, that are perpetuall prisoners, still
mewed up according to the custome of the place, have
little else beside their household businesse, or to play with
their children, to drive away time, but to dally with their
cats, which they have *in deliciis*, as many of our Ladies
and Gentlewomen use Monkies and little Doggs.

ROBERT BURTON
The Anatomy of Melancholy (1621. Edition 1632)

GEESE

Their watch and warde is good and gainfull, being indeed
better than that of the dogge, as hath beene shewed long
agoe by the geese of the Capitoll in Rome, who awaking
the souldiers and standing watch, were the cause that the
enimie was repulsed and driven backe : againe, she
declareth when winter draweth nigh by her continuall
squeaking and crying, she layeth egges, hatcheth goslings,
affoordeth feathers twise a yeere for the bed, for writing,
and for shaftes, which are gathered at the spring and
Autumne.

CHARLES ESTIENNE, *La Maison Rustique* (1572)
Trans. Richard Surflet (1600)

The householder shall make choice for the keeping of his bees of some fit and secret place in his Garden of Pleasure, in the bottome of some valley if it be possible, to the end they may the more easily rise on high to fly abroad to get their food, as also for that when they be laden, they descend the more easily downward with their load. But let us see to it especially that the place be open to the South sun, and yet notwithstanding, neither exceeding in heat nor in cold, but temperate ; and that the same by hill, wall, or some other rampart be defended from windes and tempests, and so also as that they may flie their sundrie and severall waies for to get diversitie of pastures, and so againe may returne to their little cottages laden with their composition of hony ; and againe in such a place, as wherein there is great quantitie of thyme, organie, ivie, winter savorie, wild thyme, rosemary, sage, corne-flag or gladdon, gilleflowres, violets, white lilies, roses, flowre-gentill, basil, saffron, beanes, poppie, melilot, milfoile and other sweet herbs.

Ibid.

HARES

Puss grew presently familiar, would leap into my lap, raise himself upon his hinder feet, and bite the hair from my temples. . . . He was ill three days, during which time I nursed him . . . and by constant care and trying him with a variety of herbs, restored him to perfect health. No creature could be more grateful than my patient after his recovery; a sentiment which he most significantly expressed, by licking my hand. . . . It was visible, from many symptoms which I have not room to enumerate, that he was happier in human society than when shut up with his natural companions. . . . You will not wonder, Sir, that my intimate acquaintance with these specimens of their kind has taught me to hold the sportsman's amusement in abhorrence : he little knows what amiable creatures he persecutes, of what gratitude they are capable, how cheerful they are in their spirits, what enjoyment they have of life, and that, impressed as they seem with a peculiar dread of man, it is only because man gives them peculiar cause for it.   WILLIAM COWPER

Letter to the *Gentleman's Magazine* (June 1784)

BYRONIC ZOO

Lord B.'s establishment consists, besides servants, of ten horses, eight enormous dogs, five cats, an eagle, a crow, and a falcon; and all these, except the horses, walk about the house, which every now and then resounds with their unarbitrated quarrels, as if they were the masters of it. . . .

After I have sealed my letter, I find that my enumeration of the animals in this Circaean palace was defective, and that in a material point. I have just met on the grand stair-case five peacocks, two guinea-hens, and an Egyptian crane. I wonder who all these animals were, before they were changed into these shapes.

PERCY BYSSHE SHELLEY

Letter to Thomas Love Peacock (Ravenna, 1821)

Neither can I but admire what I find recorded in the historie of the Netherlands, of a Sea-woman who was taken up in the streights of a broken dike near to the towns of *Campen* and *Edam*, brought thither by a sea-tempest and high tide, where floating up and down and not finding a passage out again (by reason that the breach was stopped after the floud) was espied by certain women and their servants as they went to milk their kine in the neighbouring pastures, who at the first were afraid of her, but seeing her often they resolved to take her, which they did ; and bringing her home, she suffered her self to be clothed, fed with bread, milk, and other meats, and would often strive to steal again into the sea, but being carefully watched she could not : moreover she learned to spinne, and perform other pettie offices of women, but at the first they cleaned her of the sea-mosse which did stick about her. She was brought from *Edam* and kept at *Harlam*, where she would obey her mistris, and (as she was taught) kneel down with her before the crucifix, never spake, but lived dumbe and continued alive (as some say) fifteen years ; then she died. This is credibly reported by the Authour of that history, by the writer of the Chronicles of Holland, and in a book called the *Theatre of cities*. They took her in the yeare of our Lord 1403.

JOHN SWAN
Speculum Mundi (1635)

PLAY-GOING

REASONS FOR GOING TO THE PLAY

The *Play-House* is an inchanted Island, where nothing
appears in reality what is, nor what should be. 'Tis
frequented by persons of all degrees and equalities whatsoever, that have a great deal of idle time lying upon their
hands and can't tell how to employ it worse. Here *Lords*
come to laugh, and to be laughed at for being there, and
seeing their qualities ridicul'd by every triobolary poet.
Knights come hither to learn the amorous Smirk, the
alamode Grin, the antick Bow, the new-fashioned
Cringe, and how to adjust their Phiz. . . . Hither come the
Country-Gentlemen to shew their shapes, and trouble the
Pit with their Impertinence about Hawking, Hunting,
their handsome Wives, and their Housewifery. . . . Here
the Ladies come to shew their Cloathes.

TOM BROWN
Amusements Serious and Comicall (1700)

SUCH A SET OF BEINGS!

" Bear me, some God, O quickly bear me hence,
To wholesome solitude, the nurse of———"

"Sense," I was going to add in the words of Pope, till I recollected that *pence* had a more appropriate meaning, and was as good a rhyme. This apostrophe broke from me on coming from the opera, the first I ever *did*, the last I trust I ever *shall* go to. For what purpose has the Lord of the universe made His creature man with a comprehensive mind? Why make him a little lower than the angels? Why give him the faculty of thinking, the power of wit and memory; and, to crown all, an immortal and never-dying spirit? Why all this wondrous waste, this prodigality of bounty, if the mere animal senses of sight and hearing (by which he is not distinguished from the brutes that perish) would have answered the end as well; and yet I find the same people are seen at the opera every night—an amusement written in a language the greater part of them do not understand, and performed by such a set of beings! . . . Going to the Opera, like getting drunk, is a sin that carries its own punishment with it, and that a very severe one.

HANNAH MORE
Letter to her Sister (1775)

MORTIFYING THE POETS

MELLEFONT: But does your Lordship never see Comedies?
LORD FROTH: O yes, sometimes—But I never laugh.
MEL.: No?
LORD F.: Oh no,—Never laugh indeed, Sir.
CARELESS: No! why what d'ye go there for?
LORD F.: To distinguish myself from the Commonalty,

517

and mortifie the Poets; the Fellows grow so conceited, when any of their foolish Wit prevails upon the Side-Boxes.—I swear—he, he, he, I have often constrained my inclination to laugh—he, he, he, to avoid giving them encouragement.

WILLIAM CONGREVE
The Double-Dealer (1694)

FAIR WENCHES

From the first age the *Theater* hath bin,
Even like a trap to take faire wenches in.
Frequent the Tilt-yard, for there oft-times are
Clusters of people thronging at the barre.
Thou shalt not need there with thy fingers beckon,
Of winking signes, or close nods doe not reckon:
But where thy Mistris sits doe thou abide,
Who shall forbid thee to attaine her side,
As neare as the place suffers see thou get,
That none betwixt thee and her selfe beset:
If thou beest mute and bashfull, I will teach
How to begin, and breake the ice of speech.
Aske whose that horse was, what he was did guide
    him,
Whence comes he, if he well or ill did ride him.
Which in the course of barriers best did do,
And whom she likes, him doe thou favour to.

OVID
Art of Love (2 B.C.)
Trans. Thomas Heywood (1600?)

In our assemblies at playes in *London*, you shall see suche heaving and shooving, suche ytching and shouldring, to sitte by women; Suche care for their garments, that they bee not trode on; Such eyes to their lappes, that no chippes light in them: Such pillowes to their backes, that they take no hurte: Such masking in their eares, I knowe not what: Such giving them Pippins to passe the time: Suche playing at foote Saunt without Cardes: Such ticking, such toying, such smiling, such winking, and such manning them home, when the sportes are ended, that it is a right Comedie, to marke their behaviour, to watche their conceites.

STEPHEN GOSSON
The Schoole of Abuse (1579)

PRISON

A HOME FROM HOME

The doctor then proposed that I should be removed into the prison infirmary; and this proposal was granted. . . . The infirmary was divided into four wards, with as many small rooms attached to them . . . and one of these, not very providently (for I had not yet learned to think of money) I turned into a noble room. I papered the walls with a trellis of roses; I had the ceiling coloured with clouds and sky; the barred windows I screened with Venetian blinds; and when my bookcases were set up with their busts, and flowers and a pianoforte made their appearance, perhaps there was not a handsomer room on that side the water. . . . Charles Lamb declared there was no other such room, except in a fairy tale.

But I possessed another surprise; which was a garden. There was a little yard outside the room, railed off from another belonging to the neighbouring ward. This yard I shut in with green palings, adorned it with a trellis, bordered it with a thick bed of earth from a nursery, and even contrived to have a grass-plot. The earth I filled with flowers and young trees. There was an apple-tree, from which we managed to get a pudding the second year. As to my flowers, they were allowed to be perfect. Thomas Moore, who came to see me with Lord Byron, told me he had seen no such heart's-ease. I bought the Parnaso Italiano while in prison, and used often to think of a passage in it while looking at this miniature piece of horticulture: Here I wrote and read in fine weather, sometimes under an awning. In autumn, my trellises were hung with scarlet-runners, which added to the flowery investment. I used to shut my eyes in my arm-chair, and affect to think myself hundreds of miles off. . . .

I entered prison the 3rd of February 1813, and removed to my new apartments the 16th of March, happy to get out of the noise of the chains. When I sat amidst my books, and saw the imaginary sky overhead, and my paper roses about me, I drank in the quiet at my ears as if they were thirsty. . . .

These rooms, and the visits of my friends, were the bright side of my captivity. . . . My friends were allowed to be with me till ten o'clock at night. . . . Even William Hazlitt, who there first did me the honour of a visit, would stand interchanging amenities at the threshold. . . . The Lambs came to comfort me in all weathers, hail or sunshine, in daylight and in darkness, even in the dreadful frost and snow of the beginning of 1814.

LEIGH HUNT
Autobiography (1850)

WRITING HISTORY

Sir *Walter* was left to his Majesties mercy, who thought him too great a Malecontent to have his Freedom, and probably too innocent to lose his Life. Therefore to the Tower he is confin'd, but permitted to enjoy *Libera Custodia* ; where he improv'd his Imprisonment to the greatest advantage of Learning and Inquisitive Men. Since his Majesty had civilly buried him, and as it were banish'd him this World, he thought it no Treason to disturb the Ashes of former times, and bring to view the Actions of deceased Heroes. . . . After some time past there, he was delivered of that great *Minerva*, the *History of the World* ; a Book which for the exactness of its Chronology, Curiousness of its Contexture and Learning of all sorts, seems to be the Work of an Age. An History which never yet met with a Detractor, and was the Envy, if some Authors may be credited, of King James himself, who thought none could out-do him at the Pen.

LIFE OF SIR WALTER RALEIGH
(*Prefaced to* 1687 *edition of the History of the World*)

When Acrisius inquired of the oracle how he should get male children, the god said that his daughter would give birth to a son who would kill him. Fearing that, Acrisius built a brazen chamber under ground, and there imprisoned Danae. However, she was seduced, some say by Proteus . . . but some say that Zeus had intercourse with her in the shape of a stream of gold which poured through the roof. When Acrisius afterwards learned that she had got a child Perseus, he would not believe that she had been seduced by Zeus.

APOLLODORUS
The Library (c. 1st Century A.D.)

LITERARY INDUSTRY

In prison Boethius composed his work on the Consolations of Philosophy ; and Grotius wrote his Commentary on Saint Matthew, with other works. . . .

Buchanan, in the dungeons of a monastery in Portugal, composed his excellent Paraphrases of the Psalms of David.

Cervantes composed the most agreeable book in the Spanish language during his captivity in Barbary. . . .

Louis the Twelfth, when Duke of Orleans, was long imprisoned in the Tower of Bourges : applying himself to his studies, which he had hitherto neglected, he became, in consequence, an enlightened monarch.

Margaret, queen of Henry the Fourth, King of France,

confined in the Louvre, pursued very warmly the studies of elegant literature, and composed a very skilful apology for the irregularities of her conduct. . . .

The plan of the *Henriade* was sketched, and the greater part composed, by Voltaire during his imprisonment in the Bastile ; and the *Pilgrim's Progress* of Bunyan was performed in the circuit of a prison's walls.

Howell, the author of *Familiar Letters*, wrote the chief part of them, and almost all his other works, during his long confinement in the Fleet prison. . . .

Lydiat, while confined in the King's Bench for debt, wrote his Annotations on the Parian Chronicle, which were first published by Prideaux. . . .

The learned Selden, committed to prison for his attacks on the divine right of tithes and the king's prerogative, prepared during his confinement his *History of Eadmer*, enriched by his notes.

Freret, when imprisoned in the Bastile, was permitted only to have Bayle for his companion. His dictionary was always before him, and his principles were got by heart. To this circumstance we owe his works, animated by all the powers of scepticism.

Sir Willian Davenant finished his poem of Gondibert during his confinement by the rebels in Carisbrook Castle. . . .

De Foe, confined in Newgate for a political pamphlet, began his " Review," a periodical paper. . . .

Wicquefort's curious work " On Ambassadors " is dated from his prison, where he had been confined for state affairs. He softened the rigour of those heavy hours by several historical works.

ISAAC DISRAELI

Curiosities of Literature (1791–1823)

I now write to you from my Confinement in Newgate, where I have been since Monday last was sennight, and where I enjoy myself with much more Tranquillity than I have known for upwards of a Twelvemonth past; having a Room intirely to myself, pursuing the Amusements of my Poetical Studies, uninterrupted, and agreeably to my mind. I thank the Almighty, I am now all collected in myself; and though my Person is in Confinement, my Mind can expatiate on ample and useful Subjects with all the freedom imaginable. I am now more conversant with the Nine than ever; and if instead of a Newgate Bird, I may be allow'd to be a Bird of the Muses, I assure you, Sir, I sing very freely in my Cage; somtimes indeed in the Plaintive notes of the Nightinghale; but at others in the cheerfull strains of the Lark.

RICHARD SAVAGE
Letter to a Friend (1743)

NAIL-CARVING

The publisher of a Leyden Gazette, who had printed a satire on Louis XIV, was secretly seized in Holland, brought away from thence, and shut up in a cage at St. Michael. . . . This cage was . . . of strong bars of wood. . . . On some of the bars were figures and landscapes, which are said to have been cut by this unhappy man with his nails.

SHOLTO AND REUBEN PERCY
Anecdotes (1826)

Grotius having taken part in the political disputes which agitated his native country in the early part of the 17th century, was condemned to imprisonment for life in the Castle of Louvestein. The malice of his persecutors was, however, fortunately disappointed by the ingenuity of his wife. Having obtained permission to remove some books from the prison, she sent a large chest for the purpose ; but instead of books, she deposited a more valuable treasure, the illustrious Grotius himself ; and . . . he was thus enabled to make his escape.

Nothing more strongly marks the genius and fortitude of Grotius than the manner in which he employed his time during his imprisonment. . . . He resumed his law studies, which other employments had interrupted. He gave a portion of his time to moral philosophy, which induced him to translate the ancient poets collected by Stoboeus, and the fragments of Menander and Philemon. Every Sunday was devoted to reading the Scriptures, and to writing his Commentaries on the New Testament. . . . He composed his treatise in Dutch verse on the Truth of the Christian Religion. Sacred and profane authors occupied him alternately.

Ibid.

LIBERTY AND LOVE

You can't imagine, my friend, the charm of a prison, where one has only to account to one's own heart for the employment of one's time. No tiresome distractions, no

troublesome sacrifices, no petty cares, none of those duties
. . . none of those conflicts of law and social prejudice
with the dearest inspirations of one's nature. No jealous
eye spies on the expression of what one feels, or on the
occupation one has chosen; no-one suffers from one's
melancholy or from one's inactivity; no-one expects
effort from one, or exacts sentiments which are not at
one's command. Given up to oneself, to truth, without
obstacles to conquer or battles to sustain, one can, without wounding the rights or the affections of any one at
all, abandon one's soul to its own integrity, find again
one's moral independence on the breast of a seeming
captivity, and exercise it with a fullness from which social
encounters almost always detract. I was not even allowed
to seek that independence, and to relieve myself thus of
the charge of the happiness of another . . . events have
procured for me that which I could not have obtained
without a sort of crime. How I cherish the irons in which
I am free to love you with undivided mind, and to occupy
myself with you all the time! Here, all other obligation is
superseded; I owe myself only to him who loves me, and
deserves so well to be loved. Follow your career generous-
ly, serve your country, save liberty; all your actions are
a joy to me, and your career is my triumph. . . . I thank
heaven for having substituted my present chains for
those which I wore before. . . . If I am to gain no more,
let me keep this situation until my complete deliverance
from a world given over to injustice and misfortune. . . .

I have better air here than at the Abbaye, and I can go,
when I choose, into the pleasant appartment of the *Con-
cierge*. . . . I usually stay in my cell. It is large enough to
contain a chair beside the bed. At a little table I read,
draw and write, your portrait on my breast or under my

eyes. I thank heaven for having known you, for having let me taste the inexpressible happiness of loving, and of being loved with that generosity, that delicacy, which vulgar souls will never know, and which are above all their pleasures. . . .

Goodbye, man the most loved by the most loving woman!

MADAME ROLAND
Letter to François Buzot
(Prison of Sainte-Pélagie, 1793)

TACITUS

In prison, as elsewhere, Madame Roland beguiled her leisure with books and flowers. Tacitus was then her favourite author, and her consciousness of her own talents made her conceive the idea of writing the annals of France, but this plan did not materialise.

J. REVENEL
Introduction to Mémoires de Mme Roland (1840)

A FORGER PETTED

Mr Ryland, the artist, who was executed in 1789 for forgery, so conciliated the friendship of the governor of Tothill Fields Bridewell, where he was confined, that he not only had the liberty of the whole house and garden, but when the other prisoners were locked up of an evening the governor used to take him out with him, and range the fields to a considerable distance.

SHOLTO AND REUBEN PERCY
Anecdotes (1826)

The Marquis de la Fayette and several French officers . . . were long confined in the castle of Olmutz. . . . Their apartments were so constructed that they were within hearing of each other when standing at the windows of their respective chambers. . . . There is at Paris a number of tunes called the airs of the Pont de Neuf, or those popular ballads that were sung at the corners of the streets. To strike up a few of the notes was to recall to memory the words that accompanied them. The captives of Olmutz gradually composed for themselves a vocal vocabulary, by whistling these notes at their windows ; and this vocabulary, after a short time, became so complete, and even rich, that two or three notes from each air formed their alphabet and effected their intercourse. By this means they communicated news to each other concerning their families, the progress of the war etc ; and when, by good fortune, one of them had procured a gazette, he *whistled* the contents of it to his partners in suffering. *Ibid.*

KITES, CROWS, AND CONDUITS

He was a close prisoner in the Tower, tempore regis Jacobi, for speaking too boldly in the Parliament House of the king's profuse liberality to the Scots. He made a comparison of a conduit, whereinto water came, and ran-out afarre-off. " Now," said he, " this pipe reaches as far as Edinborough." He was kept a close prisoner there, i.e., his windowes were boarded up. Through a small chinke he sawe once a crowe, and another time, a kite; the sight whereof, he sayd, was a great pleasure to him. He, with much adoe, obtained at length the favour to have his little son Bennet to be with him ; and he then made this distich, viz :—

Parvule, dum puer es, nec scis incommoda linguae,
Vincula da linguae, vel tibi vincla dabit.

JOHN AUBREY
Brief Lives : John Hoskyns (c. 1680)

FREEDOM OF SOUL AND OF LOVE

When love with unconfined wings
Hovers within my gates ;
And my divine *Althea* brings
To whisper at the grates ;
When I lye tangled in her haire,
And fettered to her eye,
The birds, that wanton in the aire,
Know no such liberty.

When flowing cups run swiftly round
With no allaying *Thames*,
Our carelesse heads with roses bound,
Our hearts with loyal flames ;
When thirsty grief in wine we steepe,
When healths and draughts go free,
Fishes, that tipple in the deepe,
Know no such libertie.

When (like committed linnets) I
With shriller throat shall sing
The sweetnes, mercy, majesty,
And glories of my King.

When I shall voyce aloud, how good
He is, how great should be,
Inlarged winds, that curle the flood,
Know no such liberty.

Stone walls doe not a prison make,
Nor iron bars a cage ;
Mindes innocent and quiet take
That for an hermitage ;
If I have freedome in my love,
And in my soule am free,
Angels alone that sore above
Enjoy such liberty.

RICHARD LOVELACE
To Althea. From Prison (1642)

ROCKS, SEAS, AND GARDENS

Shut up Close-Prisner in *Mount-Orgueil Pile*,
A lofty Castle, within Jersie Isle,
Remote from Friends, neere three years space,
    where I
Had *Rockes, Seas, Gardens*, dayly in mine Eye,
Which I oft viewed with no small delight.
These pleasing *Objects* did at last invite
Me to contemplate in more solemnewise
What usefull *Meditations* might arise
From each of them, my soule to warme, feast,
    cheere,
And unto *God, Christ, Heaven*, mount more neare.
In which pursuite, I found such inward Joyes,
Such Cordiall Comforts, as did over-poise

My heaviest Crosses, Losses, and supply
The want of all *Foes* did me then deny ;
Give me assurance of a sweete Returne
Both from my *Exile*, *Prison*, and mine *Urne* :
Revive my cold dead Muse, and it inspire
Though not with brightest, yet with *Sacred* fire.

WILLIAM PRYNNE
*Mount-Orgueil, or Divine and Profitable Meditations,
Raised from the Contemplation of these three Leaves of
Natures Volume, Rockes, Seas, Gardens* (1654)

A FRIEND'S VISIT

This Lord *Middleton* had a great Friendship with the
Laird *Bocconi*, and they had made an Agreement, that the
first of them that Died should appear to the other in
Extremity. The Lord *Middleton* was taken Prisoner at
Worcester Fight, and was Prisoner in the *Towre* of *London*,
under Three Locks. Lying in his Bed pensive, *Bocconi*
appear'd to him ; my Lord Middleton asked him if he
were dead or alive ? he said, Dead, and that he was a
Ghost ; and told him, that within Three Days he should
escape, and he did soe, in his Wife's Cloaths. When he
had done his Message, he gave a Frisk, and said,

> *Givenni, Givanni,* 'tis very strange,
> In the World to see so sudden a Change.

And then gathered up and vanished.

JOHN AUBREY
Apparitions (*Miscellanies*) (1696)

When we were come to *Bridewell*, we were not put up into the great Room in which we had been before : but into a low Room, in another fair Court, which had a Pump in the Middle of it. And here, we were not shut up as before : but had the Liberty of the Court, to walk in ; and of the Pump, to wash or drink at. And, indeed, we might easily have gone quite away, if we would ; there was a Passage through the Court into the Street : but we were true and steady prisoners, and looked upon this Liberty arising from their Confidence in us, to be a kind of *paroll* upon us ; so that both Conscience and Honour stood now engaged for our true imprisonment. . . .

And this Priviledge we enjoyed, by the Indulgence of our Keeper, whose Heart God disposed to Favour us : so that both the Master and his Porter were very civil, and kind to us, and had been so indeed all along. For when we were shut up before, the Porter would readily let some of us go home in an Evening, and stay at Home till next Morning, which was a great Conveniency. . . .

Under this easie Restraint, we lay till the Court sate at the Old-Baily again.

THOMAS ELLWOOD
History of his Life (1714)

CONTEMPLATION AND STUDY

Art in prison ? Make right use of it. . . . Where may a man contemplate better than in solitarinesse or study more than in quietnesse ? . . . *Severinus Boethius* never writ so elegantly as in prison, *Paul* so devoutly, for most of his

Epistles were dictated in his bands; It brings many a lewd riotous fellow home, many wandering rogues it settles, that would otherwise have been like raving Tygers, ruined themselves and others. ROBERT BURTON
The Anatomy of Melancholy (1621. Edition 1632)

A Concert

An officer was confined in the Bastile; he begged the governor to permit him the use of his lute. . . . After a few days, this modern Orpheus . . . was greatly astonished to see frisking out of their holes great numbers of mice, and descending from their woven habitations crowds of spiders, who formed a circle about him. . . . He was petrified with astonishment. Having ceased to play, the assembly . . . immediately broke up. As he had a great dislike to spiders, it was two days before he ventured again to touch his instrument. At length . . . he recommenced his concert, when the assembly was far more numerous than at first. Having thus succeeded in attracting this company, he . . . begged the keeper to give him a cat, which he . . . let loose at the very instant when the little hairy people were most entranced. ISAAC DISRAELI
Curiosities of Literature (1792–1817)

The Bastile

And as for the Bastile! the terror is in the word—— Make the most of it you can, said I to myself, the Bastile is but

another word for a tower—and a tower is but another word
for a house you can't get out of—— . . . but with nine
lives a day, and pen and ink and paper and patience,
albeit a man can't get out, he may do very well within
—at least for a month or six weeks.

LAURENCE STERNE, *A Sentimental Journey* (1768)

BETTER THAN A SHIP

He said, " No man will be a sailor who has contrivance
enough to get himself into a jail. . . . A man in a jail has
more room, better food, and commonly better company."

JAMES BOSWELL, *Life of Johnson* (1791)

RAIN

THE BENEFIT OF IRRIGATION

In April, and the springtime, his lorship [Bacon] would,
when it rayned, take his coach (open) to receive the benefit
of irrigation, which he was wont to say was very wholsome
because of the nitre in the aire and the *universall spirit of
the world.*

JOHN AUBREY, *Brief Lives : Francis Bacon* (c. 1680)

RAMBLING

But the most pleasant of all outward pastimes is . . . to make a pretty progresse, a merry journy now and then with some good companions, to visit friends, see citties, Castles, Townes, . . .

> To see the pleasant fields, the christall fountaines,
> And take the gentle air among the mountaines :

To walke amongst Orchards, Gardens, Bowres, Mounts, and Arbors, artificiall wildrenesses, greene thickets, Arches, Groves, Lawnes, Rivulets, Fountaines, and such like pleasant places . . . Brooks, Pooles, Fishponds, betwixt wood and water, in a faire meadow, by a river-side . . . to disport in some pleasant plaine parke, run up a steepe hill sometimes, or sit in a shady seat, must needs be a delectable recreation. . . . *S. Bernard,* in the description of his Monastery, is almost ravished with the pleasure of it. *A sicke man* (saith he) *sits upon a greene banke, and when the dog-starre parcheth the Plaines, and dries up rivers, he lies in a shadie bowre,* . . . *and feeds his eyes with variety of objects, hearbs, trees ; to comfort his misery, hee receaves many delightsome smells, and fills his ears with that sweet and various harmony of Birds : Good God* (saith he) *what a company of pleasures hast thou made for man !*

ROBERT BURTON

The Anatomy of Melancholy (1621. Edition 1632)

READING

MODERATION

Bookes are delightfull ; but if by continuall frequenting
them, we in the end lose both health and cheerfulnesse
(our best parts) let us leave them. I am one of those who
thinke their fruit can no way countervaile this losse.

MICHEL DE MONTAIGNE, *Essays* (1580)
Trans. John Florio (1603)

READING BY BIRD-LIGHT

There is a kind of Bird in *America,* that yields such a
light, you may read by it in the darkest night.

B. DE FONTENELLE, *A Plurality of Worlds*
Trans. John Glanvill (1688)

READING THE BIBLE

A Spanish author says, that if a person should come to
his bishop to ask for leave to read the Bible . . . the bishop
should answer him from Matthew, ch. xx. v. 20, " *You*

536

know not what you ask." And indeed, he observes the nature of this demand indicates an *heretical disposition*.

The reading of the Bible was prohibited by Henry VIII, except by those who occupied high offices in the state ; a noble lady or gentlewoman might read it in " their garden or orchard " or other retired places ; but men and women in the lower ranks were positively forbidden to read it, or to have it read to them, under the penalty of a month's imprisonment. ISAAC DISRAELI

Curiosities of Literature (1791–1823)

READING PLATO AND POETRY

. . . . the smooth Elegiack Poets . . . whom both for the pleasing sound of their numerous writing, which in imitation I found most easie, and most agreeable to natures part in me and for their matter . . . I was so allur'd to read, that no recreation came to me better welcome. . . . If I found those authors anywhere speaking unworthy things of themselves, or unchaste of those names which before they had extolled, this effect it wrought with me, from that time forward their art I still applauded, but the men I deplor'd ; . . . Next (for heare me out now Readers) that I may tell ye whether my younger feet wander'd ; I betook me among those lofty Fables and Romances, which recount in solemn canto's the deeds of Knighthood. . . . So that even those books which to many others have bin the fuell of wantonnesse and loose living, I cannot thinke how unlesse by divine indulgence, prov'd to me so many incitements as you have heard, to the love and stedfast observation of that vertue which abhorres the society of

537

bordello's. Thus from the Laureat fraternity of Poets, riper yeares and the ceaselesse round of study and reading led me to the shady spaces of philosophy, but chiefly to the divine volumes of *Plato*, and his equall *Xenephon*. Where if I should tell ye what I learnt of chastity and love, I meane that which is truly so, whose charming cup is only vertue, which she bears in her hand to those who are worthy. . . .

JOHN MILTON
An Apology against a Pamphlet call'd A Modest Con-
futation of the Animadversions upon the Remonstrant
against Smectymnuus (1642)

READING ROMANCES

Parthenissa is now my company, my Brother sent it downe, and I have almost read it. Tis handsome language. You would know it to be writt by a person of good quality though you were not tolde it, but on the whole I am not very much taken with it, the Story's have too neer a resemblance with those of other Romances, there's nothing of new or surprenant in them, the Ladys are all soe kinde they make no sport, and I meet only with one that tooke mee by doing a handsome thing. . . . She was in a beseiged Towre, and perswaded all those of her sexe to go out with her to the Enemy (which were a barbarous People) and dye by theire swordes, that the provisions of the Towne might last the longer for such as were able to doe service in defending it. But how angry was I to see him spoile this againe, by bringing out a letter this woman left behinde her for the Governour of the Towne, where she discovers a passion for him and makes that the reason why she did it. I confesse I have no patience with our faiseurs de Roman, when they make women court. It will never enter my head that tis possible any woman can Love where she is not first Loved, and much lesse that if they should doe that, they could have the face to owne it. . . . Another fault I finde too is the stile, tis affected. . . . But perhaps I like it the worse for having a peece of Cyrus by mee, that I am hugely pleased with, and that I would faine have you read, i'le send it you. . . .

DOROTHY OSBORNE
Letter to Sir William Temple (1654)

READING NOVELS

JULIA has buried her Husband, and married her Daughters, since that she spends her time in reading. She is always reading *foolish* and *unedifying* Books : She tells you every time she sees you, that she is almost at the End of the silliest Book, that ever she read in her life ; that the best of it is, it is very long, and serves to dispose of a good deal of her time. She tells you that all *Romances* are sad Stuff, yet is very impatient till she can get all that she can hear of. Histories of *Intreague* and *Scandal* are the Books that *Julia* thinks are always too short. If *Julia* was to drink *Drams* in private, and had no Enjoyment of her self without them, she would not tell you this, because she knows it would be plainly telling you that she was a *poor disordered Sot*. See here therefore the Weakness of *Julia* ; she would not be thought to be a Reprobate, yet she lets you know that she lives upon *Folly*, and *Scandal*, and *Impertinence*, in her *Closet*, that she cannot be in *private* without them, that they are the only Support of her dull Hours, and yet she does not perceive, that this is as plainly telling you, that she is in a *miserable, disordered, reprobate* State of Mind.

WILLIAM LAW, Christian Perfection (1726)

READING RICHARDSON

Oh Richardson! remarkable genius! thou shalt always form my reading. If compelled by bitter necessity . . . if my means are insufficient to educate my children, I will sell my books, but thou shalt remain! yes, thou shalt rest in the same class with Moses, Homer, Euripides, and Sophocles, to be read turn by turn.

DENIS DIDEROT

READING FIELDING

I never saw Johnson really angry with me but once. I alluded to some witty passages in *Tom Jones*, he replied, " I am shocked to hear you quote from so vicious a book. I am sorry to hear you have read it ; a confession which no modest lady should ever make. I scarcely know a more corrupt work ! " He went so far as to refuse to Fielding the great talents which are ascribed to him, and broke out into a noble panegyric on his competitor, Richardson ; who, he said, was as superior to him in talents as in virtue ; and whom he pronounced to be the greatest genius that had shed its lustre on this path of literature."

HANNAH MORE, Memoirs (1780)

Fielding being mentioned, Johnson exclaimed, " he was a blockhead " ; and upon my expressing my astonishment at so strange an assertion, he said, " What I mean by his being a blockhead is that he was a barren rascal." Boswell. " Will you not allow, Sir, that he draws a very natural picture of human life ? " Johnson. " Why, Sir, it is of very low life. Richardson used to say, that had he not known who Fielding was, he should have believed him to be an ostler. Sir, there is more knowledge of the heart in one letter of Richardson's, than in all *Tom Jones.* . . . Erskine. " Surely, Sir, Richardson is very tedious." Johnson. " Why, Sir, if you were to read Richardson for the story, your patience would be so much fretted that you would hang yourself. But you must read him for the sentiment, and consider the story as only giving occasion to the sentiment."

JAMES BOSWELL, *Life of Johnson* (1792)

Reading a Bawdy Book

Jan. 13*th*, 1668. Stopped at Martin's, my bookseller, where I saw the French book which I did think to have had for my wife to translate, called " L'escholle des filles," but when I come to look in it, it is the most bawdy lewd book that ever I saw, . . . so that I was ashamed of reading it, and so away home.

Feb. 8*th*. To my bookseller's, and there staid an hour, and bought the idle rogueish book, " L'escholle des filles " ;

which I have bought in plain binding, avoiding the buying of it better bound, because I resolve, as soon as I have read it, to burn it, that it may not stand in the list of books, nor among them, to disgrace them if it should be found.

Feb. 9*th* (Lord's Day). I to my chamber, where I did read through " L'escholle des filles," a lewd book, but what do no wrong once to read for information sake. . . . And after I had done it I burned it, that it might not be among my books to my shame, and so at night to supper and to bed.

SAMUEL PEPYS, *Diary*

READING PETRARCH

I have spent a stupid day in reading the Abbé de Sade's Memoirs of Petrarch. What a feeble whipster was this Petrarch, with all his talents ! To go dangling about, for the space of twenty years, puffing and sighing after a little coquette, whose charms lay chiefly in the fervour of his own imagination, and the art she had to keep him wavering between hope and despondency—at once ridiculous and deplorable—that he might write Sonnets in her praise ! Did you ever read his *Rime* ? I find it quite impossible to admire them sufficiently : to me they seem a very worthless employment for a mind like Petrarch's—he might have built a palace, and he has made some dozen snuff-boxes with invisible hinges—very pretty certainly—but very small and altogether useless. But the Italians call him *divine*, and that is everything.

THOMAS CARLYLE
Letter to Jane Welsh (1822)

I think I heard you say you did not think very highly of
Corinne. You must read it again : nobody with a heart and
soul can fail to admire it. I never read a book in my life
that made such an impression on me. I cried *two whole
hours* at the conclusion, and in all likelihood I might have
been crying to this minute, but for an engagement to a
party in the evening, where prudential considerations
required that my eyes should be visible.—Have you read
Nigel ? I think wondrous little of it. I am exceedingly
obliged to you for *Sismondi*. I have only read the first
volume, but like it very much. . . .

Are you not pleased with *Bracebridge Hall* ? He is a
witty, amiable sort of person Mr Irving ; but Oh, he
wants fire ; and he is *far too happy* for me. Dear Byron,
sinner as he is, there is nobody like him. I have got his
likeness. . . . I can scarcely help crying when I look at it,
and think I may chance to go out of the world without
seeing its original.

JANE WELSH
Letters to Thomas Carlyle (1822)

Ill-judged Reading

Metrodorus, Valerius Probus, Aulus Gellius, Pedianus,
Boethius, and a hundred others, to be acquainted with
whom might show much reading and but little judgment.

OLIVER GOLDSMITH
Inquiry into the Present State of Polite Learning (1759)

FOOLISH READING

March 19*th*, 1668. And so home to read a little more in last night's book, with much sport, it being a foolish book.

SAMUEL PEPYS
Diary

MEWED IN A LIBRARY

Heinsius, the keeper of the Library at *Leyden* in *Holland*, was mewed up in it all the yeare long, and that which to thy thinking should have bred a loathing caused in him a greater liking. *I no sooner* (saith he) *come into the Library, but I bolt the doore to me excluding lust, ambition, avarace, and all such vices, whose nurse is idlenesse, the Mother of ignorance, and Melancholy her selfe, and in the very lap of eternity, amongst so many divine soules, I take my seat, with so lofty a spirit and sweet content, that I pitty all our great ones, and rich men that know not this happinesse.*

ROBERT BURTON
The Anatomy of Melancholy
(1621. Edition 1632)

FRIENDS' MANUSCRIPTS

Mr Johnson did not like that his friends should bring their manuscripts for him to read, and he liked still less to read them when they were brought. . . . " Alas, Madam ! " (continued he) how few books are there of which one ever can possibly arrive at the *last* page ! Was there ever yet

any thing written by mere man that was wished longer by
its readers, excepting Don Quixote, Robinson Crusoe, and
the Pilgrim's Progress. . . .

HESTHER PIOZZI
Anecdotes of Dr. Johnson (1785)

READING BURNET

Learning is sunk so very low, that I am most certainly
inform'd that nothing is now hardly read but Burnett's
romance or libel, call'd by him *The History of his own
Times*, 'Tis read by men, women, and children. Indeed, it
is the common table-book for ladies as well as gentlemen,
especially such as are friends to the revolution scheme.

THOMAS HEARNE
Diary (March 19, 1734)

READING ONE'S OWN BOOKS

I have lately perused all my own Philosophicall Writings
which the more seriously I have consydered by so much
the more assured I am of the truth of those maine conclusions they hold out to the world. And those that will
be ignorant, if they find so great felicity in it, lett them
be so.

HENRY MORE
Letter to Lady Conway (1661)

REPARTEE

EMINENTLY SUCCESSFUL

Johnson was once eminently successful in this form of contest : A fellow having attacked him with some coarse raillery, Johnson answered him thus, " Sir, your wife, under pretence of keeping a bawdy-house, is a receiver of stolen goods."

JAMES BOSWELL, *Life of Johnson* (1791)

RESPECT FROM LOWER ORDERS

Dr Johnson sat with Mrs Thrale, Lady Ladd, and me, for an hour or two. The subject was given by Lady Ladd ; it was the respect due from the lower class of the people.

" I know my place," said she, " and I always take it : and I've no notion of not taking it. But Mrs Thrale lets all sort of people do just as they've a mind by her."

" Ay," said Mrs Thrale, " why should I torment and

worry myself about all the paltry marks of respect that consist in bows and courtesies ?—I have no idea of troubling myself about the manners of all the people I mix with."

" No," said Lady Ladd, " so they will take all sorts of liberties with you. I remember, when you were at my house, how the hair-dresser flung down the comb as soon as you were dressed, and went out of the room without making a bow."

" Well, all the better," said Mrs Thrale ; " for if he had made me one, then thousand to one if I had seen it. I was in as great haste to have done with him, as he could be to have done with me. I was glad enough to get him out of the room ; I did not want him to stand bowing and cringing."

" If any man had behaved so insolently to me," answered she, " I would never again have suffered him in my house."

" Well," said Mrs Thrale, " your Ladyship has a great deal more dignity than I have ! Dr Johnson, we are talking of the respect due from inferiors ;—and Lady Ladd is of the same side you are."

" Why, madam," said he, " subordination is always necessary to the preservation of order and decorum."

" I protest," said Lady Ladd, " I have no notion of submitting to any kind of impertinence: and I never will bear either to have any nod to me, or enter a room where I am without bowing."

" But, madam," said Dr Johnson, " what if they will nod, and what if they will not bow ?—how then ? "

" Why, I always tell them of it," said she.

" Oh, commend me to that ! " cried Mrs Thrale ; " I'd sooner never see another bow in my life, than turn dancing-master to hair-dressers."

The doctor laughed his approbation, but said that every man had a right to a certain degree of respect, and no man liked to be defrauded of that right.

" Well, sir," said Mrs Thrale, " I hope you meet with respect enough."

" Yes, madam," answered he, " I am very well contented."

" Nay, if you ain't, I don't know who should be ; for I believe there is no man in the world so greatly respected."

FANNY BURNEY
Diary (1778)

RURAL

OXFORDSHIRE SQUIRE

You have now, at length, left scouring the *Watch* and teizing the *Exchange-women*, bid adieu to *Bourdeaux*, and taken up with *Barrel-ale*. You are all the morning gallopping after a *Fox* ; all the Evening in a smoaky Chimney-corner, recounting whose Horse leap'd best, was oftenest in with the Dogs, and how readily *Lightfoot* hit the cooling Scent, and reviv'd your drooping Spirits with a prospect of more Diversion ; which some Men, who think themselves as wise in the Enjoyment of this World, as all the men in *Oxfordshire*, are pleas'd to term meer fatigue. And I believe your own Footman would not ride so far and so hard, to fetch a good Dinner, as both of you do to see the

Death of a stinking Beast. . . . Does not a Masque give a more Christian-like chase, and conclude in more satisfaction than the Animal you wot of ? I saw your Letters to some of our *Club*, and laugh'd not a little at the strangeness of your Style ; it smelt of filthy *Tobacco*, and was stain'd with your dropping Tankard. You acquainted 'em at large with the Situation of your Mansion-House ; how a knot of branching *Elms* defended it from the *North-wind* ; that the *South-Sun* gave you good *Grapes*, and most sort of *Wall-fruits*; your *Melons* came on apace, and you had hopes of much good Fruit this *Summer*. After all, in *Covent-garden* Market, we can buy, in one quarter of an hour, better Plants than yours, and richer *Melons*, for Groats apiece, than you have been poring over this three Months. You thank'd 'em for some News, that was so old we hardly could imagine what you meant, till *Tom*, who has all the *Gazets* and *Pamphlets* lock'd up in his Heart, as *David* did the Commandments, disclosed the Mystery to us. I pity your new State indeed : Your Gazets are as stale as your Drink ; which, tho' brew'd in *March*, is not broach'd till *December*. The chief Topicks of Discourse (for Conversation you have none) are Hawks, Horses, and Hounds ; every one of 'em as much God's Image as he that keeps them. . . . This you call a seasonable retreat from the *Lewdness* of *London*, to enjoy a Calm and Quiet Life : Heaven knows, you drink more there, and more ignoble and ungenerous Liquors than we in Town; for yours is down-right *Drinking*. . . . Well, 'tis Six, and I must to the *Club*, where we will pity your Solitude, and drink your Prosperity, in a Cup that is worth a Stable of *Horses* and a Kennel of *Hounds*. So adieu.

CAPTAIN AYLOFFE
Letter to a Friend in the Country (1696)

Are you so determined to spend your time now in Lucania, now in Campania ? . . . Why not sometimes return to Rome, where there are dignities, honours, and friendships both greater and less. For how long do you intend to play the lord, wake and sleep when you like, never wear shoes or full dress, and be free all day ?

PLINY THE YOUNGER, *Letter to Praesens* (c. 100)

UNDER THE BEECH TREE

Look, under that broad *Beech tree* I sate down when I was last this way a fishing, and the birds in the adjoining grove seemed to have a friendly contention with an Eccho, whose dead voice seemed to live in a hollow cave, neer to the brow of that Primrose hill, there I sat viewing the silver streams glide silently towards their center, the tempestuous sea ; yet somtimes opposed by rugged roots, and pibble stones, which broke their waves, and turned them into foam : and somtimes viewing the harmlesse lambs, some leaping securely in the cool shade, whilst others sported them selves in the cheerful sun ; and others were craving comfort from the swolne udders of their bleating Dams. As I thus sate, these and other sights had so fully possest my soul, that I thought, as the Poet has happily exprest it,

> I was for that time lifted above earth,
> And possest joies not promis'd in my birth.

IZAAK WALTON, *The Compleat Angler* (1653)

550

The very being in the country, that life it selfe is a sufficient recreation to some men, to enjoy such pleasures as
those old Patriarkes did. *Dioclesian*, the Emperor, was so
much affected by it, that he gave over his scepter, and
turned Gardner.

ROBERT BURTON
The Anatomy of Melancholy (1621. Edition 1632)

COUNTRY PLEASURES

DORINDA : You share in all the Pleasures that the Country
affords.
MRS SULLEN: Country Pleasures! Racks and Torments!
dost think, Child, that my Limbs were made for leaping of
Ditches, and clambring over Stiles ; or that my Parents
wisely foreseeing my future Happiness in Country-
Pleasures, had early instructed me in rural Accomplishments of drinking fat Ale, playing at Whisk, and smoaking
Tobacco with my Husband ; or of spreading of Plaisters,
brewing of Diet-drinks, and stilling Rosemary-Water,
with the good old Gentlewoman my Mother-in-Law ?
DOR. : I'm sorry, Madam, that it is not more in our power
to divert you ; I cou'd wish, indeed, that our Entertainments were a little more polite, or your Taste a little less
refin'd : But pray, Madam, how came the Poets and
Philosophers, that labour'd so much in hunting after
Pleasure, to place it at last in a Country Life ?
MRS SUL. : Because they wanted Money, Child, to find

out the Pleasures of the Town : Did you ever see a Poet
or Philosopher worth ten Thousand Pound ? if you
can shew me such a Man, I'll lay you Fifty Pound you'll
find him somewhere within the weekly Bills.—Not that I
disapprove rural Pleasures, as the Poets have painted
them ; in their Landschape every *Phillis* has her *Coridon*,
every murmuring Stream, and every flowry Mead gives
fresh Alarms to Love.—Besides, you'll find that their
Couples were never marry'd.

GEORGE FARQUHAR
The Beaux' Stratagem (1707)

HAPPY PEOPLE

Phoebe drest like beauty's queen,
Jellicoe in faint pea-green,
Sitting all beneath a grot
Where the little lambkins trot.

Maidens dancing, loves a-sporting,
All the country folks a-courting,
Susan, Johnny, Bob and Joe,
Lightly tripping in a row.

Happy people, who can be
In happiness compar'd with ye ?
The pilgrim with his crook and hat
Sees your happiness complete.

WILLIAM BLAKE
An Island in the Moon (1784)

552

Mr Chute tells me you have taken a new house in Squireland, and have given yourself up for two years more to port and parsons. I am very angry, and resign you to the works of the devil or the Church, I don't care which. You will get the gout, turn Methodist, and expect to ride to Heaven upon your own great toe. . . . Will you end like a fat farmer, repeating annually the price of oats and discussing stale newspapers ?

HORACE WALPOLE
Letter to George Montagu (1768

GENTLEMEN SALVAGES

ISABELLE : Sir *Timerous*, I wish you well ; but he I marry must promise me to live at *London* : I cannot abide to be in the Country, like a wilde beast in the wilderness, with no Christian Soul about me.

SIR TIMEROUS : Why I'll bear you company.

ISABELLE : I cannot endure your early hunting matches there ; to have my sleep disturbed at break of day, with heigh *Fowler Fowler*, there *Venus*, ah *Beauty* ! and then a serenade of deep mouth'd curres, to answer the salutation of the Huntsman, as if hell were broke loose about me : and all this to meet a pack of Gentleman Salvages to ride all day like mad men, for the immortal fame of being first in at the Hares death : to come upon the spur after a trayl at four in the afternoon to destruction of cold meat and cheese,

553

with your leud company in boots ; fall a drinking till
Supper time, be carried to bed, rop'd out of your Seller,
and be good for nothing all the night after.   JOHN DRYDEN
The Wilde Gallant (1669)

FIT FOR THE COUNTRY

" Yet, Sir, (said I) there are many people who are content
to live in the country." JOHNSON. " Sir . . . they who are
content to live in the country, are *fit* for the country."

JAMES BOSWELL
Life of Johnson (1791)

LAUGHTER

When the green woods laugh with the voice of joy,
And the dimpling stream runs laughing by ;
When the air does laugh with our merry wit,
And the green hill laughs with the noise of it ;

When the meadows laugh with lively green,
And the grasshopper laughs in the merry scene,
When Mary and Susan and Emily
With their sweet round mouths sing " Ha, Ha, He ! "

When the painted birds laugh in the shade,
Where our table with cherries and nuts is spread,
Come live, and be merry, and join with me,
To sing the sweet chorus of " Ha, Ha, He ! "

WILLIAM BLAKE
Laughing Song (1784)

554

I am much better off in my own part of the country, where I am very distinguished, than lost in Paris and submerged at Versailles.

COMTE DE BUSSY RABUTIN
Letter to Corbinelli (1686)

MILKMAIDS

To Portholme, seeing the country-maids milking their cows there, they being there now at grass, and to see with what mirth they come all home together in pomp with their milk, and sometimes they have musique to go before them.

SAMUEL PEPYS
Diary (Oct. 13, 1662)

GOING RUSTIC

I now hold the pen for my Lord *Bolingbroke*, who is reading your Letter between two Haycocks ; but his attention is somewhat diverted by casting his Eyes on the Clouds, not in admiration of what you say, but for fear of a Shower. . . . As to the Return of his Health and Vigour, were you here, you might inquire of his Hay-makers ; but as to his Temperance, I can answer that (for one whole day) we have had nothing for Dinner but Mutton-broth, Beans and Bacon, and a Barn-door Fowl.

555

Now his Lordship is run after his Cart, I have a moment left to myself to tell you, that I overheard him yesterday agree with a Painter for 200 l. to paint his Country-Hall with Trophies of Rakes, Spades, Prongs, etc., and other Ornaments, merely to countenance his calling this Place a Farm.

ALEXANDER POPE
Letter to Dean Swift (1728)

A SHORT WALK

LADY : Will you see a fayre Meadowe ? Is it not a great comfort to the eye to see so great varyetie of flowers ? and then cast your eye upon that little hill, looke how the little lambs doe skip on the grasse ! . . . The Sonne did not shine heare this day, for the grasse is yet with dewe. . . . What sweet noyse this water maketh among the pible stones, it doth enchaunte me almost to sleep . . . maydens, gather some water cresses, it biteth upon the tongue like pepper. . . .

CHARLOTTE : Heare how the small birds doe chatter their sweete tunes, would to God I had one of them ! I would set him in the fayrest Cage that I could get.

MASTER OUYT-AIGU : What Mistris, would you be so cruell as to deprive him of his libertie ? Ô deere libertie ! God grant me alwaies the key of the fieldes, I would like it better, then to be in bondage in the fayrest wainscotted or tapistried Chamber.

DU VAULT-L'AMOUR : I knowe a gentle-woman, which above all birds loveth a Swallowe, and hath no contentment but when she enjoyeth either the sight or the voyce of it.

MISTRIS DU PONT GAILLARD : Yet so it is, that it is an unconstant and wandering bird, and that hath no pleasant voyce.

OUYT-AIGU : But the comming of it is pleasing, for it doth denounce the spring-time, is a very good Architector, and hath great care of her little ones.

LADY : Now seeing that she whome you say loveth her so well, I pray God she may have his company to her content : but in the mean while let us retyre us for it is verye hotte : let us goe to the Orchard, and then we will rest in the garden. . . .

PIERRE ERONDELL
The French Garden (1605)

THE MERRY COUNTRY LAD

Who can live in heart so glad,
As the merrie countrie lad ?
Who upon a faire greene balke
May at pleasures sit and walke ?
And amidde the Azure skies,
See the morning Sunne arise ?
While he heares in every spring,
How the Birdes doe chirpe and sing :
Or, before the houndes in crie,
See the Hare go stealing by :
Or along the shallow brooke,
Angling with a baited hooke :
See the fishes leape and play,
In a blessed Sunny day :

557

Or to heare the Partridge call,
Till shee have her Covye all : . . .
Then the Bee to gather honey,
And the little blacke-haird Cony,
On a banke for Sunny place,
With her fore-feete wash her face :
Are not these with thousandes moe,
Than the Courts of Kinges doe knowe ?

NICHOLAS BRETON
The Passionate Shepheard (1604)

SAGA GROWTH

SPREADING STORIES

He had a trick sometimes to goe into Westminster hall
in a morning in Terme time, and tell some strange story
(sham) and would come hither again about 11 or 12 to
have the pleasure to heare how it spred ; and sometimes
it would be altered, with additions, he could scarce
knowe it to be his owne.

JOHN AUBREY
Brief Lives : Thomas Chaloner (c. 1680)

SATISFACTORY
ENGAGEMENTS

THE SHEPHERD AND HIS LOVE

At Shearing time she shall commaund,
The finest fleece of all my wooll :
And if her pleasure but demaund,
The fattest from the leane to cull.
She shall be mistresse of my store :
Let mee alone to worke for more.

My cloake shall lie upon the ground,
From wet and dust to keepe her feete :
My pipe with his best measures found,
Shall welcome her with musicke sweete.
And in my skrippe, some cates at least :
Shall bid her to a Sheapheards feast.

My staffe shall stay her, in her walke,
My dog shall at her heeles attend her :
And I will holde her with such talke,
As I doe hope shall not offend her,
My Eawes shall bleate, my Lambes shall play,
To shew her all the sport they may.

Why I will tell her twentie thinges,
That I have heard my mother tell :

Of plucking of the Buzzards winges,
For killing of her Cockerell,
And hunting Rainard to his denne,
For frighting of her sitting Hen.

How she would say, when shee was young,
That Lovers were ashamde to lie :
And truth was so on everie tongue,
That Love ment naught but honestie.
And Sirra (quoth shee) then to me
Let ever this thy lesson be.

Looke when thou lovest, love but one,
And let her worthy be thy love :
Then love her in thy heart alone,
And let her in thy passions proove,
Aglaia all that in thy minde,
Within thy heart her love shall finde.

And as shee bad, I have obeyed,
I love in heart but one alone :
Whose worthines my wits dismaid,
In finding such a worthy one.
As in *Aglaia* all doth proove,
All under heaven my only love.

And in that love to live and die,
And die, but in that love to live :
And love that cannot live to lie,
Shall for my truth this warrant give :
My life or death, to save or lose,
Shall in her love be to dispose.

Her eyes shall be my Sunne to guide me,
Her hand shall holde me by the hearte,
Her censure onely shall decide me :

What I protest in everie parte.
In heart to serve and love her so,
As under heaven to love no moe. . . .

And I will tell her such fine tales,
As for the nonce, I will devise :
Of Lapwinges and of Nightingales :
And how the Swallow feedes on flies.
And of the Hare, the Fox, the Hound,
The Pastor and the Medow ground.

And of the springes, and of the wood,
And of the Forrestes and the Deere,
And of the rivers and the floods,
And of the mirth and merrie cheere,
And of the lookes and of the glaunces,
Of Maides and young men in their daunces :

Of clapping handes, and drawing gloves,
And of the tokens of loves truth,
And of the pretty Turtle Doves,
That teach the billinge trickes of youth.
And how they kindely ought to wooe,
Before the tother thing they doe.

NICHOLAS BRETON, *The Passionate Shepheard* (1604)

THE HAPPY NIGHT

On a time the amorous Silvy
Said to her Shepheard, Sweet, how do you ?
Kisse mee this once, and then God b' wee you,
      My sweetest deare.
Kisse me this once, and then God b' wee you,
For now the morning draweth neare.

With that, her fairest bosome shewing,
Opening her lips, rich perfumes blowing,
She said, Now kisse me and be going,
    My sweetest deare.
Kisse me this once and then be going,
For now the morning draweth neare.

With that the Shepheard wak'd from sleeping,
And spying where the day was peeping,
He said Now take my Soule in keeping,
    My sweetest deare.
Kisse me and take my Soule in keeping,
Since I must go now, day is neare.

ANON (1622)

SIMON AND SUSAN

SIMON :   O Mine owne sweet heart,
        and when wilt thou be true :
    Or when will the time come,
        that I shall marry you,
    That I may give you kisses,
        one, two or three,
    More sweeter then the hunny,
        that comes from the Bee.

SUSAN :   My Father is unwilling
        that I should marry thee,
    Yet I could wish in heart,
        that so the same might be :
    For now me thinks thou seemest,
        more lovely unto me :
    And fresher then the Blossomes,
        that bloomes on the tree.

SIMON :   Thy mother is most willing,
                and will consent I know,
           Then let us to thy Father
                now both together goe :
           Where if he give us his good will,
                and to our match agree :
           Twill be sweeter then the hunny
                that comes from the Bee.

SUSAN :   Come goe, for I am willing,
                good fortune be our guide :
           From that which I have promised,
                deare heart, Ile never slide :
           If that he doe but smile,
                and I the same may see,
           Tis better then the blossomes,
                that bloomes upon the tree.

SIMON :   But stay heere comes my Mother,
                weele talke with her a word :
           I doubt not but some comfort,
                to us she may afford :
           If comfort she will give us,
                that we the same may see,
           Twill be sweeter then the hunny,
                that comes from the Bee.

SUSAN :   O Mother we are going
                my Father for to pray,
           That he will give me his good will,
                for long I cannot stay.
           A young man I have chosen
                a fitting match for me,

More fayrer then the blossomes
that bloomes on the tree.

MOTHER : Daughter thou art old enough
to be a wedded wife,
You maydens are desirous
to lead a marryed life.
Then my consent good daughter
shall to thy wishes be,
For young thou art as blossomes
that bloome upon the tree.

SIMON : Then mother you are willing
your daughter I shall have :
And *Susan* thou art welcome
Ile keepe thee fine and brave.
And have those wished blessings
bestowed upon thee,
More sweeter then the honey
that comes from the Bee.

SUSAN : Yet Simon I am minded
to lead a merry life,
And be as well maintained
as any Citie wife :
And live a gallant mistresse
of maidens that shall be
More fayrer then the blossomes
that bloome upon the tree.

SIMON : Thou shalt have thy Caudles,
before thou dost arise :
For churlishnesse breeds sicknesse
and danger therein lies.

Young lasses must be cherisht
    with sweets that dainty be,
Farre sweeter then the honey
    that commeth from the Bee.

MOTHER : Well said good Son and Daughter,
    this is the onely dyet
To please a dainty young wife,
    and keepe the house in quiet.
But stay, here comes your father,
    his words I hope will be
More sweeter then the blossomes
    that bloome upon the tree.

FATHER : Why how now daughter Susan
    doe you intend to marry ?
Maydens in the old time
    did twenty winters tarry.
Now in the teenes no sooner
    but you a wife will be
And loose the sweetest blossome
    that bloomes upon thy tree.

SUSAN : It is for my preferment
    good father say not nay,
For I have found a husband kinde
    and loving every way :
That still unto my fancy
    will evermore agree,
Which is more sweet then honey
    that comes from the Bee.

MOTHER : Hinder not your daughter,
    good husband, lest you bring

Her loves consuming sicknesse,
    or else a worser thing.
Maydens youngly married
    loving wives will be
And sweet as is the honey
    which comes from the Bee.

SIMON :   Good father be not cruell,
    your daughter is mine owne :
Her mother hath consented
    and is to liking growne.
And if your selfe will give then,
    her gentle hand to me,
Twill sweeter be then honey
    that comes from the Bee.

FATHER :   God give thee joy deare Daughter,
    there is no reason I
Should hinder thy proceeding,
    and thou a mayden die :
And after to lead Apes in hell,
    as maidens doomed be :
That fairer are then blossomes
    that bloome upon the tree.

SIMON :   Then let's unto the Parson
    and Clerke to say Amen :

SUSAN :   With all my heart good *Simon*,
    we are concluded then,
My father and my mother both
    doe willingly agree
My *Simon's* sweet as honey
    that comes from the Bee.

> You Maidens and Bachelors
> we hope will lose no time,
> Which learne it by experience
> that youth is in the prime,
> And dally in their hearts desire
> young married folkes to be
> More sweeter then the blossomes
> that bloome upon the tree.

Ibid. (c. 1620)

How It Should be Done

MADELON : Father, here is my cousin, who will tell you too that marriage ought never to occur except after other experiences. A lover, to be agreeable, must know how to utter fine sentiments, to express what is sweet, tender and passionate, and his courtship must be in due form. First, he must see at church, or on a walk, or at some public function, the person with whom he falls in love ; or be taken to her house by a relation or friend, and come away dreamy and melancholy. For a time he hides his passion from the beloved object, but nevertheless pays her several visits, on which he does n't fail to bring up some question of gallantry that exercises the wits of the company. The day of the declaration arrives ; it should usually be made in an alley of some garden, while the company is a little way off; and it is followed by prompt anger, which is shown by our flush, and which, for a time, banishes the lover from our presence. Presently he finds means of appeasing us, of accustoming us insensibly to the talk of his passion,

567

and of drawing from us that avowal which takes so much trouble. After that come adventures, the rivals who place themselves in the way of an established attachment, the persecutions of fathers, jealousies caused by false appearances, reproaches, despairs, abductions, and the rest of it. That's how things are managed in the right style, and those are the rules which, in proper love affairs, can't be dispensed with. But to come without any preamble to conjugal union, make no other love than the marriage contract, and seize romance only by its tail,—once more, father, there can be nothing more like a business deal than this procedure, and I feel heart-sick at the very thought of it.

GORGIBUS : What the devil is this kind of talk ? This is the grand style with a vengeance !

JEAN BAPTISTE MOLIÈRE
Les Précieuses Ridicules (1659)

MR DARCY AND ELIZABETH

On first hearing it, Mrs Bennett sat quite still, and unable to utter a syllable. Nor was it under many, many minutes, that she could comprehend what she heard, though not in general backward to credit what was for the advantage of her family, or that came in the shape of a lover to any of them. She began at length to recover, to fidget about in her chair, get up, sit down again, wonder, and bless herself.

" Good gracious ! Lord bless me ! only think ! dear me ! Mr Darcy ! Who would have thought it ? And is it really true ? Oh, my sweetest Lizzy ! how rich and how great you will be ! What pin-money, what jewels, what carriages you will have ! Jane's is nothing to it—nothing at all. I am so pleased—so happy. Such a charming man ! so handsome ! so tall ! Oh, my dear Lizzy ! pray apologise for my having disliked him so much before. I hope he will overlook it. Dear, dear Lizzy. A house in town ! Everything that is charming ! Three daughters married ! Ten thousand a year ! Oh Lord ! what will become of me ? I shall go distracted."

This was enough to prove that her approbation need not be doubted ; and Elizabeth . . . soon went away. But before she had been three minutes in her room, her mother followed her.

" My dearest child," she cried, " I can think of nothing else. Ten thousand a year, and very likely more ! 'Tis as good as a lord ! And a special licence—you must and shall be married by a special licence. But, my dearest love, tell me what dish Mr Darcy is particularly fond of, that I may have it to-morrow."

JANE AUSTEN
Pride and Prejudice (1813)

THE BALLET OF BALLETS OF SALOMON : CALLED IN LATYNE, CANTICUM CANTICORUM

Lyke as the apple tree amonge the trees of the wod, so is my beloved among the sonnes. My delite is to sit under his shadowe, for his frute is swete unto my throte. He bringeth me in to his wyne celler, and loveth me specially well. Refresh me with grapes, comforte me with apples, for I am sycke of love. His lefte hande lyeth under my head, and his ryghte hand embraceth me. . . .

Methinke I heare the voyce of my beloved ; lo, there

569

commeth he hopping upon the mountaynes, and leaping over the litle hylles. My beloved is like a roo or a yong hart. Beholde he standeth behynde our wall, he loketh in at the wyndowe, and pepeth thorowe the grate.

My beloved answered and sayd unto me, O stand up my love, my dove, my beautiful, and come: for loe the wynter is now past, and the rayne is awaye and gone. The flouers are come up in the feilde, the twisting time is come, the voyce of the turtle is heard in our land, the fig tree bryngeth forth her fygges, the vynes bare blossoms, and have a good smell. O stande up, my love, my beautifull, and come O my dove out of the caverns of the rocks, out of the holes of the wall : O let me see thy countenance and heare thy voyce, for swete is thy voyce and fayre is thy face. . . . My love is myne and I am his, which fedeth among the lilyes untyl the daye break, and tyl the shadowes be gone. Come agayne privyly (O my beloved) lyke as a Roo or a yong Hart, unto the mountaynes. . . .

As for my love, he is whyte and redde coloured, a syngular person among many thousandes ; his heed is the most fine gold, the lockes of his heer are busshed, browne as the evening : his eyes are as the eyes of doves by water brookes, wasshen with mylke and remayning in a plenteous place : his chekes are like a garden bed, wherin the Apotecaryes plante all maner of swete thynges : his lyppes drop as the flouers of that most principall Myrre, his handes are full of golde rynges and precious stones. His body is as the pure yvory, deckt over with Saphirs : his legges are as the pyllers of marble, set upon sockett of gold. His face is as Libanus, and as the beautie of the Cedar trees : his throte is swete, yea he is altogither lovely. Such one is my love, O ye daughters of Jerusalem, such one is my love. . . .

Thou art pleasaunt (O my love) even as lovelynesse it self, thou art fayre as Jerusalem, glorious as an army of men with their banners. . . . Thy heavye lockes are lyke a flocke of goates upon the mount of Galaad. Thy teth are lyke a flock of shepe that be clypped, which go out of the washynge place ; where every one beareth two twyns, and not one unfrutefull among them. Thy chekes are lyke a pece of a pomgranate, besydes that which lyeth hyd wuthin. There are three score quenes, foure score con-cubynes, and yong women without nomber. But one is my dove, my darling.

SALOMONS BALLET
Trans. Miles Coverdale
Bible (1539)

MIRABELL AND MILLAMANT

MILLAMANT : . . . Ah, I'll never marry, unless I am first made sure of my Will and Pleasure.

MIRABELL : Would you have 'em both before Marriage ? Or will you be contented with the first now, and stay for the other 'till after Grace ?

MILL. : Ah don't be impertinent—My dear Liberty, shall I leave thee ? My faithful Solitude, my darling Contemplation, must I bid you then Adieu ? . . . —My Morning Thoughts, agreeable Wakings, indolent Slumbers, all ye *douceurs*, ye *Someils du Matin*, adieu—I can't do't, 'tis more than impossible—Positively *Mirabell*, I'll lye a-bed in a Morning as long as I please.

MIR. : Then I'll get up in a Morning as early as I please.

MILL. : Ah ! Idle Creature, get up when you will—And d'ye hear, I won't be call'd Names after I'm marry'd ; positively I won't be call'd Names.

MIR. : Names !

MILL. : Ay, as Wife, Spouse, my Dear, Joy, Jewel, Love, Sweet-heart, and the rest of that nauseous Cant, in which Men and their Wives are so fulsomly familiar,—I shall never bear that. Good *Mirabell*, don't let us be familiar or fond, nor kiss before Folks, like my Lady *Fadler* and Sir *Francis* : Nor go to *Hide-Park* together the first *Sunday* in a new Chariot, to provoke Eyes and Whispers ; And then never be seen there together again, as we were proud of one another the first Week, and asham'd of one another ever after. Let us never Visit together, nor go to a Play together, but let us be very strange and well-bred : Let us be as strange as if we had been marry'd a great while, and as well-bred as if we were not marry'd at all.

MIR. : Have you any more Conditions to offer ? Hitherto your Demands are pretty reasonable.

MILL.: Trifles,—As Liberty to pay and receive Visits to and from whom I please; to write and receive Letters, without Interrogatories or wry Faces on your part ; to wear what I please, and chuse Conversation with regard only to my own Taste ; to have no Obligation on me to converse with Wits that I don't like, because they are your Acquaintance; or to be intimate with Fools, because they may be your Relations. Come to Dinner when I please, dine in my Dressing-Room when I'm out of Humour, without giving a Reason. To have my closet inviolate ; to be sole Empress of my Tea-table, which you must never presume to approach without first asking leave. And lastly where-ever I am, you shall always knock at the Door before you come in. These Articles subscrib'd, if I continue to endure you a little longer, I may by degrees dwindle into a Wife.

MIR. : Your Bill of Fare is somewhat advanc'd in this latter Account. Well, have I Liberty to offer Conditions—That when you are dwindled into a Wife, I may not be beyond measure enlarg'd into a Husband.

MILL. : You have free leave, propose your utmost, speak and spare not.

MIR. : I thank you. *Inprimis* then, I covenant that your Acquaintance be general; that you admit no sworn Confident, or Intimate of your own Sex; no she Friend to skreen her Affairs under your Countenance, and tempt you to make Trial of a mutual Secresie. No Decoy-Duck to wheadle you a *fop*—scambling to the Play in a Mask—Then bring you home in a pretended Fright, when you think you shall be found out. And rail at me for missing the Play, and disappointing the Frolick which you had to pick me up and prove my Constancy.

MILL. : Detestable *Inprimis*! I go to the Play in a Mask!

MIR. : *Item*. I article, that you continue to like your own Face, as long as I shall: And while it passes currant with me, that you endeavour not to new Coin it. To which end, together with all Vizards for the Day, I prohibit all Masks for the Night, made of Oil'd-skins and I know not what—Hog's bones, Hare's Gall, Pig Water, and the Marrow of a roasted Cat. In short, I forbid all Commerce with the Gentlewoman in *what-d'ye-call-it* Court. *Item*. I shut my doors against all Bauds with Basket and penny-worths of *Muslin, China, Fans, Atlasses*, etc.—*Item*, when you shall be Breeding——

MILL. : Ah! Name it not.

MIR. : Which may be presum'd, with a Blessing on our Endeavours—

MILL. : Odious Endeavours!

MIR. : I denounce against all strait Lacing, squeezing for a Shape, 'till you mould my Boy's Head like a Sugar-Loaf; and instead of a Man-child, make me Father to a Crooked-Billet. Lastly, to the Dominion of the *Tea-Table* I submit.—But with provisio, that you exceed not in your Province; but restrain yourself to native and simple Tea-Table Drinks, as *Tea*, *Chocolate*, and *Coffee*. As likewise to Genuine and Authoriz'd Tea-Table Talk—Such as mending of Fashions, spoiling Reputations, railing at absent Friends, and so forth—But that on no Account you encroach upon the Mens Prerogative, and presume to drink Healths, or toast Fellows; for prevention of which, I banish all *Foreign Forces*, all Auxiliaries to the *Tea-Table*, as *Orange-Brandy*, all *Anniseed*, *Cinamon*, *Citron*, and *Barbado's-Waters*, together with *Ratafia* and the most noble spirit of *Clary*. But for *Cowslip-Wine*, *Poppy-Water*, and all *Dormitives*, those I allow.—These Proviso's admitted, in other things I may prove a tractable and complying Husband.

MILL. : O horrid *Proviso's*! filthy strong Waters! I toast Fellows, Odious Men! I hate your odious *Proviso's*.

MIR. : Then we're agreed. Shall I kiss your Hand upon the Contract? and here comes one to be a witness to the Sealing of the Deed.

Enter MRS FAINALL

MILL. : *Fainall*, what shall I do? Shall I have him? I think I must have him.

574

MRS FAIN. : Ay, ay, take him, take him, what shou'd you do ?

MILL. : Well then—I'll take my Death I'm in a horrid Fright—*Fainall*, I shall never say it—Well—I think—I'll endure you.

MRS FAIN. : Fy, fy, have him, have him, and tell him so in plain terms : For I am sure you have a Mind to him.

MILL. : Are you ? I think I have—and the horrid Man looks as if he thought so too—Well, you ridiculous thing you, I'll have you—I won't be kissed, nor I won't be thank'd— Here, kiss my hand tho'—So hold your Tongue now, don't say a Word.

WILLIAM CONGREVE
The Way of the World (1700)

A HIGH-MINDED PAIR

One day when he was there, looking upon an odde by-shelf, in her sister's closett, he found a few Latine bookes ; asking whose they were, he was told they were her elder sister's, whereupon, inquiring more after her, he began first to be sorrie she was gone before he had seene her. . . . Then he grew to love to heare mention of her, and the other gentlewomen who had bene her companions, used to talke much to him of her, telling him how reserv'd and studious she was, and other things which they esteem'd no advantage ; but it so much inflam'd Mr. Hutchinson's desire of seeing her, that he began to wonder at himselfe that his heart, which had ever had such an indifferency for the most excellent of womankind, should have such strong impulses towards a stranger he never saw; and certainly it was of the Lord, (though he perceiv'd it not), who had ordein'd him, thro' so many various providences, to be yoak'd with her in whom he found so much satisfaction. There scarcely past anie day, but some accident or some discourse still kept alive his desire of seeing this gentlewoman. . . . One day there was a greate deale of company mett at Mr. Coleman's, the gentleman's house where he tabled, to heare the musick, and a certeine song was sung . . . and gave occasion to some of the company to mention an answer to it, which was in the house, and upon some of their desires read: a gentleman saying 'twas believ'd that a woman in the neighbourhood had made it, it was presently inquir'd who? whereupon a gentleman, then present . . . sayd, there were but two women that could be guilty of it, whereof one was . . . Mrs. Apsley. Mr. Hutchinson, fancying something of rationallity in the sonnett, beyond the customary reach of a shee-witt, allthough, to speak truth, it signified very little, addrest himself to the gentleman, and told him, he could scarcely believe it was a woman's, whereupon this gentleman, who was a man of good understanding and expression, and inspir'd with some passion for her himselfe, which made him regard all her perfections through a multiplying glasse, told Mr. Hutchinson, that . . . he was confident it was Mrs. Apsley's only, for she had sence above all the rest. . . . Mr. Hutchinson hearing all this, sayd . . . I cannot be at rest till this ladie's returne, that I may be acquainted with her; the gentleman replied, Sir, you must not expect that, for she is of an humour she will not be acquainted with any of mankind, and however this song is stolen forth, she if the nicest creature in the world of suffering her perfections to be knowne, she shuns the converse of men as the plague, she only lives in the enjoyment of herself, and has not the humanitie to communicate that happiness to any of our sex. " Well," sayd Mr. Hutchinson, " but I will be acquainted with her " ; and indeed the information of this reserv'd humour pleas'd him, more than all elce he had heard, and fill'd him now with thoughts, how he should attaine the sight and knowledge of her. . . . This at length he obteined ; but his heart, being prepossesst with his owne fancy, was not free to discerne how little there was in her to answer so greate an expectation. She was not ugly, in a carelesse riding-habitt she had a melancholly negligence both of herselfe and others, as if she neither affected to please others, nor tooke notice of anie thing before her : yet spite of all her indifferency, she was surpriz'd with some unusuall liking in her soule, when she saw this gentleman, who had haire, eies, shape, and countenance enough to begett love in any one at the first, and these sett of with a gracefull and generous mine, which promis'd an extraordinary person ; he was at that time, and indeed always very neatly habited, for he wore good and rich clothes, and had variety of them, and had them well suited and every way answerable. . . . He found withall, that though she was modest, she was accostable, and willing to entertaine his acquaintance. This soone past into a mutuall friendship betweene them, and though she innocently thought nothing of love, yett was she glad to have acquir'd such a friend. . . . Mr. Hutchinson, on the other side, having bene told, and seeing how she shun'd all other men, and how civilly she entertain'd him, believ'd that a secret power had wrought a mutuall inclination betweene them, and dayly frequented her mother's house, and had the opportunitie of conversing with her in those pleasant walkes, which, at that sweete season of the spring, invited all the neighbouring inhabitants to seeke their joyes ; where, though they were never alone, yet they had every day opertunity for converse with each other, which the rest shar'd not in, while every one minded their owne delights. . . . He in the meanewhile prosecuted his live, with so much discretion, duty, and honor that at the length, through many difficulties, he accomplisht his designe. I shall passe by all the little amorous relations, which if I would take the paynes to relate, would make a true history of a more handsome management of love then the best romances describe ; for these are to be forgotten as the vanities of youth, not worthy of mention among the greater transactions of his life. There is this only to be recorded, that never was there a passion more ardent and lesse idolatrous ; he lov'd her better than his life, with inexpressible tendernesse and kindnesse, had a most high obliging esteeme of her, yet still consider'd honour, religion, and duty, above her, nor ever suffer'd the intrusion of such a dotage as should blind him from marking her imperfections ; these he looked upon with such an indulgent eie as did not abate his love and esteeme of her, while it augmented his care to blott out all those spotts which might make her appeare lesse worthy of that respect he pay'd her ; and thus indeed he soone made her more equall to him than he found her ; for she was a very faithfull mirror, reflecting truly, though but dimmely, his owne glories upon him, so long as he was present. . . . 'Twas not her face he lov'd, her honor and her vertue were his mistresses, and these (like Pigmalion's) images of his owne making. . . . That day that the friends on both sides met to conclude the marriage, she fell sick of the small pox, which was many wayes a great triall upon

578

him ; first, her life was allmost in desperate hazard, and
then the disease, for the present, made her the most
deformed person that could be seene, for a greate while
after she recover'd ; yett he was nothing troubled at it, but
married her as soone as she was able to quitt the chamber
when the priest and all that saw her were affrighted to
looke on her : but God recompenc'd his justice and
constancy, by restoring her, though she was longer than
ordinary before she recover'd, as well as before. One thing
is very observable, and worthy imitation in him ; although
he had as strong and violent affection for her as any man
had, yet he declar'd it not to her till he had first acquainted
her father. . . . At length, to the full content of all, the thing
was accomplish'd, and on the third day of July, in the
1638, he was married to Mrs. Lucy Apsley, the second
daughter of Sr. Allen Apsley, late liftenant of the Tower
of London, at St. Andrew's church in Holborne.

LUCY HUTCHINSON
Memoirs of Life of John Hutchinson (c. 1665)

WILLIAM AND DOROTHY

Nothing can alter the resolution I have taken of settling
my whole stock of happinesse upon the affection of a
person that is deare to mee whose kindnesse I shall
infinitly preffer before any other consideration whatsoever, and I shall not blush to tell you, that you have
made the whole world besydes soe indifferent to mee,
that if I cannot be yours they may dispose mee how they
please, H.C. will be as acceptable to me as any body else.

DOROTHY OSBORNE
Letter to Sir William Temple (1653)

A PRETTY RIDDLE

Down in a Garden sat my dearest love
Her skin more soft than down of Swan,
More tender hearted than the Turtle Dove,
And far more kinde than bleeding Pellican ;
I courted her, she rose, and blushing said,
Why was I born to live, and die a Maid ?
With that I pluckt a pretty Marygold,
Whose dewy leaves shut up when day is done,
Sweeting (I said) arise, look and behold,
A pretty Riddle I'le to thee unfold.
These leaves shut in as close as cloyster'd Nun,
Yet will thye open when they see the Sun.
What mean you by this Riddle Sir, she said,
I pray expound it : Then I thus began,
Are not Men made for Maids, and Maids for Men ?
With that she chang'd her colour, and grew wan,
Since now this Riddle you so well unfold,
Be you the Sun, I'le be the Marygold.   ANON

Song 70 : *New Academy of Compliments* (c. 1630)

THE LOST NYMPH

Tell me you wandering spirits of the Ayre,
Did you not see a Nimph more bright, more faire
Then beauties darling, or of parts more sweet
Than stolne content ? If such a one you meet
   Wait on her hourely where so e're she flies,
   And cry, and cry, *Amintas* for her absence dies.

Go search the Vallies, pluck up every Rose,
You'l find a scent, a blush of her in those :

Fish, Fish for Pearle, or Corrall, there you'l see
How orientall all her colours bee :
    Go call the Ecchoes to your ayde, and cry,
    Chloris, Chloris, for that's her name for whom I dy.

But stay a while, I have inform'd you ill,
Were she on earth, she had been with me still :
Go fly to Heaven, examine every Sphere,
And try what Star hath lately lighted there ;
    If any brighter than the Sun you see,
    Fall down, fall down and worship it, for that is
    shee.

ANON
Select Musicall Ayres and Dialogues (1672)

SCEPTICISM

HERODOTUS DOUBTS

Besides many other stories which the Hellenes tell without due consideration, this tale is especially foolish which
they tell about Heracles. . . . I for my part am of the opinion
that the Hellenes when they tell this tale are altogether
without knowledge of the nature and customs of the
Egyptians. . . . Besides this, how is it possible that
Heracles, being one person only . . . should slay many
myriads ? Having said so much of these matters, we pray
that we may have grace from both the gods and the
heroes for our speech. . . .

I do not believe this tale either, that nature produces one-eyed men which in all other respects are like other men. . . .

These bald-headed men say (though I do not believe it) that the mountains are inhabited by men with goats' feet ; and that . . . others are found who sleep through six months of the year. This I do not admit at all as true. . . .

As to the feathers of which the Scythians say the air is full . . . the opinion which I have is this :—in the parts beyond this land it snows continually. . . . Now whosoever has seen close at hand snow falling thickly knows what I mean without further explanation. . . .

It is said of them by the Scythians . . . that once in every year each of the Neuroi becomes a wolf for a few days, and then returns to his original form. For my part I do not believe them when they say this, but they say it nevertheless, and swear it moreover. . . .

I marvel if the tale is true which is reported, for it is said that he dived into the sea at Aphetai and did not come up till he reached Artemision, having traversed here somewhere about eighty furlongs through the sea. Now there are told about this man several other tales which seem likely to be false, but some also which are true : about this matter however let it be stated as my opinion that he came to Artemision in a boat.

HERODOTUS (5th cent. B.C.)
Trans. G. C. Macaulay

PLINY TOO

That men may be transformed into wolves, and restored again to their former shape, we must confidently beleeve

582

to be a lowd lie, or else give credit to all those tales which
we have for so many ages found to be meere fables. . . .
A wonder it is to see, to what passe these Greekes are
come in their credulity : there is not so shamelesse a lye
but it findeth one or other of them to uphold and maintaine it.

PLINY THE ELDER, *Natural History* (c. 77)
Trans. Philemon Holland (1601)

THE STRANGE RELATIONS OF AUTHORS

The strange relations made by Authors, may sufficiently
discourage our adherence unto Authority, and which if
we believe we must be apt to swallow anything. . . .

The common opinion of the Ostrich . . . or Sparrow-
Camel, conceives that it digesteth Iron ; and this is confirmed by the affirmations of many. . . . Notwithstanding
upon enquiry we find it very questionable, and the nega-
tive seems most reasonably entertained ; whose verity
indeed we do the rather desire, because hereby we shall
relieve our ignorance of one occult quality. . . .

We shall not, I hope, disparage the Resurrection of our
Redeemer, if we say the Sun doth not dance on Easter
Day. And though we would willingly assent unto any
sympathetical exultation, yet cannot conceive therein
any more than a Tropical expression. Whether any such
motion there were in that day wherein Christ arised,
Scripture hath not revealed, which hath been punctual
in other records concerning solar miracles : and the
Areopagite that was amazed at the Eclipse, took no notice
of this. . . .

And though it be said that poyson will break a Venice glass, yet have we not met with any of that nature. . . .

The story of the wandering Jew is very strange, and will hardly obtain belief. . . .

Unto some it hath seemed incredible what Herodotus reporteth of the great Army of Xerxes, that drank whole rivers dry. And unto the Author himself it appeared wondrous strange. . . .

That Annibal eat or brake through the Alps with Vinegar, may be too grossly taken. . . .

That Archimedes burnt the ships of Marcellus, with speculums of parabolical figures, at three furlongs . . . sounds hard unto reason. . . .

SIR THOMAS BROWNE, Pseudodoxia Epidemica (1646)

LOUD LIARS

Many have held opinion that Pliny and Aulus Gellius were loud liars, when they wrote and published, that there lived a certain kinde of people in Scythia, which had Dogs heads, and that they howled like dogs, instead of speaking as other men doe. JOHN BULWER

Anthropometamorphosis, or the Artificial Changeling (1650)

NO SUCH THING

I feel that we should say most times : There is no such thing. MICHAEL DE MONTAIGNE, Essays (1580)

Trans. John Florio (1603)

You seem sollicitous about that pretty thing called soul. I do protest you I know nothing of it, not whether it is, nor what it is, nor what it shall be. Young scholars and priests know all that perfectly. For my part I am but a very ignorant fellow.

F. M. A. DE VOLTAIRE

Letter to James Boswell (Feb. 1765, *after Boswell's visit to Ferney and in reply to a letter continuing their theological controversy*)

SERMONS

A Democratic Sermon

God forgive mee I was as neer Laughing Yesterday where I should not : would you beleeve that I had the grace to goe heare a sermon upon a week day . . . and Mr Marshall was the man that preached, but never any body was soe defeated, hee is soe famed that I expected rare things from him and seriously I listned to him at first with as much reverence and attention as if hee had bin St Paul. And what doe you think hee told us ? why that if there were no kings no Queens noe Lord's no Lady's noe Gentlemen nor Gentlewoman, in the world, twould bee noe losse at all to God Almighty. This wee had over some forty times which made mee remember it whither

585

I would or not, the rest was much at this rate, enterlarded with the prittyest od phrases that I had the most adoe to look soberly enough for the place I was in that ever I had in my life ; hee do's not preach soe always sure ; if hee do's I cannot beleeve his Sermon's will doe much toward's the bringing any body to heaven, more than by Excercising there Patience. Yet I'le say that for him, hee stood stoutly for Tyth's, though in my opinion few deserved them lesse than hee, and it may bee hee would bee better without them.

DOROTHY OSBORNE, *Letter to Sir William Temple* (1653)

PREACHING TO THE JEWS

A sermon was preach'd to the Jewes at Ponte Sisto, who are constrain'd to it till the houre is don ; but it is with so much malice in their countenances, spitting, hum'ing, coughing, and motion, that it is almost impossible they should heare a word from the preacher. A conversion is very rare.

JOHN EVELYN, *Diary* (Jan. 7, 1645)

KEEPING THE DEAN IN ORDER

Leave that alone ! To your text, Mr Dean ! To your text ! Leave that. We have heard enough of that. To your subject !
QUEEN ELIZABETH

(*To the Dean of St Paul's when he preached against images in churches*)

586

May 14. 1669.

Most of the company gone, and I going, I heard by a gentleman of a sermon that was to be there ; [Lambeth Palace] and so I staid to hear it, thinking it serious, till by and by the gentleman told me it was a mockery, by one Cornet Bolton, a very gentleman-like man, that behind a chair did pray and preach like a Presbyter Scot that ever I heard in my life, with all the possible imitation in grimaces and voice. And his text about the hanging up their harps upon the willows ; and a serious good sermon too, exclaiming against Bishops, and crying up of my good Lord Eglinton, till it made us all burst ; but I did wonder to have the [Arch] Bishop at this time to make himself sport with things of this kind, but I perceive it was shewn him as a rarity ; and he took care to have the room door shut, but there was about twenty gentlemen there, and myself, infinitely pleased with the novelty.

Nov. 16. 1661.

So to church again, and heard a simple fellow upon the praise of Church musique, and exclaiming against men's wearing their hats on in the church, but I slept part of the sermon, till latter prayer and blessing and all was done without waking which I never did in my life.

April 1. *ib.*

Staid to hear a sermon ; but, it being a Presbyterian one, it was so long, that after above an hour of it we went away, and I home and dined.

Christmas Day, ib.

Bishop Morley preached upon the song of the Angels ... Methought he made but a poor sermon, but long, and reprehending the mistaken jollity of the Court for the true joy that shall and ought to be on those days, he particularized concerning their excess in plays and gaming, ... Upon which it was worth observing how far they are come from taking the reprehensions of a bishopp seriously, that they all laugh in the chappell when he reflected on their ill actions and courses. He did much press us to join these publique days of joy, and to hospitality. But one that stood by whispered in my ear that the Bishopp himself do not spend one groat to the poor himself.

SAMUEL PEPYS
Diary

REFRESHMENT

At the 2 howers sermons at St Pauls crosse the preacher to refresh him and continue his voyce was used to stoope down in the pulpitt and drinck.

SIR THOMAS BROWNE
Miscellaneous Writings (undated)

PREACHING LIKE AN ANGEL

His Majestie appointed him a day to preach to him. And though his Majestie and others expected much from him, yet he was so happy (which few are) as to satisfie and

588

exceed their expectations : preaching the Word so, as shewed he was possest with those joyes that he labored to distill into others : A Preacher in earnest, weeping sometimes for his Auditory, some with them, always preaching to himselfe like an Angel from a cloud, though in none : carrying some (as St. *Paul* was) to Heaven, in holy raptures ; and enticing others, by a sacred art and courtship, to amend their lives ; here picturing a vice so as to make it ugly to those that practised it ; and a vertue so, as to make it beloved, even by those that lov'd it not ; and all this with a most particular grace, and an unimitable fashion of speaking.

IZAAK WALTON
The Life and Death of Dr. Donne
(1640 and 1670 editions)

A Good Riddance

I have liv'd to see both Greek and Latin almost entirely driven out of the Pulpit, for which I am heartily glad.

JONATHAN SWIFT
Letter to a Young Gentleman (1721)

If I Were A Clergyman

Now I felt that if I composed and preached sermons, I should by no means compose myself to the Vicar's threadbare subjects—should preach the Wrath of God, and sound the last Trump in the ears of my Hell-doomed

589

congregation, cracking the heavens and dissolving the world with the eclipses and earthquakes of the great Day of Judgement. Then I might refresh them with high and incomprehensible Doctrines, beyond the reach of Reason —Predestination, Election, the Co-existence and Co-eternities of the incomprehensible Triad. And with what a holy vehemence would I exclaim and cry out against all forms of doctrinal Error—all the execrable hypotheses of the great Heresiarchs ! Then there would be many ancient and learned and out-of-the-way Iniquities to denounce and splendid, neglected Virtues to inculcate—Apostolic Poverty, and Virginity, that precious jewel, that fair garland, so prized in Heaven, but so rare, it is said, on earth.

For in the range of creeds and morals it is the highest peaks that shine for me with a certain splendour : it is towards those radiant Alps that, if I were a Clergyman, I should lead my flock to pasture.

LOGAN PEARSALL SMITH
Trivia (1918)

THE SWEETEST WORDS

And never was I more glad after a long sermon on a cold day to come to those dear words—" Now to God the Father," and " The Peace of God,"—words which were for so many years the sweetest to me in the whole Church service, and which I shall love as long as I live.

ROBERT SOUTHEY
Letter to Captain Southey, R.N. (1812)

SHOWING OFF

PARTRIDGE FOR DINNER

The Gentlemen Criolians or natives of *Chiapa* . . . as
presumptuous they are and arrogant, as if the noblest
bloud in the Court of *Madrid* ran through their veines.
It is a common thing amongst them to make a dinner only
with a dish of Frixoles in black broath, boyled with pepper
and garlicke, saying it is the most nourishing meat in all
the *India's* ; and after this so stately a dinner they will
be sure to come out to the street-dore of their houses, to
see and to be seen, and there for halfe an houre will they
stand shaking off the crums of bread from their cloaths,
bands, (but especially from their ruffes when they used
them) and from their mustachoes. And with their tooth-
pickers they will stand picking their teeth, as if some
small Partridge bone stuck in them ; nay if a friend passe
by at that time, they will be sure to find out some crum
or other in their mustacho (as if on purpose the crums of
the table had been shaken upon their beards . . .) and
they will be sure to vent out some non-truth, as to say,
A Senor que linds perdiz he comido oy, O Sir, what a dainty
Partridge have I eat to-day, where as they picke out

nothing from their teeth but a black husk of a dry frixole or Turkey bean.—

The English-American ; his travail by sea and land (1648)

It Seemed to Him

Now Sir William would sometimes, when he was pleasant over a glasse of wine with his most intimate friends—e.g. Sam. Butler (author of Hudibras) etc.—say, that it seemed to him that he writt with the very spirit of Shakespeare, and seemd contented enough to be thought his son. He would tell them the story as above, in which way his mother had a very light report.

JOHN AUBREY
Brief Lives : Sir William Davenant (c. 1680)

Lucullus

He was a vaine man in his ordinarie service at his borde, not only in that his beddes whereon he fedde, were covered with rich carpettes of purple, and him selfe served in gold and silver vessell set with pretious stones, and that there was dauncing, musicke, playes, and other such like pastimes of ordinary : but also for that he was continually served with all sortes of fine dainty dishes, with workes of pastry, bancketing dishes, and frute curiously wrought and prepared, which only made him to be wonderd at of men of simple understanding and mean condicion. . . .

In such thinges therefore did Lucullus lavishly and riotously spend his goods, like spoyles in dede gotten of slaves and barbarous peple.

PLUTARCH
Lives (c. 100)
Trans. Sir Thomas North (1579)

A FIRE-EATING CAPTAIN

SIR JOSEPH WITOLL : By the Lord *Harry*, Mr *Sharper*, he's a brave a Fellow as *Cannibal*, are not you, Bully-Back ?

SHARPER : *Hannibal* I believe you mean, Sir Joseph.

CAPTAIN BLUFFE : Undoubtedly he did, Sir ; faith *Hannibal* was a very pretty Fellow—but Sir *Joseph*, Comparisons are odious—*Hannibal* was a very pretty Fellow in those Days, it must be granted—but alas Sir ! were he alive now, he would be nothing, nothing in the Earth.

SHARPER : How Sir ! I make a doubt, if there be at this Day a greater General breathing.

BLUFFE : Oh excuse me, Sir ; have you serv'd abroad, Sir ?

SHARP. : Not I really, Sir.

BL. : Oh I thought so—Why then you can know nothing, Sir : I am afraid you scarce know the History of the late War in *Flanders*, with all its particulars.

SH. : Not I, Sir, no more than publick Letters, or *Gazettes* tell us.

BL. : Gazette ! Why there agin now—Why, Sir, there are not three Words of Truth, the Year round, put into the Gazette—I'll tell you a strange thing now as to that—

593

You must know, Sir, I was resident in *Flanders* the last Campaign, had a small Post there ; but no matter for that—Perhaps, Sir, there was scarce any thing of moment done but an humble Servant of yours, that shall be nameless, was an Eye Witness of—I won't say had the greatest share in't. Tho' I might say that too, since I name no Body you know—Well, Mr *Sharper*, would you think it ? In all this time—as I hope for a Truncheon—this rascally Gazette-writer never so much once mention'd me—Not once by the Wars—Took no more notice, than as if Nol. Bluffe had not been in the Land of the Living.

Sh. : Strange !

Sir Jo. : Yet by the Lord *Harry* 'tis true Mr *Sharper*, for I went every Day to Coffee-Houses to read the Gazette my self.

Bl. : Ay, ay, no matter—You see, Mr *Sharper* after all I am content to retire—Live a private Person—*Scipio* and others have done it. . . . .

Sir J. : Ay, this damned Modesty of yours—Agad if he would put in for't he might be made General himself yet.

Bl. : Oh fie, no Sir *Joseph*—You know I hate this.

Sir J. : Let me but tell Mr *Sharper* a little, how you eat Fire once out of the Mouth of a Cannon—agad he did ; those impenetrable Whiskers of his have confronted Flames——

Bl. : Death, what do you mean, Sir *Joseph* ?

Sir J. : Look you know, I tell you he's so modest he'll own nothing.

Bl. : Pish you have put me out, I have forgot what I was about. Pray hold your Tongue and give me leave.

WILLIAM CONGREVE
The Old Batchelor (1693)

Swimming the Hellespont

This morning I *swam* from Sestos to *Abydos*. . . . The current renders it hazardous;—so much so that I doubt whether Leander's conjugal affection must not have been a little chilled in his passage to Paradise I . . . crossed the " broad Hellespont " in about an hour and ten minutes.

LORD BYRON
Letter to Henry Drury (1810)

The Froth of Ostentation

All his humor rises up into the froth of ostentation; which if it once settle, falles downe into a narrow roome. If the excesse be in the understanding part, all his wit is in print; the Presse hath left his head emptie; yea, not only what he had, but what he could borrow without leave. If his glorie be in his devotion, he gives not an Almes but on record; and if he have once done well, God heares of it often; for upon every unkindnesse hee is readie to upbraid him with his merits. . . . Or, if a more gallant humour possesse him, hee weares all his land on his backe, and walking high, looks over his left shoulder, to see if the point of his rapier follow him with a grace. Hee is proud of another mans horse; and wel mounted, thinks every man wrongs him, that looks not at him. A bare head in the street doth him more good than a meales meat. Hee sweares bigge at an Ordinarie, and talkes of the Court with a sharpe accent; neither vouchsafes to name anie not honourable, nor those without some terme of familiaritie, and likes well to see the hearer looke upon him amazedly ; as if he sayd, How happie is this man that is so great with great ones ! Under pretence of seeking for a scroll of newes, hee drawes out an handfull of letters, indorsed with his owne stile, to the height ; and halfe reading every title, passes over the latter part, with a murmur ; not without signifying, what Lord sent this, what great Ladie the other ; and for what sutes : the last paper (as it happens) is his newes from his honourable friend in the French Court. In the midst of dinner, his Lacquay comes sweating in, with a sealed note from his creditour, who now threatens a speedie arrest, and whispers the ill newes in his Masters eare, when hee aloud names a Counsellor of State, and prefesses to know the imployment. The same messenger hee calles with an imperious nod, and after expostulation, where he hath left his fellowes, in his eare sends him for some new spur-leathers or stockings, by this time footed, and when he is gone halfe the roome, recalles him, and sayth aloud, *It is no matter, let the greater bagge alone till I come ;* and yet againe calling him closer, whispers (so that all the table may hear) *that if his crimson sute be readie against the day, the rest need no haste.* He picks his teeth when his stomacke is emptie, and calles for Pheasants at a common Inne. You shall find him prizing the richest jewels, and fairest horses, when his purse yeelds not money enough for earnest. He thrusts himselfe into the prease before some great Ladies ; and loves to be seene neere the head of a great traine. His talke is how many Mourners hee furnish't with gownes at his fathers funerals, how many messes ; how rich his coat is, and how ancient, how great his alliance : what challenges hee hath made and answered ; what exploits at *Cales* or *Nieuport* : and when

596

hee hath commended others buildings, furnitures, sutes, compares them with his owne. When hee hath undertaken to be the Broker for some rich Diamond, he weares it, and pulling off his glove to stroke up his haire, thinks no eye should have any other object. Entertaining his friend, he chides his Cooke for no better cheere, and names the dishes he meant, and wants. To conclude, hee is ever on the stage, and acts still a glorious part abroad. . . . He is a Spanish souldier on an Italian Theater ; a bladder full of winde, a skin full of words ; a fooles wonder, and a wise mans foole.

JOSEPH HALL
Characters of Vertues and Vices (1608)

THAT WAY MADNESS LIES

If we consult the Collegiates of *Moorfields*, we shall find most of them are beholden to their Pride for their introduction into that magnificent Palace. I had some Years ago the Curiosity to enquire into the particular circumstances of these whimsical Freeholders, and learned from their own Mouths the Conditions and Character of each of them. Indeed, I found that all I spoke to were Persons of Quality. There were at that time five Duchesses, three Earls, two Heathen Gods, an Emperor, and a Prophet. There were also a great Number of such as were locked up from their Estates, and others who concealed their Titles. A Leather-seller of Taunton whisper'd me in the Ear, That he was the Duke of *Monmouth* ; but begged me not to betray him. At a little distance from him sat a

Taylor's Wife, . . . I presumed to ask her, Who she was ?
And was answered, *My Lady Mayoress.* . . .

I was resolved to guard myself against a Passion which
makes such Havock in the Brain, and produces so much
Disorder in the Imagination. For this Reason I have
endeavoured to keep down the secret Swellings of
Resentment, and stifle the very first Suggestions of Self-
Esteem.

RICHARD STEELE

Lucubrations of Isaac Bickerstaff. Tatler No. 127
(1709)

TARTARIN GOES LION-HUNTING

Suddenly, towards ten o'clock, there was a great move-
ment in the crowd. The garden gate turned violently on
its hinges.

" It's he ! It's he ! " people cried.

It was he.

When he appeared on the threshold, two cries of
astonishment went up from the crowd.

" He's a Turk ! "

" He's got spectacles ! "

Tartarin of Tarascon, in fact, had conceived it to be his
duty, since he was going to Algeria, to assume Algerian
costume. Large puffed trousers of white linen, small tight
jacket with metal buttons, two feet of red sash round the
stomach, the neck bare, the face shaved, on the head a
huge red fez, and a blue streamer of immense length !
With this, two heavy guns, one on each shoulder, a great
hunting-knife in the sash, a cartridge pouch on the

stomach, a revolver balancing in a leather pocket on the hip. That was all. . . .

Ah, pardon me, I forgot the spectacles ; an enormous pair of blue goggles which came in very aptly to correct anything that might be a little too fierce in our hero's get-up.

" Long live Tartarin ! Long live Tartarin ! " shouted the people. The great man smiled, but did not bow, because of the guns which hindered him. For the rest, he knew now how to keep popular favour ; possibly in the depths of his soul he cursed his dreadful countrymen who were forcing him to depart, to leave his pretty little home, with its white walls and its green shutters. . . . But of this one saw nothing.

Calm and proud, though rather pale, he walked along the street . . . and briskly took the road to the railway station.

ALPHONSE DAUDET
Tartarin de Tarascon (1872)

A SCHOLAR-MOUNTEBANK

He is indeed a kind of Schollar-Mountebank . . . trickt out in all the accoutrements of Learning, . . . he heares you not till the third knocke, and then comes out very angry, as interrupted. You find him in his Slippers, and a Pen in his eare. . . . His Table is spred wide with some Classicke Folio, which is as constant to it as the carpet, and hath laid open in the same Page this halfe yeere. . . . His pocket is seldome without a Greeke Testament, or Hebrew Bible, which hee opens only in the Church, and that when

599

some stander by lookes over. He has his sentences for Company, some scatterings of *Seneca* and *Tacitus*, which are good upon all occasions. If he reads any thing in the morning, it comes up all at dinner ; and as long as that lasts, the discourse is his. Hee is a great *Plagiarie* of Taverne-wit, and comes to sermons onely that hee may talke of *Austin*. . . . He talkes much of *Scaliger* and *Casaubone*, and the Jesuites, and prefers some unheard-of Dutch name before them all. He has verses to bring in upon these and these hints, and it shall goe hard but he will wind in his opportunity.

JOHN EARLE
Micro-cosmographie (1628)

SHOWS

WHAT SO PLEASANT

What so pleasant as to see some Pageant or Sight goe by, as at Coronations, Weddings, and such like Solemnities, to see an Embassadour or a Prince met, received, entertained, with Masks, Shewes, Fireworks, &c. . . . To behold a battle fought, like that of *Cressy*, or *Agincourt*. . . . To see one of *Caesar's* triumphs in old *Rome* revived, or the like. . . . So infinitely pleasant are such Shewes, to the sight of which often times they will come hundreds of miles, give any money for a place, and remember many

yeares after with singular delight. *Bodine*, when he was
Embassador in *England*, said he saw the Noblemen go in
their Robes to the Parliament House . . . he was much
affected with the sight of it. *Pomponius Columna* . . . saw
13 *Frenchmen* and so many *Italians* once fight for a whole
Army : . . . the pleasantest sight that ever he saw in his
life. Who would not have been affected with such a
Spectacle ? . . . The very reading of Feasts, Triumphs,
Interviews, Nuptialls, Tilts, Turnaments, Combats, and
Monomaches, is most acceptable and pleasant.

ROBERT BURTON
The Anatomy of Melancholy (1621. Edition 1632)

MONEY'S WORTH

To see a strange out-landish Fowle,
A quaint Baboon, an Ape, an Owle,
A dancing Beare, a Gyants bone,
A foolish Ingin move alone,
A Morris-dance, a Puppit-play.
Mad *Tom* to sing a Roundelay,
A Woman dancing on a Rope,
Bull-baiting also at the *Hope* ;
A Rimers Jests, a Juglers cheats,
A Tumbler showing cunning feats,
Or Players acting on the Stage—
There goes the bounty of our Age :
    But unto any pious motion,
      There's little coine and lesse devotion.

HENRY FARLEY
(1621)

SHOPPING

The Pedlar

1.

Who is it will repaire,
　　or come and see my packet :
Where there's store of Ware,
　　if any of you lacke it,
view the Fayre.

2.

Faire Maydens come and see,
　　If heere be ought will please you :
And if we can agree,
　　Ile give you just your due,
Or nere trust me.

5.

Farre-fetcht *Indian* ware,
　　and *China* hard to enter :
Which to get is rare,
　　costs many lives to venter,
we nere care.

6.

From *Venice* Citie comes
    great store of rare Complection,
From western Iles your Gummes
    to keep Teeth from infection,
and from Rhewmes.

7.

Heere is a water rare,
    will make a wench that's fiftie,
For to look more fayre
    then one that wants of twenty,
stil'd from the Ayre.

8.

A Perriwig to weare,
    or Cover for bare places :
If you have lost your heare,
    full many one it graces :
tis not deare.

9.

Heeres Poking stickes of steele,
    and Christall Looking Glasses :
Here globes that round will wheele
    to see each one that passes,
Dildo Dill.

10.

Pomado for your Lips,
    to make them soft and ruddy :
And sweet as Cipres chips,
    a lustre like a Ruby
soone it gets.

11.

Heres Bracelets for your arm
  of Corall, or of Amber :
A Powder that will Charme
  or bring one to your Chamber,
tis no harme.

15.

Rebatoes, Tyres, and Rings,
  Sissers and a Thimble :
And many pretty thinges,
  to keepe your fingers nimble,
weaving stringes.

17.

Balles of Camphyre made,
  to keepe your face from pimples :
An Unguent that's alayd,
  you never shall have wrinckles,
if a Mayde.

18.

Spunges for your face,
  or Sope that came from *Turkey* :
Your favour it will grace,
  if that you be not durty,
in no place.

19.

Rich imbroydered Gloves,
  to draw upon your white hand :
Or to give your Loves,
  a Ruffe or falling band,
my pretty Doves.

604

22.

Pinnes both white and red,
   of all sortes and all sizes :
Plumbes and Ginger bread,
   my Wares of divers prizes,
Bookes to read.

23.

Venice Glasses fine,
   were newly made in London :
To drinke your Beere or Wine,
   come now my Pack's undone,
speake betime.

24.

Lawne and Cambricke pure.
   as good as e're was worne :
Like yron it will dure,
   untill that it be torne,
be you sure.

25.

Heer's many other thinges,
   As Jewes trumps, pipes, and Babies :
St. *Martins* Beades and Ringes,
   and other toyes for Ladyes,
knots and stringes.

27.

And as my Ware doth prove,
   so let me take your mony :
My pretty Turtle Dove,
   that sweeter is then hony,
which is Love ;   ANON
    The Pedler opening his Pack (c. 1620)

SHOP-GIRL : Madame, what doth it please you to have ?
Would ye have any faire linnen cloath ? Mistris, see what
I have, and I will showe you the fayrest linnen cloath in
London, if you do not like it, you may leave it, you shall
bestowe nothing but the looking on, The payne shall be
ours to showe them you.

LADY : Into what Shop shall we goe ?

MASTER DU VAULT-L'AMOUR : Madame, will it please you
to enter into this Shop ? . . .

LADY : How sell you the Ell of this Cambricke ?

SHOP-GIRL : I knowe you have so good Judgement in
linnen cloath, that I dare not showe you any for good,
unlesse it were so : there needes no replye to such a Lady
as you are, you may say your pleasure, the Cambricke
will cost you twentie shillings the Ell.

LADY : Truly it lacketh no price : And if thinges be so
much worth as those which sell them, doe make them to
be : your Cambricke is very good, for you holde it at a
good price, But yet I will not give so much tho.

SHOP-GIRL : How much will it please you to give then
Madame ? to the end that I may have your Custome ?

LADY : I will give you fifteene shillings, If you will take
my money make shorte, for I have other busines then to
tarye heere.

SHOP-GIRL : Truely Madame I would be verye sorie to
denie you if I could give it at that price, but in truth
I cannot, unles I should lose by it.

LADY : I will give you sixteene, and not one halfpeny more.
Mistris Du Pont-galliard, is it not enough ?

MISTRESSE DU PONT-GALLIARD : Me thinketh it Madame

that you offer too much, as of me, I would not give so much.

LADY : Let us goe then to the shop on the other side. . . .

SHOP-GIRL : Madame, if you finde any better, I am content to give you mine for nothing.

LADY : Let it be as good as it will, yet you shall not have of me a penye more for it, for I have offred too much alreadie.

SEMPSTER : Madame, I am content to lose in it, of the price that I sell it to others, in hope that you will buye of us when you shall have need : how many Elles will it please you to have ?

LADY : Halfe a dossen Elles. . . Make good measure. Master Du Vault-l'amour, I pray you to buye for me yonder wastcoate that I see in that other shop, for if I cheapen it, they will over price it me by the halfe, As for you, they knowe you have better skill in it. Joly pay for this cloath. Now, are you payed and contented ?

SEMPSTER : Yes Madame, I most humbly thanke you. Beleeve me you have bestowed your money very well, and you have good cheap. Will you buye no shirts, ruffes, Falling bandes, handkerchers, night-coyfes, Falles, sockes, edged lace, Boote-hosen wrought, Or any other thing that we have ? All is at your commaundement.

LADY : Not for this time I thanke you, farewell my she friend.

SEMPSTER : Madame, God have you in his keeping.

LADY : Page goe see if the Coach be ready, Runne quickly. Coach-man we must alight in Cheapside, at the Mercers and Gold-smiths.

PIERRE ERONDELL
The French Garden (1605)

There be many Witches at this day in Lapland, who sell
winds to Mariners for money.

THOMAS FULLER
The Profane State : The Witch (1642)

BUYING MAIDENS

In every village once in each year it was done as follows :—
When the maidens grew to the age for marriage, they . . .
brought them in a body to one place, and round them stood
a company of men: and the crier caused each one severally
to stand up, and proceeded to sell them, first the most
comely of all, and afterwards . . . the most comely after her.
. . . Now all the wealthy men of the Babylonians who were
ready to marry vied with one another in bidding for the
most beautiful maidens ; those however of the common
sort who were ready to marry did not require a fine form,
but they would accept money together with less comely
maidens.

HERODOTUS
History (5th cent. B.C.)
Trans. G. C. Macaulay

THE SINGLE LIFE

BETTER STILL

It is very agreeable to beget children, but, by Hercules, it's much more agreeable still to be free.

PLAUTUS, Miles Gloriosus (C. 225 B.C.)

HOW FREE, HOW HAPPY, HOW HEAVENLY

" Art thou young ? Then match not yet ; if old, match not at all." . . . And therefore . . . still make answere to thy friends that importune thee to marry, *adhuc intempestivum*, 'tis yet unseasonable, and ever will be.

Consider withall how free, how happy, how secure, how heavenly, in respect, a single man is, as he said in the Comoedie . . . " that which all my neighbours admire and applaud me for, account so great an happinesse, I never had a wife " ; consider how contentedly, quietly, neatly, plentifully, sweetly, and how merrily he lives ! hee hath no man to care for but himselfe, none to please, no charge, none to controll him, is tied to no residence, no cure to serve, may goe and come, when, whether, live where he will, his owne master, and doe what he list himselfe. Consider the excellency of Virgins ; *Virgo coelum meruit*, a virgin merits heaven, marriage replenisheth the earth,

Up   609

but virginity Paradise ; Elias, Eliseus, John Baptist, were batchelors : Virginity is a pretious Jewel, a faire garland, a never-fading flowre, for why was *Daphne* turned to a green bay-tree, but to shew that virginity is immortall ? . . . Virginity is a fine picture, as *Bonaventure* calls it, a blessed thing in itselfe, and if you will believe a Papist, meritorious. And although their be some inconveniences, irksomenesse, solitarinesse, &c. incident to such persons, *quae aegro assideat et curet aegrotum, fomentum paret,* embracing, dalliance, kissing, colling, &c, those furious motives and wanton pleasures a new-married life most part enjoyes ; yet they are but toyes in respect, easily to be endured, if conferred to those frequent encombrances of marriage. Solitarinesse may be otherwise avoided with mirth, musick, good company, businesse, imployment ; . . . for their good nights, he shall have good dayes. . . . Thinke of these things, conferre both lives, and consider last of all these commodious prerogatives a Batchelor hath, how well he is esteemed, how hartily welcome to all his friends. . . . But if thou marry once, . . . bethinke thy selfe what a slavery it is, what a heavy burden thou shalt undertake, how hard a taske thou art tyed to . . . and how continuate, what squalor attends it, what irksomenesse, what charges . . . besides a Myriade of cares, miseries, and troubles.

ROBERT BURTON, *Anatomy of Melancholy* (Edition 1632)

ROVING ABOUT

SIR ABEL HANDY : Where will you go ? I'll go anywhere you like—Will you go to Bath, or Brighton, or Petersburgh, or Jerusalem, or Seringapatam ? all the same to me—we single fellows—we rove about—nobody cares for us—we care for nobody.

THOMAS MORTON, *Speed the Plough* (1800)

CELIBATE

I would be married, but I'de have no Wife,
I would be married to a single Life.

RICHARD CRASHAW, *Delights of the Muses* (1646)

FREE TO MAKE VISITS

I hope in a few days to be at leisure, and to make visits. Whither I shall fly is matter of no importance. A man unconnected is at home everywhere ; unless he may be said to be at home nowhere.

SAMUEL JOHNSON, *Letter to Joseph Simpson* (1759)

WEDDINGS IN HEAVEN

Because the blush of modesty, and youth without blemish were your inclination, because you tasted none of the pleasures of the marriage bed, behold, the honours of the virgin are kept for you. With your bright head chapleted by a glittering crown, and bearing the delightful shade of a branch of palm, you will eternally celebrate immortal nuptials ; where song is, and the lyre rages, mingled with happy dances, and festal orgies are celebrated with the thyrsus of Sion.

JOHN MILTON
Epitaphium Damonis (1639) (Translated)

I am attracted to perpetual spinsterhood not by prejudice, but rather by natural inclination.

QUEEN ELIZABETH
(To Ambassador of the Duke of Würtemberg)

SLOTH

A SLOTHFUL MAN

He loves still to have the Sun witnesse of his rising ; and lies long more for lothnesse to dresse him, then will he sleepe : and after some streaking and yawning, calles for dinner, unwashed ; which having digested with a sleepe in his chaire, he walks forth to the bench in the Market-place, and looks for companions ; whomsoever he meets, he stayes with idle questions, and lingring discourse : how the daies are lengthened, how kindly the weather is, how false the clocke, how forward the Spring, and ends ever with *What shall we doe* ? . . . When all the people are gone from Church, hee is left sleeping in his seat alone. . . . When he is warned on a Jurie, hee had rather pay the mulct than appeare. All but that which Nature will not permit, he doth by a deputie. . . . He had rather freeze then fetch wood, and chuses rather to steale then worke, to begge then take paines to steale, and in many things to

612

want then begge. Hee is so loth to leave his neighbors fire, that he is faine to walke home in the darke and if he be not lookt to, weares out the night in the chimney-corner.

JOSEPH HALL
Characters of Vertues and Vices (1608)

A SORT OF INDOLENCE

Johnson told me that " Taylor was a very sensible acute man, and had a strong mind ; that he had great activity in some respects, and yet such a sort of indolence, that if you should put a pebble upon his chimney-piece you would find it there, in the same state, a year afterwards."

JAMES BOSWELL
Life of Johnson (1791)

THE TRUE STATE OF MAN

Hang work !

I wish that all the year were holiday ; I am sure that indolence,—indefeasible indolence—is the true state of man, and business the invention of the old Teazer, whose interference doomed Adam to an apron and set him a-hoeing. Pen and ink, and clerks and desks, were the refinements of this old torturer some thousand years after, under pretence of " Commerce allying distant shores, promoting and diffusing knowledge, good," etc. etc.

CHARLES LAMB
Letter to William Wordsworth (1805)

613

SMOKING

DELIGHTSOME DRUNKENNESS

This herbe is called Nicotiana of the name of an ambassadour which broght the first knowledge of it into this realme. . . .

The Spaniards call it Tabaco. Some call it the holy herbe, because (as I thinke) of his holy and marvueilous effects. . . . Notwithstanding it were better to call it Nicotiana, after the name of the Lord which first sent it into France, to the end that we may give him the honour which he hath deserved of us, for having furnished our land with so rare and singular an herbe. . . .

The inhabitance of Florida doe feede themselves a certain space with the fume of this herbe (whatsoever a certaine new Cosmographer say to the contrary, who seeketh by his lies to triumph over us in this respect) which they take at the mouth, by meanes of certaine small hornes.

And the truth hereof we gather from them which have beene in Florida, and by mariners comming daily from the Indies, which hanging about their neckes little pipes or hornes made of the leaves of the date tree, or of reedes, or of rushes, at the endes of which little hornes there are

614

put and packt many drie leaves of this plant, writhen together and broken. They put fire to this end of the pipe,
receiving and drawing in with their breath at their mouth
wide open, so much of this fume as possibly they can,
and affirme thereupon that they finde their hunger and
thirst satisfied, their strength recovered, their spirites
rejoyced, and their braine drencht with a delightsome
drunkennesse.

CHARLES ESTIENNE, La Maison Rustique (1572)
Trans. Richard Surflet (1600)

Against Plague

I have been told that in the last great plague at London
none that kept tobacconist's shops had the plague. It is
certain, that smoking it was looked upon as a most
excellent preservative. In so much that even children
were obliged to smoak. And I remember, that I heard
formerly Tom Rogers . . . say, that when he was, when
the plague raged, a school-boy at Eaton, all the boys of
that school were obliged to smoak in the school every
morning, and that he was never whipped so much in his
life as he was one morning for not smoaking.

THOMAS HEARNE, Diary (Jan. 21, 1721)

Against Execution

He tooke a pipe of tobacco a little before he went to the
scaffold, which some formall persons were scandalized

at, but I thinke 'twas well and properly donne, to settle his spirits.

JOHN AUBREY, *Brief Lives : Sir Walter Raleigh* (c. 1680)

THE MAGIC DRUG

Here could I tell you how upon the seas
Some men have fasted with it fortie daies, . . .
How a dull Cynick by the force of it
Hath got a pleasing gesture and good wit . . .
How many Cowards base and recreant
By one pipes draught were turned valiant,
And after in an artificiall mist
Have overthrowne their foes before they wist :
How one that dreamt of a Tabacco roll
Though sick before, was straight made perfect
    whole.

ANON. *The Metamorphosis of Tabacco* (1602)

A GENTLEMAN-LIKE SMELL

Homer of *Moly* and *Nepenthe* sings,
Moly the Gods most soveraigne Hearbe divine,
Nepenthe Heavens drinke most gladnesse brings,
Hearts griefe expels, and doth the wits refine
But this our age another world hath found,
From whence an hearbe of Heavenly power is
    brought.
Moly is not so soveraigne for a wound,
Nor hath *Nepenthe* so great wonders wrought.

It is *Tobacco*, whose sweet substantiall fume
The hellish torment of the teeth doth ease,
By drawing downe, and drying up the rewme,
The Mother and the Nurse of each disease.
It is *Tobacco* which doth colde expell,
And cleares the obstructions of the Arteries,
And surfets threatning Death digesteth well,
Decocting all the stomackes crudities.
It is *Tobacco* which hath power to clarifie
The clowdie mists before dim eyes appearing,
It is *Tobacco* which hath power to rarifie
The thick grose humour which doth stop the
    hearing.
The wasting Hectique, and the Quartain Fever,
Which doth of Physique make a mockerie,
The gowt it cures, and helps ill breaths for ever,
Whether the cause in Teeth or stomacke be.
And thoug ill breaths were by it but confounded,
Yet that Medicine it doth Farre excell,
Which by sir *Thomas Moore* hath bin propounded,
For this is thought a Gentleman-like smell.

SIR JOHN DAVIES, Of Tobbacco (1586)

A LOATHSOME CUSTOM

For *Tobacco* being a common herbe, which (though under divers names) growes almost everywhere, was first found out by some of the barbarous *Indians*, to be a Preservative or Antidot against the Pockes, a filthy disease, whereunto these barbarous people are (as all men know) very much subject. . . . And now, good Countrey men let us (I pray you) consider what honour or policie can moove us to imitate the barbarous and beastly manners of the wilde, godlesse and slavish *Indians*, especially in so vile and stinkinge a custom ? Shall wee that disdaine to imitate the maners of our neighbour *France* . . . and that cannot endure the spirit of the *Spaniards* . . . shall we, I say, without blushing abase our selves so farre, as to imitate these beastly *Indians*, slaves to the *Spaniards* refuse to the world, and as yet aliens to the holy Covenant of God ? Why doe we not as well imitate them in walking naked as they do ? in preferring glasses, feathers, and such toyes, to golde and precious stones, as they do ? yea, why do we not denie God and adore the Devill, as they doe ? . . .

Is it not both great vanitie and uncleanessee that at the table, a place of respect, of cleanlinesse, of modestie, men should not be ashamed to sit tossing of *Tobacco pipes*, and puffing of the smoke of *Tobacco* one to another, making the filthy smoke and stinke thereof to exhale athwart the dishes and infect the aire, when, very often, men that abhor it are at their repast ? . . . And is it not a great vanitie, that a man cannot heartily welcome his friend now, straight they must bee in hand with *Tobacco* ? . . . He but that will refuse to take a pipe of *Tobacco* among his fellowes, (though by his own election he would rather feele the savour of a Sinke) is accounted peevish and no good company, even as they doe with tippling in the cold Eastern Countries. . . .

A custome lothsome to the eye, hatefull to the Nose, harmfull to the braine, dangerous to the Lungs, and in the blacke stinking fume thereof, neerest resembling the horrible Stigian smoke of the pit that is bottomlesse.

KING JAMES I

A Counterblaste to Tobacco (1604)

The *Indian* weede withered quite,
Greene at noon, cut downe at night ;
Shows thy decay, all flesh is hay :
Thus thinke, then drinke, *Tobacco.*

The Pipe that is so lilly-white,
Shews thee to be a mortall Wight,
And even such gone with a touch :
Thus thinke, then drinke *Tobacco.*

And when the Smoake ascends on high,
Thinke thou behold'st the Vanitie
Of worldly stuffe, gone with a puffe ;
Thus thinke, then drinke *Tobacco.*

And when the Pipe grows foule within,
Think on the Soule defil'd with Sinne,
And then the Fire it doth require :
Thus thinke, then drinke *Tobacco.*

The Ashes that are left behinde
May serve to put thee still in minde,
That unto Dust returne thou must :
Thus thinke, then drinke *Tobacco.*

THOMAS JENNER, *The Soule's Solace* (1631)

A LIBEL

And as one said, but falsely, the bodies of such Englishmen as are so much delighted with this plant, did seeme to degenerate into the nature of the Savages.

WILLIAM CAMDEN, *Annales* (trans. 1625)

AN EXHORTATORY LETTER TO AN OLD LADY THAT SMOAK'D TOBACCO

Madam,

Tho' the ill-natur'd world censures you for smoaking, yet I would advise you, Madam, not to part with so innocent a diversion : in the first place, it is healthful, and as Galen, *de usu partium,* rightly observes, is a sovereign remedy for the tooth-ach, the constant persecutor of Old Ladies. Secondly, tho' it be a heatthenish weed, it is a great help to Christian meditations ; which is the reason, I suppose, that recommends it to your parsons ; the generality of whom can no more write a sermon without a pipe in their mouth than a Concordance in their hands : besides, every pipe you break may serve to put you in mind of Mortality, and shew you upon what slender accidents man's Life depends. I know a Dissenting Minister who on fast-days used to mortify upon a Rump of Beef, because it put him, as he said, in mind that all flesh was grass ; but I'm sure much more is to be learnt from Tobacco : it may instruct you that riches, beauty, and all the glories of the World vanish like a Vapour. Thirdly, it is a pretty play-thing : a pipe is the same to an old woman that a gallant is to a young one. . . . Fourthly and lastly, it is fashionable, at least 'tis in a fair way of becoming so ; cold tea, you know, has been a long while in reputation at court, and the gill as naturally ushers in the pipe as the forward-bearer walks before the Lord Mayor.

I am your Ladyship's humble servant.

TOM BROWN
Letter to an Old Lady (c. 1690)

Little Tube of mighty Pow'r,
Charmer of an idle Hour,
Object of my warm Desire,
Lip of wax and eye of fire :
And they snowy taper waist,
With my finger gently brac'd ;
And they pretty swelling crest,
With my little Stoper press'd,
And the sweetest bliss of blisses
Breathing from thy balmy kisses.
Happy thrice and thrice agen,
Happiest he of happy men ;
Who when agen the night returns,
When agen the Paper burns ;
When agen the cricket's gay,
(Little cricket, full of play)
Can afford his tube to feed
With the fragrant *Indian* weed ;
Pleasure for a nose divine,
Incense of the God of Wine.
Happy thrice, and thrice agen,
Happiest he of happy men.

ISAAC HAWKINS BROWNE, *A Pipe of Tobacco* (1735)

GOOD FOR EVERY ONE

Tabacco that excellent plant, the use thereof . . . the world
cannot want, is that little shop of Nature, wherein her

whole workeman-ship is abridg'd, where you may see
Earth kindled into fire, the fire breath out an exhalation
which entring in at the mouth walkes through the Regions
of a mans brayne, drives out all ill Vapours but itselfe
drawes downe all bad Humours by the mouth, which in
time might breed a Scabbe over the whole body if already
they have not ; a plant of singular use, for on the one
side ; Nature being an Enemie to Vacuitie and emptines,
and on the other, there beeing so many empty braynes
in the World as there are, how shall Natures course be
continued ? How shall these empty braines be filled, but
with ayre, Natures immediate instrument to that purpose ? If with ayre, what so proper as your fume : what
fume so healthfull as your perfume ? what perfume so
soveraigne as Tabacco ? Besides the excellent edge it gives
a mans wit, (as they can best judge that have been present
at a feast of Tabacco where commonly all good Witts are
conforted) what varietie of discourse it begetts ? What
sparkes of wit it yeelds, it is a world to heare : as likewise
to the courage of a man. . . . For the diseases of the Court,
they are out of the Element of Garlick to medicine ; to
conclude as there is no enemy to Tabacco but Garlick,
so there is no friend to Garlick but a sheeps head and so
I conclude.

GEORGE CHAPMAN
Monsieur D'Olive (1606)

MOST DIVINE

BOBADILLA : Signior beleeve me . . . I have been in the
Indies (where this herbe growes) where neither myselfe,

nor a dozen Gentlemen more (of my knowledge) have received the taste of any other nutriment in the world for the space of one and twentie weekes, but Tabacco onely. Therefore it cannot be but 'tis most divine. Further . . . it makes an Antidote, that (had you taken the most deadly poysonous simple in all Florence) it should expell it, and clarifie you, with as much ease as I speak . . . I professe myselfe no quack-salver ; only thus much : by Hercules I doe holde it, and will affirme it (before any Prince in Europe) to be the most soveraigne and pretious herbe, that ever the earth tendred to the use of man.

. . . .

COB : By gods deynes : I marle what pleasure or felicitie they have in taking this rogish Tabacco : it's good for nothing but to choke a man, and fill him full of smoake and imbers : there were foure died out of one house last weeke with taking of it, and two more the bell went for yester-night, one of them (they say) will ne're scape it, he voyded a bushell of soote yester-day, upward and downe-ward. . . . I'ld have it present death, man or woman, that should but deale with a Tabacco pipe ; why, it will stifle them all in th' end as many as use it ; it's little better than rats bane.

BEN JONSON
Every Man in his Humor (1601)

WHOLESOME

The Physicall and chirurgicall uses of it are not a few ; and being teken in a pipe it helpeth aches in any part of the

bodie ; being good also for the kidneys by expelling wind.
But beware of cold after it ; neither take it wantonly, nor
immoderately . . . for we see that the use is too frequently
turned into an abuse, and the remedie is proved a disease ;
and all through a wanton and immoderate use. For *Omne
nimium vertitur in vitium.*

> *To quaffe, roar, swear and drinke Tobacco well,*
> *Is fit for such as pledge sick healths in hell :*
> *Where wanting wine, and ale, and beer to drink,*
> *Their cups are filled with smoke, fire, fume and stink.*

. . . The women of America (as *Gerard* mentions in his
Herball) do not use to take *Tobacco*, because they perswade
themselves it is too strong for the constitution of their
bodies : and yet some women of England use it often, as
well as men . . . It is said that Sir *Francis Drakes* mariners
brought the first of this herb into England in the year
1585, which was in the 28 yeare of Q. Elizabeth.

JOHN SWAN
Speculum Mundi (1635)

A CIGAR

Sublime tobacco ! which from East to West
Cheers the Tar's labour or the Turkman's rest ;
Which on the Moslem's ottoman divides
His hours, and rivals opium and his brides ;
Magnificent in Stamboul, but less grand,
Though not less loved, in Wapping and the Strand ;
Divine in hookahs, glorious in a pipe,
When tipp'd with amber, mellow, rich and ripe ;

Like other charmers, wooing the caress,
More dazzlingly when daring in full dress ;
Yet they true lovers more admire by far
Thy naked beauties—give me a cigar !

LORD BYRON, The Island (1823)

PRESERVES FROM VACUITY

" Smoking has gone out. To be sure, it is a shocking thing, blowing smoke out of our mouths into other people's mouths, eyes and noses, and having the same thing done to us. Yet I cannot account why a thing which requires so little exertion, and yet preserves the mind from total vacuity, should have gone out. Every man has something by which he calms himself : beating with his feet, or so."

JAMES BOSWELL, Life of Johnson (1791)

SNACKS BETWEEN MEALS

ROAST PIG

Of the Rev. William Collier, B.D. . . . I have previously spoken, as having taken an emigrant Countess under his protection. He had been Tutor of the college [Trinity], and was for nearly twenty years Professor of Hebrew ; he was an admirable classic, and particularly well versed in modern languages (at that time a very rare accomplishment in the University). Collier led a most dissolute life ; he was also a notorious *gourmand*. An anecdote I had from his own mouth will prove his title to the latter character.

" When I was last in town," said he, " I was going to dine with a friend, and passed through a small court, just as a lad was hanging up a board on which was this tempting inscription—" *A roast pig this instant set upon the table !* " The invitation was irresistible—I ordered a quarter; it was *very delicate* and *very delicious*. I despatched a second and a third portion, but was constrained to leave one quarter behind, as my dinner hour was approaching, and my friend was remarkably punctual." (1798)

HENRY GUNNING
Reminiscences of Cambridge (1852)

A LOAF BEFORE DINNER

A very working head, in so much that, walking and meditating before dinner, he would eate-up a penny loafe, not knowing that he did it.

JOHN AUBREY
Brief Lives : Thomas Fuller (c. 1680)

OYSTERS

From thence I rowed to another port, called by the naturals *Piche*, and by the Spaniardes *Tierra de Brea*. In the way betweene both were divers little brooks of fresh water, and one salt river that had store of oisters upon the branches of the trees, and were very salt and wel tasted. Al their oisters grow upon those boughs and spraies, and not on the ground : the like is commonlie seene in the West Indies and else where.

SIR WALTER RALEIGH
The Discoverie of Guiana (1596)

SALTS

A dose of salts has the effect of a temporary inebriation, like light champagne, on me.

LORD BYRON
Diary (Jan. 6, 1821)

GROG

Read Diodorus Siculus—turned over Seneca and some other books. Wrote some more of the tragedy. Took a glass of grog. After having ridden hard in rainy weather, and scribbled, and scribbled again, the spirits (at least mine) need a little exhilaration, and I don't like laudanum now as I used to do. So I have mixed a glass of strong waters and single waters, which I shall now proceed to empty. . . . The effect of all wines and spirits upon me is, however, strange. It *settles*, but it makes me gloomy.

Ibid.
(Jan. 14, 1821)

I have drank as many as fifteen bottles of soda-water in one night, after going to bed, and been still thirsty—calculating, however, some lost from the bursting out and effervescence and overflowing of the soda-water in drawing the corks, or striking off the necks of the bottles in mere thirsty impatience.

Ibid. (Feb. 2, 1821)

SALTS

How do you manage? I think you told me, at Venice, that your spirits did not keep up without a little claret. I *can* drink, and bear a good deal of wine (as you may recollect in England) : but it don't exhilarate—it makes me savage and suspicious. Laudanum has a similar effect ; but I can take much of *it* without any effect at all. The thing that gives me the highest spirits (it seems absurd, but true) is a dose of *salts*—I mean in the afternoon, after their effect. But one can't take *them* like champagne.

Ibid. Letter to Thomas Moore (1821)

DRAMS

The solicitations of sense are always at hand, and a dram to a vacant and solitary person is a speedy and seducing relief.

HESTHER PIOZZI
Anecdotes of Dr. Johnson (1786)

A dew-bite and breakfast, a stay-bite and dinner, a mummet and a crummet, and a bite after supper.

ANON. *A Centenarian's recipe for long life*

WINE EXTRAORDINARY

A good, formall, precise Monister in the Isle of Wight us't to say that a glasse or two of wine extraordinarie would make a man praise God with much alacritie.

SIR NICHOLAS L'ESTRANGE
Merry Jests and Conceits (1630–55)

GRUEL

MR. WOODHOUSE : " You must go to bed early, my dear, and I recommend a little gruel to you before you go. You and I will have a nice basin of gruel together. My dear Emma, suppose we all have a little gruel."

Emma could not suppose any such thing, knowing as she did that both the Mr Knightleys were as unpersuadable on that article as herself, and two basins only were ordered. . . .

The gruel came, and supplied a great deal to be said— much praise and many comments—undoubting decision of its wholesomeness for every constitution, and pretty severe philippics upon the many houses where it was never met with tolerable.

JANE AUSTEN, *Emma* (1816)

" What should you say to a drop o' beer, gen'l'men ? " suggested the mottle-faced man. . . .

" And a little bit o' cold beef," said the second coach-man.

" Or a oyster," added the third, who was a hoarse gentleman, supported by very round legs.

" Hear, hear ! " said Pell, " to congratulate Mr. Weller on his coming into possession of his property : eh ? ha ha ! "

" I'm quite agreeable, gen'l'men," answered Mr Weller. " Sammy, pull the bell." . . .

Where everybody took so active a part, it is almost invidious to make a distinction : but if one individual evinced greater prowess than another, it was the coach-man with the hoarse voice, who took an imperial pint of vinegar with his oysters, without betraying the least emotion.

CHARLES DICKENS
Pickwick Papers (1836)

TEA

I suppose no person ever enjoyed with more relish the infusion of that fragrant leaf than Johnson. The quantities which he drank of it at all hours were so great, that his nerves must have been uncommonly strong not to have been extremely relaxed by such an intemperate use of it. He assured me, that he never felt the least inconvenience from it.

JAMES BOSWELL
Life of Johnson (1791)

Though he usually eat seven or eight large peaches of a morning before breakfast began, and treated them with proportionate attention after dinner again, yet I have heard him protest that he never had quite as much as he wished of wall-fruit, except once in his life, and that was ... at Ombersley, the seat of my Lord Sandys.

HESTHER PIOZZI, *Anecdotes of Dr. Johnson* (1786)

TARTS, CUSTARDS, CHEESECAKES

They [the Presbyterians and Independents] would also entertaine each other in their chambers with edibles, and somtimes ... at a cook's house that had a back-way, and be very merry and frolicsome. Nay, such that had come from Cambridg and had gotten fellowships would be more free of entertainment than any, and instead of a cup of college beare and stir'd machet which use to be the antient way of entertaining in a College at 3 or 4 in the afternoon, they would entertaine with tarts, custards, cheescaks, or any other junkets that were in season; and that fashion continued among the generalitie till the restauration.

ANTHONY WOOD, *Life and Times* (1659)

ROLLS, ALE, AND RHENISH WINE

About every 3 houres his man was to bring him a roll and a pott of ale to refocillate his wasted spirits. So he studied and dranke, and munched some bread; and this maintained him till night; and then he made a good supper. Now he did well not to dine, which breakes of one's fancy, which will not presently be regained: and 'tis with invention as a flux—when once it is flowing, it runnes amaine; if it is checked, flowes but *guttim*: and the like for perspiration—check it, and 'tis spoyled. Goclenius, professor at —— in Germany, did better; he kept bottles of Rhenish wine in his studie, and when his spirits wasted, dranke a good rummer of it.

JOHN AUBREY
Brief Lives : William Prynne (1680)

SORORAL

AFTER THE PARTY

A girl said to her sister, late, when their friends had gone :
" I wish there were no men on earth, but we alone.

" The beauty of your body, the beauty of your face—
That now are greedy flames, and clasp more than themselves in light,
Pierce awake the drowsing air and boast before the night—
Then should be of less account than a dark reed's grace,
All Summer growing in river mists, unknown—
The beauty of your body, the beauty of my own.

632

When we two talk together, the words between us pass
across long fields, across drenched upland fields of grass,
like words of men who signal with flags in clear weather.
When we two are together, I know before you speak
your answers, by your head's turn and shadows on your
    cheek—
running of wind on grass, to bring out thoughts together.

We should live as though all day were the day's first hour,
all light were the first daylight, that whistles from so far,
that still the blood with distance. We should live as
    though
all seasons were the earliest Spring, when only birds are
    mating,
when the low, crouched bramble remembers still the
    snow,
and woods are but half unchained from the Winter's
    waiting.
We should be gay together, with pleasures primrose-cool,
scattered, and quick as Spring's are, by thicket and chill
    pool.

"Oh, to-night," the girl said, " I wish that I could sit
all my life here with you, all my life unlit.
To-morrow I shall love again the Summer's valour,
heavy heat of noon, and the night's mysteries,
and love, like the sun's touch, that closes up my eyes—
to-morrow : but to-night," she said, as night ran on,
I wish there was no love on earth but ours alone."

E. J. SCOVELL
A Girl to her Sister (1932)

SMELLS

AIR OF EDEN

                          Now purer aire
Meets his approach, and to the heart inspires
Vernal delight and joy, able to drive
All sadness but despair : now gentle gales
Fanning their odoriferous wings dispense
Native perfumes, and whisper whence they stole
Those balmie spoiles. As when to them who sail
Beyond the *Cape of Hope*, and now are past
Mozambic, off at Sea North-East windes blow
Sabean Odours from the spicie shoare
Of Arabie the blest, with such delay
Well pleas'd they slack thir course, and many
    League
Cheard with those odorous sweete the Fiend
Who came thir bane, though with them bett
    pleas'd
Then *Asmodeus* with the fishie fume,
That drove him, though enamoured, from t
    Spouse.
Of *Tobits* Son.

JOHN MILT
Paradise Lost, Book IV (16

. . within scent of those fragrant orchards which are on
is coast, full of princely retirements for the sumptuous-
sse of their buildings, and noblenesse of their planta-
ons, especially those at St Pietro d'Arena; from whence,
e wind blowing as it did, might perfectly be smelt the
culiar joys of Italy in the perfumes of orange, citron,
d jassmine flowers, for divers leagues seaward.

JOHN EVELYN, *Diary* (October 1644)

AIR OF LONDON

r, I prepare in this short Discourse an expedient . . . to
nder not only Your Majesties Palace, but the whole City
ewise, one of the sweetest and most delicious Habita-
ns in the World; . . . by improving those Plantations
ich Your Majesty so laudably affects . . . as upon every
ntle emission through the Aer, should so perfume the
jacent places with their breath; as if, by a certain
arm, or innocent Magick, they were transferred to that
rt of Arabia, which is therefore styled the Happy, be-
use it is amongst the Gums and precious Spices. Those
o take notice of the scent of the Orange-flowers from
Rivage of Genoa, and St Pietro dell' Arena; the Blos-
nes of the Rosemary from the Coasts of Spain many
agues off at Sea; or the manifest and odoriferous waft
ich flow from Fontenay and Vaurigard, even to Paris, in
season of Roses, with the contrary Effects of those less
asing Smells from other accidents, will easily consent
what I suggest: And I am able to enumerate a Catalogue

of native Plants, and such as are familiar to our Count
and Clime, whose redolent and agreeable Emissions wou
even ravish our senses, as well as perfectly improve ar
meliorate the Aer about London. . . . Such as are (for i
stance amongst many others) the *Sweet-brier*, all the *Per*
clymenas and *Woodbinds* ; the Common *white* and *yell*
Jessamine, both the *Syringas* or *Pipe trees* ; the *Guelde*
rose, the *Musk*, and all other *Roses* ; *Genista Hispanica*
. . . *Bayes*, *Junipier* . . . *Lavender* : but above all *Rosemar*
the *Flowers* whereof are credibly reported to give the
scent above thirty Leagues off at Sea, upon the coasts
Spain ; and at some distance towards the Meadow sic
Vines, yea *Hops*. . . . For there is a very sweet smelli:
Sally, and the blossoms of the *Lime-tree* are incomparab
fragrant ; in brief, whatever is odoriferous and refreshir

JOHN EVEL\

Fumifugium : Or the Smoake of London Dissipated (166

GARDEN SMELLS

And because the Breath of Flowers is farre Sweeter
the Aire (where it comes and goes, like the Warbling
Musick) then in the hand, therfore nothing is more
for that delight then to know what be the Flowers a
Plants that doe best perfume the Aire. Roses Damask a:
Red are fast Flowers of their Smels ; So that you m
walke by a whole Row of them, and finde Nothing of th
Sweetnesse ; Yea though it be in a Mornings Dew. Bay
likewise yeeld no Smell as they grow. Rosemary littl
Nor Sweet-Marjoram. That, which above all Otl
yeelds the Sweetest Smell in the Aire, is the Violet .

ext to that is the Muske-Rose. Then the Strawberry-
eaves dying, which yeeld a most Excellent Cordiall
mell. Then the Flower of the Vines ; It is a little dust,
ke the dust of a Bent, which growes upon the Cluster,
the First comming forth. Then Sweet-Briar. Then Wall-
lowers, which are very Delightfull, to be set under a
arler, or Lower Chamber Window ... Then the Flowers
the Lime-Tree. Then the Hony-suckles, so they be
mewhat a farre off. . . . But those which Perfume the
ire most delightfully, not passed by as the rest, but being
roden upon and Crushed, are Three : That is Burnet,
ilde-Time, and Water-Mints. Therefore, you are to set
hole Allies of them, to have the Pleasure when you walk
Tread. . . .

FRANCIS BACON, *Essays. Of Gardens* (1625)

SMELLING ONE'S DINNER

vas saying to a friend . . . that I did not like goose ; one
ells it so while it is roasting, said I. " But you, Madam,"
plies the Doctor) " have been at all times a fortunate
man, having always had your hunger so forestalled by
lulgence, that you never experienced the delight of
elling your dinner beforehand."

HESTHER PIOZZI, *Anecdotes of Dr Johnson* (1786)

SMELLS THAT ALLURE SPIRITS

od Spirits are delighted and allured by sweet Per-
nes, as rich Gums, Frankincense, Salt, &c. which was

637

the reason that the Priests of the *Gentiles*, and also th
Christians, used them in their Temples, and Sacrifices
and on the contrary, Evil Spirits are pleased and allure
and called up by Suffumigations of *Henbane*, &c., stin
ing Smells, &c., which the Witches do use in their Co
juration. JOHN AUBREY, *Miscellanies* (169

SMELLS THAT INTOXICATE

It is said that other trees have been discovered by the
which yield fruit of such a kind that when they ha
assembled together in companies in the same place a
lighted a fire, they sit round in a circle and throw some
it into the fire, and they smell the fruit which is thrown o
as it burns, and are intoxicated by the scent as the Hellen
are with wine, and when more of the fruit is thrown on th
become more intoxicated, until at last they rise up
dance and begin to sing. This is said to be the manner
their living. HERODOTUS, *History* (5th cent. B.
Trans. G. C. Macaul

MR TATTLE'S SCENT

MRS FORESIGHT : Well, but Miss, what are you so ov
joy'd at ?
MISS : Look you here, Madam, then, what Mr *Tattle*
given me—Look you here, Cousin, here's a Snuff-Bo
nay, there's Snuff in't ;—here, will you have any—
good ! how sweet it is—Mr *Tattle* is all over sweet,

638

erruke is sweet, and his Gloves are sweet—and his
Handkerchief is sweet, pure sweet, sweeter than Roses—
smell him, Mother . . . He gave me this Ring for a Kiss.

TATTLE : O fie Miss, you must not kiss and tell.

MISS : Yes ; I may tell my Mother—And he says he'll
give me something to make me smell so—Oh pray lend
me your Handkerchief—Smell, Cousin ; he says, he'll
give me something that will make my smocks smell this
way—Is it not pure ?—It's better than Lavender mun—
I'm resolv'd I won't let Nurse put any more Lavender
among my Smocks.

WILLIAM CONGREVE, Love for Love (1695)

SOLITUDE

THE HERMIT

Whereas the Hermit leades a sweet retyred life,
From Villages repleate with ragg'd and sweating Clownes,
And from the loathsome ayres of smoky cittied Townes.

  · · · · ·

Then as the Hermet comes out of his homely Cell,
There from all rude resort he happily doth dwell :
Who in the strength of youth, a man at Armes hath been ;
As one who of this world the vilenesse having seene
Retyres him from it quite ; and with a constant mind
Mans beastliness so loathes, that flying humane kind,

The black and darksome nights, the bright and gladson
    dayes
Indifferent are to him, his hope on God that staies.
Each little Village yeelds his short and homely fare :
To gather wind-falne sticks, his great'st and onely care
Which every aged tree still yeeldeth to his fire.
    This man, that is alone a King in his desire,
By no proud ignorant Lord is basely over-aw'd . . .
His free and noble thought nere envies at the grace
That often times is given unto a Baud most base,
                    . . . but absolutely free,
His happy time he spends the works of God to see,
In those so sundry hearbs which there in pleanty grow
Whose sundry strange effects he onely seeks to knowe.
And in a little Maund, beeing made of Oziars small,
Which serveth him to doe full many a thing withall,
He very choicely sorts his Simples got abroad.

MICHAEL DRAYTO

Poly-Olbion. Song XIII (161

LUCULLUS SUPS WITH LUCULLUS

Another time, when he happened to sup alone, and s
but one table and a very moderate provision, he called t
servant who had the care of these matters, and express
his dissatisfaction. The servant said, he thought as nobo
was invited, his master would not want an expensi
supper. " What ! " said he, " didst thou not know tl
this evening Lucullus sups with Lucullus ? "

PLUTAR

Lives (c. 100). Trans. J. and W. Langhorne (17

This (says he) is one of the thousand reasons which ought to restrain a man from drony solitude and useless retirement. Solitude (added he one day) is dangerous to reason, without being favourable to virtue : . . . those who resist gaiety, will be likely to fall a sacrifice to appetite ; . . . Remember (continued he) that the solitary mortal is certainly luxurious, probably superstitious, and possibly mad.

HESTHER PIOZZI
Anecdotes of Dr Johnson (1786)

NONE TO TROUBLE US

As for *Alcmoeon*, he made his abode and residence upon the muddy banke, which the river *Achelous* had newly gathered and cast up, . . . to avoid the pursute (as the Poets say) of the Furies ; but in my conceit rather, because he would decline the offices of State, civill magistrates, seditious broiles, and biting calumniations sib to furies in hel, he chose such a streight and narrow place to inhabit, where he might leade a life in quietnesse and repose, secured from all such busie affaires. . . . In mine opinion, there is no reason that a man (unlesse he be very much besotted and transported with the vaine wind of popularity) when he is confined and enclosed within an island, should complaine of fortune . . . but rather praise her. . . . You may oftentimes there enjoy fully your rest and repose . . . for whereas when we are haply playing at dice, or otherwise keeping close at home, there will be some of these sycophants or busie priers and envious searchers into all our actions, ready to draw us out of our houses of

pleasure in the suburbs, or out of our delightsome
gardens, to make our appearance judicially in the common
place, or to perform our service and give attendance in the
Court : there will be none such about to saile into the
Island where thou art confined for to trouble thee ; none
will come to thee to demaund or crave any thing, to
borrow monie, to request thy suretie-ship, or thy assistance for to second him in the sute of any office . . . unlesse
peradventure some of thy best friends onely and nearest
kinsfolke, of meere love and affectionate desire to see thee,
saile over for thy sake ; for the rest of thy life besides is
permitted to be as safe as a sanctuarie, not subject to any
spoile, trouble, or molestation.

PLUTARCH
Morals (c. 100)
Trans. Philemon Holland (1603)

PROPHESY IN THE WILDERNESS

Before I left *London*, I fained an hundred agreeable
Melancholy Pleasures, with which I might Fool away a
Retirement, but now I detest being alone. . . . Of this I
am sure, that God Almighty rather than be alone created
the Devil, and Man rather than be alone chose a Wife.
Whatever advantage I have lost by my Country Life, I
believe I have gain'd the gift of Prophesy in the Wilderness, for I foretold the Poem with which A—— has
visited us.

WALTER MOYLE
Letter to John Dennis (1695)

SPRING

PASSION AND ECSTASY

Time, turning eternally, round, now that the spring grows
warm calls again the young west winds. Earth, renewed,
puts on her brief youth, and already the ground, unbound
from frost, grows sweetly green. Am I wrong, or do my
songs also gain renewed strength, and is genius the reward
of spring ? . . . My breast stirs and burns with secret
passion, and frenzy and holy sounds move me to the
depths. Apollo himself comes, I see his locks twined with
laurel of Peneus, Apollo is coming himself. . . . What high
music does my spirit sound through my open lips ? What
does this madness, this holy inspiration, bring forth ? Of
spring, who has inspired me, I will sing, thus repaying
her her gifts. . . .

Earth, revived, lays aside loathèd age, and desires,
Phoebus, to enter thy embrace. She both desires and is
worthy, for what is lovelier than she, as, luxuriantly
all-bearing, she stretches out her breast, and breathes
forth the harvests of Arabia, and from her beautiful mouth
pours the gentle balsam and the roses of Paphos ? . . .

Thus lascivious Earth breathes forth her passion, and
all the mob of creatures run after their mother's example.

Now truly Cupid runs roaming over the world. . . . And now he is striving to conquer the unconquered Diana herself. . . . Young men shout the marriage song about marble cities, and the shore and the hollow rocks echo Io Hymen ! Hymen comes, richly and beautifully adorned. . . . Now the Satyrs too, when twilight rises, fly in a swift band about the flowery country, and Sylvanus, chapletted with his own cypress, the god half goat, the goat half god. The Dryads, who have lain hid beneath ancient trees, now wander over the lonely fields. Through the sown fields and thickets Maenalian Pan runs riot . . . and desirous Faunus preys after some Oread, while the nymph takes thought for herself on fearful feet, and now she hides, and hiding, ill-sheltered, would fain be seen ; she flees, and fleeing, wishes herself caught. . . .

O Phoebus, drive thy swift yoked steeds as slowly as thou canst, and let not the spring haste by.

JOHN MILTON
Elegia Quinta. In Adventum Veris (1628)
(Translated)

THE MIRTHFUL QUIRES

When *Phoebus* lifts his head out of the Winteres wave
No sooner doth the Earth her flowerie bosome brave,
At such time as the Yeere brings on the pleasant Spring,
But Hunts-up to the Morne the feathered *Sylvans* sing :
And in the lower Grove as on the rising Knole,
Upon the highest spray of every mounting pole,

Those Quirristers are pearcht with many a speckled
  breast.
Then from her burnisht gate the goodly glittring East
Guilds every lofty top which late the humorous Night
Bespangled had with pearle to please the Mornings sight.
On which the mirthfull Quires with their cleere open
  throats
Unto the joyfull Morne so straine their wobling notes
That Hills and Valleys ring, and even the echoing Ayre
Seemes all composed of sounds about them every where.

MICHAEL DRAYTON
Poly Olbion. Song XIII (1613)

THE VERNAL SUN

The Almond flourisheth, the Birch trees flowe,
the sad Mezereon Cheerefully doth Blowe.
The flourie sonnes before their fathers seen,
and snayles beginne to Crop the Mandrake green.
The vernall sunne with Crocus gardens fills,
with Hyacinths, Anemones, and Daffodills :
The hazell Catskins now delate and fall,
and Paronychions peep upon each wall.

SIR THOMAS BROWNE (?)
(Date unknown)

SPRUNKING

A New Name for an Ancient Thing

This sprunking is a Dutch word, the first as we hear of
that Language that ever came in fashion with Ladies.

Ladies' Dictionary (1694)

Fictitious Hair

You deceive us with faked hair represented by an oint-
ment, Phoebus, and your bald scalp is covered with
locks painted on it. MARTIAL

Epigrams. Book VI. 57 (c. 84)

Improving the Face

Learn, girls, what attentions improve the face, and by what
means your beauty may be kept up. . . . What is cultivated
pleases. . . . Do not trust [for inspiring love] to herbs,
or to mixed juices, nor try the noxious poison of an
enamoured mare. . . .

Learn how . . . your faces can shine fair. Strip barley . . . from its husk. Let an equal quantity of vetch be soaked in ten eggs : but let the stripped barley weigh two pounds. When this has been dried by the winds let the slow she-ass break it on the rough mill-stone : pound up with it the first horns that fall from a lively stag. . . . Add twelve narcissus bulbs without their sheaths . . . gums and Tuscan seed . . . and let nine times as much honey go with it. Whoever shall apply such a prescription to her face will shine smoother than her own mirror. Neither hesitate to parch pale lupin seeds, and with them beans that puff out the body. . . . Blemishes on the face disappear before a remedy from the plaintive birds-nest ; they call it Halcyonea. . . . It is good to add fennel to fragrant myrrh . . . as much as one hand can hold of dried roses. . . . On these pour cream of barley. . . . Placed for a short time on your soft face, it will leave plenty of colour over all the countenance. I have seen some one pound up poppies wetted with cold water, and smear them on her tender cheeks. OVID

De Medicamine Faciei Liber (c. 10 B.C.)

SCANDALISING CHRISTIANS

Those women who paint their faces with rouge and their eyes with purple, whose faces, coated with plaster and spoilt by too much whiteness, remind us of idols, who, if by chance they shed a careless tear, show a furrow, . . . who pile themselves a head out of the hair of others, these are they who scandalise the eyes of Christians.

ST JEROME
Letter to Marcella (384)

A Dishonest Artifice

As to the use of pigments by women in colouring the face, in order to have a ruddier or a fairer complexion, this is a dishonest artifice, by which I am sure that even their own husbands do not wish to be deceived.

ST AUGUSTINE, *Letter to Possideus* (c. 400)

Those Tawny Women

It hath towards the south part of the river, great quantities of . . . divers berries, that die a most perfect crimson and Carnation : And for painting, all *France*, *Italy*, or the east *Indies*, yeild none such : For the more the skyn is washed, the fayrer the cullour appeareth, and with which, even those brown and tawnie women spot themselves, and cullour their cheekes.

SIR WALTER RALEIGH, *Discoverie of Guiana* (1596)

Painful Beauty

Who hath not heard of her at Paris, which only to get a fresher hew of a new skin, endured to have her face flead all over ? There are some who, being sound, and in perfit health, have had some teeth puld-out, thereby to frame a daintier or more pleasing voyce, or to set them in better order ? How many examples of paine or smarte have we of that kind and sex ? What can they not doe ? What will they not doe ? What feare they to doe ? So they may but hope for some amendment of their beautie ?

Vellere queis cura est albos a stirpe capillos,
Et faciem dempta pelle referre novam.

Who take great care to root out their gray haire,
And skin flead-off a new face to repaire.

I have seene some swallow gravell, ashes, coales, dust,
tallow, candles and for the-nonce, labour and toyle themselves to spoile their stomacke, only to get a pale-bleake
colour. To become slender in wast, and to have a straight
spagnolized body what pinching, what girding, what cing-
ling will they not indure; Yea sometimes with yron-plates,
with whale-bones, and other such trash, that their very
skin, and quicke flesh is eaten in and consumed to the
bones ; Whereby they sometimes worke their owne death.

MICHEL DE MONTAIGNE
*Essays : That the taste of goods or evils doth greatly
depend on the opinion we have of them* (1580)
Trans. John Florio (1603)

FACE-DECORATIONS

The *Bramines* of *Agra* mark themselves in Forehead, Ears,
and Throat, with a kind of yellow geare which they grind,
and every morning they do it, and so do the women. The
Gentiles of *Indostan*, men and women both, paint on their
foreheads and other parts of their faces, red and yellow
spots. The *Cygnanians* are of a horrid aspect, much like
the people called *Agathyres*, of whom the poet *Virgil*
speaketh, for they were all painted and spotted with sundry
colours, and especially with black and red . . . they paint
themselves from the forehead even unto the knees. . . .

A man would think them to be Divels incarnate broke out of Hell, they are so like hell-hounds. I am sure they violate and impudently affront Nature. . . . The *Virginian* women rase their Faces and whole Bodies with a sharp iron which makes a stamp in curious knots, and drawes the proportions of Fowls, Fishes, or Beasts ; then with Painting of sundry lively Colours they rub it into the stamp, which will never be taken away. . . . The *Egyptian-Moores*, both men and women, for love of each other distain their Chins with knots and flowers of blew, made by the pricking of the skin with needles, and rubbing it over with ink and the juice of an herb. . . . The *Arabian* women . . . paint their Faces, Breasts, Armes, and Hands, with a certain azured colour, thinking that they are very handsome after this manner.

Our *English* ladies, who seeme to have borrowed many of their Cosmetical conceits from barbarous Nations, are seldome known to be contented with a Face of God's making, for they are either adding, detracting, or altering continually. Sometimes they thinke they have too much colour, then they take much Physique to make them look pale and faire : Now they have too little colour, then Spanish-Paper, Red-Leather, and other Cosmetical Rubriques must be had. Yet for all this, it may be the skins of their Faces do not please them, off they go with Mercury-water, and so they remain like peeled ewes, until their Faces have recovered a new Epidermis. Sometimes they want a Mole to set off their beauty, such as *Venus* had, then it is well if one Black-Patch will serve to make their Faces remarkable, for some fill their Visages full of them, varied into all manner of shapes and figures, which is as odious and senseless an affectation as ever was used by any barbarous Nation in the world. . . . Effeminate

Gallants . . . of late have begun to vie patches and beauty-spots, nay painting, with the most tenderest and phantastical Ladies . . . to the . . . high dishonour and abasement of the glory of mans perfection.   JOHN BULWER
Anthropometamorphosis : or, The Artificial
Changeling (1650)

EYE-BROWS

In the West Indies, the Cumanans pluck off all the haire of their *Eye-brows*, taking great pride and using much superstition in that unnatural depilation. . . . Of old time, the women when their Eye-brows were long and broad, they made them narrow, subtile, and arched either with Pinsers or Sissers, and when they were yellow or white, they made them black with Soot, as you may read in *Tertullian, Plautus, Athenaeus, Clemens Alexandinus*, and others. . . . The *American* women do with a certain Fucus paint their *Ey-browes*, which they lay on with a pencil : A thing also usual with *Frenchwomen*, who have little modesty.   *Ibid.*

EYE-LIDS

The *Brasileans* . . . pull off and eradicate the Haire growing on their Eye-lids. The *Turks* have a black powder . . . which with a fine pencil they lay under their Eye-lids, which doth colour them black, whereby the White of the Eye is set off more white : with the same powder also they colour the hairs of their Eye-lids.   *Ibid.*

They of *Cape Lopos Gonfalues*, both men and women, use sometimes to make one of their Eyes white, the other red or yellow.

Ibid.

NOSES

The Tartarian women cut and pare their *Noses* between their Eyes, that they may seem more flat and saddle-nosed, leaving themselves no Nose at all in that place, annointing the very same place with a black oyntment; which sight seemed most ugly in the eyes of Friar *William de Rubraquins*, a Frenchman, and his companions.

Ibid.

EARS

The *Macuas*, . . . weare their Eares bored round with many holes, in which they have pegs of wood, slender like knitting-needles . . . which make them look like hedge-hogs; this is part of their gallantry, for if they are sad, or crossed with any disaster, they have all these holes open. In *Peru*, the greatest Eares are ever esteemed the fairest, which with all Art and Industry they are continually stretching out; and a man . . . sweareth to have been in a Province of the East Indies, the people so careful to make them great, and so to load them with heavy Jewels, that at great ease he could have thrust his arme thorow one of their Eare-holes.

Ibid.

TEETH

The people of *Molalia* . . . account Red Teeth a great
beautie, and therefore they colour their Teeth Red with
Beetle. . . . The women of . . . *Orissa* in *India* . . . in a
foolish pride black their Teeth, because Dogs teeth
(forsooth) are white. In Cariaian the women use to gild
their teeth.

Ibid.

ARMS, HANDS, AND NAILS

The *Persins* . . . illustrate their Arms and Hands, their
Legs and Feet, with painted flowers and birds. . . . They
paint their nails party-coloured white and vermelion. The
Turkes paint their long nails red, and our Merchants that
live there conform unto the custome. In the Kingdom of
Goer, they paint their Nails yellow : and the nobler any
one is, so much the longer his Nails : so that he is the best
Gentleman whose Nails appears like Eagles claws.

Ibid.

SUBMARINE TOILET

My Cabinets are Oyster-shells,
In which I keep my Orient-Pearls,
To open them I use the Tide,
As Keys to Locks, which opens wide,
The Oyster-shells, then out I take ;

Those, Orient-Pearls and Crowns do make ;
And modest Coral I do wear,
Which blushes when it touches air.
On Silver-Waves I sit and sing,
And then the Fish lie listening :
Then sitting on a Rocky Stone,
I comb my Hair with Fishes bone.
The whil'st *Apollo*, with his Beams,
Doth dry my Hair from wat'ry streams.
His Light doth glaze the Water's face,
Make the large Sea my Looking-Glass ;
So when I swim on Waters high,
I see my self as I glide by :
But when the Sun begins to burn,
I back into my Waters turn,
And dive unto the bottom low :
Then on my head the Waters flow
In Curled waves and Circles round ;
And thus with Waters am I Crown'd.

MARGARET CAVENDISH, DUCHESS OF NEWCASTLE
The Convent of Pleasure (1668)

TINTING THE NAILS

The nayles are also of a substance tingible and outwardly
colourable, . . . as I have seen in the Dominions of the
Turk, where some not only guild the nayles, butt many
colour them of a reddish colour which may bee anywhere
performed by the powder of Alcanna or Cua steeped in
a cloath to lay it upon the nayles some howers, butt this
is no long lasting colour and must be renewed sometimes,

and if it were, yett the nayles, growing in length, would at last carye it off.

SIR THOMAS BROWNE
Letter to his son Edward (1679)

A LADY'S REQUIREMENTS

And Spanish paper, Lip and Cheek
With Spittel sweetly to belick :
Nor therefore spare in the next place
The pocket *sprunking* Looking-glass :
Calembuc combs in pulvil case
To set and trim the hair and face :
And that the cheeks may both agree,
Plumpers to fill the cavity. . . .
   The table miroir, one glue pot,
One for Pomatuma, and what not ?
Of washes, unguents, and cosmeticks ;
A pair of silver candlesticks ;
Snuffers and snuff-dish ; boxes more,
For powders, patches, waters store,
In silver flasks, or bottles, cups
Cover'd, or open, to wash chaps. . . .
Of other waters, rich and sweet,
To sprinkle Handkerchief is meet ;
D'ange, orange, *mill-fleur*, myrtle,
Whole quarts the Chamber to bequirtle. . . .
Thus rigg'd the Vessel, and equipp'd,
She is for all Adventures shipp'd.

JOHN EVELYN (AND HIS DAUGHTER MARY)
*Mundus Muliebris, or the Ladies Dressing-Room
Unlock'd* (1690)

But perhaps, with a panting heart, you carry your piece
before a woman of quality. She gives the labours of your
brain to her maid to be cut into shreds for curling her hair.

F. M. A. DE VOLTAIRE
Letter to M. Le Février

PREPARING FOR THE PARTY

And now unveil'd, the Toilet stands display'd,
Each silver Vase in mystic order laid.
First, rob'd in white, the Nymph intent adores,
With head uncover'd, the Cosmetick pow'rs,
A heav'nly Image in the glass appears,
To that she bends, to that her eyes she rears ;
Th' Inferior Priestess, at her altar's side,
Trembling begins the sacred rites of Pride.
Unnumber'd treasures ope at once, and here
The various off'rings of the world appear ;
From each she nicely culls with curious toil
And decks the Goddess with the glitt'ring spoil.
This casket India's glowing gems unlocks,
And all Arabia breathes from yonder box.
The tortoise here and elephant unite,
Transform'd to combs, the speckled and the white.
Here files of pins extend their shining rows,
Puffs, Powders, Patches, Bibles, Billets-doux.
Now awful Beauty puts on all its arms ;
The fair each moment rises in her Charms

Repairs her smiles, awakens ev'ry grace,
And calls forth all the wonders of her face.

ALEXANDER POPE
The Rape of the Lock (1712)

NATURE'S INCIVILITY OUTDONE

Yet, uncivil as Nature has been, they seem resolved to outdo her in unkindness ; they use white powder, blue powder, and black powder, for their hair, and a red powder for the face on some particular occasion.

They like to have the face of various colours, as among the Tartars of Koreki, frequently sticking on, with spittle, little black patches on every part of it, except on the tip of the nose, which I have never seen with a patch. You'll have a better idea of their manner of placing these spots, when I have finished the map of an English face patched up to the fashion, which shall shortly be sent to increase your curious collection of paintings, medals, and monsters.

OLIVER GOLDSMITH
*Letters from a Citizen of the World to his Friends in
the East* (1762)

A FOOLISH QUESTION

Why do they adorn themselves with so many colours of hearbs, fictitious flowers, curious needleworks, quaint devices, sweet-smelling odours, with those inestimable riches of pretious stones, pearls, rubies, diamonds, emeralds, etc ? Why do they crown themselves with gold and silver, use coronets, and tires of several fashions, deck themselves with pendants, bracelets, ear-rings, chains, girdles, rings, pins, spangles, embroyderies, shadows, rabatoes, versicolor ribbands ? Why do they make such glorious shews with their scarfs, feathers, fans, masks, furs, laces, tiffanies, ruffs, falls, calls, cuffs, damasks, velvets, tinsels, cloth of gold, silver, tissue ? with colours of heaven, stars, planets ? the strength of metals, stones, odours, flowers, birds, beasts, fishes, and whatsoever *Afrika, Asia, America,* sea, land, art, and industry of man can afford ? Why do they use and covet such novelty of invention, such new-fangled tires, and spend such inestimable summs on them ? *To what end are those crisped, false hairs,* painted faces, as the *Satyrist observes.* . . . Why are they like so many *Sybarites,* or *Neroes Poppaea, Assuerus* concubines, so costly, so long a dressing as *Caesar* were marshalling his army, or an hawk in pruning ? . . . *A Gardiner takes not so much delight and pains in his garden, an horse man to dress his horse, scour his armour,* a Marriner about his ship, a merchant his shop and shop-book, as they do about their faces, and all those other parts : such setting up with corks, streighting with whale-bones ; why is it but as a day-net catcheth Larks, to make yong men stoop unto them ?

ROBERT BURTON
Anatomy Of Melancholy (1621. Edition 1632)

STREET MUSIC

BARREL ORGAN

Oh ! there is an organ playing in the street—a waltz too !
I must leave off to listen. They are playing a waltz which
I have heard ten thousand times at the balls in London,
between 1812 and 1815. Music is a strange thing.

LORD BYRON, *Diary* (Feb. 2, 1821)

STREET DANCERS

The sister of St Damian appeared to him after her death,
and said . . . " Once, standing in mine own chamber, I
listened with a certain sweetness to the songs of them
that danced in the streets, for which I did no penance
during my earthly life ; wherefore I must now be punished
for fifteen days in purgatory."

JOANNES HEROLT, *Promptuarium* (c. 1500)

BALLADS

After he [Bishop Corbet] was D. of Divinity, he sang ballads at the Crosse at Abingdon on a market-day. He and

some of his camerades were at the taverne by the crosse. . . .
The ballad singer complaynd, he had no custome, he
could not putt-off his ballades. The jolly Doctor putts-off
his gowne, and putts-on the ballad singer's leathern jacket,
and being a handsome man, and had a rare full voice, he
presently vended a great many, and had a great audience.

JOHN AUBREY, *Brief Lives : Richard Corbet* (c. 1680)

BEGGING TO THE TABOR

In Herefordshire, and parts of the marshes of Wales, the
Tabor and Pipe were exceedingly common. Many beggars
beg'd with it, and the peasants danced to it in the church-
yard on holydays and holyday-eves. The Tabor is derived
from the Sistrum of the Romans.

Ibid. Remains of Gentilism and Judaism (1687)

SUNDAY

CHURCH OF ENGLAND

*The King's Majesty's Declaration to his Subjects Concern-
ing Lawful Sports to be used.*

Whereas We did justly in Our Progresse through
Lancashire rebuke some *Puritanes* and *Precise People*, . . .

in the prohibiting and unlawfull punishing of Our good people for using their lawfull recreations and honest exercises upon Sundays and other Holy-days, after the afternoone Sermon or Service ; We now finde, that two sortes of people wherewith that countrey is much infested (We mean *Papists* and *Puritanes*) have maliciously traduc'd and calumniated those Our just and honourable proceedings. . . . We have therefore thought good hereby to cleer and make Our Pleasure to be manifested to all Our good people in those partes. . . .

We heard the generall complaynt of Our people, that they were barred from all lawfull recreation and exercise upon the Sundaye's afternoone, after the ending of all Divine Service. Which cannot but produce two evills. . . . This prohibition barreth the common and meaner sort of people from using such exercises as may make their body's more able for war, when We, or Our Successours shall have occasion to use them : and in place therof setts up filthie tipplings and drunkennesse, and breedes a number of idle and discontented speeches in their ale-houses. For when shall the common people have leave to exercise, if not upon the Sundayes and Holy-dayes, seeing they must apply their labour and win their living in all workingdayes ? . . .

Our Pleasure is, . . . *That after the end of Divine Service, Our good People be not disturb'd, letted, or discourag'd from any lawfull recreation, such as Dancing (either men or women) Archery for men, Leaping, Vaulting, or any other such harmlesse recreations ; nor from having of May Games, Whitsun Ales, and Morris Dances, and the setting up of May Poles, and other sports therwith used : so as the same bee had in due and convenient time, without impediment or neglect of Divine Service. And, That women shall have leave to carry*

Rushes to the Church for the decoring of it, according to their olde custome.

But whithal, *We doe here account stil as prohibited, all unlawfull games, to be us'd upon Sundayes onely; as Beare and Bull Baitings; Interludes; and at all times, in the meaner sorte of people by Law prohibited, Bowling.*

And likewise, *We bar from this benefit and libertie, all such knowne Recusants, either men or women, as will abstaine from comming to Church or Divine Service:* beeing therfor unworthy of any lawfull recreation after the said Service, that wil not first come to the Church and serve GOD.

Prohibiting in like sorte, the said recreation to any that, though conforme in Religion, are not present in the Church . . .

Our Pleasure likewise is, *That they to whom it belongeth in Office shall present and sharply punish all such, as in abuse of this Our libertie, will use these Exercises before the ends of all Divine Services for that day.*

And We, likewise, straitly commaund, *That every person shall resort to his owne Parish Church to heare Divine Service; and each Parish, by it selfe, to use the said recreation after Divine Service*, Prohibiting likewise, *Any offensive weapons to be carryed or us'd in the said times of recreation.*

KING JAMES I
(1618)

DR JOHNSON'S

Dr Johnson enforced the strict observance of Sunday. "It should be different," (he observed,) "from another day. People may walk, but not throw stones at birds. There may be relaxation, but there should be no levity." . . .

" Sunday," (said he) " was a heavy day to me when I was a boy. My mother confined me on that day, and made me read *The Whole Duty of Man.*"

JAMES BOSWELL
Life of Johnson (1791)

I seldom frequent card-tables on Sunday.

SAMUEL JOHNSON
Rambler (1750–52)

LONDONERS'

Sunday, October 20, 169–. Great jangling of Bells all over the City from eight to nine. Psalms murder'd in most Parishes at ten. Abundance of Doctrines and Uses in the Meetings and no Application. Vast consumption of Roast Beef and Pudding at one. Afternoon sleepy in most Churches. Score of Handkercheifs stolen in *Paul's* at three. Informers busy all day long. Night not so sober as might be wish'd.

Sunday, Oct. 27. Taylors curs'd for not bringing the fine Cloathes home at the promis'd Hour. Great Ogling at *Covent-Garden* Church and other places, from ten to twelve. A She-Quaker holds forth in her Stays in *Grace-Church-Street*, to the great Cramping of the Spirit.

Ministers preach against Sin, but the People still Practice it, and are like to do so to the end of the Chapter.

Sunday, Nov. 3. Beggars take up their respective Posts in *Lincoln-Inn Fields* and other Places, by seven, that they may be able to praise God in Capon and *March* beer at Night. Parish-Clerks liquor their Throats plentifully at eight, and chaunt out Hopkins most melodiously about ten. Sextons, Men of great Authority most part of the Day, whip Dogs out of the Church for being Obstreperous. Great Thumping and Dusting of the Cushion at *Salter's Hall*, about eleven ; one would almost think the Man was in Earnest, he lays so Furiously about him. A most Refreshing Smell of Garlick at *Spitalfields* and *Soho* at twelve. Country-fellows staring at the two Wooden Men in *St Dunstans* from one to two, to see how Notably they Strike the Quarters. The great Point of Predestination settled in *Russel-Court* about three, and the People go home as Wise as they came thither. A merrie Farce, call'd the *Confusion of Babel*, acted at surly *Wat's* Coffee-House in the Evening, and lasts from five till ten. Great Squabbling, Buzzing, and Prating, from the *Baronet's Club*, down to the noisy Footman below. Terrible Swearing in the Kitchen for the Boys not brining the vile *Derby* in time. Beef call'd for at every Table, and Mrs Cook most highly importun'd for a Carrot.

Sunday, Nov. 17. Surgeons knock'd up by twelve Penny Customers at seven and hinder'd, as they say, from going to Church ; but ten to one whether they wou'd have gone thither, tho' no body had visited 'em. Dumplings far exceeding those of *Norfolk*, at the *Half-Moon* in *Cheapside*, and the *Rose* by *Temple-Bar* at eleven. Citizens whet away their Stomachs, and judiciously censure the Sermon, in most Taverns about twelve ; in the Strength of Roast-Beef and the Sunday Bottle of Claret, give their Wives a Comfortable Refreshment on the Couch about two ; beget Block-heads to continue the City-Breed. A Magistrate with a Golden Chain about his Neck snores Inordinately in a Coventicle at three. Tradesmens Wives treat their Children in the Farthing Pye-Houses at four. Not one Physitian at Church, except the City-Bard, within the Bills of Mortality.

TOM BROWN
Comical View of London and Westminster (169–)

THE COUNTRYMAN'S

I am always very well pleased with a Country *Sunday* ; and think if keeping holy the Seventh Day were only a human Institution, it would be the best Method that could have been thought of for the polishing and civilizing of Mankind. It is certain the Country-People would soon degenerate into a kind of Savages and Barbarians, were there not such frequent Returns of a stated Time, in which the whole Village meet together with their best Faces, and in their cleanliest Habits, to converse with one another upon indifferent subjects, hear their Duties explained to them, and join together in Adoration of the Supreme Being. *Sunday* clears away the Rust of the whole Week, not only as it refreshes in their Minds the Notions of Religion, but as it puts both the Sexes upon appearing in their most agreeable Forms, and exerting all such Qualities as are apt to give them a Figure in the Eye of the Village. A Country-Fellow distinguishes himself as much in the *Church-yard* as a Citizen does upon the *Change*, the whole Parish-Politicks being generally discussed in that Place either after Sermon or before the Bell rings.

JOSEPH ADDISON
Spectator (1711)

THE CLERGYMAN'S

Thou art a day of mirth :
And where the week-dayes trail on ground,
Thy flight is higher, as thy birth.
O, let me take thee at the bound,
Leaping with thee from sev'n to sev'n,
Till that we both, being toss'd from earth,
    Flie hand in hand to heav'n !

GEORGE HERBERT
Sunday. From The Temple (1633)

MISS HANNAH MORE'S

Thank my dear Dr S. for his kind and seasonable admonitions on my last Sunday's engagement at Mrs Montagu's. Conscience had done its office before ; nay, was busy at the time : and if it did not dash my cup of pleasure to the ground, infused at least a tincture of wormwood into it. I *did* think of the alarming call, " What doest thou here, Elijah ? " . . .

Perhaps you will say I ought to have thought of it

666

again to-day, when I tell you I have dined abroad ; but
it is a day I reflect on without those uneasy sensations one
has when one is conscious it has been spent in trifling
company. I have been at Mrs Boscawen's. Mrs Montagu,
Mrs Carter, Mrs Chapone, and myself only were admitted.
We spent the time, not as wits, but as reasonable creatures ;
better characters, I trow. The conversation was sprightly
but serious. I have not enjoyed an afternoon so much
since I have been in town. There was much sterling sense,
and they are all ladies of high character for piety ; of
which, however, I do not think their visiting on Sundays
any proof : for though their conversation is edifying, the
example is bad.

HANNAH MORE
Letter to her Sister (1775)

MR PEPYS'S

Nov. 3rd, 1661. (Lord's day.) This day I stirred not out, but
took physique, and it did work very well, and all the day
as I was at leisure I did read in Fuller's Holy Warr, which
I have of late bought, and did try to make a song in praise
of a liberall genius (as I take my own to be) to all studies
and pleasures, but it not proving to my mind I did reject
it and so proceeded not in it. At night my wife and I
had a good supper by ourselves of a pullet hashed, which
pleased me much to see my condition come to allow ourselves a dish like that, and so at night to bed.

April 14, 1667. (Lord's day.) Up, and to read a little in my
new History of Turkey, and so with my wife to church,

and then home, where is little Michell and my pretty Betty and also Mercer, and very merry. A good dinner of roast beef. After dinner I away to take water at the Tower, and thence to Westminster, where Mrs Martin was not at home. So to White Hall, and there walked up and down, and among other things visited Sir G. Carteret, and much talk with him.... From him to St Margaret's Church, and there spied Martin, and home with her . . . but fell out to see her expensefullness, having bought Turkey work, chairs, etc. By and by away home, and there took out my wife and the two Mercers and two of our maids, Barker and Jane, and over the water to Jamaica House, where I never was before, and there the girls did run for wagers over the bowling-green ; and there with much pleasure spent little, and so home, and they home, and I to read with satisfaction in my book of Turkey, and so to bed.

SAMUEL PEPYS
Diary

DEVILISH PASTIMES

PHILOPONUS : The Sabboth daie of some is well observed, namely, in hearing the blessed worde of God read, preached, and interpreted ; in private and publique praiers ; in singing of godly psalmes ; in celebrating the sacraments ; and in collecting for the poore and indigent, which are the true uses and endes whereto the Sabbaoth was ordained. But other some spend the Sabbaoth day (for the most parte) in frequenting of baudy stage plaies and enterludes ; in maintayning lordes of misrule (for so they call a certaine kinde of plaie which they use) in Maie games, church ales, feastes, and wakesses; in pyping, dauncying, dicyng, carding, bowlyng, tenisse playing; in bear baytyng, cocke fightyng, hawkyng, hunting, and suche like; in keeping of fayres and markettes on the Sabbaoth; in keepyng of courtes and leetes; in foote ball playing, and such other devilish pastymes; in readyng of lascivious and wanton bookes, and an infinite number of suche like practises and prophane exercises used upon that day, whereby the Lorde God is dishonoured, his Sabaoth violated, his word neglected, his sacramentes contemned, and his people mervailously corrupted, and caried away from true vertue and godlines.

SPUDEUS : You will be deemed too too stoicall, if you should restraine menne from those exercises uppon the Sabbaoth, for they suppose that that day was ordained and consecrate to that ende and purpose, onely to use what kinde of exercises they thinke good themselves; and was it not so?

PHILIP STUBBES
The Anatomy of Abuses (1583)

A LIVELY SUNDAY

PHILOPONUS : Firste, all the wilde heades of the Parishe, conventyng together, chuse them a Ground Capitaine (of mischeef), whom they innoble with the title of my Lorde of Misserule, and hym they crown with great solemnitie, and adopt for their kyng. This kyng anoynted, chuseth for the twentie, fourtie, three score, or a hundred lustie guttes like to hymself to waite uppon his lordely majestie, and to guerde his noble persone. Then every one of these his menne he investeth with his liveries of greene, yellowe, or some other light wanton colour. And as though that were not (baudie) gaudy enough, I should saie, they bedecke themselves with scarffes, ribons, and laces, hanged all over with golden rynges, precious stones, and other jewelles ; this doen, they tye about either legge twentie or fourtie belles, with riche hande-kercheefes, in their handes, and somtymes laied a crosse over their shoulders and neckes, borrowed for the moste parte of their pretie mopsies and loovyng bessies, for bussyng them in the darcke. Thus all thinges sette in order, then have they their Hobbie horses, Dragons, and other antiques, together with their baudie pipers and thunderyng drommers, to strike up the Devilles Daunce withall ; then marche these heathen companie towardes the churche and churcheyarde, their pipers pipyng, their drommers thonderyng, their stumppes dauncyng, their belles iynglyng, their handkerchefes swyngyng about their heades like madmen, their Hobbie horses and other monsters skirmishyng amongest the throng ; and in this sorte they goe to the churche (though the minister bee at praier or preachyng), dauncyng and swingyng their handkercheefes over their heades, in the churche, like devilles incarnate, with suche a confused noise, that no man can heare his owne voice. Then the foolishe people they looke, they stare, they laugh, they fleere, and mount upon formes and pewes, to see these goodly pageauntes, solemnized in this sort. Then after this, aboute the churche they goe againe and againe, and so forthe into the churche-yarde, where they have commonly their Sommer halles, their bowers, arbours, and banquetyng houses set up, wherein they feaste, banquet, and daunce all that daie, and (peradventure) all that night too. And

670

thus these terrestrial furies spend the Sabbaoth daie ! . . .
SPUDEUS : This is a horrible prophanation of the Sabbaoth
(the Lorde knoweth), and more pestilent then pestilence
it self.

Ibid.

SECRET BOWLS

The Puritan faction did begin to increase in those dayes
and especially at Emmanuel College . . . They preached up
very strict keeping and observing the Lord's day ; made,
upon the matter, damnation to breake it, and that 'twas
lesse sin to kill a man. . . . Yet these hypocrites did bowle
in a private green at their colledge every Sunday after
sermon.

JOHN AUBREY
Brief Lives : Lancelot Andrewes
(c. 1680)

A CHEERFUL SHROPSHIRE VILLAGE

In the Village he liv'd in, not a Sermon was to be heard
from Year to Year. And the Service was run over very
Cursorily and Irreverently ; and when that was done, the
rest of the Lord's Day was profanely spent by the whole
Town in Dancing under a May-Pole, and a great Tree.

EDMUND CALAMY
*Abridgement of Mr. Baxter's History of his Life and
Times* (1702)

That Luxury and Excess men usually practise upon this Day . . . dividing the time between God and their Bellies, when, after a gluttonous meal, their senses dozed and stupefied, they retire to God's House to sleep out the Afternoon.

JONATHAN SWIFT
Sermon upon Sleeping in Church

TAKING UMBRAGE

A GOD IS OFFENDED

What is that Land, says he, the Waves embrace ?
(And with his Finger pointed at the Place ;)
Is it one parted Isle which stands alone ?
How nam'd ? and yet methinks it seems not one.
To whom the watry God made this Reply ;
'Tis not one Isle, but five ; distinct they lie ;
'Tis Distance which deceives the cheated Eye.
But that *Diana's* Act may seem less strange,
These once proud *Naiads* were, before their Change.
'Twas on a Day more solemn than the rest,
Ten Bullocks slain, a sacrificial Feast :

The rural Gods of all the Region near
They bid to dance, and taste the hallow'd Cheer.
Me they forgot : Affronted with the Slight,
My Rage, and Stream swell'd to the greatest Height;
And with the Torrent of my flooding Store,
Large Woods from Woods, and Fields from Fields
   I tore.
The guilty Nymphs, Oh ! them rememb'ring me,
I, with their Country, wash'd into the Sea :
And joining Waters with the social Main,
Rent the gross Land, and spit the firm Champagne.
Since, the *Echinades*, remote from Shore
Are view'd as many Isles, as Nymphs before.

OVID
Metamorphoses (c. 5 B.C.)
Trans. Mr. Vernon (1717 ?)

THRIFT

THE PROVIDENT INDIAN

The *Orenoqueponi* bury not their wives with them, but
their jewels, hoping to injoy them againe.

SIR WALTER RALEIGH
The Discoverie of Guiana (1596)

A Cheap Evening

Here I met with Osborne and with Shaw and Spicer, and we went to the Sun Tavern in expectation of a dinner . . . at which we were very merry, while in came Mr. Wade and his friend Capt. Moyse . . . and here we staid till seven at night. . . . I by having but 3d in my pocket made shift to spend no more, whereas if I had had more I had spent more as the rest did, so that I see it is an advantage to a man to carry little in his pocket.

SAMUEL PEPYS
Diary (Feb. 17, 1660)

After Christmas

This night making an end wholly of Christmas, with a mind full satisfied with the great pleasures we have had by being abroad from home, and I do find my mind so apt to run to its old want of pleasures, that it is high time to betake myself to my late vows, which I will to-morrow, God willing, perfect and bind myself to, that so I may, for a great while, do my duty, as I have well begun, and increase my good name and esteem in the world, and get money, which sweetens all things, and whereof I have much need. So home to supper and to bed, blessing God for his mercy to bring me home, after much pleasure, to my house and business with health and resolution to fall hard to work again.

Ibid.
(Twelfth Day, 1663)

The Athenians might fairly except against the practise of Democritus to be buried up in honey ; as fearing to embezzle a great commodity of their Countrey, and the best of that kinde in Europe.

SIR THOMAS BROWNE
Hydrotaphia (1658)

THE PARSIMONIOUS MAN

When hee returnes from his field, he asks, not without rage, what became of the loose crust in his cupboard, and who hath rioted among his leekes ? He never eats good meals, but on his neighbors trencher. . . . Once in a yeere perhaps, he gives himselfe leave to feast ; . . . and when his guests are parted, talkes how much every man devoured, and how many cups were emptied, and feeds his familie with the moldie remnants a moneth after. . . . In his short and unquiet sleepes hee dreames of theeves, and runnes to the dore.

JOSEPH HALL
Characters of Vertues and Vices (1608)

TRAVEL

To Lie in Diverse Inns

For Peregrination charmes our senses with such unspeakable and sweet variety, that some count him unhappy that never travelled, a kinde of prisoner, and pitty his case that from his cradle to his old age beholds the same still; still, still, the same, the same : insomuch that *Rhasis* . . . doth not only commend but enjoyne travell, and such variety of objects, to a melancholy man, *and to lie in diverse Innes, to bee drawne into severall companies.* . . .

He that should be admitted on a sudden to the sight of such a Palace as that of *Escuriall* in *Spaine*, or to that which the *Moores* built at *Granada*, *Fontainebleau* in *France*, the *Turkes* gardens in his *Seraglio*, wherein all manner of birds and beasts are kept for pleasure, Wolves, Beares, Lynces, Tigers, Lyons, Elephants, &c. . . . the Pope's *Belvedere* in *Rome* . . . or that *Indian* King's delightsome garden in *Ælian* . . . could not choose . . . but be much recreated for the time. . . . To take a boat in a pleasant evening, and with musicke to rowe upon the waters, which *Plutarch* so much applaudes, *Ælian* admires upon the river *Peneus*, in those *Thessalian* fields beset with greene Bayes, where Birds so sweetly sing that passengers, enchanted as it were with their heavenly musicke, . . . forget forthwith all labours, cares, and griefe : or in a *Gundilo* through the grand *Canale* in *Venice*, to see those goodly Palaces, must needs refresh and give content to a melancholy dull spirit.

ROBERT BURTON
The Anatomy of Melancholy (1621. Edition 1632)

OFF TO THE BERMUDAS

Where the remote *Bermudas* ride
In th' Oceans bosome unespy'd
From a small Boat, that row'd along,
The listning Winds receiv'd this Song.

" What should we do but sing his Praise
That led us through the watry Maze,
Unto an Isle so long unknown,
And yet far kinder than our own ?
Where he the huge Sea-Monsters wracks,
That lift the Deep upon their Backs.
He lands us on a grassy Stage ;
Safe from the Storms, and Prelat's rage.
He gave us this eternal Spring,
Which here enamells every thing ;
And sends the Fowl's to us in care,
On daily Visits through the Air.
He hangs in shades the Orange bright,
Like golden Lamps in a green Night.
And does in the Pomegranates close,
Jewels more rich than *Ormus* show's.

677

He makes the Figs our mouths to meet;
And throws the Melons at our feet.
But Apples plants of such a price,
No Tree could ever bear them twice.
With Cedars, chosen by his hand,
From *Lebanon* he stores the Land.
And makes the hollow Seas, that roar,
Proclaime the Ambergris on shoar.
He cast (of which we rather boast)
The Gospels Pearl upon our Coast.
And in these Rocks for us did frame
A Temple, where to sound his Name.
O let our Voice his Praise exalt,
Till it arrive at Heavens Vault :
Which thence (perhaps) rebounding, may
Eccho beyond the *Mexique Bay*."

Thus sang they in the *English* boat,
An holy and a chearful Note,
And all the way, to guide their Chime,
With falling Oars they kept the time.

ANDREW MARVELL
Bermudas (pub : 1681)

SEEING THE CONTINENT

Towards Venice we progress, and tooke Roterdam in our
waie, that was cleane out of our waie, there we met with
aged learnings chiefe ornament, that abundant and super-
ingenious clarke *Erasmus*, as also with merrie Sir *Thomas*

Moore our Countriman, who was come purposely over a little before us, to visite the said grave father *Erasmus* : what talke, what conference wee had then, it were here superfluous to rehearse. . . .

So we left them to prosecute their discontented studies, and make our next journey to Wittenberg. . . .

To the Emperours court wee came, where our entertainment was every way plentiful, carouses we had in whole galons in sted of quart pots. Not a health was given us but contained well neere a hogshead. The customes of the countrie we were eager to bee instructed in, but nothing wee coulde learne but this, that ever at the Emperours coronation there is an oxe roasted with a stag in the belly, and that stag in his belly hath a kid, and that kid is stufte full of birds. Some courtiers to wearie out time, would tell us further tales of *Cornelius Agrippa*, and howe when Sir *Thomas Moore* our countryman was there, he shewed him the whole destruction of Troy in a dreame. How the Lord *Cromwell* being the kings Embassador there, in like case in a perspective glasse hee set before his eyes king *Henrie* the eight, with all his Lordes on hunting in his forrest at Windsore. . . .

Though the Emperours court, and the extraordianarie edifiing companie of *Cornelius Agrippa* might have bin argumentes of waight to have arrested us a little longer there, yet Italy still stuck as a great moate in my masters eie, he thought he had travelled no further than Wales, till he had tooke survey of that countrie which was such a curious molder of wits.

To cut off blind ambages by the high way side, we made a long stride and got to Venice in short time.

THOMAS NASHE
The Unfortunate Traveller (1594)

Travellers gain Rest, but by coming Home,
Men at Home mope, till that Abroad they come ;
Thus is Love of Variety, Man's curse,
Which us to such a Love of Change does force.

WILLIAM WYCHERLEY
The World Unmask'd (1704)

COACHING AT THE HAGUE

Mr Creed and I went in the fore part of a coach wherein
were two very pretty ladies, very fashionable and with
black patches, who very merrily sang all the way and that
very well, and were very free to kiss the two blades that
were with them. I took out my flageolette and piped.

SAMUEL PEPYS
Diary (May 14, 1660)

WALPOLE IN THE ALPS

.

We were eight days in coming hither from Lyons ; the
four last in crossing the Alps. Such uncouth rocks, and
such uncomely inhabitants! My dear West, I hope I shall
never see them again! At the foot of Mount Cenis we were
obliged to quit our chaise, which was taken all to pieces
and loaded on mules ; and we were carried in low arm-
chairs on poles, swathed in beaver bonnets, beaver gloves,

beaver stockings, muffs and bear-skins. When we came to the top, behold the snows fallen! and such quantities, and conducted by such heavy clouds that hung glouting, that I thought we could have never have waded through them. The descent is two leagues, but steep and rough as O——'s father's face, over which, you know, the devil walked with hobnails in his shoes. But the dexterity and nimbleness of the mountaineers are inconceivable : they run with you down steeps and frozen precipices, where no man, as men are now, could possibly walk. We had twelve men and nine mules to carry us, our servants and baggages, and were above five hours in this agreeable jaunt !

HORACE WALPOLE
Letter to Richard West from Turin (1739)

COASTING DOWN THE RIVIERA

We lay at Canes, which is a small port on the Mediterranean ; here we agreed with a seaman to carry us to Genoa, and . . . embarqed on the 12th. . . . We coasted within two leagues of Antibes, which is the utmost towne in France. Thence by Nice, a citty in Savoy, built all of brick, which gives it a very pleasant appearance towards the sea . . .

We sailed by Mentone and Ventimiglia, being the first citty of the Republiq of Genoa ; supped at Oneglia, where we anker'd and lay on ashore. The next morning we coasted in view of the Isle of Corsica, and St Remo, where the shore is furnished with evergreens, oranges, citrons, and date-trees . . . The next morning by Diano, Araisso, famous for the best corall fishing, growing in aboundance on the rocks, deep and continually covered by sea. By Albengo and Finale, a very faire and strong towne, belonging to the King of Spayne, for which reason a monsieur in our vessell was extreamely afraide, as was the patron of our barke, for they frequently catch French prizes as they creepe by these shores to go into Italy ; he therefore ply'd both sayles and oars, to get under the protection of a Genoese gally that pass'd not far before us, in whose company we sayl'd as far as the Cape of Savona, a towne built at the rise of the Appenines : for all this coast (except a little of St Remo) is a high and steepe mountainous grounde, consisting all of rock-marble, without any grasse, tree, or rivage, formidable to look on . . . The rock consist of all sorts of the most precious marbles.

Here, on the 15th, forsaking our gally, we encountered a little foule weather, which made us creepe *terra, terra,* as they call it . . . but our patron, striving to double the point of Savona, making out into the wind put us into greate hazard ; for blowing very hard from land betwixt those horrid gapps of the mountaines, it set so violently, as rais'd on the suddaine so great a sea that we could not recover the weather shore for many houres, insomuch that, what with the water already enter'd, and the confusion of fearful passengers (of which one who was an Irish bishop, and his brother, a priest, were confessing some as at the article of death) we were almost abandoned to despaire, our pilot himselfe giving us up for lost. And now, as we were weary with pumping and laving out the water, almost sinking, it pleas'd God on the suddaine to appease the wind, and with much ado and greate perill we recover'd the shore, which we now kept in view.

JOHN EVELYN
Diary (October 1644)

Jan. 29, 1645. . . . The Via Appia is here a noble prospect ; having before consider'd how it was carried through vast mountaines of rocks for many miles, by most stupendious labor : here it is infinitely pleasant, beset with sepulchres and antiquities, full of sweete shrubbs in the invironing hedges. At Fondi, we had oranges and citrons for nothing, the trees growing in every corner, charged with fruite.

We descried Mount Caeculus, famous for the generous wine it heretofore produc'd, and so rid onward the Appian Way, beset with myrtils, lentiscus, bayes, pomegranads, and whole groves of orange-trees, and most delicious shrubbs, till we came to Formiana, where they shewed us Cicero's Tomb, standing in an olive grove; for here that incomparable orator was murther'd. I shall never forget how exceedingly I was delighted with the sweetnesse of this passage, the sepulchre mixed with all sorts of verdure ; besides being now come within sight of the noble citty; Cajeta, which gives a surprizing prospect along the Tyrrhen Sea, in manner of a theatre. . . .

Feb. 8. Now we enter'd the haven of the Baiae, where once stood that famous towne, so called from the companion of Ulysses here buried ; not without greate reason celebrated for one of the most delicious places that the sunn shines on, according to that of Horace :

Nullus in Orbe locus Baiis prælucet amœnis.

Though, as to the stately fabrics, there now remaine little save the ruines, whereof the most entire is that of Diana's Temple, and another of Venus. Here were those famous pooles of lampreys that would come to hand when called by name, as Martial tells us. On the sum'ite of the rock stands a strong castle garrisoned to protect the shore from Turkish pyrates. . . . It was once the retiring place of Julius Ceasar. . . .

Returning toward the Baiae, we again pass the Elyssian Fields, so celebrated by the poetes, nor unworthily, for their situation and verdure, being full of myrtils and sweete shrubbs, and having a most delightful prospect toward the Tyrrhen Sea. . . .

Having well satisfied our curiosity among these antiquities, we retired to our felucca, which rowed us back againe towards Pozzolo, at the very place of St Paule's landing. Keeping along the shore, they shewed us a place where the sea water and sands did exceedingly boyle. Thence, to the island Nesis, once the fabulous Nymph ; and thus we leave the Baiae, so renowned for the sweete retirements of the most opulent and voluptuous Romans. They certainly were places of uncommon amoenitie, as their yet tempting site, and other circumstances of natural curiosities, easily invite me to believe, since there is not in the world so many stupendious rarities to be met with, as in the circle of a few miles which environ these blissfull aboades.

Ibid.

HUSBAND-HUNTING IN THE INDIES

LUCIA : What will this come to ? What can it end in ? You have persuaded me to leave dear *England*, and dearer *London*, the place of the World most worth living in, to follow you a Husband-hunting into *America* : I thought Husbands grew in these Plantations.

CHARLOTTE : Why, so they do, as thick as Oranges, ripening one under another. Week after week they drop into some Woman's mouth : 'Tis but a little patience, spreading your Apron in expectation, and one of 'em will fall into your Lap at last.

LUCIA : Ay, so you say indeed.

THOMAS SOUTHERNE
Oroonoko (1696)

A TRAVELLER'S PRIVILEGE

You must allow him the Priviledge of a Travelleur, and he dos not abuse it, his lyes are as pleasant harmlesse on's as lyes can bee, and in noe great number considering the scope hee has for them ; there is one in Dublin now that ne're saw much further, has tolde mee twice as many (I dare swear) of Ireland.

DOROTHY OSBORNE
Letter to Sir William Temple (1654)

BIRDS AND FRUIT IN GUIANA

On the banks of these rivers were divers sorts of fruits good to eate, flowers and trees of that varietie as were sufficient to make ten volumes of herbals, we releeved our selves manie times with the fruits of the countrey, and

685

sometimes with foule and fish: we sawe birds of all colours, some carnation, some crimson, orange tawny, purple, greene, watched, and of all other sorts both simple and mixt, as it was unto us a great good passing of the time to beholde them, besides the reliefe we found by killing some store of them with our fouling pieces.

SIR WALTER RALEIGH
The Discoverie of Guiana (1596)

A COACH TO ONE'S SELF

The coache was gone before I came ... But being sett on my journy I hired a whole Coache to my selfe which cost me 4£, but it was the best bestowed money ... that ever I layd out, for the ayre being cool and fresh, and the coach to be opened before as well as on the sydes, I quaff'd off whole coachfulls of fresh ayr, without the pollution or the interruption of the (?) of any person. This had been an exceeding pleasant journy had not the remembrance of the misfortunes of some near relations of mine inter-mixt my wine with wormwood. But however I have most firmly concluded againe to my self in this ayry journy two of the main Theories of my Enchiridium Metaphysicum.

HENRY MORE
Letter to Lady Conway (1671)

TAPESTRY ANIMALS

.... The testimonies you give, and which I well recollect, of the juvenile huntings of the great Prince of Tuscany, and the slaughter he used to make of game in tapestry.... It was Ferdinand who, on going out of the drawingroom, always made an effort, or at least motion with his leg, that indicated a temptation to mount a horse in tapestry that hung near the door. It may, indeed, be a disorder in the family, and it may run in the blood to have an itch after tapestry animals. I am sure I wish I had a rage for riding and shooting my furniture, by a genealogic disorder, instead of the gout.   HORACE WALPOLE
Letter to Sir Horace Mann (1770)

TAVERNS

The Throne of Felicity

I have heard him assert, that a tavern-chair was the throne of human felicity.—" As soon," said he, " as I enter the door of a tavern, I experience an oblivion of care, and a freedom from solicitude : when I am seated, I find the master courteous, and the servants obsequious to my call; anxious to know and ready to supply my wants : wine there exhilarates my spirits, and prompts me to free conversation and an interchange of discourse . . . I dogmatize and am contradicted, and in this conflict of opinions and sentiments I find delight."

SIR JOHN HAWKINS
Life of Johnson (1787)

WILLS COFFEE-HOUSE

Would to God I could laugh with you for one hour or two at all the ridiculous things that have happen'd at *Wills Coffee-House* since I left it. 'Tis the merriest place in the World. Like *Africa*, every day it produces a Monster.

WALTER MOYLE
Letter to William Congreve (1695)

OVER A POT &C.

Some mens whole delight is to take Tobacco, and drinke day long in a Taverne or Ale-house, to discourse, sing, all jest, roare, talk of a Cock and a Bull over a pot &c.

ROBERT BURTON
The Anatomy of Melancholy
(1621. Edition 1632)

688

At Danby Wisk, in the north riding of Yorkshire, it is the custom for the parishioners, after receiving the Sacrament, to goe from church directly to the ale-house, and there drink together, as a testimony of charity and friendship.

JOHN AUBREY
Remains of Gentilism and Judaism
(1687)

VANITY

HAPPINESS

But what ? A Sot cannot help his Vanity. Agreed : But then it makes him so much happier than he deserves to be that he may well be contented to pay for it.

JOHN DENNIS
Letter to Walter Moyle
(pub. 1696)

VIRTUE

Chastity

ELDER BROTHER :
>   Vertue could see to do what vertue would
>   By her own radiant light, though Sun and Moon
>   Were in the flat Sea sunk. . . .
>   'Tis chastity, my brother, chastity :
>   She that has that, is clad in compleat steel,
>   And like a quiver'd Nymph with Arrows keen
>   May trace huge Forrests, and unharbour'd Heaths,
>   Infamous Hills, and sandy perilous wildes, . . .
>   Som say no evil thing that walks by night
>   In fog, or fire, by lake, or moorish fen, ...
>   Hath hurtfull power o're true Virginity. . . .
>   Hence had the huntress *Dian* her dred bow
>   Fair silver-shafted Queen for ever chaste,
>   Wherewith she tam'd the brindled lioness
>   And spotted mountain pard, . . .
>   So dear to Heav'n is Saintly chastity,
>   That when a soul is found sincerely so,
>   A thousand liveried Angels lacky her,
>   Driving far off each thing of sin and guilt,
>   And in cleer dream, and solemn vision
>   Tell her of things that no gross ear can hear.

JOHN MILTON, *Comus* (1634)

SPIRIT:

> Mortals that would follow me,
> Love vertue, she alone free,
> She can teach ye how to clime
> Higher then the Spheary chime ;
> Or if Vertue feeble were,
> Heav'n it self would stoop to her.

Ibid.

UNSELFISHNESS

I only feel persecution bitterly because I bitterly lament the depravity and mistake of those who persecute.

PERCY BYSSHE SHELLEY
Letter to Lord Byron (1817)

NOT SPEAKING AGAINST PEOPLE

It is a principle with me never to give others to understand any thing against an acquaintance, not only which I would not give, but which I *have* not given himself to understand ; a principle to which this book will have furnished no exception. It may be judged by this, how little I have been in the habit of speaking against any body, and what a nuisance it is to me to do it now.

LEIGH HUNT
Lord Byron and some of his Contemporaries
(1828)

All nobilitie
(But pride, that schisme of incivilitie)
She had, and it became her ! she was fit
T'have knowne no envy, but by suffring it !
She had a mind as calme, as she was faire ;
Not tost or troubled with light Lady-aire :
But kept an even gate, as some streight tree
Mov'd by the wind, so comely moved she.
And by the awfull manage of her Eye
She swaied all bus'nesse in the Familie.
To one she said, Doe this, he did it ; So
To another, Move : he went ; to a third, Go,
He run, and all did strive with diligence
T'obey, and serve her sweet Commandements.
She was in one, a many parts of life ;
A tender *Mother*, a discreeter *Wife*,
A solemne *Mistresse*, and so good a *Friend*,
So charitable, to religious end
In all her petite actions, so devote
As her whole life was now become one note
Of Pietie, and private holinesse.

BEN JONSON

*Eupheme, or the Faire Fame of that truly-noble Lady,
the Lady Venetia Digby* (1633 ?)

RESISTING TEMPTATION

Thence I home ; but Lord ! how it went against my heart
to go away from the very door of the Duke's play-house,

and my Lady Castlemayne's coach, and many great coaches there, to see " The Siege of Rhodes." I was very near making a forfeit, but I did command myself, and so home to my office, and there did much business to my good content, much better than going to a play, and then home to my wife, who is not well with her cold, and sat and read a piece of Grand Cyrus in English by her, and then to my chamber and to supper, and so to bed.

SAMUEL PEPYS
Diary (May 21st, 1667)

Its Rewards

And now his life was a Shining light among his old friends : now he gave an ocular testimony of the strictness and regularity of it ;

Nor did he preach onely, but as S. *Paul* advised his Corinthians to be followers of him as he was of Christ ; so he also was an ocular direction to them by a holy and harmlesse conversation.

Their love to him was expresst many wayes ; for (besides the faire lodgings that were provided and furnisht for him) other curtesies were daily accumulated, so many, and so freely, as though they meant their gratitude (if possible) should exceed, or at least equall his merits. In this love-strife of desert and liberality, they continued for the space of three yeares ; he constantly and faithfully preaching, they liberally requiting him.

IZAAK WALTON
The Life and Death of Dr. Donne
(1640 and 1670 editions)

VISITS

Entertaining Julius Caesar

O, I don't repent my heavy-weight guest ! For it went very pleasantly. But when he arrived at Philippus's on the second evening of the Saturnalia, the villa was so full of soldiers that there was scarcely a dining-room empty for Cæsar himself to sup in : two thousand men, forsooth ! ... On the third day of the Saturnalia he stayed with Philippus till one o'clock, and admitted no one ; doing accounts, I think, with Balbus. Then he walked on the shore. After two, the bath. He was annointed, and took his place at the table. He was taking emetics, so he ate and drank freely and boldly, and the dinner was not only very splendid and sumptuous, but

> " well cooked,
> And seasoned with good talk, indeed, quite gay."

Further, his attendants were entertained very lavishly in three diningrooms. The freedmen of lower grade and the slaves lacked nothing. But the upper ranks were entertained most elegantly. In short, we were seen to be men of the world. But he is not a guest to whom one would say, " Please come again on your way back." Once is enough. We had no serious conversation, but much literary. In short, he was pleased and had a good time. He said he should spend a day at Puteoli and another at Baiae.

Now you have the tale of my hospitality, or billeting, I might call it ; troublesome, but not annoying.

CICERO
Letter to Atticus (B.C. 45)

Out-Staying Welcome

Prudent Telemachus began to address them : Suitors of my mother, you insolent bullies, let us please ourselves now with feasting. . . . But in the morning let us all go down and sit in assembly, that I may firmly tell you this, that you are to go out of this house, and busy yourselves with other feasts, devouring your own substance, and taking turns at one another's houses. But if it seems to you more appropriate to consume without redress the goods of one man, then waste on ; but I will call upon the eternal gods, and if Zeus grants that deeds be punished, then you shall perish in this house unavenged.

HOMER
Odyssey. Book I

A Charming Time

I have passed the most delightful time in the most beautiful country in the company of Tonantius Ferreolus and Apollinaris, the most charming hosts in the world. Their estates march together, the houses are not far apart ... The hills above the houses are under vines and olives ... Every morning began with a flattering rivalry between the two hosts, as to which of their kitchens should first smoke for the refreshment of their guest ... From the first moment we were hurried from one pleasure to another. Hardly had we entered the vestibule of either house, when we saw two opposed pair of partners in the ball-game. ... In another place one heard the rattle of dice boxes ... in yet another were books. ... They were so arranged that the devotional works were near the ladies' seats ; where the master sat were those ennobled by the great style of Roman eloquence. ... The dinner was short, but abundant. ... Amusing and instructive anecdotes accompanied our potations ; wit went with the one sort, and learning with the other. To be brief, we were entertained with decorum, refinement and good cheer. ... The siesta over, we took a short ride to sharpen our jaded appetites for supper. ... I could tell you of suppers fit for a king : it is not my sense of shame, but simply want of space, which sets a limit to my revelations.

BISHOP SIDONIUS APOLLINARIS
Letter to Donidius (461–7)
Trans. T. Hodgkin (1892)

STAYING WITH THE SQUIRE

Why, if any of my friends come to see me, I entertain them with a good table and a bottle of good champaign ; and for their diversion I show them some sport. We have

allwayes some thing or other in season in the field, either
hunting or shooting, or setting or fishing. We never want
game of one sort or another, and if they are men of books
and talk learnedly, that's out of my way, and I say to
'em, " Come let's go visit the vicar," so away we go to
the parsonage, and the Doctor has a good library, and,
what is better than all his books, keeps a cup of good
liquor, as he calls it, for second-rate drinking.

DANIEL DEFOE
The Compleat Gentleman (1729)

A DISAPPOINTING SUPPER

To sup with thee thou didst me home invite ;
And mad'st a promise that mine appetite
Sho'd meet and tire, on such lautitious meat
The like not *Heliogabalus* did eat :
And richer Wine wo'dst give to me (thy guest)
Than Roman *Sylla* powr'd out at his feast.
I came ; ('tis true) and look't for Fowle of price,
The bastard *Phenix* ; bird of *Paradice* ;
And for no less than Aromatick Wine
Of *Maydens-blush*, commixt with *Jessamine*.
Cleane was the herth, the mantle larded jet ;
Which wanting *Lar*, and smoke, hung weeping wet ;
At last, i' th' noone of winter, did appeare
A ragd-soust-neats-foot with sick vineger :
And in a burnisht Flagonet stood by
Heere small as Comfort, dead as Charity.
At which amaz'd, and pond'ring on the food,
How cold it was, and how it child my blood,

I curst the master ; and I damn'd the souce ;
And swore I'de got the ague of the house.
Well, when to eat thou dost me next desire,
I'le bring a Fever, since thou keep'st no fire.

ROBERT HERRICK
The Invitation (1648)

CALLING ON THE POOR

We went to every house in the place, and found each a scene
of the greatest ignorance and vice. We saw but one Bible in
all the parish, and that was used to prop a flower-pot !

HANNAH MORE
Letter to Mr Wilberforce (1791)

CALLING ON THE RICH

George Hotel, Cheddar.

I was told we should meet with great opposition if I did
not try to propitiate the chief despot of the Village, who is
very rich, and very brutal ; so I ventured into the den of
this monster, in a country as savage as himself, near
Bridgewater. He begged I would not think of bringing any
religion into the country ; it was the worst thing in the
world for the poor, for it made them lazy and useless. In
vain did I represent to him that they would be more
industrious as they were better principled. . . . I made
eleven more of these agreeable visits ; and, as I improved

in the art of canvassing, had better success. Miss Wilberforce would have been shocked, had she seen the petty
tyrants whose insolence I stroked and tamed, the ugly
children I fondled, the pointers I stroked and caressed, the
cyder I commended, and the wine I swallowed. . . . Patty,
who is with me, says she has good hopes that the hearts
of some of these rich poor wretches may be touched;
they are at present as ignorant as the beasts that perish,
intoxicated every day before dinner, and plunged in such
vices as make me begin to think London a virtuous place.

Ibid. (1789)

AT BORELAND

Now and then a visit to Penfillan or somewhere has afforded
a little variety to my existence. The week before last I
spent with my Uncle George at Boreland; and such a
week! There was no amusement within doors, and the
weather precluded the possibility of finding any without.
The only book in the house (*Coelebs in Search of a Wife*)
was monopolized by a young lady who, I strongly suspect, had come there upon Coelebs's errand; and the rest
of us had no sort of weapon whatever to combat time with.
For four whole days I had nothing for it but to count the
drops of rain that fell from the ceiling into a basin beneath;
or to make a " burble " of my watchchain, for the satisfaction of undoing it. Oh Plato, Plato! what tasks! At
length in a phrensy of ennui I mounted a brute of a horse
that could do nothing but trot, and rode thirty-two miles
just for diversion. I left the good people at Boreland
wondering, when it would be fair? they had wondered for

four days, and when I came back they were still wondering. How few people retain their faculties in rainy weather!

JANE WELSH
Letter to Miss Stodart (1822)

A CHRISTMAS VISIT

The preparing and the going abroad in such weather . . .
were evils, were disagreeables at least, which Mr John
Knightley did not by any means like : he anticipated
nothing in the visit that could be at all worth the purchase ;
and the whole of their drive to the vicarage was spent by
him in expressing his discontent.

" A man," said he, " must have a very good opinion of
himself when he asks people to leave their own fire-side,
and encounter such a day as this, for the sake of coming to
see him. He must think himself a most agreeable fellow ;
I could not do such a thing. It is the greatest absurdity—
actually snowing at this moment ! The folly of not allow-
ing people to be comfortable at home—and the folly of
people's not staying comfortably at home when they can !
If we were obliged to go out on such an evening as this,
by any call of duty or business, what a hardship we should
deem it ;—and here are we, probably with rather thinner
clothing than usual, setting forth voluntarily, without
excuse, in defiance of the voice of nature, which tells man,
in every thing given to his view or his feelings, to stay
at home himself, and keep all under shelter that he can ;—
here are we setting forward to spend five dull hours in
another man's house, with nothing to say or to hear that

was not heard or said yesterday, and may not be said or heard again to-morrow. Going in dismal weather, to return probably in worse ;—four horses and four servants taken out for nothing but to convey five idle, shivering creatures into colder rooms and worse company than they might have had at home." . . . " Christmas weather," observed Mr Elton. " Quite seasonable : and extremely fortunate we may think ourselves that it did not begin yesterday, and prevent this day's party. . . . This is quite the season, indeed, for friendly meetings. At Christmas every body invites their friends about them, and people think little of even the worst weather. I was snowed up at a friend's house once for a week. Nothing could be pleasanter. I went only for one night, and could not get away till that very day se'nnight."

Mr John Knightley looked as if he did not comprehend the pleasure, but said only, coolly, " I cannot wish to be snowed up a week at Randalls."

JANE AUSTEN
Emma (1816)

FROM AN ANGEL

Haste hither *Eve*, and worth thy sight behold
Eastward among those Trees, what glorious shape
Comes this way moving ; seems another Morn
Ris'n on mid-noon ; som great behest from Heav'n
To us perhaps he brings, and will voutsafe
This day to be our Guest. But goe with speed,
And what thy stores contain, bring forth and poure
Abundance, fit to honour and receive

701

Our Heav'nly stranger ; . . .
To whom thus *Eve. Adam*, earths hallowd mould,
Of God inspir'd, small store will serve, where store,
All seasons, ripe for use hangs on the stalk ; . . .
   So saying, with dispatchful looks in haste
She turns, on hospitable thoughts intent
What choice to chuse for delicacie best,
What order, so contriv'd as not to mix
Tastes, not well joynd, inelegant, but bring
Taste after taste upheld with kindliest change,
Bestirs her then, and from each tender stalk
Whatever Earth all-bearing Mother yeilds
In *India* East or West, or middle shoare
In *Pontus* or the *Punic* Coast, or where
Alcinous reign'd, fruit of all kindes, in coate,
Rough, or smooth rin'd, or bearded husk, or shell
She gathers, Tribute large, and on the board
Heaps with unsparing hand ; for drink the Grape
She crushes, inoffensive moust, and meathes
From many a berrie, and from sweet kernels prest
She tempers dulcet creams, nor these to hold
Wants her fit vessels pure, then strews the ground
With Rose and Odours from the shrub unfum'd.
Mean while our Primitive great Sire, to meet
His god-like Guest, walks forth, without more train
Accompani'd then with his own compleat
Perfections in himself was all his state.

JOHN MILTON
Paradise Lost, Book V (1667)

WEALTH

EXCESS

He left a vast estate to his son, Sir Francis (I thinke ten thousand pounds per annum) ; he lived like a hog, but his son John was a great waster, and dyed in his father's time.

He was the greatest howse-keeper in England ; would have at Littlecote 4 or 5 or more lords at a time. His wife (Harvey) was worth to him, I thinke, 60000 li., and she was as vaine as he, and she sayd that she had brought such an estate, and she scorned but she would live as high as he did ; and in her husband's absence would have all the women of the countrey thither, and feast them, and make them drunke, as she would be herselfe. They both dyed by excesse ; and by luxury and cosonage by their servants, when he dyed, there was, I thinke, a hundred thousand pound debt.

Old Sir Francis, he lived like a hog, at Hownstret in Somerset. . . . I remember this epitaph was made on Mr John Popham :

> Here lies he who not long since
> Kept a table like a prince,
> Till Death came, and tooke away.
> Then ask't the old man, What's to pay ?

JOHN AUBREY, *Brief Lives : Sir John Popham* (c. 1680)

He ranges beyond his pale, and lives without compasse. His expense is measured not by abilitie, but will. His pleasures are immoderate, and not honest. . . . The vulgar sort call him bountiful, and applaud him while he spends. . . . While he is present, none of the wealthier guests may pay ought to the shot, without much vehemencie, without danger of unkindnesse. Use hath made it unpleasant to him, not to spend. . . . When he looks into the wealthie chest of his father, his conceit suggests, that it cannot be emptied ; and while hee takes out some deale every day, hee perceives not any diminution ; and when the heape is sensibly abated, yet still flatters himselfe with enough. . . . He doth not so much bestow benefits as scatter them. . . . Hee hath so dilated himselfe with the beamses of prosperitie, that he lies open to all dangers.

JOSEPH HALL
Characters of Vertues and Vices (1608)

ALL I SAW

The Streets seem'd paved with golden Stones, . . .

Rich Diamonds, and Pearl, and Gold
    Might evry where be seen ;
Rare Colors, yellow, blew, red, white, and green
    Mine Eys on every side behold :
All that I saw, a Wonder did appear,
      Amazement was my Bliss :
    That and my Wealth met evry where.
      No Joy to this !

For Property its self was mine,
  And Hedges, Ornaments :
Walls, Houses, Coffers, and their rich Contents,
  To make me Rich combine.
Cloaths, costly Jewels, Laces, I esteem'd
  My Wealth by others worn,
  For me they all to wear them seem'd,
    When I was born.   THOMAS TRAHERNE
          Wonder : Poems of Felicity (? 1656–66)

KING SOLOMON

And the Kyng made sylver and goulde at Jerusalem as
plenteous as stones and Cedar trees as plenty as the mul-
berry trees that growe in valeyes.   *Chronicles ii*
    Trans. by William Tyndale. *Matthew's Bible* (1537)

BARABAS

*Enter Barabas in his Counting-House, with heapes of gold
                  before him*
JEW :
  . . . Fye ; what a trouble 'tis to count this trash.
  Well fare the *Arabians*, who so richly pay
  The things they traffique for with wedge of gold,
  Whereof a man may easily in a day
  Tell that which may maintaine him all his life. . . .
  Give me the Merchants of the *Indian* Mynes,
YP   705

That trade in mettall of the purest mould ;
The wealthy *Moore*, that in the *Easterne* rockes
Without controule can picke his riches up,
And in his house heape pearle like pibble-stones ;
Receive them free, and sell them by the weight,
Bags of fiery *Opals*, *Saphires*, *Amatists*,
Jacints, hard *Topas*, grasse-greene *Emeraulds*,
Beauteous *Rubyes*, sparkling *Diamonds*. . . .
This is the ware wherein consists my wealth :
And thus me thinkes should men of judgement frame
Their meanes of traffique from the vulgar trade,
And as their wealth increaseth, so inclose
Infinite riches in a little roome. . . .
But who comes heare ? How now.

Enter a Merchant

MERCH. :
   Barabas, thy ships are safe,
   Riding in *Malta* Rhode : And all the Merchants
   With other Merchandize are safe arriv'd. . . .

Enter a second Merchant

2 MERCH. :
   Thine Argosie from *Alexandria*,
   Know *Barabas*, doth ride in *Malta* Rhode,
   Laden with riches, and exceeding store
   Of *Persian* silkes, of gold, and Orient Perle. . . .

JEW :
   Well, goe
   Thus trowles our fortune in by land and sea
   And thus are wee on every side inrich'd :

CHRISTOPHER MARLOWE
The Jew of Malta (1590)

Encouraging Trade

HANDY JUN. : I suppose she has found out the use of money.

SIR ABEL : Yes ; I'll do her the justice to say she encourages trade.—Why, do you know, Bob, my best coal-pit won't find her in white muslins—round her neck hangs a hundred acres at least ; my noblest oaks have made wigs for her ; my fat oxen have dwindled into Dutch pugs and white mice ; my India bonds are transmitted into shawls and otto of roses ; and a magnificent mansion has shrunk into a diamond snuff-box.

THOMAS MORTON
Speed the Plough (1800)

Gallies, Virgins, and Negroes

CALAPINE :
    Amongst so many crownes of burnisht gold,
    Choose which thou wilt, all are at thy command,
    A thousand Gallies mann'd with Christian slaves
    I freely give thee, which shall cut the straights,
    And bring Armados from the coasts of Spaine,
    Fraughted with golde of rich *America* :
    The Grecian virgins shall attend on thee,
    Skilful in musicke and in amorous laies :
    As faire as was *Pygmalions* Ivory gyrle,
    Or lovely *Io* metamorposëd.
    With naked Negros shall thy coach be drawen,
    And as thou rid'st in triumph through the streets,
    The pavement underneath they chariot wheels

With Turky Carpets shall be covered :
And cloath of Arras hung about the walles,
Fit objects for thy princely eie to pierce.
A hundred Bassoes cloath'd in crimson silk
Shall ride before thee on Barbarian Steeds :
And when thou goest, a golden Canapie
Enchac'd with pretious stones, . . .
And more than this, for all I cannot tell.

CHRISTOPHER MARLOWE
Tamburlaine the Greate (1588)

EMPEROR OF GUIANA

I thought good to insert part of the 120 chapter of *Lopez*
in his generall historie of the *Indies*, wherein he describeth
the court and magnificence of *Guaynacapa*, auncestor to the
Emperour of *Guiana*, whose very words are these. . . .
That is, All the vessels of his home, table, and kitchin were
of gold and silver, and the meanest of silver and copper for
strength and hardnes of the mettal. He had in his ward-
roppe hollow statues of gold which seemed giants, and the
figures in proportion and bignes of all the beastes, birdes,
trees, and hearbes, that the earth bringeth forth : and of
all the fishes that the sea or waters of his kingdome
breedeth. Hee had also ropes, budgets, chestes and troughs
of golde and silver, heapes of billets of golde that seemed
woode, marked out to burne. Finally there was nothing in
his countrey, whereof hee had not the counterfeat in gold :
Yea, and they say, The *Ingas* had a garden of pleasure in
an iland neere *Puna*, where they went to recreate themselves, when they would take the ayre of the sea, which

had all kind of garden hearbes, flowers and trees of Gold
and Silver, an invention and magnificence, til then never
seene : Besides all this, he had an infinite quantitie of
silver and gold unwrought in *Cuzco*.

SIR WALTER RALEIGH
The Discoverie of Guiana (1596)

Obvious

Riches are for Spending.

FRANCIS BACON
Essayes : Of Expence (1597)

Mammon

Moralists and Church Fathers have named it the root of all
Evil, the begetter of hate and bloodshed, the sure cause of
the soul's damnation. It has been called "trash," "muck,"
" dunghill excrement," by grave authors. The love of it
is denounced in all Sacred Writings ; we find it repre-
hended on Chaldean bricks, and in the earliest papyri.
Buddha, Confucius, Christ, set their faces against it; and
they have been followed in more modern times by
beneficed Clergymen, Sunday School Teachers, and the
leaders of the Higher Thought. But have the condemna-
tions of all the ages done anything to tarnish that bright
lustre ? Men dig for it ever deeper into the earth's intes-
tines, travel in search of it farther and farther to arctic
and unpleasant regions.

In spite of all my moral reading, I must confess that I
like to have some of this gaudy substance in my pocket.

Its presence cheers and comforts me, diffuses a genial warmth through my body. My eyes rejoice in the shine of it ; its clinquant sound is music in my ears. Since I then am in his paid service, and reject none of the doles of his bounty, I too dwell in the House of Mammon. I bow before the Idol and taste the unhallowed ecstasy.

How many Altars have been overthrown, and how many Theologies and heavenly Dreams have had their bottoms knocked out of them, while He has sat there, a great God, golden and adorned, and secure on his unmoved throne ?

LOGAN PEARSALL SMITH
Trivia (1918)

GETTING AND SPENDING

He left an estate of eleaven thousand pounds per annum. Sir John Danvers, who knew him, told me that when one told him his sonnes would spend the state faster then he gott it, he replyed, " they cannot take more delight in spending of it then I did in the getting of it."

JOHN AUBREY
Brief Lives : Sir Edward Coke (c. 1680)

TWIRING AND LOLLING

PHILLIS : Alas ! Alas ! it is a sad thing to walk. Oh Fortune ! Fortune !

TOM : What ! a sad thing to walk ? Why, Madam *Phillis*, do you wish yourself lame ?

PHILLIS : No, Mr *Tom*, but I wish I were generally carry'd on a Coach or Chair, and of a Fortune neither to stand nor go, but to totter, or slide, to be short-sighted, or stare, to fleer in the Face, to look distant, to observe, to overlook, yet all become me, and if I was rich, I could twire and loll as well as the best of them. Oh *Tom* ! *Tom* ! is it not a pity, that you shou'd be so great a Coxcomb, and I so great a Coquet, and yet be such poor Devils as we are ?

RICHARD STEELE, The Conscious Lovers (1722)

FAIR, FINE AND PERFECT

If she be rich, then she is fair, fine, absolute and perfect, then they burn like fire, they love her dearly, like pig and pye, and are ready to hang themselves if they may not have her.   ROBERT BURTON

The Anatomy of Melancholy (1621. Edition 1632)

HAVING THE STUFF

THOMAS : But has she got the stuff, Mr. Fag ? Is she rich, hey ?

FAG : Rich !—Why, I believe she owns half the stocks ! Zounds ! Thomas, she could pay the national debt as easily as I could my washerwoman ! She has a lap-dog that eats out of gold,—she feeds her parrot with small pearls,—and all her thread-papers are made of bank-notes !

RICHARD SHERIDAN, The Rivals (1775)

As I sat in the café I said to myself,
They may talk as they please about what they call pelf,
They may sneer as they like about eating and drinking,
But help it I cannot, I cannot help thinking
How pleasant it is to have money, heigh ho !
How pleasant it is to have money !

ARTHUR HUGH CLOUGH
Poems (1849)

WEDDINGS

Sir Clipesby and Lady Crew

3.

See where she comes ; and smell how all the street
Breathes Vine-yards and Pomgranats : O how sweet !
 As a fir'd Altar, is each stone,
 Perspiring pounded Cynamon.
  The Phenix nest,
Built up of odours, burneth in her breast.
 Who therein wo'd not consume
His soule to Ash-heaps in that rich perfume ?
  Bestroaking Fate the while
  He burnes to Embers on the Pile.

712

4.

Himen, O Himen ! Tread the sacred ground ;
Shew thy white feet, and head with Marjoram crown'd....

5.

Glide by the banks of Virgins then, and passe
The Shewers of Roses, lucky foure-leav'd grasse :
    The while the cloud of younglings sing,
    And drown yee with a flowrie Spring :
        While some repeat
Your praise, and bless you, sprinkling you with Wheat :
    While that others doe divine ;
Blest is the Bride, on whom the Sun doth shine !
      And thousands gladly wish
    You multiply, as doth a Fish.

7.

And now y'are enter'd : see the Codled Cook
Runs from his *Torrid Zone*, to prie, and look,
    And blesse his dainty Mistresse : see,
    The Aged point out, This is she,
        Who now must sway
The House (Love shield her) with her Yea and Nay :
    And the smirk Butler thinks it
Sin, in's Nap'rie, not to express his wit ;
    Each striving to devise
  Some gin, wherewith to catch your eyes.

8.

To bed, to bed, kind Turtles, now, and write
This the short'st day, and this the longest night ;
    But yet too short for you : 'tis we,
    Who count this night as long as three,
        Lying alone,

Telling the Clock strike Ten, Eleven, Twelve, One.
Quickly, quickly, then prepare;
And let the Young-Men and the Bride-maids share
Your garters; and their joynts
Encircle with the Bride-grooms Points. . . .

11.

And to enchant yee more, see every where
About the Roofe, a *Syren* in a Sphere;
(As we think) singing to the dinne
Of many a warbling *Cherubim* : . . .

16.

All now is husht in silence; *Midwife-moone*
With all her *Owl-ey'd* issue begs a boon
Which you must grant; that's entrance; with
Which extract, all we can call pith
And quintiscence
Of Planetary bodies; so commence
All faire *Constellations*
Looking upon yee, That two Nations
Springing from two such Fires,
May blaze the vertue of their Sires.

ROBERT HERRICK
*A Nuptiall Song, or Epithalamie, on Sir Clipseby Crew
and his Lady* (1648)

LORD AND LADY HAYES

Now hath *Flora* rob'd her bowers
To befrend this place with flowers;
Strowe aboute, strowe aboute,
The Skye rayn'd never kindlyer Showers.

714

Flowers with Bridalls well agree,
Fresh as Brides and Bridgromes be.
　　Strowe aboute, strowe aboute,
And mixe them with fit melodie.
Earth hath no Princelier flowers
Then Roses white, and Roses red,
But they must still be mingled.
And as a Rose new pluckt from *Venus* thorne
So doth a Bride a Bride groomes bed adorne.

Divers divers Flowers affect
For some private deare respect,
　　Strowe about, strow about,
Let every one his owne protect.
But hees none of *Floras* friend,
That will not the Rose commend.
　　Strow about, strow about,
Let Princes princely flowers defend.
Roses, the Gardens pride,
Are flowers for love and flowers for Kinges.
In courts desir'd, and Weddings.
And as a Rose in *Venus* bosome worne,
So doth a Bridegroome his Brides bed adorne. . .

Who is the happier of the two,
　　A maide or wife ?
Which is more to be desired
　　Peace or strife ?
What strife can be where two are one,
Or that delight to pine alone ?
None such true freindes, none so sweet life,
As what betweene the man and wife.
A maide is free, a wife is tyed.
No maide but faine would be a Bride.

Why live so many single then ?
Tis not, I hope, for want of men ?
The bow and arrow both may fit,
And yet tis hard the marke the hit.
He levels faire that by his side
Laies at night his lovely Bride.
Sing Io : Hymen, Io : Io : Hymen.

THOMAS CAMPION
*Maske . . . in honour of the Lord Hayes, and his
Bride* (1607)

SIR THOMAS AND LADY SOUTHWELL

VI

Behold ! how *Hymens* Taper-light
Shews you how much is spent of night....
 See, see the Bride-grooms Torch
 Half wasted in the porch.
 And now those Tapers five,
 That shew the womb shall thrive :
 Their silv'rie flames advance,
 To tell all prosp'rous chance
Still shall crown the happy life
Of the good man and the wife.

XII

Virgins, weep not ; 'twill come, when,
As she, so you'l be ripe for men.
Then grieve her not, with saying
She must no more a Maying :

Or by Rose-buds devine
Who'l be her Valentine.
Nor name those wanton reaks
Y'ave had at Barly-breaks.
But now kisse her, and thus say,
Take time Lady while ye may.

XVI

On your minutes, hours, dayes, months, years,
Drop the fat blessing of the sphears.
    That good, which Heav'n can give
    To make you bravely live,
    Fall, like a spangling dew
    By day and night on you.
    May Fortunes Lilly-Hand
    Open at your command ;
With all luckie Birds to side
With the Bride-groom, and the Bride.

XVII

Let bounteous Fate your spindles full
Fill, and winde up with whitest wooll.
    Let them not cut the thred
    Of life, until ye bid.
    May Death yet come at last ;
    And not with desp'rate haste
    But when ye both can say,
    Come, Let us now away.
Be ye to the barn then born,
Two, like two ripe shocks of corn.

ROBERT HERRICK
*An Epithalamie to Sir Thomas Southwell and his
Ladie. Hesperides* (1648)

I saw the marriage of the trapper in the open air in the
    far west, the bride was a red girl,
Her father and his friends sat near cross-legged and
    dumbly smoking, they had moccasins to their feet
    and large thick blankets hanging from their shoulders,
On a bank lounged the trapper, he was drest mostly in
    skins, his luxuriant beard and curls protected his
    neck, he held his bride by the hand,
She had long eyelashes, her head was bare, her coarse
    straight locks descended upon her voluptuous limbs
    and reach'd to her feet.

WALT WHITMAN
Song of Myself (1855)

WOODS

PLEASURE AND PASTIME

But the chiefe pleasure and pastime which commeth by
wilde woods, is, that being joyned to your house and
champion habitation, (which is the place, where it must
be seated or planted) it is pleasant to the sight : for by his

diversity of greenenesse, it marvellously delighteth, and with great contentment recreateth the sight.

The second pleasure or pastime is, that the woods (beeing neere unto your lodging) are alwaies full of all sorts of pretie birds, which sing sommer and winter all the day long, and the most part of the night, as nightingales and such other like, whereby their songs become joifull and delightsome to the eare, and so there is a pleasure and great contentment to the eare even to them in the house if it be neere unto.

Another pleasure is, that in the said woods there are alwaies great store of wood coists, popingjaies, stares, cranes and other sorts of birds, which make you pastime to see them flie : and there may also pleasure be reaped in taking of them with little engines, as, with a call, nets the tonnell, or other such like.

The fourth is, that in the woods are to be had conies hares, squirrels, and other sorts of small beasts pleasant to behold, and of great service for provision of vittaile.

The fifthe is, that in hot seasons you may purchase a coole aire within the said woods, as those which will cover and defend you from the injurie and vexation of the sunne, and contrariwise cooling you whether the heate will or no : and therein you have also to behold a comfortable greenenesse, both upon the boughes and ground, which keepeth his grasse greene through the coolenesse and shadow of the trees.

The sixth, is, that in winter being in the said woods, you are out of the injurie and force of the winds and great cold, because they breake them off : and further in these woods you are solitaire, and may use your leasure, in reading, writing or meditating upon your affaires, without being disquieted or distracted, or drawne to cast your sight abroad over any far distant place or countrie, in as much as the sight cannot pearse through the boughes or bushes.

CHARLES ESTIENNE
La Maison Rustique (1572)
Trans. Richard Surflet (1600)

PROFIT AND DELIGHT

But inward round, in rowes there stand
As well for profit, as delight,
The Trees of Orchard, and the Wood. . . .

HENRY PEACHAM
Minerva Brittanna (1612)

XENOPHILISM

THE FRENCH AIR

PHILOTIS : Count Rhodophil's a fine gentleman indeed, madam ; and, I think, deserves your affection.

MELANTHA : Let me die but he's a fine man ; he sings and dances en *Français*, and writes the *billets-doux* to a miracle.

PHIL. : And those are no small talents, to a lady that

understands and values the French air, as your Ladyship does.

MEL. : How charming is the French air, and what an *étourdi bête* is one of our untravelled islanders ! When he would make his court to me, let me die but he is just Æsop's ass, that would imitate the courtly French in his addresses ; but, instead of those, comes pawing upon me, and doing all things so *maladroitly*. . . .

Enter Palamede.

PAL. : . . . I want many things, madam, to render me accomplished ; and the first and greatest of them is your favour.

MEL. : Let me die, Philotis, but this is extremely French. . . . A gentleman, sir, that understands the grand monde so well, who has haunted the best conversations, and who, in short, has voyaged, may pretend to the good graces of a lady.

PAL. : (aside) Hey-day ! *Grand monde ! Conversation ! voyaged !* and *good graces !* I find my mistress is one of those that run mad in new French words.

MEL. : I suppose, sir, you have made the tour of France ; and, having seen all that's fine there, will make a considerable reformation in the rudeness of our court : For let me die, but an unfashioned, untravelled, mere Sicilian, is a *bête* ; and has nothing in the world of an *honnête homme*.

PAL. : I must confess, madam, that——

MEL. : And what new minuets have you brought over with you ? their minuets are to a miracle ! And our Sicilian jigs so dull and sad to them !

PAL. : For minuets, madam——

MEL. : And what new plays are there in vogue ? And who

danced best in the last grand ballet? Come, sweet
servant, you shall tell me all.

PAL. (aside): Tell her all? Why she asks all, and will
heare nothing.—To answer in order, madam, to your
demands——

MEL.: I am thinking what a happy couple we shall be!
For you shall keep up your correspondence abroad, and
everything that's new writ, in France, and fine, I mean all
that's delicate and *bien tourné*, we will have first.

JOHN DRYDEN
Marriage à la Mode (1673)

RUSSIAN BALLET

The Russians, hearing the great respect we have for
Foreign Dancing, have lately sent over some of their best
Ballarins, who are now practising a famous Ballat, which
will be suddenly danced at the *Bear-garden*.

GEORGE ETHEREGE
The Man of Mode (1676)

FRENCH FASHIONS

I have much wondered why our English above other
nations should so much doat upon new fashions, but more
I wonder at our want of wit, that wee cannot invent them
ourselves, but when one is growne stale runne presently
over into France, to seeke a new, making that noble and

flourishing kingdome the magazin of our fooleries: and for this purpose many of our tailors lye leger there, and ladies post over their gentlemen ushers, to accoutre them and themselves as you see.

HENRY PEACHAM
The Truth of our Times (1638)

Salute to all Foreigners

I hear emulous shouts of Australians pursuing the wild
    horse,
I hear the Spanish dance with castanets in the chestnut
    shade, to the rebeck and guitar,
I hear continual echoes from the Thames,
I hear fierce French liberty songs,
I hear of the Italian boat-sculler the musical recitative
    of old poems,
I hear the locusts in Syria as they strike the grain and
    grass with the showers of their terrible clouds,
I hear the chirp of the Mexican muleteer, and the bells
    of the mule,
I hear the Arab muezzin calling from the top of the
    mosque, . . .
I hear the cry of the Cossack, and the sailor's voice
    putting to sea at Okotsk, . . .
I hear the Hebrew reading his records and psalms,
I hear the rhythmic myths of the Greeks, and the strong
    legends of the Romans, . . .
I hear the Hindoo teaching his favorite pupil the loves,
    wars, adages, transmitted safely to this day from
    poets who wrote three thousand years ago. . . .

You whoever you are!

You daughter or son of England!

You of the mighty Slavic tribes and empires! You Russ in Russia!

You dim-descended, black, divine-soul'd African, large, fine-headed, nobly form'd, superbly destin'd, on equal terms with me!

You Norwegian! Swede! Dane! Icelander! you Prussian!

You Spaniard of Spain! you Portuguese!

You Frenchwoman and Frenchman of France!

You Belge! you liberty-lover of the Netherlands! (you stock whence I myself have descended);

You sturdy Austrian! you Lombard! Hun! Bohemian! farmer of Styria!

You neighbor of the Danube!

You working-man of the Rhine, the Elbe or the Weser! you working-woman too!

You Sardinian! you Bavarian! Swabian! Saxon! Wallachian! Bulgarian!

You Roman! Neapolitan! you Greek!

You lithe matador in the arena at Seville!

You mountaineer living lawlessly on the Taurus or Caucasus!

You Bokh horse-herd watching your mares and stallions feeding!

You beautiful-bodied Persian at full speed in the saddle shooting arrows to the mark!

You Chinaman and Chinawoman of China! you Tartar of Tartary! . . .

You Jew journeying in your old age through every risk to stand once more on Syrian ground!

You other Jews waiting in all lands for your Messiah!

You thoughtful Armenian . . . !
You sheiks . . . !
You Thibet trader . . . !
You Japanese . . . !
All you continentals of Asia, Africa, Europe, Australia,
    indifferent of place ! . . .
Health to you ! good will to you all, from me and America
    sent ! . . .
You Hottentot with clicking palate ! you woolly-hair'd
    hordes ! . . .
You dwarf'd Kamtschatkan, Greenlander, Lapp !
You Austral negro, naked, red, sooty, with protrusive lip,
    groveling, seeking your food !
You Caffre, Berber, Soudanese !
You haggard, uncouth, untutor'd Bedowee !
You plague-swarms in Madras, Nankin, Kaubul, Cairo !
You benighted roamer of Amazonia ! you Patagonian !
    you Feejeeman !
I do not prefer others so very much before you either,
I do not say one word against you, . . .
Salut au monde ! . . .
Toward you all, in America's name,
I raise high the perpendicular hand, I make the signal. . . .

WALT WHITMAN
Salut au Monde ! (1856)

XENOPHOBIA

Hating the Dutch

Holland, that scarce deserves the name of land,
As but th' off-scouring of the British sand, ...
This indigested vomit of the sea
Fell to the Dutch by just propriety.
   Glad, then, as miners who have found the oar,
They, with mad labour, fish'd the land to shoar;
And div'd as desperately for each piece
Of earth, as if 't had been of ambergreece;
Collecting anxiously small loads of clay,
Less then what building swallows bear away;
Or then those pills which sordid beetles roul,
Transfusing into them their dunghil soul. . . .
   Yet still his claim the injur'd ocean laid,
And oft at leap-frog ore their steeples plaid : . . .
A daily deluge over them does boyl;
The earth and water play at level-coyl.
The fish oft-times the burger dispossest,
And sat, not as a meat, but as a guest,
And oft the Tritons and the sea-nymphs saw
Whole sholes of Dutch serv'd up for Cabillau;
Or, as they over the new level rang'd,
For pickled herring, pickled *heeren* chang'd. . . .

Therefore Necessity, that first made kings,
Something like government among them brings. . . .
'Tis probable Religion, after this,
Came next in order, which they could not miss ; . . .
Sure when Religion did itself imbark,
And from the East would Westward steer its ark,
It struck, and splitting on this unknown ground,
Each one thense pillag'd the first piece he found :
Hence Amsterdam, Turk-Christian-Pagan-Jew,
Staple of sects, and mint of Schisme grew ; . . . .
In vain for Catholicks our selves we bear ;
The universal church is only there. . . .
How fit a title clothes their governours,
Themselves the hogs, as all their subjects bores ! . . .

ANDREW MARVELL
Character of Holland (1672)

HATING THE SPANISH

In contemplacion of all which things, who would not be incouraged to proceed in this Voiage, having in a maner none other enemyes but these Spaniards, abhorred of God and man ?

SIR WALTER RALEIGH
Of the Voyage for Guiana (c. 1598)

HATING THE FRENCH

Frenchmen are not human beings, and must under no circumstances be dealt with as such. If a German nevertheless lowers himself to treat a Frenchman humanly, he is only doing it in order not to come down to the level of the French.

The German must therefore avoid having any voluntary dealings with a Frenchman, as otherwise he is dirtying himself and the German people indelibly.

Pforzheimer Anzeiger
(1933)

His reply to the person who complimented him on its [the Dictionary's] coming out . . . mentioning the ill success of the French in a similar attempt, is well known ; and, I trust has been often recorded : " Why, what would you expect, dear Sir (said he) from fellows that eat frogs ? "

HESTHER PIOZZI
Anecdotes of Dr Johnson
(1786)

HATING THE BABYLONIANS

Remember the children of Edom, O Lord, in the day of Jeruṣalem ; how they said, Downe with it, downe with it, even to the ground.
O daughter of Babylon, wasted with misery : yea, happy shall he be that rewardeth thee, as thou hast served us.
Blessed shall he be that taketh thy children : and throweth them against the stones.

Psalm 137. *Book of Common Prayer*
Trans. Miles Coverdale (1611 edition)

728

To the banisht Earle I came to render thankes, when thus
he examined and schoold me.

Countriman, tell me what is the occasion of thy
straying so farre out of *England*, to visit this strange
nation ? If it bee languages, thou maist learne them at
home, nought but lasciviousnesse is to bee learnt here.
Perhaps to be better accounted of than others of thy condition, thou ambitiously undertakest this voyage : these
insolent fancies are but *Icarus* feathers, whose wanton
waxe melted against the Sunne will betray thee into a sea
of confusion.

The first traveller was *Cain*, and he was called a vagabond runnagate on the face of the earth. . . .

God had not greater curse to lay upon the *Israelites*, than
by leading them out of their owne countrey to live as slaves
in a strange land. That which was their curse, we Englishmen count our chiefe blessednes, hee is no bodie that hath
not traveld : wee had rather live as slaves in another land,
croutch and cap, and be servile to everie jelous Italians
and proud Spaniards Humor, where we may neither speak
looke nor doo anie thing but what pleaseth them : than live
as freemen and Lords in our owne Countrey.

He that is a traveller must have the backe of an asse to
beare all, a tung like the taile of a dog to flatter all, the
mouth of a hogge to eate what is set before him, the eare
of a merchant to heare all and say nothing : and if this be
not the highest step of thraldome, there is no libertie or
freedome. . . . .

If thou doost but lend half a looke to a *Romans* or
Italians wife, thy porredge shalbe prepared for thee, and

cost thee nothing but thy lyfe. Chance some of them breake a bitter jest on thee, and thou retortst it severely, or seemest discontented : goe to they chamber, and provide a great blanket, for thou shalt be sure to be visited with guests in a mask the next night, when in kindness and courtship thy throat shall be cut, and the dooers returne undiscovered. . . .

What is there in *Fraunce* to bee learned more than in *England*, but falshood in fellowship, perfect slovenrie, to love no man but for my pleasure, to sweare *Ah par la mort Dieu*. . . . I have knowen some that have continued there by the space of halfe a dozzen yeares, and when they come home, they have hid a little weerish leane face under a broad French hat, kept a terrible coyle with the dust in the streete in their long cloakes . . . and spoke English strangely. Nought els have they profited by their travell, save learnt to distinguish of the true *Burdeax* Grape, and knowe a cup of neate *Gascoigne* wine from wine of *Orleans* . . . . and walk melancholy with their Armes folded.

From Spaine what bringeth our Traveller ? A scull crowned hat of the fashion of an olde deepe porringer, a diminutive Aldermans ruffe. . . . A soldier and a braggart he is (thats concluded) he jetteth strouting, dancing on hys toes with his hands under his sides. If you talk with him, he makes a dishcloth of his owne Countrey in comparison of *Spaine*, but if you urge him more particularly wherein it exceeds, he can give no instance but in *Spaine* they have better bread than any we have : when (pore hungrie slaves) they may crumble it into water well inough . . . for they have not a good morsell of meate except it be salt piltchers to eat with it all the yere long : and which is more, they are poore beggars, and lye in fowle straw everie night.

Italy the Paradice of the earth, and the Epicures heaven, how doth it forme our yong master? It makes him to kiss his hand like an ape, cringe his necke like a starveling, and play at hey passe repasse come aloft when he salutes a man. From thence he brings the art of atheisme, the art of epicurising, the art of whoring, the art of poysoning, the art of Sodomitrie. The onely probable good thing they have to keepe us from utterly condemning it is, that it maketh a man an excellent Courtier, a curious carpet knight : which is, by interpretation, a fine close leacher, a glorious hipocrite. It is nowe a privie note amonst the better sort of men, when they would set a singular marke or brand in a notorious villaine, to say, he hath beene in *Italy*.

With the Dane and the Dutchman I will not encounter, for they are simple honest men, that ... doe nothing but fill bottomles tubs, and will be drunke and snort in the midst of dinner: he hurts himself only that goes thither, he cannot lightly be damned, for the vintners, the brewers, the malt-men, and alewives pray for him. . . . But lightly a man is nere the better for their prayers, for they commit all deadly sin for the most part of them in mingling their drinke, the vintners in the highest degree. . . .

THOMAS NASHE
The Unfortunate Traveller (1594)

Thos old *Hebrews* esteemed the whole world *Gentiles* ; the *Greeks* held all Barbarians but themselves ; our modern *Italians* account of us as dull *Transalpines* by way of approach, they scorn thee and thy country, which thou so much admirest. 'Tis a childish humour to hone after

731

home, to be discontent at that which others seek; to prefer, as base *Icelanders and Norwegians* doe their own ragged Island before *Italy* or *Greece*, the Gardens of the world. There is a base Nation in the North, saith *Pliny*, called *Chauci*, that live amongst rockes and sands by the sea side, feede on fish, drinke water; and yet these base people account themselves slaves in respect when they come to *Rome*.

ROBERT BURTON
The Anatomy of Melancholy (1621. Edition 1632)

HATING GERMAN FIDDLERS

The players being denied coming to Oxford by the Vice-Chancellor, and that very rightly, tho' they might as well have been here as Handell and his lowsy crew, a great number of foreign fidlers.

THOMAS HEARNE
Diary (July 6th, 1733)

ACKNOWLEDGMENTS

I should like to thank, for permission to use copyright material, the following authors, authors' representatives, and publishers : Mr. David Garnett and Messrs. Chatto & Windus, *A Rabbit in the Air* ; Mr. Stuart Gilbert and Messrs. Desmond Harmsworth, *Night Flight* ; Mr. T. Hodgkin and the Oxford University Press, translation of a letter of *Sidonius* ; the family of Gerard Manley Hopkins and the Oxford University Press, *A Vision of the Mermaids*, and *The Stars* ; Mr. Robert Lynd and Messrs. Methuen & Co., *Happy England* ; Miss E. J. Scovell, *A girl and her sister* ; Mr. Logan Pearsall Smith and Messrs. Constable & Co., *Trivia* and *More Trivia* ; Mr. R. E. Tickell and Messrs. Constable & Co., *Thomas Tickell* ; Mrs. Woolf and the Hogarth Press, *Orlando* ; Mr. Thomas Wright and Messrs. Everett & Co., *The Life of Sir Richard Burton* ; Messrs. Macmillan, G. C. Macaulay's translation of *Herodotus* ; Messrs. Constable & Co., Emerson's *Journal* ; Professor Findlay and Messrs. Longman's, *Chemistry in the Service of Man* ; and the Trustees of the British Museum for leave to use various B.M. MSS. I am also very grateful to Miss Marjorie Hope Nicholson and the Yale University Press for permission to use Miss Nicholson's edition of the *Conway Letters* in quoting from these. Finally, I should like gratefully to acknowledge the skilful, valuable and unwearying help of Miss D. E. Marshall.

733

INDEX OF AUTHORS AND TRANSLATORS

738

739

740

742

743

INDEX OF FIRST LINES
OF VERSE

Printed in Great Britain by
The Camelot Press Ltd., London and Southampton